BANKS AND REMEDIES:
SECOND EDITION

Series Consultant Editor
Prof. Joseph J. Norton, S.J.D, D.Phil.

ALSO IN THIS SERIES:

European Banking Law: the Banker–Customer Relationship
SECOND EDITION
by Ross Cranston and contributors
(1999)

Banking Regulation and the Bank of England
by Christos Hadjiemmanuil
(1996)

Banks, Liability and Risk
SECOND EDITION
by Ross Cranston and contributors
(1995)

The Single Market and the Law of Banking
SECOND EDITION
by Ross Cranston and contributors
(1995)

Cross-Border Electronic Banking
by Joseph J. Norton and contributors
(1995)

Environmental Liability for Banks
by Joseph J. Norton and contributors
(1995)

International Asset Securitisation
by Joseph J. Norton and contributors
(1995)

Banks: Fraud and Crime
by Joseph J. Norton and contributors
(1994)

Bank Regulation and Supervision in the 1990s
by Joseph J. Norton and contributors
(1991)

BANKS AND REMEDIES

SECOND EDITION

EDITED BY

WILLIAM BLAIR QC

3 Verulam Buildings, Visiting Professorial Fellow, Centre for Commercial Law Studies, Visiting Professor, London School of Economics and Political Science

PUBLISHED JOINTLY WITH
THE CENTRE FOR COMMERCIAL LAW STUDIES AND
THE LONDON INSTITUTE OF INTERNATIONAL
BANKING, FINANCE AND DEVELOPMENT LAW

LLP

LONDON HONG KONG
1999

LLP Professional Publishing
(a trading division of the
Informa Publishing Group Ltd)
69–77 Paul Street
London EC2A 4LQ
Great Britain

EAST ASIA
LLP Asia
Sixth Floor, Hollywood Centre
233 Hollywood Road
Hong Kong

First published 1992
Second edition 1999

British Library Cataloguing in Publication Data
A catalogue record
for this book is available
from the British Library

ISBN 1-85978-653-7

Typeset in 10/12 Sabon
by Mendip Communications Ltd,
Frome, Somerset
Printed in Great Britain by
WBC Limited,
Bridgend, Mid-Glamorgan

INTRODUCTION

An efficient financial system depends ultimately on the availability of effective remedies. This may be taken for granted in developed economies, but its importance has become widely recognised in the context of international reform generally. As has been said by the IMF:

Efficient banking ... requires a "credit culture"—an environment in which credit contracts are customarily honoured and enforced, in the context of a legal and judicial system that facilitates the enforcement of financial contracts, loan recovery, realisation of collateral, and bankruptcy. In some countries serious weaknesses in the judicial systems can negate improvements in corporate government and official oversight.[1]

This basic point is as valid in England as anywhere else. Finance is predicated on the assumption that contracts will be fulfilled, and that in the event of non-fulfilment the courts can be relied upon to enforce the contract according to its terms, and provide as efficient a system for execution of judgments as is reasonably possible. The concentration of international finance in centres such as New York and London is due to various factors, and the existence of an effective and responsive system of commercial law is high on the list. Lack of commercial sophistication in the law, and even more damaging, a compromised rule of law, undermines the confidence which finance needs if it is to thrive. That is not to say that recovery rights are untrammelled, or that social considerations do not enter the equation. The business of banking increasingly revolves around social considerations, particularly at the retail level. Self-evidently, a financial institution must take a different approach to the enforcement of a home loan than a derivatives contract with another financial institution. But the basic point is still there: a financial system needs the support of effective remedies, and it is the business of lawyers, courts and the substantive law to provide it.

This book was first published in 1992 under the distinguished editorship of Professor Ross Cranston. On his appointment as Solicitor-General, the task passed to me. I am extremely grateful to the group of contributors, all of them

1. *Towards a Framework for Financial Stability*, International Monetary Fund, Washington DC, January 1998, p. 14 (prepared by Staff Team led by David Folkerts-Landau and Carl Johan Lindgren).

practitioners or academics of high standing, who have updated their contributions to the first edition, and in some cases produced entirely new contributions. Together they provide an informed insight into the range of remedies available to banks in England, Europe and the United States.

Substantive law always moves on, but since 1992 a number of trends are discernible as regards banks and remedies. First, remedies have to be considered on an increasingly cross-border basis. At one level, this may result from the litigation of a single matter in a number of different jurisdictions. For example, the courts of one country may be invoked to support litigation in another country by freezing orders. At the self-help level, it is often impossible to ascertain the effectiveness of set-off rights without reference to the substantive and insolvency laws of more than one country. Similar considerations apply in the regulatory field. Second, banks increasingly view the remedies available to them through a wider perspective than merely litigation through the courts. This does not necessarily reflect dissatisfaction with court procedures. In part, it is a response to an increased awareness of reputational risk. Reputational risk used to be limited to the perception of a bank's ability to repay its depositors. Now, senior bankers must be increasingly preoccupied with public perception of the way in which their institutions conduct their business. In this context, mediation or arbitration, and the various Ombudsmen schemes available, may present a more attractive alternative to the courts of law for certain types of dispute. Third, at the operational level, banks are taking a critical look at the way in which legal services are delivered to them. Legal services are increasingly viewed in the same way as any other service, and those providing them are required to meet objective standards of efficiency and cost.

Prior to reviewing the contributions made by individual authors, there is one other development to note; 26 April 1999 is not a day which litigation lawyers in England and Wales will readily forget. On that day, an entirely new set of procedural rules came into force in the form of the Civil Procedure Rules. Though the reform was long in gestation, the speed of introduction of the new rules was remarkable. They had only been available in final form for a few months, and were in a number of respects incomplete. It is impossible to imagine a change of this nature being introduced in this manner in a system with state and federal components. When the dust settles, there may be considerable advantages to financial institutions in the new regime. For heavy litigation, all the best features of the Commercial Court have been preserved. On the other hand, a more critical approach will be taken to the discovery process, where litigation can prove particularly burdensome and expensive. Litigants will have to justify the need to require institutions to disclose their records en masse. A further innovation is that costs on interlocutory applications are generally to be assessed and paid forthwith. A litigant will now have a much clearer view of its costs exposure as the litigation proceeds. Lawyers will be expected to provide sharper appraisals of the need for interlocutory relief, and the costs consequences of seeking that relief. At the other end of the spectrum, the reforms adopt concrete measures to cut both the time and cost of litigation at the retail level. The effectiveness of these reforms will inevitably depend on the efficiency of their implementation. In principle, however, an institution like a bank with a considerable volume of claims should be well placed to take advantage of the savings in time and cost which the rules are capable of presenting.

Chapter 1 is concerned with the big picture. In his landmark publications on financial law, Philip Wood has expounded the core concepts on which the law is built, and in particular the functions and policies behind these concepts. He has broken new ground in identifying the ideas that lie behind the rules, and describing how they are dealt with in different legal systems round the world. In chapter 1, he applies this approach to a series of subjects that touch on remedies and risk: insolvency, security, title finance, set-off, divided ownership, assignment, lifting the veil of incorporation and judicial rescue. The theme is the flexibility and diversity of commercial law. Wood points out that insolvency law is fundamental to commercial and financial law, and the foundation of security and guarantees. His comparative approach enables discernible pro-creditor and pro-debtor groups to be identified among the world's jurisdictions. More broadly, the self-help aspect of remedies is explored in its most characteristic form, namely set-off. Since the publication of his work on *English and International Set-Off*, this doctrine has been the subject of sustained international attention. In particular, the importance of finality in payment and securities settlement systems has resulted in many jurisdictions adopting rules intended to permit internal set-off procedures to prevail over insolvency rules that would otherwise apply.

In chapter 2, David Waksman explains the new Civil Procedure Rules in force in England and Wales which have already been referred to above. Out of the mass of detail he identifies eight areas of practice of particular importance to banks: statements of case, judgments in default, summary judgment and related applications, freezing injunctions, costs, offers to settle, case management and proceedings in the commercial court. He highlights a number of the features of the new regime, including so-called "front loading" by which more detailed case preparation is expected at an earlier stage of proceedings than was formerly the case, and the case management process which envisages judges assuming a pro-active, rather than the traditional reactive, role. His verdict is that provided that banks are properly prepared for the litigation of their claims at an early stage, they should benefit considerably from the changes in civil procedure.

In chapter 3, Richard Salter QC demonstrates how closely the remedies available to banks are bound up with the substantive rules that govern the relationship between bank and customer. He identifies a number of different "rights" open to a bank under the general law. A bank has the right to demand repayment; to combine accounts; a right of lien; the right to close the account; to enforce security; and to assist in a rescue. Each of these rights and the circumstances in which they are exercisable span some of the basic aspects of the banker–customer relationship. In many ways, his exposition shows that it is the nature of the remedies that defines the relationship, distinguishing it (for example) from a simple contract of loan.

In chapter 4, David Baker and Nicola Anstey describe the rules applying as to disclosure (discovery) of documents in contentious litigation, as those rules affect banks and financial institutions. They point out that the increased scope for pre-action disclosure will in some cases help a party to establish whether it has a sufficiently solid case to justify instituting proceedings. Cases will be won and lost on disclosure, as they were on discovery, but the authors explain that the role played in disclosure under the new rules is somewhat different and starts much earlier. The authors' prediction is that banks involved in large-scale litigation may be expected to provide full disclosure similar to that which was expected under the old rules, the differences lying in the criteria for assessing which documents to disclose, and the manner in which the documents will be obtained, the latter point focusing on the type and extent of the search required. They show that the effect of the disclosure rules in principle is one thing, the working through of the rules in practice is another. From a practical perspective, the distinctive role of banks as deposit-takers, financial advisers and record keepers inevitably draws them into litigation even if they are not primarily involved as claimant or defendant.

Chapter 5 by Lawrence Collins, which describes the way in which cross-border court orders affect banks, has been updated by Matthew Morgan of the Centre for Commercial Law Studies. Mr Collins explains that the need for cross-border cooperation between courts and enforcement agencies is greater than ever. On the other hand, he shows that real issues as to privacy and confidentiality arise, and courts in any particular country are bound by practical considerations of territoriality. In England, by contrast to some jurisdictions, the presence of assets here was not generally considered in itself sufficient to found jurisdiction. Whilst the principle remains, its practical significance has been reduced by the introduction in 1997 of rules giving the English courts broad latitude to provide interim relief in support of claims proceeding abroad. This is an important step towards a rational approach to cross-border fraud.

In cases of corporate failure or malfeasance official remedies are often as important as private ones. The Department of Trade and Industry has wide powers of investigation. In chapter 6, Ian Taylor describes what has in the past proved an effective remedy, namely inquiries by inspectors under section 432(2) of the Companies Act 1985. The utility of this procedure has been adversely affected by the controversial decision of the European Court of Human Rights in the *Saunders* case. The author explains that the court ruled that Mr Saunders had been deprived of his rights to a fair hearing because of the use at his trial of evidence in the form of transcripts of DTI interviews which he had been compelled to give: this was said to violate the principle of privilege against self-incrimination. There are other public remedies, including confidential statutory enquiries, mostly under section 447 of the Companies Act 1985, and inspections under section 177 of the Financial Services Act 1986 (insider dealing).

It would be an exaggeration to describe European Community law as all-pervasive. Nevertheless, it is striking how in recent years it has moved from a focus on competition issues to a much wider remit with fundamental implications for everybody including financial institutions. In chapter 7, Maurice Sheridan and Richard Brent describe the impact of European law in the banking field, pointing out that it will be further accentuated by the advent of the single currency. They identify areas such as consumer protection law (including, for example, the directive on cross-border transfers and the far-reaching Unfair Terms in Consumer Contracts Directive) in addition to competition and jurisdictional issues. Their chapter shows that European Community law tends to be more about remedies against banks, rather than remedies in their favour. On the other hand, the authors describe the potential for uniform rules presented by the Insolvency Convention, albeit in flawed form. A new consolidating Banking Directive has been promised by the Commission, and the authors foresee that the trend towards an increasingly integrated banking system in Europe will bring with it a set of Europe-wide remedies for banks. Uniformity may be hard to achieve, and many would argue that subsidiarity is to be preferred. Nevertheless, the gradual reality of a single market in banking and financial services will make the present legal patchwork increasingly obsolete.

The United States has possibly the most highly developed system of remedies both judicial and non-judicial of any country in the world. Non-US financial institutions often view the prospect of joinder to US litigation with alarm. In chapter 8, Gary Born and Joseph Profaizer explain and demystify the course of pre-trial proceedings in the US courts from the perspective of international commercial lawyers. The interplay between the state and federal judicial systems (often particularly opaque to foreign litigants) is expounded as is the role of pleadings, jurisdiction, service of process, forum selection and discovery (including practical means of resisting discovery). There is an important discussion of the principles applicable to extra-territoriality in the discovery process, a subject that is quite capable of bringing foreign banks into collision with the US judicial process. Most foreign banks are now well aware that where, for example, as is often the case local confidentiality rules inhibit compliance with a discovery order, an appropriate and timely response is required to avoid risking the imposition of sanctions which could seriously interfere with their business interests within the United States.

Until recently, a chapter on arbitration would have been out of place in a book dealing with banking remedies. Traditionally, arbitration has not been favoured in commercial finance since financial institutions take the view that the amount due is ascertained, and there is no room for "splitting the difference". Financiers expect repayment in full, and this generally outweighs the admitted disadvantage of litigation (e.g. cost, delay, publicity, etc). On the other hand, arbitration procedure in the UK was reformed by the Arbitration Act 1996 well before the reforms to civil procedure in the courts, the aim being to reduce delay and costs and impose on arbitrators a duty to control the process. Arbitration may not, perhaps, produce the clarity of result expected from litigation, but its utility in the financial field is being reassessed. In chapter 9, Professor William Park brings his international arbitration experience to bear in describing the role that arbitration is capable of playing in banking and finance. He points out that enforcement can be an important advantage (because of the wide reach of the New York Arbitration Convention). He describes the process of securities arbitration in the United States, which has greatly increased since two leading decisions of the US Supreme Court at the end of the eighties. Practical guidance is given about the arbitration process as it applies to financial institutions. Professor Park's exposition leads to the conclusion that in a number of types of banking transaction (for example OTC derivatives transactions in which basic details may be in dispute such as the amount owing and the method of calculation) arbitration may become increasingly common.

Realisation of security is one of the most fundamental of all remedies. It is the means by which a creditor transforms a juridical advantage into hard cash. The main distinction is between "self-help" systems (such as that of England), and systems in which some form of judicial intervention is required, for example a judicial auction of the secured assets. In his classic account of receiverships, Professor Robert Pennington describes how on default a creditor with the benefit of a floating charge is entitled to appoint receivers who take over the debtor's business with a view to obtaining repayment. As chapter 10 makes clear, this is a particularly valuable remedy as regards corporate debtors (particularly smaller businesses), because until default the debtor has full use of its assets, and upon default the bank has the right to appoint a receiver without the court's intervention. Though many jurisdictions recognise concepts similar to the floating charge (for example the civil law enterprise charge), rules differ widely, and the English law solution is particularly effective. On the other hand, as Professor Pennington explains, the exercise of the right to appoint a receiver can be problematic, and in practice a bank is unlikely to use it except as a last resort.

In chapter 11, Gerald Nels Olson shows that in many situations the best remedy available to a bank is to support a debtor in trouble. Though written from a US perspective, he cites guidelines issued by the Hong Kong Association of Banks in 1998 to the effect that when it becomes known that a debtor company is experiencing financial problems, banks' initial attitude should be one of support. They should not withdraw facilities or hastily put the company into receivership, or issue writs demanding payment. The author describes the evolution of insolvency law as a backdrop against which the consensual workout has developed. His description of the basic principles of loan restructures are applicable generally, and show that lawyers will provide a more effective service to their bank clients if they have an appreciation of the regulatory, accounting, financial, economic and practical banking techniques required to make a workout successful. The underlying issue is how to enhance the prospects of a failing business whilst at the same time protecting the banks' security. The practical advice which chapter 11 contains applies to all restructurings, and demonstrates the extent to which a successful response to problem loans depends on a detailed understanding of the borrower's overall financial position.

If a workout is impractical, a bank must consider a more formal remedy. In chapter 12, Hamish Anderson describes the UK approach to administration and insolvency. He points out that perhaps the most important practical distinction between the UK and US approaches to ailing companies is that under the UK system, the court will only appoint a licensed insolvency practitioner to be administrator: the concept of debtor in possession currently plays no part in English or Scottish law. Administration unlike receivership requires a court order. The author explains that an advantage of administration is that the order is more likely to be recognised in foreign jurisdictions, that creditors are precluded from repossessing goods except with the administrator's consent and that security ranking in priority to the debenture cannot be enforced without the administrator's consent. Banks are in a position to block an unwanted administration since no order can be made if a receiver has been appointed prior to the hearing. The author concludes that historically insolvency procedures were intended to realise assets and distribute them to creditors: now there is an understanding that the best solution is to rehabilitate business and save jobs. The policy issue is how to combine that objective with the need to provide creditors with an effective remedy, which is the essential underpinning of a healthy financial system.

The final chapter consists of a timely review by Professor Johannes Köndgen of Germany's new insolvency law, the Insolvenzordnung of 5 October 1994 which came into effect on 1 January 1999 (InsO). This entirely replaced the Bankruptcy Code of 1877, and as Professor Köndgen explains, marked a new approach in Germany to questions of rehabilitation and insolvency. The InsO shifts the emphasis from the goal of fair distribution of the debtor's assets to the goal of providing an economically efficient realisation procedure with a minimum of transaction costs. It is clear from Professor Köndgen's exposition that the secured bank creditor's position differs significantly from that which subsists under English law. Holders of non-possessory collateral must make a contribution to "liquidation expenses". The InsO provides for an automatic stay of individual remedies in the hands of secured creditors or in respect of the collection of receivables assigned as security. Realisation of non-possessory collateral other than reserved ownership is assigned to the administrator who is authorised to postpone realisation of moveables while they are needed to carry on the debtor's business.

Thus the new German code (which is likely to be influential in emerging economies in Eastern Europe) places the emphasis more on the rehabilitation of the business, in contrast with the English approach which generally favours the financier. The reaching of a balance between these two objectives—the need to preserve and restore businesses in trouble on the one hand, and the need on the other hand to provide adequate remedies to the banks and institutions which provided the capital in the first place—underlies much of the philosophical content of this area of the law. Whilst the balance differs in different legal systems the availability of effective remedies to banks and other financial institutions remains an important policy goal.

WILLIAM BLAIR

CONTENTS

CONTRIBUTORS

HAMISH ANDERSON: Partner and Solicitor, Norton Rose, London.

NICOLA ANSTEY: Solicitor, Lovell White Durrant, London.

DAVID BAKER: Partner and Solicitor, Lovell White Durrant, London.

WILLIAM BLAIR QC: Barrister, 3 Verulam Buildings, London; Visiting Professorial Fellow, Centre for Commercial Law Studies; Visiting Professor, London School of Economics and Political Science.

GARY B. BORN: Partner and Attorney, Wilmer, Cutler & Pickering, London and Berlin.

RICHARD BRENT: Barrister, 3 Verulam Buildings, London.

LAWRENCE COLLINS QC: Partner and Solicitor, Herbert Smith, London; Fellow, Wolfson College, Cambridge; Visiting Professor, Queen Mary & Westfield College, University of London.

JOHANNES KÖNDGEN: Professor of Law, University of Bonn, Germany; formerly Judge, Court of Appeals, Hamburg, Germany.

GERALD NELS OLSON: Senior Fellow, London Institute of International Banking, Finance and Development Law; Associate Executive Director, Institute of International Banking and Finance, Southern Methodist University.

WILLIAM W. PARK: Professor of Law, Boston University; Counsel, Ropes & Gray; Vice President, London Court of International Arbitration; Arbitrator, Claims Resolution Tribunal for Dormant Accounts in Switzerland; Sometime Fellow, Selwyn College, Cambridge.

ROBERT R. PENNINGTON: Emeritus Professor of Commercial Law, University of Birmingham.

JOSEPH R. PROFAIZER: Attorney and Solicitor, Wilmer, Cutler & Pickering, London.

RICHARD SALTER QC: Barrister, 3 Verulam Buildings, London.

MAURICE SHERIDAN: Barrister, 3 Verulam Buildings, London.

IAN TAYLOR: Partner and Solicitor, Freshfields, London.

DAVID WAKSMAN: Barrister, Fountain Court Chambers, London.

PHILIP WOOD: Partner and Solicitor, Allen & Overy, London; Visiting Professor, Centre for Commercial Law Studies, Queen Mary & Westfield College, University of London.

TABLE OF CASES

TABLE OF UK STATUTES

TABLE OF UK STATUTORY INSTRUMENTS AND PRACTICE DIRECTIONS

STATUTORY INSTRUMENTS

PRACTICE DIRECTIONS

TABLE OF EUROPEAN LEGISLATION

COMMISSION NOTICES ETC.

COUNCIL REGULATIONS

DECISIONS

DIRECTIVES

TREATIES

TABLE OF INTERNATIONAL LEGISLATION

GERMANY

HONG KONG

JAPAN

LIECHTENSTEIN

TABLE OF INTERNATIONAL CONVENTIONS AND RULES

TABLE OF INTERNATIONAL CONVENTIONS AND RULES

RULES

CHAPTER 1

REMEDIES AND RISK: INTERNATIONAL COMPARISONS

1.1 In financial transactions one party or the other has to bear the legal risk, and the choice is often hard to make. It is the law which decides who it is to be. This chapter gives some examples of the choices that legal systems have made in deciding who carries that risk in the context of banking and finance.

INSOLVENCY—A SUGGESTED SCALE

1.2 In providing a suggested scale, one is mainly concerned with showing international bankruptcy comparisons, because bankruptcy is the biggest source of trouble. On an insolvency there is not enough money to go round and so the law has to decide whether to throw the risk on to the debtor or on to creditors. The world's jurisdictions can be divided roughly into three groups:

1. pro-creditor;
2. pro-debtor;
3. not interested—these are a few (former) communist and fundamentalist Muslim states.

1.3 Bankruptcy is fundamental to commercial and financial law and numerous major doctrines in commercial law which really matter (beyond the most basic and primitive rules of contract) are in some way or another traceable back to what happens on insolvency.

1.4 Insolvency law is, for example, one of the foundations of when title passes in a contract of sale, and it is the foundation of security and guarantees. There is no point in allowing retention of title if it fails on insolvency because the whole object of retention of title is that it should succeed on insolvency. There is no point in having a law of pledge if the pledge is set aside or its enforcement frozen on the bankruptcy of the debtor since the only reason for taking the pledge is to protect the creditor against that bankruptcy. There is no point in having ease of set-off between parties if it does not function on insolvency because that is precisely when one party wishes to be protected against the default of the other. The efficacy of corporate law is much reduced if it is ineffective to protect the owners or managers when the corporation becomes insolvent—one of the basic objectives of corporate law is not merely to achieve administrative or mechanistic convenience but to protect those who capitalise and manage the enterprise against the failure of the venture. The strength of a law of unjust enrichment or recovery of wrongful takings is weakened if it does not operate to give a proprietary recovery on insolvency, since that is usually when it is really needed.

1.5 It is possible to construct a more detailed scale of jurisdictions according to whether they are pro-debtor or pro-creditor in their legal rules. A pro-creditor jurisdiction seeks to help a creditor to escape the debacle, e.g. as follows:

(a) by recognising a wide security or a set-off, while a pro-debtor jurisdiction seeks to aggrandise the debtor's estate, e.g. by restricting security, refusing insolvency set-off, setting aside title finance, such as hire purchase (so that the leased asset is treated as belonging to the lessee on his bankruptcy),
(b) by refusing divided ownership and the trust (so that trust assets go to the trustee's creditors),
(c) by clawing back all payments and transfers by the insolvent member in long suspect periods with a minimum of defences available to creditors (so that transactions are unsafe and the formal insolvency is retroactive),
(d) by promoting corporate rehabilitation procedures (thereby making the consensus rescue more difficult), and
(e) by allowing the insolvent estate to insist on the performance of profitable contracts by the counterparty but allowing it to repudiate the unprofitable contracts ("cherry-picking").

These labels are simplistic and the scaling itself is unreliable and subjective: it is not possible to be scientifically accurate.

1.6 It is usually the case that the law has to decide the winner and the loser, the victor and the victim. This is why the law is ultimately so ruthless. It is particularly ruthless on insolvency because of the profound effect that insolvency has upon people's lives, upon business dealings and upon the economy.

1.7 One may attempt to rank some of the senior jurisdictions on a scale according to whether their corporate insolvency laws are pro-creditor or pro-debtor. One on the scale is extreme pro-creditor. Ten on the scale is extreme pro-debtor. A tentative scale is as follows:

1. Hong Kong, Singapore and other English-influenced states (nearly 80 of them);
2. Australia, England, Ireland;
3. Netherlands (and former Dutch states like Indonesia), Norway, Switzerland;
4. Scotland, Japan, Korea, New Zealand, Sweden, Germany;
5. United States, Canada (Quebec more pro-debtor);

6. Austria, Denmark, South Africa (and related states like Botswana and Zimbabwe);
7. Italy;
8. Greece, Portugal, Spain, most of Latin America;
9. Belgium, Luxembourg, many former French colonies;
10. France.

Apart from those at the exteme ends of one and ten, it would be quite legitimate to move others up or down a rung or two in the scale.

1.8 Suffice it to say here that the scaling overrides the civil code/common law classification and certainly overrides any classification based upon whether a state is developed or undeveloped. It is surprising to note that, on the basis of the criteria used, most traditional English jurisdictions are on the extreme pro-creditor end of the scale and that France is on the extreme pro-debtor end, even though England and France are both neighbouring Western European industrialised countries sharing a common outlook.

1.9 The scaling is based upon a variety of criteria, notably the scope and efficiency on bankruptcy of security and of title finance, such as retention of title and financial leasing; the availability of insolvency set-off; the aggressiveness of corporate rehabilitation statutes; the recognition of the trust and the ownership of assets in the possession of the debtor as opposed to reputed ownership; the armoury of the veil of incorporation; the attitude to preferential transfers; and the attitude to contract and lease rescission on insolvency.

1.10 The scale is not based on the actual culture of a jurisdiction: law and culture are often diffeent. For example, it is not true to say that the people of France are extreme pro-debtor and the people of England extreme pro-creditor. But their legal systems are. History often dictates that the law loses touch with the culture. Something may now be said about some of these criteria.

SECURITY

Generally

1.11 The attitude to security is a leading criterion and is primarily dictated by insolvency policies.

1.12 Security is employed in every conceivable context in international finance: universal security to secure finance for a project, security over goods to finance trade, margin collateral to secure dealings on futures and options exchanges, security over investments to support bank finance for the transfer of investments in clearing-houses for investment securities, security to central banks in payment systems or for overnight overdrafts, mortgages of ships and aircraft to finance the purchase money, even the humble lien, which everybody recognises, to protect the supplier who has not been paid—the vendor, the repairer, the warehouseman, the custodian, the crew, the airport. The use of investment security collateral is now immense in financial markets.

1.13 The rationale of security is to protect the creditor against the insolvency of the debtor. The policies in favour include, for example, that security is desirable to mitigate the risk of cascade or domino insolvencies, to encourage capital to finance ventures, to facilitate a debt restructuring if a project gets into difficulties and to reduce the cost of credit. The ethical basis is that he who pays for the assets should have the right to the asset and that the conditional security right is a fair exchange for the credit. The desire to protect the impecunious and unsophisticated debtor from himself and from the money lender is at odds with the realities of modern wholesale finance provided by responsible institutions: in most developed jurisdictions, the small debtor is adequately covered by consumer protection laws.

1.14 The opposing policies are that security violates the equality principle on bankruptcy and defeats small creditors. Those subscribing to this view maintain that we should be aiming at more creditor equality, not a complex ladder of priorities. It is also said that creditors are paid for the risk.

1.15 The point remains that security which is ineffective on insolvency is futile. Accordingly a jurisdiction which inhibits enforcement by insolvency freezes or deprioritises the security below preferential creditors or rehabilitation expenses reduces the effectiveness of the transaction.

1.16 When one surveys the international reception of security, one is staggered by the disparities. There is not the remotest consensus. One group of states allows a universal monopolistic security over all the assets of the debtor, allows it to reach future assets, including assets coming into existence after the bankruptcy of the debtor, imposes no ceremonial formalities to warn the debtor, holds the debtor to any agreement that he may not prepay and hence shake off the security, imposes no limits on who may take the security, permits the security to cover all future debt without stating a maximum amount, allows the secured creditor to sell the collateral without court intervention, and permits the secured creditor privately to appoint a possessory manager to run the business without selling and on terms that the creditor is not responsible for the conduct of the manager. This group comprises about 80 English-based states and is joined, with qualifications, by the United States, Sweden, Finland and Russia, amongst others—the main difference being that most of these latter countries do not permit possessory receivership.

1.17 The proponents of this pro-creditor system will argue that the regime also protects debtors because a well-secured bank is likely to stay with the situation longer, because the business can be sold as a whole without the devastation of value caused by piecemeal sale, and because possessory management on a default via a receiver enables the business to be continued pending sale so that, again, its value is not lost by an abrupt stoppage while the secured creditor goes through a time-consuming and expensive court-initiated public auction procedure. They aver that enforcement is in any event a last resort and that banks in practice are disinclined to pounce unless all is lost, so that judicial protectionism of corporate debtors is not necessary.

1.18 Yet another group of states rejects this approach. They allow security over land, as practically everybody does, but make it difficult to take security over goods, receivables, contracts and investments. They do so either by prohibiting the security altogether or else by imposing onerous initial formalities, levying unrealistic documentary taxes, excluding security for future debt or revolving credits, insisting on a maximum amount, down-grading the security below priority creditors (taxes, bankruptcy costs, employees) so that one never knows what it is worth, and by placing obstacles in the way of enforcement, such as the cumbersome and expensive judicial public auction, compulsory grace periods and freezes on enforcement. These countries include the more traditional members of the Napoleonic group, subject to wide exceptions especially in the case of legally advanced countries.

TITLE FINANCE

1.19 Title finance is an alternative to security and an assessment of a jurisdiction's view about security should also include its view about title finance. For example, the English nineteenth-century bills of sale legislation prohibited non-possessory chattel mortgages by individuals but were side-stepped by the title finance technique of hire purchase: the result is that credit based on assets is available to consumers. Austria is very hostile to security (even now a non-possessory chattel mortgage of an aircraft is not possible in Austria), but is very receptive to title finance: the aircraft can be finance leased.

1.20 In title finance the financier has title or ownership of the asset, as opposed to a mortgage or security interest. A favoured form is the financial lease, widely used for aircraft and other large pieces of equipment. The financier buys the equipment from the manufacturer and then leases it to the operator for its full useful life. Instead of repaying a loan plus interest, the lessee-operator pays rentals which together amount to the original capital cost plus interest. Effectively the lessor is secured since, if the lessee defaults, the financier can cancel the lease and sell the equipment, accounting to the lessee for any surplus, in the same way that a mortgagee sells the mortgaged asset and, after repayment of the loan, pays any excess back to the mortgagor. Indeed, the operator could instead have borrowed the money to buy the asset, e.g. an aircraft, and mortgaged the aircraft to the lender to service the loan. The substantive business effect would be very similar to a finance lease.

1.21 Other forms of title finance are widely used, for example in relation to trade finance. These forms include retention of title, and the discounting or factoring of commercial receivables. Other classic forms include sale and leaseback and sale and repurchase ("repos"). Repos are commonly used for investment securities and are of enormous importance in financial markets. A similar concept is harnessed for stock borrowings.

1.22 The rationale of these asset-based transactions varies. But in essence they have the commercial effect of security and indeed most of them are designed to avoid the archaic obstacles of pledge laws. The attitude of courts and legislators to quasi-security has ranged from enthusiasm to hostility, a diversity of view which is often inconsistent with the attitude of the jurisdiction concerned to security generally. Some countries are glad to find an escape from the cage of mortgages and hence, by subterfuge, support form over substance. Others are displeased that the birds are flying out and seek to rebolt the gate: they recharacterise the transaction as security with the result that it often fails for non-compliance with a pledge rule. The central point at issue is not whether title finance is similar to security—which it is—but whether the law should permit legal ingenuity to overcome restrictive legal rules which are ill-adapted to modern conditions: the absurd English Bills of Sale Acts are a classic example.

SET-OFF AND NETTING

Set-off as a litmus test

1.23 Set-off is one of the leading, and most accurate, indicators of pro-debtor or pro-creditor attitudes to insolvency; it is a litmus test of jurisdictions. For example, in English-based countries, set-off is restricted as between solvent parties. This favours payment to creditors like banks, lessors and sellers who wish to be paid without deduction so as to maintain cash flow and to support the "pay now, litigate later" principle. But it is compulsory on insolvency—favouring payment to creditors who are thereby paid by the defaulter, even though they are unsecured. By contrast, in most Napoleonic jurisdictions solvent set-off is liquid between solvent parties (favouring debtors) but prohibitied on insolvency (augmenting the debtor's estate and hence favouring debtors). The contrast could not be more complete.

Security function of set-off

1.24 Set-off avoids circuity of payment and achieves the aim of judicial economy by avoiding multiplicity of proceedings. But the main effect of set-off is that a debtor with a set-off is in substance "secured" in that the debtor's cross-claim can be paid or discharged by setting it off against the creditor's claim. Thus a bank can discharge a loan owed to it by setting it off against a deposit owed by the bank. The set-off discharges both claims.

1.25 Since claims are a major form of property nowadays and since creditors are often also debtors to the same counterparty, the law of set-off is of paramount importance in international financial affairs, almost as important as the law of security interests. The most common cases of set-off in other contexts include set-off by banks of loans against deposits; set-off between institutions in financial markets such as the inter-bank deposit market; netting of foreign exchange, swaps, futures, securities and repo contracts; and set-off in centralised payment systems. Netting usually involves both a cancellation of contracts and a set-off of resulting losses and gains. The amounts involved are immense and the reduction in exposures achieved by set-off, with resulting reduction in credit costs, and cascade risks threatening the integrity of the financial system, are correspondingly large.

1.26 But this short list should not disguise the persuasiveness of set-off in financial and business affairs: wherever there are a series of contracts between parties, there is a potential for set-offs, and even single contracts containing reciprocal obligations give rise to a set-off possibility—banking, sales, insurances, leasing, custodianship, transportation, services.

Policies of insolvency set-off

1.27 The old classical view espoused by the Napoleonic jurisdictions is that insolvency set-off is a violation of the *pari passu* principle because a creditor with a set-off gets paid in full, and that the set-off is like an unpublicised security interest causing assets to disappear on bankruptcy.

1.28 The arguments in favour of set-off are:

(a) it is unjust that the defaulter should insist on payment, but not pay himself;
(b) set-off helps creditors escape the debacle and hence mitigates the knock-on or cascade effect of bankruptcy;
(c) set-off reduces exposures and hence the cost of credit;
(d) set-off avoids circuitry and hence reduces costs;
(e) set-off prevents the debtor from being bankrupted on a debt he does not owe, if the overall position is taken into account; if he has this admittedly legitimate relief, he should not be in a better position than the creditor.

1.29 As to the view that set-off is effectively an unpublished security interest, it is not practical to require creditors who have reciprocal claims to publish this fact. There are many other cases where it is accepted that it is not realistic to publicise the fact that assets will be removed or depleted on insolvency, e.g. repossessions of leased assets, cancellation of contracts and forfeitures of mortgaged assets where it is too expensive or burdensome to require filing or registration. Financial statements themselves are based on the necessary assumption that the enterprise will continue as a going concern: a bankruptcy break-up sale results in a dramatic collapse of values and extinction of goodwill, so that creditors dealing with an enterprise must accept that bankruptcy is a spoliator of value, a devastation far in excess of anything that set-off can inflict. The "secrecy" argument therefore appears unconvincing.

1.30 In any event, whatever view one may take about the policies, the fact of the matter is that if set-off is to be of any value as a form of "security" it must stand up on insolvency, which is the time that the protection is really needed.

States allowing insolvency set-off

1.31 The majority of international opinion favours the grant of wide insolvency set-off although there is variation in the detail.

1.32 States allowing insolvency set-off by statute include the following.

(a) *Europe*: Austria, Denmark, England, Germany, Guernsey (but only if the parties have contracted for it), Ireland (North and Republic), Isle of Man, Italy, Jersey, Liechtenstein, Netherlands, Poland, Scotland (case law—no statute) and Switzerland.

(b) *North America*: Canada (including Quebec since the Federal bankruptcy legislation overrides the Napoleonic bar on insolvency set-off), and the United States (including Louisiana which is also a Napoleonic state where the Bankruptcy Act 1978, s.553 overrides, although there are contrary decisions). Note that there is a stay on set-off under the Canadian Bankruptcy and Insolvency Act 1992, s.65.1(1) amending the insolvency set-off in BA s.75(3).

(c) *Scandinavia*: Finland, Norway, Sweden. There are corporate rehabilitation stays in Finland and Sweden.

(d) *Latin America*: Panama.

(e) *Middle East*: Cyprus, Israel.

(f) *Asia and Pacific*: Australia, China, Hong Kong, India, Japan, South Korea, Malaysia, New Zealand, Pakistan, Singapore, Sri Lanka, Thailand.

(g) *Africa*: Liberia (probably, although there is no statute), Nigeria, Zambia and probably some or all of the former British colonies (except South Africa).

(h) *Caribbean*: Bahamas, Bermuda, Cayman Islands.

1.33 The position in the Arabian states in the Middle East, such as Saudi Arabia, is often uncertain because of the absence of a developed bankruptcy law.

1.34 The position in the former USSR states appears unclear. The new bankruptcy laws in Russia, Belarus, Khazakhstan and the Ukraine do not mention insolvency set-off: it is likely that set-off is not available.

States refusing insolvency set-off

1.35 In those jurisdictions which do not permit insolvency set-off, the general principle subject to local variations is that the reciprocal claims must satisfy the conditions of the solvent set-off rules prior to the relevant insolvency date. For instance, in the case of independent set-off both claims must be mutual, liquidated, matured and legally payable, or they must have been set off by contract prior to the insolvency date under a contract entered into prior to the preferential suspect period. Generally a contract which removes an obstacle to set-off, such as illiquidity, multicurrency or immaturity, must remove the bar prior to the suspect period and the claims must be eligible for set-off before the relevant insolvency date pursuant to the contract.

1.36 If the claims do not satisfy these requirements by the relevant date, there can be no set-off and the creditor must pay the cross-claim into the insolvent's estate and prove for the claim owed to him by the insolvent. Hence if a bank owes a term deposit maturing after the insolvency date and is owed a term loan accelerated before the insolvency date, there is no set-off and the bank must pay in the term deposit and prove for the accelerated loan—something of a disaster. The bar is also unfortunate for netting agreements.

1.37 The group of non-allowing states comprise:

(a) *Europe*: France (Art. 107 of the Decree of December 27, 1985), Belgium, Luxembourg, Spain, Greece, Portugal.
(b) *Middle East*: Egypt, Kuwait (probably, but there is no statutory provision), Bahrain (Art. 86 of the Banking and Composition Law No. 11 of 1987).
(c) *Latin America*: Argentina (CC Art. 862, Art. 134 of the Bankruptcy Law 1955), Brazil, Chile, Colombia, Mexico (Art. 128 of the Bankruptcy Law).
(d) Africa: South Africa and (probably) various other states originally part of the French or Belgian dominions, e.g. Francophone north, west and central African states.

Exceptional insolvency set-offs in refusing states

1.38 There are three main exceptions to the general bar on insolvency set-off in the refusing states.

(a) *Current account set-off*. It seems to be universally true that current account set-off is available in the refusing states on the rationale that debits and credits are but one account eligible for compensation on termination of the banker–customer relationship on insolvency.
(b) *Transaction set-off*. There appears to be wide acceptance of the notion in the non-allowing states that transaction set-off is permitted because it would be intolerable that, for example, an insolvent should be able to claim the price without bringing into account damages for delay or defective performance.
(c) *Netting statutes*. An increasing number of the refusing countries have introduced netting statutes to protect financial markets. These include

France, Belgium, Luxembourg, South Africa and Spain. These statutes are extremely technical. The trouble with the compromise approach is that the sheer complexity of carve-outs can itself produce systemic risks—only a real expert can follow the detail and the carve-outs quickly become out-of-date.

Set-off as general indicator

1.39 Although these are generalisations which are subject to exceptions, a country which does not have insolvency set-off is also usually hostile to security and makes it difficult to take non-possessory security over movables, has expansive attitudes to the preferential reach of preferential transfers made in the suspect period, has a low opinion of the veil of incorporation as a protection against insolvency, disapproves of attempts by suppliers to protect themselves against insolvency by retention of title and the like and requires that assignment of debts be notified to the debtor if those assignments are to be effective on the insolvency of the seller. The test is therefore quite useful in terms of litmus paper.

DIVIDED OWNERSHIP: THE TRUST

Recognition of the trust

1.40 It is not difficult to operate a modern commercial system of law without divided ownership, namely the trust. The essence of the trust is that ownership is divided between the nominal, representative, legal or titular holder of the asset—the trustee—and the real beneficial owner. If the trustee becomes insolvent, then the beneficial owner can claim the property ahead of the creditors of the insolvent trustee and the property is not expropriated. The essence of the trust is its validity on the bankruptcy of the trustee: a trust invalid on bankruptcy is pointless and dangerous.

1.41 There is nothing strange about the idea of split ownership. A warehouse which holds furniture for depositors is a trustee in this sense, although everyone, including the common law states, flinch from applying the trust language and prefer instead something safe, like "bailment". Hence, the idea itself is quite routine and indeed it seems that virtually all states permit divided ownership for goods.

1.42 Examples of the use of the trust in international finance are:

— trusts of specific securities or of fungible securities held by custodians for the collective benefit of depositors of those securities in clearing houses, e.g. Euroclear, Cedel, the US Depository Trust Corporation and many others—the amounts involved are stupendous;

- trustees of bonds for the benefit of bondholders;
- syndicate agents which hold the security for the benefit of the syndicate banks;
- collective investment schemes, such as investment funds and unit trusts;
- subordination trusts of the proceeds of the junior debt and trusts of the proceeds of letters of credit;
- third-party beneficiary contracts, e.g. exculpation clauses in syndicate loan agreements protecting employees of the agent bank;
- trusts of the benefit of contracts held by market agents for outside clients as principal, protecting the principal if the agent should become insolvent;
- securitisations and equipment trusts in asset-based finance.

1.43 The trust was rejected by the civilian countries on account mainly of false wealth plus an assembly of other rationalisations, despite the fact that it was an institution developed by the classical Romans and was much in evidence in Europe prior to Napoleon's time, e.g. in family law (the usufruct of the husband or the parent). The Napoleonic rejection seems to have been motivated partly by a desire to simplify property, to grant the citizen the absolute right of enjoyment and disposition of property freed from feudal burdens, and to promote capitalism. It was also feared that secret ownership could disrupt commercial dealings (sale and mortgages), although it is perfectly possible to subordinate the secret owner in commercial transactions but to give him a proprietary claim on the insolvency of the trustee.

1.44 When the German jurists settled the BGB, the view which predominated was that *in rem* proprietary rights must be registered publicly and that there could be no proprietary *in rem* right effective on insolvency without this publicity. This was against the spirited advice of the Germanist professor at Berlin, Otto von Gierke (1841–1921), who described it as a "horrible legal blunder".

1.45 But it is not true to say that civil countries do not have the trust at all and that it is purely a common law institution. A different word is used in civilian countries—*in rem* remedy or vindication or revindication or fiduciary ownership.

1.46 A number of civilian countries have directly absorbed the Anglo-American trust, either by statute or case law, usually by statute. Examples are South Africa, Japan, Liechtenstein and Panama. Secondly, many civilian countries have installed the trust where it was felt to be useful. Examples are:

1. the holding in trust of fungible investment securities by central depositories in Austria, Belgium (Euroclear), Germany, Luxembourg (Cedel) and the Netherlands;
2. an exemption in favour of banks allowing them to act as custodian trustees in some Latin American countries;

3. the acceptance of fiduciary ownership in the Chilean Civil Code drafted by the Venezuelan Andrés Bello and subsequently adopted by Ecuador (1860), Colombia (1873) and a number of central American states;
4. the trust by a bankrupt agent of his claim for the sale price against the third party buyer for the benefit of his principal (most countries have this);
5. various other direct actions;
6. the French third party beneficiary contract, the *stipulation pour autrui*; and
7. trusts in connection with securitisations, e.g. Argentina in the 1990s.

1.47 Interesting examples of the acceptance of the trust by Napoleonic countries include the adoption of the trust by Quebec in 1879 to sanction gifts for McGill University and the Fraser Institute in Montreal, its adoption by Louisiana in 1882 to allow Paul Tulane's gifts to Tulane University (followed by bank trusteeship in 1902, bondholder trustees in 1914 and trusts of land in 1938), and the remarkable French case of *De Renesse* v. *Robineau*, D 1928, 2, 121 where the court validated a legacy for the creation of a foundation to provide for the poor widows and orphans of the Banque de France and, in case of a shortage in this class of beneficiaries, to the poor orphans and widows of the Crédit Lyonnais.[1]

1.48 Nevertheless, these are all exceptions to the general rule, enacted to meet special situations and limited to the scope of the statutory dispensation. Thus in Austria and Germany the statutory *Sammelverwahrung* (collective ownership) is restricted to certain classes of securities (not all securities) under the Depotgesetz (Custody Act). Almost uniformly in the civil countries, for example, a syndicate agent cannot hold the security as trustee for the banks, with the result that it is not possible to novate bank debt on a change of participants without discharging the security.

1.49 In any event, it seems to be true that, outside the common law states, the constructive trust and tracing, e.g. of moneys wrongfully taken away from the real owner or of mistaken payments, is uniformly rejected, so that this is an important test of a legal system's orientation. The refusal of tracing effectively torpedoes the law of restitution and unjust enrichment.

ASSIGNMENT OF DEBTS

Notification of assignments of debts

1.50 An important criterion is whether a sale of a debt is effective on the bankrupcty of the seller if the sale is not notified to the debtor. This is different

1. See Vera Golgár, "Why no trusts in the civil law?", 2 *American Journal of Comparative Law* 204 (1953).

from whether the notice is desirable for priority against competing assignees, for directing the debtor to pay the assignee and the like. The test is relevant because of the economic importance of ease of transfers of claims, either by sale or by security assignment. A rule which requires notification to the debtor is based on false wealth—the seller is not dispossessed, even though other creditors cannot possibly know whether their debtor's debtors have been notified and how. The rule is also influenced by other policies, notably a desire to protect debtors from a change of creditors, a desire for certainty, a wish to control trafficking in lawsuits, a wish to prevent the impecunious from assigning away their income—a medley of historical hostility to and conservation about intangible property.

1.51 The common law countries allow debts to be sold over the telephone and without notification and in this they are joined by the Germanic group. But Japan, Korea and the Scandinavian countries remain outside this group: notification to the debtor or other formality is required for validity. Most of the Napoleonic group require notification, although there has been some erosion of this, notably the Dailly Act of 1981 in France and the abolition of the rule in Belgium in 1994.

1.52 But as so often happens when a state is unwilling to surrender an age-old policy, the carve-outs in the refusing states tend initially to be grudging and hedged about with limits. This was evidenced by the tight rules allowing negotiability in the Geneva Conventions of 1930–1931 on negotiable instruments, a formalism which led to the rejection of the Conventions by common law states. The "notice to the debtor" rule is the main international obstacle to the dematerialisation of debt securities—which in many jurisdictions can still only escape by being wrapped up in the paper of a negotiable instrument. It is a significant brake on securitisations.

VEIL OF INCORPORATION

Candidates for personal liability

1.53 One of the fundamental decisions jurisdictions have to make is whether to honour the veil of incorporation. The test is whether the law visits personal liability on persons other than the company when it is insolvent.

1.54 The main candidates for personal liability are:

(a) the directors and officers, whether *de jure* or *de facto*;
(b) shareholders, including parent companies;
(c) other group companies, i.e. siblings or brother-sister corporations under common ownerships;
(d) financing banks (especially in the context of workouts or security enforcement);
(e) regulators.

Policies

1.55 The main attitudes which are likely to influence the transfer of responsibility for the insolvency to persons other than the company and thereby to lead to the dishonour of the veil of incorporation are:

1. The desire to prevent abuse of the corporate form. The prioritisation of an anti-fraud policy can result in an effective criminalisation of commercial law, since the financial sanction tends to be massive, even though not accompanied by a criminal taint. The real question is how punitive commercial law should be and the degree to which the society is content to absorb abuse in the interests of some higher business objective.
2. The intensity of big pocket liability, i.e. finding another pocket to pay, preferably a deep one. The big pocket may be a regulator, a shareholder, a group company or a financing bank. Directors are not usually big enough pockets. The essence of the big pocket liability is that it imposes liability on a bystander who is not primarily responsible, but who happens to be able to pay the victim and who was sufficiently involved for a case to be made out against him.
3. The desire to stop a business before it is too late. This policy shows itself in a greater readiness to fix personal liability on directors (to encourage them to apply early for bankruptcy) and in rules for the mandatory presentation of insolvency petitions if the company becomes balance sheet insolvent (as opposed to being unable to pay current debts) or loses half its capital. The theory is that creditors would be protected if business is halted before the wave of debt engulfs the assets. The opposing view is that attempts to compel an early stoppage can prevent companies from trading out of their difficulties or carrying out a private workout, and may instead force them into formal insolvency proceedings, which almost invariably have a cataclysmic effect on values, even if they are survival proceedings.

Scale of jurisdictions

1.56 It would be possible to scale jurisdictions according to whether they honour the veil of incorporation on insolvency.

1.57 Those high on the scale would be intensely loyal to incorporation and require creditors of an insolvent company to look only to the assets of that company and not to some third party. Those lowest on the scale would be intensely suspicious of incorporation and regard the corporate form more as an administrative convenience and not as a protection against insolvency. It is thought that South Africa, Switzerland and Germany have a strong veil, while France and perhaps Belgium and Spain have a weak veil, with countries like England, Australia, Japan, Scandinavian countries, the Netherlands, Ireland,

Austria, the United States and Italy ranging from a fairly strong to a fairly weak veil.

1.58 The scale would be based on weightings. The prime weighting should be given to the risk of liability being imposed on persons other than the company, mainly directors. Other subsidiary factors—which tend to be merely indicative of attitude but are not paramount in terms of legal risk or economic importance—would include rules as to the maintenance of capital (especially financial assistance for the purchase of own shares, redemption of capital, special reserves, and the action to be taken on loss of capital); conclusivity of corporate formation (economically unimportant since in practice companies are easy to form in most jurisdictions); and the minimum number of shareholders (also unimportant in practice and influenced by attitudes to the family enterprise sector and the convenient availability of the corporate privilege).

1.59 The US is difficult to characterise. Although bankruptcy law is federal, corporation law is not and there are state variations. There is no concept of wrongful trading imposing liability on directors, but on the other hand the concepts of tort liability, of stripping the veil, of equitable subordination and of lender liability appear to be quite potent in comparative terms, but this may only be because they are well publicised.

JUDICIAL RESCUE PROCEEDINGS

Rescue proceedings and private restructuring

1.60 A feature of modern insolvency law is the adoption of corporate rescue proceedings designed to resuscitate debtor companies in distress.

1.61 The alternative is a private consensual debt restructuring (workout) agreed between creditors, or more usually by bank creditors. The main advantages of formal proceedings are that they result in a statutory freeze on individual creditor enforcements and a power to bind dissentient creditors. The main disadvantages are that the public declaration of insolvency normally devastates a business, that the freeze can prejudice creditor protections and that formal proceedings are costly. Formal rehabilitation proceedings have a low rate of success—often around a mere 10 per cent of those initiated. An essential question for countries is whether to encourage the private restructuring—in which event the formal proceeding must be discouraged—or whether to opt for a formal proceeding—in which event the private restructuring is more difficult because the debtor will tend to pre-empt its creditors by forcing them into a formal proceeding. Many experienced practitioners in this field agree that the private restructuring is much faster, safer and cheaper than a formal proceeding and that a formal proceeding is a last resort to be used only if there is absolutely no alternative. The debate has been intensified by bouts of financial cataclysm where a systemic risk, e.g. the collapse of a currency or a generalised economic depression, devastates the business sector and many enterprises which are otherwise sound. Hence the desire to preserve these companies till the storm passes.

1.62 The emphasis here is on large corporations and not small one-man or family companies, which are not commonly prime actors in international finance. One may therefore dispense with debate over the economic requirements of small businesses and the protection of consumers, while recognising that they too may become the victims of debt and seek survival.

Classification of proceedings

1.63 One may in outline classify the various forms of present-day proceedings into the following groups:

- — voluntary compositions;
- — traditional compositions and moratoriums, often requiring an unrealistic immediate minimum payment to creditors;
- — corporate rehabilitation proceedings.

The first two are little used in those countries which have them and hence it is mainly the corporate rehabilitation proceedings which are of interest.

Corporate rehabilitation proceedings

1.64 Modern forms of corporate rehabilitation impose a freeze on creditor proceedings and sometimes also significantly impinge on creditor rights in the interests of preserving businesses. The rationale of the disturbance of creditor rights is that the rights are merely delayed and are reinstated if the rescue is successful so that the creditors, it is said, lose nothing. However, these rescue proceedings have had a very low rate of success, e.g. 10 per cent, so that this rationale appears to be more difficult to justify. Nevertheless, corporate rehabilitations are a useful back-stop as an alternative to final liquidation or a private workout. The real question is how tough they should be.

1.65 Examples include mild proceedings, such as:

- — in Australia the voluntary administration and deed of company arrangement under the Corporate Law Reform Act 1992;
- — in Britain, an administration under the Insolvency Act 1986;
- — in the Republic of Ireland, an examinership under the Companies (Amendment) Act 1990;
- — in Japan, the Corporate Rehabilitation Law of 1952, based on the pre-1978 US Bankruptcy Act of 1898, Chapter X. The Bankruptcy Law of 1923 was based on German ideas;
- — in Singapore the judicial management introduced by the Companies (Amendment) Act 1987 and largely based on the British administration

under IA 1986, but limited to 180 days. As in Britain, floating chargees have blocking powers;
— in Spain, the suspension of payments under the Suspension of Payments act of 1922.

1.66 There are also tough proceedings, such as:

— in Canada, the commercial reorganisation proposal under the Bankruptcy and Insolvency Act 1992 and the older but tougher Companies' Creditors Arrangement Act dating from the 1930s. Both are federal;
— in France the *redressement judiciaire* under the Law of January 25, 1985;
— in Italy, the extraordinary administration of 1979 (*amministrazione straordinaria*), which placed the bankruptcy of large enterprises in the hands of the executive, not the courts;
— in New Zealand, the statutory management under the Corporations (Investigation and Management Act) 1989;
— in the United States, Chapter 11 of the Bankruptcy Code of 1978 which is a federal statute.

Recent tougher statutes have been introduced in Belgium, Finland, Sweden and Thailand.

1.67 In practice, the crucial features in terms of economic impact are:

— freezes on set-off, netting, and contract cancellations. Freezes on contract cancellations are draconian because there are so many different contracts they can impinge upon—business life is based on contract—so that fairness is difficult to achieve because they allow the insolvent debtor to "cherry-pick", i.e. preserve contracts profitable to him and cancel loss-making contracts, because they prevent netting and because they inhibit other currently important transactions, e.g. repos;
— freezes on the enforcement of security and other interferences with the security, e.g. by super-super-priority loans;
— freezes on title finance repossessions, including finance lesses;
— right of the debtor's management to stay in possession and initiate a plan.

1.68 Everybody recognises that there must be a stay on piecemeal creditor executions by unsecured creditors and on liquidation petitions, and there can be no objection to these.

1.69 Probably the most important factor in a successful reorganisation is the ability to raise fresh money to keep the business going. Almost invariably, this will require the priming of existing creditors by giving priority to the new finance and some jurisdictions have been tempted to take away existing creditors' asset protection, e.g. security, to ensure the availability of fresh capital. Both can result in a worsening of the position of creditors if the procedure fails.

CONCLUSION

1.70 Two conclusions may be drawn from this chapter. The first is that eliminating legal risk suffered by one party usually involves casting the risk onto someone else. Almost invariably, compromises, or splitting the difference, will not provide an escape. So the choice has to be made. The second is that the difference internationally between the choices made is dramatic. It follows that the advantage of a low-risk country from the point of view of creditors can be threatened by the presence of high-risk countries. No commercial jurisdication is an island.

PHILIP WOOD

CHAPTER 2

CLAIMS BY BANKS IN THE ENGLISH COURTS: KEY ASPECTS OF PROCEDURE

INTRODUCTION

2.1 Perhaps the most important practical development for banks in English litigation since the first edition of this work has been the introduction of the new Civil Procedure Rules ("CPR"). The product of Reports on Civil Justice in 1995 and 1996 by Lord Woolf (the present Master of the Rolls), the CPR aim to increase dramatically the speed and efficiency with which claims are processed in the English courts, while at the same time saving costs. This is embodied in the CPR themselves whose "overriding objective" is that of "enabling the Court to deal with the case justly".[1] Whether such goals can be achieved remains to be seen, but there can be no doubt that the radical changes in procedure wrought by the CPR will have a very significant impact upon the way in which banks pursue their remedies through civil litigation. It is therefore appropriate that a separate chapter is now devoted to this subject.

2.2 It is likely that these changes will benefit banks. First, they are designed to eliminate or at least reduce substantially the delay which, formerly, was typical between commencing an action and having it tried, something which the defendant was only too happy to have. Equally, the new rules on pleadings, which make it incumbent on a defendant to spell out his case in positive terms, instead of hiding behind a string of denials, are bound to be of assistance to banks. In addition, the CPR will make it easier for banks to persuade a court that the case should be disposed of summarily where there is no real defence. Finally, the rules on discovery have been revised so as to restrict significantly the width of a party's disclosure obligations, which should save banks much of the time and money previously expended on finding and producing documents which were of marginal relevance at best and which were often sought by defendants interested only in "fishing expeditions" and generally slowing things down. This aspect of the CPR merits attention in its own right and is accordingly dealt with in Chapter 4.

2.3 However, there is a price to pay for these advantages, which is the fact that the aim and likely effect of the CPR is to make litigation much more

1. R. 1.1(1).

"front-end loaded" than before. In addition, there is, or is likely to be, increased judicial control of both parties, so that plaintiffs, as well as defendants, will be expected to move the case along swiftly. Finally, the obligation on the parties to consider settlement actively at the outset requires that detailed information be available from the start so as to enable a proper assessment of the merits to take place. In practical terms, therefore, banks are likely to find that they have to make their own internal enquiries at an earlier stage than they may have been used to before. This applies in particular to interviewing witnesses and recovering records from, say, the local branch involved in the case.

2.4 The CPR came into force on 26 April 1999. They are divided into "Parts" which contain the Rules setting out the general principles governing each aspect of procedure. The Rules are then supplemented by Practice Directions ("PDs") which provide more detailed guidance. Transitional provisions[2] deal with cases which were already under way by the commencement date, but it should be noted that the aim of the CPR is to subject such cases to the new regime as comprehensively and quickly as possible.[3] However, some parts of the RSC and CCR remain for the time being. These include the provisions dealing with service out of the jurisdiction, security for costs, judicial review and appeals to the Court of Appeal. The remaining parts of the RSC are now reproduced with some amendment[4] in Schedule 1 to the CPR while Schedule 2 contains the remaining parts of the CCR. The CPR (including the Practice Directions) are contained in a separate volume published as a supplement to the White Book,[5] known as *Civil Procedure*. This volume also contains notes to the CPR in the same format as those in the White Book itself. *Civil Procedure* is likely be at least one of the texts referred to by practitioners when addressing the High Court and for that reason, it will be referred to where appropriate, below.

2.5 Case law dealing with the old Rules of the Supreme Court ("RSC") and County Court Rules ("CCR") will usually be irrelevant insofar as those provisions have been replaced by the CPR.[6] Part 1 begins with the statement that "These Rules are a new procedural code".[7] According to the Introduction to *Civil Procedure*, this was intended "to give a clear message to the courts at all levels that interpretation of the Rules was to be tackled afresh without reference to earlier precedent". The Introduction goes on to point out that this will not be the case with clear and unambiguous earlier decisions (where still relevant presumably) but also that it was suspected that the Court of Appeal will try to interpret the new Rules "in the light of the culture which they seek to promote". Accordingly it will be some time before a further body of case law develops in

2. Contained in PD 51 issued pursuant to R. 51.

3. Paras 2(b), 11 and 12 of PD 51.

4. Usually just to reflect the new terminology employed by the CPR.

5. The 1999 Edition of which has the old rules as its main text.

6. This reflects cases such as *Re a Debtor (No. 1 of 1987)* [1989] 1 WLR 271, in which it was stated that the new insolvency code [i.e. the 1986 Insolvency Rules] required a fresh approach "unfettered by previous authorities", *per* Nicholls LJ at p. 276G.

7. R. 1.1(1).

respect of the interpretation and application of the new rules although it must be the hope of the draftsmen of the CPR that the simpler style and greater flexibility of the latter will mean that the Court of Appeal will be troubled less than previously by such questions.

2.6 It is neither possible nor useful to cover all aspects of the CPR here. Instead, this chapter will focus on those Parts which have particular significance for banks pursuing their remedies through the civil courts. The following areas of practice will therefore be addressed:

- Statements of case;
- Judgments in default;
- Summary judgment and related applications;
- Freezing injunctions;
- Costs;
- Offers to settle;
- Case management;
- Proceedings in the commercial court.

STATEMENTS OF CASE

Claims

2.7 The "statement of case" is the new generic name for what was previously called a pleading, but it also encompasses documents which provide information about a party's case.[8] The old writ is now replaced by a "claim form" which is the method by which all actions are to be commenced save insofar as such a method would be inconsistent with the rules and practice directions applicable to "specialist proceedings"[9] or other proceedings to which the retained rules apply.[10] This qualification is set out in paragraphs 3.3 and 3.4 of PD 7.

2.8 Particulars of claim is the new name for the Statement of Claim, and, as before, particulars of claim may either be contained in the claim form or may follow it within 14 days of service of the claim form.[11] The principal innovation in this context is the introduction of the requirement that every statement of case must be accompanied by a "statement of truth",[12] namely a statement that the party putting the document forward believes in its truth.[13] The statement may be signed either by the party themselves, their "litigation friend" or their legal representative.[14] Failure so to verify a statement of case will render it liable to be

8. R. 2.3(1).
9. As defined in Part 49.
10. See Part 50.
11. See R. 7.4(1) which provides time-limits for service following commencement which are the same as before.
12. R. 22.1(1).
13. R. 22.1(4).
14. R. 22.1(6).

struck out.[15] Furthermore, a person who makes a false statement in a statement of case without an honest belief therein will be guilty of contempt of court.[16] The ambit of the statement of truth may be quite extensive, given that the rules allow for particulars of claim to make reference to any point of law relied upon, to the name of any witness and to any document considered by the party to be necessary to his case.[17] All this emphasises the need for a bank which is bringing a claim to be sure of its ground right at the start, particularly if, as is suspected, solicitors will encourage their clients to sign the statement rather than signing it themselves.[18]

2.9 Finally, it is suggested that banks and their advisers should make use of the freedom to make reference to points of law, documents and witnesses in statements of case, if they can, because it will mean that the defendant will get a fuller picture of what are hopefully the strengths of the claim being made. That being so, the defendant may be more inclined to pay up or settle at an early stage.[18a]

Defences

2.10 Two particular points are of note in relation to the defence to a claim (still called a "defence"). First, as with the claim documents, the defence must be accompanied by a statement of truth.[19] In itself, this may give a defendant about to embark upon a sham defence some pause for thought. Second, Rule 16.5(2) provides that where a defendant denies an allegation he must state his reasons for doing so and if he intends to put forward a version of events different from that given by the plaintiff he must state his own version. This should prevent a defendant from being able to plead merely a series of denials. Once again, the need for a defendant to "set out his stall" at the beginning may encourage him to assess the merits of his own position at a much earlier stage. One final point to note which is relevant to banking litigation is the fact that if the defendant relies on a limitation defence he must give details of the expiry of the relevant period.[20]

Further information

2.11 The procedure for seeking and obtaining "further information"[21] replaces the provisions dealing with further and better particulars and interrogatories.

15. R. 22.2.
16. R. 32.14(1).
17. Which may be attached to the particulars or served at the same time.
18. Although even if a solicitor does sign, he will have to have received clear and express instructions as to the truth of the document, because that is what he will be stating.
18a. However, this does not mean that the pleading should be prolix or disproportionate to the case as a whole. See the observations of Lord Woolf MR in *McPhilemy* v. *Times*, 21 May 1999, unreported.
19. R. 22.1(1) and para. 2.1–2.3 of PD 15.
20. Para. 16.1 of PD 16.
21. Part 18.

The emphasis on "information" makes it clear that the old distinction between pleadings and evidence (behind which a party would often hide) has been dispensed with. It is submitted that this new procedure, under which a party can seek, and the court can order, a response to a question or questions about the other side's case,[22] is a far simpler procedure for obtaining details or clarification of the other side's case, but there are some caveats. First, before making any application to the court for the appropriate order, the request for information (the "request") should be made in writing by the party concerned of the other party giving a reasonable time for a response.[23] Second, the request must confine itself to seeking information reasonably necessary and proportionate to enable the party to prepare his own case.[24] This reflects the criticism of the old system of Further and Better Particulars made by Saville LJ (as he then was) in *Trust Securities* v. *McAlpine*[25] to the effect that the purpose of pleadings was not to play a game at the expense of the litigants. In addition, being a statement of case, the response to any request must be verified by a statement of truth. Once more, this reform is likely to benefit the bank which is faced with a defendant who is being coy about his case, provided that it is also remembered that the bank will be susceptible to a request concerning its claim if this has not been made entirely clear at the start.

JUDGMENTS IN DEFAULT

2.12 It is very common for a bank to find itself in a position to enter judgment in default against a defendant. Under the CPR, a default judgment can be entered or sought where particulars of claim have been served but the defendant has not acknowledged service or (as the case may be) served a defence. As with the old rules, such a judgment may be entered as an administrative act where the only claims being made are for liquidated sums or damages[26] but otherwise must be sought from the Court by application.[27]

2.13 Important changes have been made, however, in connection with the right of a defendant to set aside a default judgment. In the first place, the distinction between "regular" and "irregular" judgments has gone, to be replaced by a (different) distinction between judgments which have been "entered wrongly" and those which have not. The former category applies only to cases where:

22. R. 18.1(1).
23. Para. 1.1 of PD 18.
24. Para. 1.2 of PD 18.
25. *The Times*, 21 December 1994.
26. R. 12.4(1), which also includes in this category claims for delivery-up where the claim form gives the defendant the alternative of paying their value.
27. R. 12.4(2) and Part 23.

(a) the defendant was not in truth in default of acknowledgment of service or defence;
(b) where there was a pending application (by the defendant) to summarily dispose of the claim under Part 24;[28] or
(c) where the defendant had made a counterclaim against the claimant which he had admitted.

In such cases, the court must set the judgment aside.[29]

2.14 In all other cases, the court has a discretion. This means that where, as sometimes happens with claims by banks, judgment is entered for too much, that judgment does not now fall to be set aside as of right but will be considered as a matter of discretion. Questions about whether a judgment for too much can be saved by amendment are therefore no longer apposite. The court will simply make the appropriate adjustment on the application to set aside or any other order which appears suitable in the circumstances.

2.15 Before the court can exercise its discretion, the defendant must have a "real prospect of successfully defending the claim" or it must appear to the court that there is some other good reason why the judgment should be set aside or varied or the defendant should be allowed to defend the claim.[30] Each of these factors must be looked at in turn.

2.16 The "real prospect" test clearly reflects the reasoning in *Alpine Bulk Transport Co. Inc.* v. *Saudi Eagle Shipping Co. Inc.* [1986] 2 Lloyds Rep. 221. However, given that this decision has been the subject of differing interpretations in later cases[31] the proper approach must be to start afresh with the words as they now appear in the rule. This is of course consistent with the general position *vis-à-vis* prior case law. The particular way in which this new test should be applied in practice will emerge in a short space of time since the same phrase is used in the context of applications for summary judgment.[32] What is clear is that the standard is higher than that of a (mere) "triable issue" or "arguable defence".[33]

2.17 In theory, the court can also exercise its discretion, even in the absence of merits if there was some other good reason to set the judgment aside. It is not clear how much leeway the court will give in this respect, although the likelihood must be that "good reason" will be narrowly defined.[34] One good reason for varying a judgment in the absence of merits would, of course, exist where judgment was entered for too much. Beyond that it is difficult to say.

2.18 The question of delay is now given specific prominence as a factor to be

28. See below, 2.28 *et seq.*
29. R. 13.2
30. R. 13.3(1).
31. See, for example *Day* v. *RAC*, *The Times*, 24 November 1998.
32. See R. 24.2(a).
33. See also the notes at 13.3.1 of *Civil Procedure*.
34. The reference in R. 13.3(1)(b) to "some other *good* reason" (emphasis added) to set aside judgment may be compared with the reference in R. 24.2(b) to the requirement, in the context of summary judgment applications, that there be "no other reason" for a trial.

taken into account, by Rule 13.3(2). Indeed it is the only factor which these provisions single out as being one to which the court *must* have regard when exercising its discretion. Given the CPR's aim (among others) of dealing with cases "expeditiously"[35] this is not wholly surprising.

2.19 Finally, and as before, the court may impose terms on the setting aside or variation of any judgment in default. This is by virtue of the general power, when making an order, to impose conditions (including the payment of monies into court) conferred upon the court by Rule 3.1(3)(a).

2.20 All this suggests that the bank will be in a strong position to exploit the tactical advantage gained when the defendant has failed to comply with the time-limits concerned with acknowledging service or filing a defence.

SUMMARY JUDGMENT AND RELATED APPLICATIONS[36]

2.21 This procedure has long been a key element in banking litigation which consists very largely of straightforward debt, guarantee or related claims where there is no obvious defence.[37] Taking a case all the way to trial is time-consuming and expensive and always carries a degree of risk for the bank, even if a small risk, and there is thus a powerful incentive to dispose of the case summarily if possible. In addition, such applications are dealt with on the basis of written, not live evidence. This is a double advantage for banks, whose evidence often comes from managers or other officials who can remember little more than what is recorded in their internal records and memoranda. Such records then form the substance of the bank's evidence and the persons concerned are spared the strain of giving oral evidence.

2.22 Part 24 permits the court to give summary judgment against a defendant (as well as a claimant[38]), on the whole of a claim or on a particular issue if (a) the relevant party has no real prospect of success and (b) there is no other reason for a trial.[39] That the court is entitled to look at the persuasiveness or otherwise of the evidence before it is confirmed by paragraph 1.3 of PD 24 to the effect that an application for summary judgment against a defendant may be based on a point of law (including construction of a document) or the evidence which can reasonably be expected to be available at trial or a combination of the two.

2.23 PD 24 then makes specific reference to the approach to be taken by the

35. R. 1.1(2)(d).

36. Parts of this section previously appeared in the chapter entitled "Remedies for banks: an outline of English law" written by Richard Salter QC, in the first edition of this work.

37. Mortgage claims continue to be dealt with in the Chancery Division under a modified version of RSC Order 88, now known as R. 88 in Sch. 1 to the CPR. Under this procedure, the court is entitled at a first or subsequent hearing to make such order as it thinks fit on the claim, including judgment. Banks are reminded that there are highly specific matters which must be covered in the witness statement or affidavit where delivery of possession is sought. See R. 88.5.

38. See below, para. 2.28.

39. R. 24.2(a) and (b).

court, and provides a gloss on the test to be applied. First, paragraph 4.1 states that the court will give judgment against a defendant if (1) the claimant has shown a case which, if unanswered would entitle him to judgment and (2) the defendant has shown no reason why there should be a trial. It is submitted that requirement (1) means that the claimant will not get judgment if his claim can be seen to be defective in any event, for in this circumstance it matters not whether the defendant is able to put up any positive reason for having a trial—the claim is bound to fail anyway. The claim might fall into this category because of some technical problem or because as a matter of law it is misconceived. Requirement (2) then encompasses the two matters which the defendant must raise to avoid judgment against him, namely a reasonable prospect of success or some other reason for trial. The distinction between these two requirements is not quite the same as the distinction between the ability of a defendant under the old Order 14 procedure to show that the application against him should be dismissed for some technical reason (almost always procedural) and his ability, on the other hand to raise some matter of substance.[39a]

2.24 However, paragraph 5.1 of PD 24 then provides that the orders which may be made on an application under Part 24 include judgment on the claim or dismissal or striking out of the claim, the dismissal of the application and a conditional order.[40] The latter is an order which requires a party to pay a sum of money into court or take some specified step in relation to his claim or defence. Where the claimant is seeking judgment, it is thought that ordinarily only the first of these options will be relevant. It is not yet clear whether the decision of the House of Lords in *Yorke Motors* v. *Edwards* [1982] 1 WLR 444 will continue to have a bearing on whether the court makes a conditional order where it would otherwise be appropriate to do so but the defendant cannot afford the payment. Under this decision, the court should not make such an order where these circumstances exist because it would be tantamount to giving judgment against the defendant. The answer probably lies in the fact that the "overriding objective" stated in Rule 1.1 expressly requires the court to have regard to dealing with the case in ways which are, *inter alia*, "proportionate" to the financial position of each party and ensuring that it is dealt with fairly. In a case where the defendant has made genuine efforts to raise the sum to be paid in, or it is clear that he will not be able to raise it, the court is unlikely to order such a payment.

2.25 The Note to paragraph 5 also makes it clear that the practice of granting "leave to defend" will in any event not be followed. Accordingly, unless the court makes a conditional order, if a claimant fails to obtain summary judgment, his application will be dismissed. However, although there is no longer any such thing as "conditional leave to defend" it is clear that this is what paragraph 5.1 is purporting to provide for, albeit under a different name.

39a. It may be that this particular gloss does not survive. It has been observed that the "no prospect" test is itself clear enough.

40. It is slightly odd that such basic provisions only appear in the PD and not in the rule itself.

Whether it has been drafted entirely successfully is open to some doubt. The conditional order would state that a sum of money is to be paid into court and in default the party's statement of case will be struck out. But in the case of a claimant's application for judgment, the defendant may not have served a defence,[41] in which case he will have no defence to be struck out if the time for payment-in is expressed to expire before the time for the service of the defence. Presumably the court will interpret this part of PD 24 so as to allow the claimant to enter judgment if the money is not paid in on time.[42]

2.26 A further possible problem lies in the fact that PD 24 makes express reference to the circumstances in which the court may make a conditional order, namely, where it appears to the court to be "possible ... but improbable" that the defence will succeed. This is somewhat surprising for two reasons. First, the old rules never legislated for this expressly[43] and, it might be thought, wisely so. Second, it suggests that a defendant who has no *reasonable* prospects of success but who might nonetheless *possibly* succeed can escape judgment under Rule 24.2 by invoking paragraph 4.3 of PD 24. And it is no answer to this problem to say that even if the defendant could show a *possible* defence the court does not *have* to make a conditional order because in practice, if a defendant can afford to make a suitable payment into court and can show a possible defence, it will be difficult for the court to give judgment instead of a conditional order without appearing to act arbitrarily. It remains to be seen how the courts will deal with this. On any view it might be thought that it would have been better if paragraph 4.3 had not appeared at all. At all events, the making of a conditional order is a useful "second-best" to obtaining judgment and if a substantial sum has to be paid in by the defendant, then there will be a good chance that the claim will be settled.

2.27 At this point mention should be made of the interim payments procedure under Rule 25.6–25.9. Such a payment may be sought where

(a) the defendant has admitted liability to pay damages or some other sum to the claimant;
(b) the claimant has obtained an order that the defendant pay damages or some other sum to be assessed;
(c) the court is satisfied that if the claim went to trial the claimant would obtain judgment for a substantial amount of money; or
(d) there is a claim for possession and the court is satisfied that the defendant would in any event be liable to pay the claimant a sum in respect of the defendant's use and occupation of land.

It is thought that in practice it will only be cases which fall into category (c) which will be of interest to banks. Even here, however, it is questionable whether

41. See R. 24.4(1) and (2).
42. Which it could probably do pursuant to its general power under R. 3.1(3).
43. Although the case law referred to "shadowy" defences, or cases where the court was "very nearly" prepared to give judgment.

the interim payments procedure offers any advantage over an application for summary judgment pursuant to Part 24, bearing in mind the relaxed standard of proof which now governs applications under the latter. Furthermore, although paragraph 5.1 of PD 24 does not say so expressly, it must be the intention that the court can give judgment on a part of the claim as opposed to all of it (as before), so it is not as if an application for an interim payment is needed for that reason. Finally, the notes at 25.7.4 in *Civil Procedure* suggest that in all cases, the court will have regard to the financial position of each party. If so, this is hardly likely to benefit the bank—such considerations are not relevant to an application for summary judgment.[44]

2.28 The procedure under Part 24 is available not only to claimants but also to defendants. Accordingly, a bank which is the subject of an unmeritorious claim, perhaps as a pre-emptive strike by a customer who is about to be sued by the bank, can apply to have the claim dismissed. Since the test is the same—"no real prospect"—the bank is entitled to ask the court to assess the claimant's case in the round, including consideration of the evidence. It is likely that it will be easier for the bank to succeed here than under the former "strike-out" procedure under Order 18, rule 19 of the RSC where the courts were in practice reluctant to embark on a review of the evidence in order to conclude that the claim brought was "frivolous and vexatious" or an "abuse of the process". In cases where the bank seeks a summary dismissal of the claim, it will also be entitled to seek summary judgment upon the counterclaim for moneys owed, which will often be a feature of such cases. Even if the defendant bank does not succeed in obtaining the dismissal of the claim altogether, it is worth remembering that the court may make a conditional order, requiring the claimant to pay money into court, failing which his claim will be struck out.[45] Again, this is a most useful addition to the bank's armoury.

2.29 There is now a choice of ways in which the applicant for summary judgment or a related order can adduce evidence in support. This is a consequence of Rule 32.6(1) which provides that at hearings other than the trial evidence is to be by witness statement unless the court, a practice direction or other enactment requires otherwise. Part 22 sets out the particular requirements for the witness statement which may be drafted specifically for the hearing concerned. Rule 32.6(2), however, goes on to provide that a party may rely upon the matters set out in his statement of case or application notice if they are verified by a statement of truth. Rule 32.15(2) preserves the right of a party to adduce evidence by affidavit instead of a witness statement but any extra costs of so doing cannot be recovered unless the court so orders. In practice, it is to be expected that the principal evidence to be adduced on a summary judgment application will be by way of witness statement. The position may be otherwise where, for example, a solicitor wishes to file an affidavit summarising the points

44. At least in the absence of the making of a conditional order.
45. Para. 5.2 of PD 24.

to be made and/or conveniently collecting evidence from a number of sources.[46] In this regard, paragraph 4.2 of PD 32 makes it clear that the affidavit may contain statements made on information or belief, provided that the source is stated.

2.30 Part 24 and PD 24 lay down a detailed procedure for the hearing of applications for summary judgment. First, the respondent must not only be given 14 days' notice of the hearing date but must also be given such notice of the issues which it is proposed the court will decide. As with other interlocutory applications, the application notice must be served with the evidence to be used in support. In addition, the notice or evidence served with it must

(a) identify the points of law or documents on which the applicant relies and/or
(b) state that it is made because the applicant believes that there is no real prospect of the defence (a claim, as the case may be) succeeding, and in any event
(c) state that the applicant knows of no other reason why the disposal of the claim or issue should await trial.[47]

The significance of "and/or" is somewhat unclear in this context. Bearing in mind that under the RSC, the affidavit in support of any application for judgment had to state that the deponent believed that there was no defence to the claim, it must be that the form of statement referred to in (b) above is always required. The statement in (a) will be required as well only where there is a relevant point of law or document. The further requirement in (c) (no other reason to await trial) is new and means that the applicant must have a clear view of the case at the outset. This is a further reason for banks to assemble their case (and particularly the salient documents) at an early stage so that the requirement for this further statement may be furnished with confidence. It also means that there is nothing to be gained, and possibly much to lose (in terms of costs or adverse comment from the court) from putting in short or "formal" evidence in support of the application initially and leaving the filing of more substantial evidence until after receipt of the defendant's evidence. The proper approach is for the bank to adduce all the evidence it thinks it will need to dispose of the anticipated defence, at the start.

2.31 Evidence in opposition must be filed at least seven days before the hearing and evidence in reply at least three days before.

2.32 Applications for judgment which were defective in some way, for example because the affidavit in support did not depose to the required matters, tended to be dealt with strictly by the courts and this could lead to an application which was sound in substance failing on a technicality.[48] No special rules about

46. It should be borne in mind, however, that documents can be exhibited to a witness statement, in much the same way as they are to an affidavit. See paras 18.3–18.5 of PD 32.
47. Para. 2(3) of PD 24.
48. See, for example, *Barclays Bank* v. *Piper*, *The Times*, 31 May 1995.

this are laid down in Part 24. Instead, Rule 3.10 states that an error in procedure does not invalidate any step taken in the proceedings unless the court so orders and the court may make an order so as to rectify the error. Nonetheless, banks and their advisers should be astute to ensure that the various procedural requirements referred to above are met. They are not unduly onerous, and the court may well take the view that banks usually have the litigation experience as well as the resources to get their applications in order first time round.

2.33 Given that applications under Part 24 may be made against claimants as well as defendants, and given the width of those provisions, it might be thought that there was no need to retain the former jurisdiction to strike out pleadings. However, it re-appears in Rule 3.4 under which the court may strike out a statement of case, *inter alia*, where it discloses no reasonable grounds for bringing or defending the claim or where it is an abuse of the court's process or otherwise likely to obstruct the just disposal of the proceedings. PD 3 gives examples of cases which may fall under this part of the Rule. They include claims which are devoid of particulars, make no sense, or do not give rise to any recognisable claim in law.[49] They also include cases which are vexatious or scurrilous. Banks may wish to make use of this procedure where, as often happens, a disgruntled customer makes wild or incoherent claims against the bank in an effort to avoid paying his debts or in an attempt to gain publicity. A novel feature of PD 3 which may also assist banks is contained in paragraphs 2 and 3. These provide for the referral to a judge of claims or defences which the issuing officer believes may fall foul of Rule 3.4(2)(a) or (b). Having reviewed the documents, the judge then has the power to stay the proceedings so as to dispose of them, although he may give an opportunity to the party making the claim or defence to supply further information and/or to be heard before any order is made.

2.34 If the bank is faced with a claim or defence which appears to fall within Rule 3.4(2) it will usually be sensible for it to join any application to strike out with an application under Part 24.

FREEZING INJUNCTIONS[50]

2.35 A freezing injunction is what was formerly known as a *Mareva* injunction.[51] It is defined in Rule 25.1(1)(f) as an order (i) restraining a party from removing from the jurisdiction assets located there or (ii) restraining a party from dealing with any assets whether located in the jurisdiction or not. The freezing injunction has shown itself to be an important procedural tool in the

49. See para. 1.4.
50. Parts of this section previously appeared in the chapter entitled "Remedies for banks: an outline of English law" written by Richard Salter QC, in the first edition of this work.
51. See *Mareva Compania Naviera SA* v. *International Bulk Carriers SA* [1980] 1 All ER 213.

hands of a bank which suspects that the assets of the defendant may be dissipated before judgment is obtained so as to give the bank a hollow victory. A freezing injunction in favour of the bank does not give it any security in respect of the moneys or other assets made the subject of the injunction, nor does it give it any other kind of priority over the defendant's other creditors. Its purpose is simply to preserve the assets.

2.36 In the nature of things, freezing injunctions tend to be sought as a matter of urgency (because the assets are likely to be dealt with imminently, or may be) and in secrecy (because if the defendant has warning of the application he is likely to hasten the dissipation of the assets, or may do so). The CPR gives effect to these requirements, first by providing in Rule 25.2 that an application for an interim remedy (of which this injunction is an example) may be sought before proceedings are started, and second that a shortened timetable is available in cases of urgency and, where secrecy is essential, it is not necessary to give even informal notice to the defendant—see paragraph 4 of PD 25. Accordingly, as before, the bank can make what used to be called an *ex parte* application, now referred to simply as an application without notice.[52]

2.37 Paragraph 3.1 of PD 25 provides that applications for freezing injunctions must be supported by affidavit evidence. It is clear from paragraph 3.2 that this requirement is meant to be in contradistinction to other applications where the evidence may be contained in the application itself or statement of case (where verified by a statement of truth) or in a witness statement. It does not and cannot mean that the affidavit evidence has to be complete, or even fully drafted at the time when the application is made, though it is obviously desirable that this is so. In urgent cases, there may be no time to have the affidavit sworn and it may be produced in draft only.[53] Furthermore, there is no reason why the court should not act on what it has been told upon instructions on the basis that they are going to be embodied in an affidavit. That is often the case with telephone applications, which are provided for specifically in paragraph 4.5 of PD 25.

2.38 There is nothing in the CPR to suggest that the substantive principles which govern the grant of such injunctions have been changed. It therefore follows that the bank must satisfy two basic requirements. First, it must show that it has a good arguable case against the defendant. Second, it must show that there is a real risk of dissipation of assets. It will here be recalled that this does not mean that the bank must show that the defendant deliberately intends to frustrate the bank's claim in this way. Rather,

> the test is whether, on the assumption that the plaintiffs have shown at least "a good arguable case," the court concludes, on the whole of the evidence then before it, that the refusal of a *Mareva* injunction would involve a real risk that a judgment or award in favour of the plaintiffs would remain unsatisfied.[54]

52. See the general provisions in R. 23.4, 23.9 and 23.10 and in para. 3 of PD 23.

53. As contemplated by para. (4) of the Undertakings contained in Sch. B to the freezing injunction forms annexed to PD 25.

54. See *Ninemia Maritime* v. *Trave* [1983] 1 WLR 1412, 1422.

2.39 In an appropriate case, the court will grant the freezing injunction over defendant's assets wherever they are. However, such orders are exceptional and there is a heavy burden on the applicant to demonstrate why an order limited to assets in this jurisdiction would not be sufficient. Standard forms of order for both "domestic" and "world-wide" freezing injunctions are provided as the first two items in the Annex to PD 25 (collectively, "the practice forms").

2.40 It should be possible for the bank to obtain at the outset, and it should always seek, an order requiring the defendant to state at once (and later confirm on affidavit) what assets he has, whether in his own name or not, and their location and value. See paragraph 4 of the practice forms. This is an application of the principle that the court has jurisdiction to ensure that its principal order (i.e. that which freezes the assets) is made as efficacious as possible. That obviously requires that the applicant know where the assets are, in order to maximise the chances of preserving them, for example by putting third parties (including other banks) on notice of the granting of the injunction.

2.41 At this juncture, it is worth recalling that the court also has the power to order that specific assets be frozen on the ground that the applicants claim a proprietary interest in them, and that there is a need to preserve them pending trial. This power can be invoked in many circumstances but it may be of particular importance to the bank. This is because many claims brought by banks may be, or may be characterised as, claims to be beneficially entitled to particular assets, often through the operation of the remedy of constructive trust, occasioned by fraud or other vitiating circumstances. This can extend even to cases where the bank has paid out money under a mistake.[55] Such orders can be useful because the bank can then seek the further help of the court—for example, by obtaining an order requiring the defendant to say at once what has become of the assets concerned if they do not exist in their present form.[56] The court has jurisdiction to make such orders either pursuant to its general ability to ensure that its primary orders are effective and/or pursuant to its power to assist in the making of tracing claims.[57] The subject of such orders (to provide information as to what has happened to the assets) is not of course confined to the defendant. The same power[58] may be exercised against third parties (again, often other banks).[59]

2.42 As the practice forms make clear, if the injunction is to be granted, the bank has to comply with any order the court makes should the court subsequently decide that the freezing injunction has caused loss to the defendant for which he should be compensated (by the claimant).[60] In the normal case, the

55. See the decision of Goulding J in *Chase Manhattan Bank* v. *Israel-British Bank* [1981] Ch. 105.

56. As will usually be the case with funds which have been stolen or obtained by fraud.

57. See the dicta of Goff J in *A* v. *C* [1981] QB 956, 959.

58. Itself based on the principle laid down in *Norwich Pharmacal* v. *Customs and Excise* [1974] AC 133.

59. See *Banker's Trust* v. *Shapira* [1980] 1 WLR 1274.

60. This is likely to be the case where the freezing order was wrongly granted.

court also requires that undertaking to be fortified by security from the claimant in the form of a bank guarantee—that would seem unnecessary where the bank is itself the applicant unless perhaps its status is unclear or doubtful or it is resident outside the jurisdiction. Nonetheless, the bank should be prepared to provide such security if required. There is of course nothing to stop the court ordering that security be provided in some other way, including the setting aside or payment into court of specific funds.

2.43 There are two further factors which make it incumbent upon the bank to undertake the fullest investigation of its case possible prior to making the application. The first is the well-established obligation upon any applicant for an order in the absence of the other party (and especially one which, as here, may well be draconian in its effect) to make full and frank disclosure to the court. In practice this means that the bank should undertake a search of the files which are likely to have some bearing on the merits of the claim or other matters which may be relevant. It is not always easy to retrieve all such material at the outset, but the bank should make every effort to do so in order to comply with its obligations. The second is the prospect that under the CPR the court, on consideration of the application or shortly afterwards, for example at a later hearing attended by the defendant, will wish to make directions for the further conduct of the action then and there, in accordance with the underlying ethos of the new regime. Indeed, paragraph 2.9 of PD 23 states that the parties must anticipate that at *any* hearing the court may wish to review the case as a whole and give any necessary case management directions. The parties must be ready to assist the court in this and answer any questions the court may have.[61]

COSTS

2.44 The court has a discretion as to who pays the costs, the amount, and when they should be paid. (See Rule 44.3(1).) That said, the general rule remains that the unsuccessful party will be ordered to pay the costs of the successful party. Previously, this principle was often of little comfort to the bank because it would have to have its costs taxed, which was expensive and time-consuming, unless the defendant was prepared to agree a figure for the bank's costs which it was often reluctant to do. The major change concerning costs which is likely to be of interest to banks, is that the courts are now encouraged to assess summarily the costs awarded in favour of one side as against the other, in particular at the interlocutory stage.

2.45 Part 44.7 provides that when the court orders one side to pay the other's costs it may make a summary assessment of costs (i.e. undertaken by the tribunal hearing the application or matter in which the costs order was made) or it may order that there be a detailed assessment of costs (i.e. undertaken by a "costs

61. This is considered further below.

officer"[62]). If the costs order does not specify the method of assessment, it will be taken to be the latter.[63] However, paragraph 4.3(1) of PD 44 states that whenever the court makes an order for costs other than in respect of fixed costs (where the amount is quantified in any event) it should consider whether to make a summary assessment. This is then subject to the general rule laid down by paragraph 4.4(1) to the effect that the court will make a summary assessment (a) at the conclusion of a "fast-track" trial[64] and (b) at the conclusion of any other hearing which has lasted less than one day unless there is good reason not to. However, it should not be assumed by this that if the hearing lasts more than one day, it will not be a candidate for summary assessment. There is nothing to stop the court from assessing costs in substantial applications and it may often be sensible to do so where the party which is awarded costs prefers to have an immediate order rather than wait for taxation at the end of the case. It also has the advantage that the paying party feels the effect of the costs order straight away because Rule 44.8 provides that assessed costs must be paid within 14 days of the assessment. Both sides are therefore forced to keep uppermost in the minds all the way through what the litigation is costing. This can only encourage parties to take a realistic view of their chances of success and incline them towards settlement.

2.46 Paragraph 4.5 of PD 44 requires parties who are going to, or may, seek a costs order in their favour on a forthcoming application or matter to file and serve not less than 24 hours before it starts, a statement of costs incurred by them in respect of it. Such a statement must contain a list of the fees earners involved and the charge-out rate applied to each as well as the hours claimed. Details of disbursements (including Counsel's fees) and VAT charges are also to be given. A standard form is at Form 1 of the Schedule of Costs Forms annexed to PD 44. The very exchange of such documents may concentrate the minds of the parties.

2.47 It should be noted, however, that, as with a detailed assessment of costs, the court will summarily assess costs on either the standard or the indemnity basis. The standard basis now means first that the costs incurred must have been proportionate to the issues involved.[65] In addition, any doubts as to whether the costs were reasonably incurred or reasonable and proportionate in amount will be resolved in favour of the paying party. The indemnity basis means that any such doubts are to be resolved in favour of the party to whom the costs are to be paid. Despite this similarity to the detailed assessment procedure, summary assessments are, by definition, short hearing where the court does not enter into discussion of the minutiae of the costs. Rather, the court will take a "broad brush" approach, which means that the courts may not give very detailed reasons for the assessments they make, and may well be influenced by matters of impression. On the other hand, as one judge has already expressed it, just

62. The new name for the taxing master.
63. Para. 4.2 of PD 44.
64. Which takes place, usually, where the claim is for between £5,000 and £15,000—see R. 26.6.
65. Thereby echoing the reference to proportionality in the overriding objective at R. 1.1(2)(c).

because a broad brush is applied does not mean that the court will be a "soft touch" in respect of any application for a summary disposal. It must also be the case that the courts want to make orders which reflect the fact that the party who has the benefit of the order prefers to take less now than what might be achieved on taxation.

2.48 Having said that, detailed guidance for the court conducting the summary assessment is to be found in Rule 44.5. Circumstances to which the court must have regard include the conduct of the parties before and during the proceedings, the amount or value of any money or property involved, the importance of the matter to all the parties, the complexity of the matter, the skill, effort and specialised knowledge and responsibility of those involved, and the time spent on the case.

2.49 The commentary at 44.5.1 of *Civil Procedure* suggests that if a party fails without good reason to utilise ADR[66] its costs may be reduced on assessment on that account. Further, paragraph 3.1 of PD 44 makes the point that while the court must have regard to proportionality, the relationship between the total costs involved and the value of the claim may not always be a reliable guide. Paragraph 3.2 states that the incurring of some costs will be inevitable whatever the size of the claim, since solicitors are under no duty to undertake litigation at rates which will be uneconomic.

2.50 Once the courts have built up a body of experience of making such orders, they are likely to become very popular with commercial practitioners and their clients, certainly at the interlocutory stage, and one would imagine that banks will prefer to have the costs dealt with (hopefully in their favour) as the case goes along.

OFFERS TO SETTLE

2.51 Part of the strategy inherent in the CPR of encouraging the early settlement of claims[67] is a significant extension of provisions dealing with formal offers. Those provisions are set out in Part 36. The new regime includes two novel aspects: first, it is applied to offers made before as well as after the proceedings have begun; second, it covers the making of offers not only by the defendant but by the claimant as well. Part 36 will be examined here from the perspective of the defendant and then the claimant.

2.52 A defendant can make a formal offer to compromise proceedings which are already under way as follows. If the claim against him is a "money claim",[68] then he must make a "Part 36 Payment", the equivalent of the former payment

66. Alternative dispute resolution.

67. Itself embodied in R. 1.4(2)(e) [encouraging parties to use alternative dispute resolution] and (f) [helping the parties to settle part or all of the case].

68. This term is not defined in the CPR—it obviously covers debt and damages claims and, in addition, it is suggested that it would cover restitutionary claims as well.

into court.[69] As before, the money offered is paid into court and the claimant notified. The basic rule as to acceptance is that the claimant has 21 days in which to accept the payment.[70] If he does so, then he will be entitled to his costs up to and including the date of acceptance.[71] Part 36 is very clear about the costs consequences of a claimant not accepting a Party 36 payment and then failing to beat it at trial. The court will order him to pay the costs of the defendant as from the latest date on which the payment could have been accepted without the permission of the court "unless it considers it unjust to do so". It is submitted that the effect of this proviso is to give the court some, but not much, room for manoeuvre in unusual cases. It therefore behoves the claimant bank to consider the merits of its case very carefully when presented with a Part 36 payment. Of course, if it has by then complied with the various other provisions of the CPR which require it to make an early assessment of the case (the "front-end loading" of the litigation) it may find itself more ready to deal with this eventuality than would formerly have been the case.

2.53 Again, and as before, provision is made for the making of formal offers in respect of "non-money" claims, being the equivalent of *Calderbank* offers, except that it is now more detailed than before, when many of the principles were set out in case law rather than in the RSC themselves. Such offers are called "Part 36 offers". The time-limits and cost consequences here follow those applicable to Part 36 payments.

2.54 The fact that Part 36 applies to claimants as well is likely to be of great benefit to banks. This is because banks are often prepared to take a commercial view of the litigation and accept less than the amount of the debt in order to make a swift recovery and remove the disputed transaction from their books. Unfortunately, some defendants prove to be recalcitrant or ill-advised once litigation commences and maintain their refusal to pay what may be a very reasonable sum from their point of view. They may be forced to pay following an application under Part 24 but this will not always be so. The ability of a claimant now to make its own offer, with significant adverse financial consequences for the defendant who fails to accept it when he should, may encourage defendants to be more realistic at the outset.

2.55 The provisions of Part 36 in respect of Part 36 offers cover offers from either side, unless otherwise stated. If the offer is accepted in time, the claimant will be entitled to his costs up to the date on which notice of acceptance is served by the defendant.[72] If the offer is not accepted and at trial the claimant does better than its Part 36 offer, then Rule 36.21 provides that the court can award interest at up to 10 per cent above base rate on the moneys awarded to the claimant at trial, and in addition it can award costs on an indemnity basis for the relevant period together with interest at up to 10 per cent above base on those

69. See R. 36.3(1).
70. See R. 36.11.
71. See R. 36.13.
72. See R. 36.14.

costs. Rule 36.21(4) goes on to say that the court "will" make such orders unless it considers it "unjust" to do so. Apart from the question of what amounts to "injustice" in this context[73] it is not clear how these provisions will work, because there is a range of possible orders so far as interest is concerned both as to the period to which it should apply and the precise rate (i.e. up to 10 per cent and therefore not inevitably 10 per cent). One reading of these provisions would be that in the absence of injustice the court will order that at least some additional interest is paid, both on the award and on the costs which the court will require to be paid on an indemnity basis. It will not therefore follow as a matter of course that the court has to exercise its powers to the maximum even if a defendant could not object on the grounds of injustice if the court so chose. It is to be noted here that Rule 36.21(5) sets out particular circumstances to be taken into account when considering the question of "injustice".

2.56 Banks should make use of this ability to make formal offers of their own at an early stage. In view of the consequences of non-acceptance, they will have to be taken seriously by the defendant's legal advisers and it is highly likely that if the defendant is legally-aided, the Legal Aid Board will take particular notice of them. Once more, if the bank has already looked in detail at the merits of the case, it will have the appreciation necessary to enable it to make an informed decision about a Part 36 offer.

2.57 All of this is given added importance by the extension of the Part 36 regime (in respect of both defendants and claimants) to the situation of the parties even before proceedings are issued. This is contained in Rule 36.10 which refers to the making of an "offer to settle". In the case of a defendant, if the offer is not accepted and proceedings are commenced he must follow it up with a Part 36 payment for the same sum, which the claimant cannot then accept without the permission of the court. If the claimant is the one to have made the pre-action Part 36 offer it would seem that there is nothing further required of him if it is not accepted and he has to issue proceedings. The position at trial will then be governed by Rules 36.20 and 36.21.

2.58 If the parties are all desirous of time in which to attempt to settle a case, then the court has the power to stay the proceedings for an initial period of one month to enable this to take place. This is set out in Rule 26.4. It should be noted that this only applies where there is consent between the parties or the court decides to grant a stay of its own initiative. There is no general right given to a defendant to seek such a stay against the wishes of other parties, though no doubt at any hearing or at a case-management conference the defendant could say why it thought the court should intervene "on its own initiative". Banks will no doubt have to be vigilant to ensure that Rule 26.4 is not thereby abused by defendants who are simply looking at ways to delay the progress of the litigation.

73. See below.

CASE MANAGEMENT

2.59 A clear example of the principle of "front-end loading" embodied in the CPR is the way in which case management is dealt with. The process starts at almost the earliest possible stage—when the defendant files a defence. Once that has been done the court serves upon every party an "allocation questionnaire" which seeks basic information about the case and indications about what preparation has so far been undertaken by each side and what further procedural steps they propose to take. The claim or defence (as the case may be) can be struck out if the questionnaire is not provided—see paragraph 2.5 of Part 26.

2.60 The principal purpose of the information given pursuant to allocation questionnaires is to enable the court to allocate a particular "track" to the case. It is assumed here that the bank's claim will be substantial enough to avoid it being placed in the "fast track"[74] and so it will be placed in the "multi-track". But another important purpose of the information is to enable the court to give directions for the future progress of the case which it is intended will be given at an early stage. Indeed, Rule 29.2 provides that when allocating the case to a track, the court will also give directions or alternatively fix a case-management conference or a pre-trial review or both. Paragraph 3 of PD 29 emphasises the fact that parties to litigation must be willing to deal with the general management of the case at any stage and in particular at any hearing, regardless of the nature of the particular application for which the hearing takes place. Paragraph 5 of PD 29 backs this up by giving detailed guidance as to what the court will expect to discuss at any case-management conference (which itself may be fixed by the court on allocating the case to a track or at any time thereafter).[75] This will include reviewing the steps taken to date, deciding on future steps and seeing whether the parties have agreed as much about the conduct of the case as they can. Particular matters to be considered include whether each side has made its case clear enough to the other, whether any amendments are required, what disclosure of documents is necessary, expert evidence, the disclosure of factual evidence and whether there should be a trial of any preliminary issues.[76] The court will expect to see a legal representative of each party who is familiar with the case so that the conference can proceed meaningfully, with severe cost consequences if they are not.[77] In addition, the parties and their advisers will have to consider whether or not to provide a case-summary in advance of the hearing, as well as whether the parties themselves should attend.[78]

74. Which has an upper monetary limit of £15,000 in respect of the size of the claim, as stated above, 2.45.

75. See R. 29.2(1) and 29.3(1).

76. See para. 5.3 of PD 29.

77. R. 29.3(2) and para. 5.2 of PD 29.

78. Para. 5.6 of PD 29. See also *Matthews* v. *Tarmac*, 14 June 1999, unreported, which emphasises the need for the parties to assist the court to further the overriding objective.

2.61 The upshot of all of this is that the CPR intends much more pro-active case-management by the court (and indeed by the parties) than was the case under the old system. Banks must be prepared for this. Given their resources, the court is unlikely to be sympathetic to a claimant bank which appears not to be able or willing to embrace the new regime.

PROCEEDINGS IN THE COMMERCIAL COURT

2.62 Part 49 states that the CPR are expressed to apply to the specialist proceedings listed therein (including commercial and mercantile actions). The CPR will be "subject to the provisions of the relevant practice direction which applies to those proceedings".

2.63 Many claims made by banks are presently brought in the Commercial Court (or the Mercantile Court outside London). Of considerable importance in this context is the new version of the Commercial Court Guide ("the Guide") which came into force in tandem with the CPR but which has important differences of content or emphases. The Guide is given authority by the Commercial Court Practice Direction (49D) which supplements Part 49 of the CPR and replaces with modifications the former Order 72 of the RSC (which used to govern particular aspects of commercial actions). Paragraph 1.1 of the Commercial Court Practice Direction states that it applies to commercial claims in the Queen's Bench Division. Paragraph 9.5 states that the practice of the Commercial Court set out in the Guide should now be followed, subject to the provisions of the Commercial Court Practice Direction or any other Commercial Court Practice Direction and to any order made in any individual case.

2.64 The definition of a "commercial claim", set out in paragraph 1.2 of the Commercial Court Practice Direction, has been widened considerably in comparison with its predecessor, Order 72, rule 1(2), with the consequence that virtually all claims brought by banks will now fall within it. In particular, any case relating to "a business document or contract" is a commercial claim, as well as one which relates to banking and financial services. This, together with the difference in approach taken by the Guide, may well mean that business litigants (including banks) will come to see the Commercial Court as the natural venue in which to commence their actions.

2.65 Paragraph A2 of the Guide refers to the "overriding objective" set out in Rule 1.1 of the CPR, which is to be served by the Guide "in the specialist context of commercial cases". This foreshadows a number of points in the Guide which make it different from the CPR. This section of the chapter contains a brief overview of such of those differences as may be of particular interest or concern to banks.

2.66 First, Part D of the Guide sets out the Commercial Court's own code for case management which, save for one exception, replaces the provisions contained in Part 29 of the CPR. In addition, the claimant self-allocates by commencing proceedings in the Commercial Court, which will then be deemed to be multi-track proceedings. Accordingly, Part 26 of the CPR, which deals with allocation, does not apply. Heavy cases will be dealt with by two-judge management teams.[79] Usually, a mandatory case-management conference will be fixed to take place six weeks after service of the defence,[80] and it should be borne in mind that by then the parties will have to have produced various documents designed to assist the court, including a case memorandum and a list of issues.[81] In this sense, therefore, the "front-loading" aspect of the CPR is followed through into the Commercial Court albeit in a slightly different fashion. One useful additional feature of the Guide is that fixed trial dates will be given for most cases.[82]

2.67 Second, greater flexibility with regard to statements of case is shown. For example, there is no requirement for the claim form to be accompanied by the particulars of claim.[83] If particulars of claim are not served with the claim form, then the claimant has 28 days after acknowledgement of service in which to serve it.[84] In addition, the parties may agree an extension beyond the 28 days provided that this is in writing and notified to the court.[85] Similarly, the parties can agree extensions for the service of defences longer than the 28 days extensions permitted by Rule 15.5.[86]

2.68 Third, greater specific emphasis is given to the aim of encouraging settlement between the parties. In particular,

1. the advantages of ADR are highlighted in paragraph G1.2 and a specimen "ADR Order" is contained in Appendix 7 to the Guide, prescribing directions for the initiation of ADR and a date by which the parties' differences are to be settled, with the restoration of the case-management conference if this does not happen;
2. furthermore, paragraph G2 of the Guide provides for a procedure, in appropriate cases, where a Commercial Court judge will give a "without prejudice, non-binding, early neutral evaluation" of a dispute or a particular issue arising in it. Unless the parties otherwise agree, that judge will then play no further part in the case.

Given the need to bear in mind at all times the economics of the litigation, there may well be some cases where it will be very helpful for the bank to pursue these alternative routes.

2.69 The conclusion in respect of Commercial Court proceedings must be that banks would be well advised to consider the Commercial Court as a forum

79. Para. D3.
80. Para. D7.1.
81. Para. D6.
82. Para. D11.
83. Cf. para. 3.1 of PD 16 requiring this where practicable.
84. Cf. the 14 days from service of the claim form allowed by R. 7.4(1).
85. Para. C2.4.
86. Para. C3.4.

for their claims even where they might not have done so before. What cannot be predicted, however, is the extent to which the increased popularity of this venue itself will cause delay because of a shortage of resources to deal with the upturn in business. If this happens, banks may find themselves seeking the assistance of the Chancery Division. Though cases being heard in that division are not *per se* specialist proceedings within the meaning of Part 49 of the CPR, the advent of the CPR was also the occasion for the publication of a new Chancery Guide which incorporates all relevant practice directions. Paragraph 2.4 of the Chancery Guide states, somewhat intriguingly, that

> If a claim brought in the Chancery Division is a "commercial claim" within the meaning of paragraph 1.2 of the [Commercial Court] Practice Direction ... the Court will in general, and to the extent that it is consistent with the CPR and relative practice directions, adopt the same practices as the Commercial Court.

It is not clear how far this is intended to take on board the Commercial Court Guide in such cases. But it does emphasise the growing awareness of the courts of the need to promote access—and efficient access—to justice not only to individual litigants but also to the business community. Provided that banks are properly prepared for the litigation of their claims at an early stage, they should benefit considerably from the changes in civil procedure referred to above.

DAVID WAKSMAN

CHAPTER 3

REMEDIES FOR BANKS: AN OUTLINE OF ENGLISH LAW

3.1 When things go wrong, banks turn to the legal means they have to recover their rights, or to obtain redress for the wrongs done to them: in other words, to their legal remedies.[1] Some are matters of self-help.[2] Others require the intervention of the courts. This chapter surveys the variety of remedies which the law of England and Wales[3] makes available, and the limits which it imposes upon the exercise of some of those remedies.

THE RIGHT TO DEMAND REPAYMENT

3.2 The most fundamental remedy possessed by a lending bank is its right to ask for its money back. In modern banking practice, most lending on overdraft is made on the terms of a facility letter containing some such phrase as:

> This facility will expire on [date]. Whilst it is our present intention that this facility should remain available to you until that date and notwithstanding any other provision of this letter we nevertheless reserve the right to terminate the facility at any time by notice in writing . . .[4]

or, more commonly (if less felicitously):

> We will review this facility in six months' time, subject to normal banking terms and conditions, including the bank's right at any time to require repayment on demand . . .

1. *Webster's English Dictionary*, cited by Pearson J in *Goulandris Bros Ltd* v. *B. Goldman & Sons* [1958] QB 74, 99–100 in the course of holding that the word "remedies" in Rule D of the York-Antwerp Rules 1950 was "wide enough to cover defences as well as cross-claims, shields as well as spears, pleas as well as counts".

2. According to Professor Treitel "The policy against self-help is strongest in French law, where the Maxim '*nul ne peut se faire justice à soi-même*' (no-one is allowed to mete out justice personally) has been exceedingly influential. In that system even the process of putting a contract to an end requires, at least in theory and as a general rule, a judgment of a court. At the other extreme, in the United States of America, the Uniform Commercial Code expressly recognises 'self-help' as a 'remedy' available to an aggrieved party": *Remedies for Breach of Contract* (1988), p. 2.

3. Hereafter, simply for brevity, "English law". For similar reasons, the "English courts" means the courts of England and Wales and for "he" read "(s)he" throughout.

4. *Encyclopaedia of Forms and Precedents* (5th edn) Vol. 4, para. 138.

3.3 In the absence of special circumstances, both of these formulations are likely to be effective to reserve to the lender the right to ask for its money back whenever it wishes. Although the expression "subject to normal banking terms and conditions" is probably too vague to have any contractual effect at all,[5] "repayable on demand" normally means just that. So, in *Lloyds Bank Plc* v. *Lampert*,[6] the facility letter stated

> ... it is the Bank's present intention to make the facility available until 28 February 1997 or such later date as may from time to time be advised in writing by the Bank. All monies from time to time owing to the Bank shall be repaid no later than the agreed expiry date.

However, it also provided that "any amounts owing under this facility are repayable on demand". The Court of Appeal rejected the borrower's argument that the demand made by the bank on 10 July 1996 was premature, Kennedy LJ observing that he was

> ... wholly unpersuaded that the words "repayable on demand" in this facility letter do not mean what they say. It is in no way inconsistent for a bank or other lender to grant a facility which it and the borrower both envisage will last for some time, but with the caveat that the lender retains the right to call for repayment at any time on demand ...

3.4 In the absence of a fiduciary or other special relationship, English law does not in general impose any obligation on a lender to exercise its right to demand repayment either "in good faith", or on any basis other than that of serving its own interests.[7] However, in two sets of circumstances, the bank's right to demand repayment may be restricted.

3.5 The first is where the contract term entitling the bank to demand repayment is either unenforceable under section 3(2)(b) of the Unfair Contract Terms Act 1977[8] or not binding on the consumer under the Unfair Terms in Consumer Contracts Regulations 1994.[9]

3.6 The 1994 Regulations include in their "indicative and non-exhaustive" list of terms which *may* be regarded as unfair "Terms which have the object or effect of ... (g) enabling the ... supplier to terminate a contract of indeterminate

5. In *Williams & Glyn's Bank Ltd* v. *Barnes* (26 March 1980, unreported), Ralph Gibson J was prepared to assume, after hearing expert evidence of banking practice, that one of the usual banking conditions was that an overdraft is repayable on demand. But he went on to hold that "a reference to 'the usual banking conditions' without stating what they are, and without clear language showing that such conditions are to prevail over any other terms as to duration or termination, whether express or necessarily derived from the language used, cannot negative a term which is otherwise part of the agreement": transcript, pp. 617–618. Gibson J's approach was approved by the Court of Appeal in *Cryne* v. *Barclays Bank Plc* [1987] BCLC 548, 552.

6. [1999] 1 All ER (Comm.) 161.

7. See *China & South Sea Bank* v. *Tan* [1990] 1 AC 536, 545D, where Lord Templeman emphatically restated the principle that a mortgagee "must decide in his own interest if and when he should sell" the mortgaged property.

8. On the basis that, by relying on the term, the bank was "claim[ing] to be entitled to render a contractual performance substantially different from that which was reasonably expected", *per* Kennedy LJ.

9. SI 1994 No. 3159, made under the European Communities Act 1972 to implement Council Directive 93/13/EEC on Unfair Terms in Consumer Contracts.

duration without reasonable notice except where there are serious grounds for doing so".[10] Standard provisions in overdraft and other facility letters entitling the bank, at its discretion, to require repayment on demand from consumers appear to fall within the terms of this paragraph. Although it is stated to be

> ... without hindrance to terms by which a supplier of financial services reserves the right to terminate unilaterally a contract of indeterminate duration without notice *where there is a valid reason*, provided that the supplier is required to inform the other contracting party or parties thereof immediately,[11]

this does not rescue the situation. It merely reduces the requirement of "serious grounds" in paragraph 1(g) to that of "a valid reason", and adds the requirement of prompt notification.

3.7 It is, of course, arguable that a contract term which makes clear the "on demand" nature of an overdraft merely "defines the main subject matter of the contract" and so, "insofar as it is in plain, intelligible language", is not a matter whose fairness is to be assessed.[12] However, the extent of the "main subject matter" exception is far from clear. First of all, it could be said that the main subject-matter of an overdraft is merely the amount of the overdraft facility, leaving the repayment terms as matters whose fairness it is proper to assess. After all, there is no conceptual objection to an overdraft facility that is repayable on reasonable notice. Second, the "main subject matter" exception only applies to terms expressed "in plain, intelligible language". Not all facility letters will qualify. Third, some facility letters grant what are in substance term loans, repayable by stated instalments, yet reserve the lender's right at its discretion to require repayment on demand at any time. These provisions, designed to avoid the lender having to prove an event of default, cannot realistically be described as part of the "main subject matter" of the contract, and so would be caught by paragraph 1(g).

3.8 The second set of circumstances in which the bank's right to demand repayment may be restricted, despite the inclusion of a term providing for repayment on demand, is where that statement is simply part of the unconsidered "boiler plate" of the facility letter, and is repugnant to the specially agreed main provisions.

3.9 In *Titford Property Co. Ltd* v. *Cannon Street Acceptances Ltd*,[13] Goff J had to consider the terms of an overdraft facility granted to property developers. The bank's facility letter stated that the overdraft was "for a period of 12 months to assist you in the purchase and development" of a specified property (over which it required a legal charge). Clause 9 of the facility letter, however, also stated that all monies, whether capital or interest, were to be repayable on demand. Goff J held that the bank was not entitled to make demand before the expiry of the 12 months. The bank, in his judgment,

10. *Ibid.*, Reg. 4(4) and Sch. 3, para. 1(g).
11. *Ibid.*, Reg. 4(4) and Sch. 3, para. 2(1).
12. See *ibid.*, Reg. 3(2)(a).
13. 22 May 1975, unreported.

... could not ... with one hand grant a facility for a term for a purpose which to its knowledge clearly involves the Plaintiffs in incurring expenditure and liabilities, with a view to ultimate profit, and with the other take it away by an unqualified right to require repayment on demand at any time ... therefore, I must modify Clause 9, by reading it as subject to the provision as to the duration of this facility, or ignore it altogether ...

3.10 As the *Titford* case makes clear, the issue of whether any demand is necessary to make the money lent repayable and, if so, when such a demand may be made, is primarily a matter of construction of the express and implied terms of the contract of loan. Having considered the *Titford* decision, Ralph Gibson J put the matter in this way in *Williams & Glyn's Bank Ltd* v. *Barnes*:[14]

... in the absence of any express agreement providing for the duration of the facility, or for the date of re-payment, the Court must consider whether, according to the ordinary rules for the implication of terms into commercial contracts, any term controlling the duration of the facility or the date of repayment is to be implied. If no such term must be implied, then money lent under the facility is no more than money lent and is therefore repayable on demand ...

3.11 Since the test for implying terms is whether the implication is *necessary*,[15] not whether it is reasonable, mere knowledge on the part of the bank that the customer intends to spend all or part of the money in a business venture that will take a long time to come to fruition cannot, by itself, give rise to an implied term requiring a period of notice for repayment calculated by reference to the probable duration of the business venture.[16] Nor will a provision referring to the expected duration of the facility usually override a clause permitting immediate demand. The question of which provision is to prevail must be decided according to the normal principles of contract law.[17]

3.12 Banks will usually make loan facilities (as opposed to overdraft facilities) available on terms[18] which include "events of default", such as non-payment or insolvency, which if they occur will entitle the bank (a) to refuse further lending, and (b) to declare the outstanding balance immediately repayable. Unless these events are expressly stated, they are unlikely to be implied. So, in *Cryne* v. *Barclays Bank Plc*,[19] the Court of Appeal refused to imply into a fixed-term loan a term entitling the bank to require early repayment and/or to appoint a receiver if its security was in jeopardy.

14. Above, transcript p. 605.

15. As Lord Wilberforce put it in *Liverpool City Council* v. *Irwin* [1977] AC 239, 254: "... such obligation should be read into the contract as the nature of the contract itself implicitly requires, no more, no less: a test, in other words, of necessity ..." This stringent test was applied to the implication of terms in the contract between banker and customer in *Tai Hing Cotton Mills* v. *Liu Chong Hing Bank* [1986] AC 80, 104H–105A.

16. *Williams & Glyn's Bank* v. *Barnes* (above), transcript, p. 609.

17. *Ibid*., pp. 650–652. "If the judgment of Goff J [in the *Titford* case] ... is to be regarded as stating that in a contest for primacy between a term loan and a clause for repayment on demand, the provision for term loan must always prevail, then, with respect, I should not feel able to follow it." See also *Lloyds Bank Plc* v. *Lampert*, above.

18. See, for example, cl. 8 of the specimen Facility Letter in the *Encyclopaedia of Forms and Precedents* (5th edn), Vol. 4 at para. 153.

19. [1987] BCLC 548.

3.13 Even where there are no express events of default, a non-payment or other breach of the loan agreement will permit the lending bank to treat the contract of loan as at an end if, but only if, the default amounts to a breach of a condition of the agreement (for example, because time of payment or other performance is of the essence) or because it amounts to a repudiation of the borrower's obligations under the loan agreement. Unless time of payment is of the essence of the agreement, it may in practice be very difficult to show that persistent small delays in payment of instalments are, alone or cumulatively, sufficiently grave to amount to a repudiation.[20] The test seems to be whether the defaults in payment are such as to destroy the lender's confidence in the borrower's creditworthiness.[21] As to other events, common sense might suggest that the insolvent liquidation or personal bankruptcy of the borrower ought usually to be treated as a sufficient repudiation of a contract to repay money.[22] However, the power of a liquidator to perform *any* of the company's contracts so far as may be necessary for the beneficial winding-up of the company[23] means that the matter cannot be regarded as beyond doubt.[24] It is unlikely that the appointment of an administrator[25] or administrative receiver would be held, of itself, to amount to a repudiation of a contract of loan,[26] in the absence of special circumstances.

3.14 Service of a default notice under Part VII of the Consumer Credit Act 1974 is necessary before the creditor can become entitled, by reason of the debtor's breach of a regulated agreement[27] under that Act, to terminate the agreement, demand early repayment, treat any right conferred by the agreement on the debtor as terminated, restricted or deferred, or to enforce any security.[28]

3.15 Unless the contract of loan provides otherwise, a demand (although usual) is not a necessary element of the cause of action to recover money lent.[29]

20. See, for example, *Decro-Wall International* v. *Practitioners in Marketing Ltd* [1971] 1 WLR 361; *The Brimnes* [1975] QB 929.

21. See *per* Salmon LJ in *Decro-Wall* (above), at p. 369.

22. Because, in the case of a contract to repay money, the fact of insolvency demonstrates that the borrower is unable to carry the contract out: see *Re Phoenix Bessemer Steel Co. ex parte Carnforth Haematite Iron Co.* (1876) 4 Ch. D 108 (declaration of insolvency); *Mees* v. *Duffus* (1901) 6 Com. Cas. 165 (declaration of insolvency); *Baker* v. *Lloyds Bank* [1920] 2 KB 322 (insolvency of indorser of bill); *Re National Benefit Assurance Co. Ltd* [1924] 2 Ch. 339 (insolvency of insurer).

23. Insolvency Act 1986, ss.165, 167, and Sch. 4, para. 5. The trustee in bankruptcy of an individual has similar powers, under s.314 and Sch. 5, para. 1.

24. The liquidation of a company is not generally a repudiation, without more, of its contractual obligations: see *British Waggon Co.* v. *Lea* (1880) 5 QBD 149.

25. Who may, after all, have been appointed specifically for the purpose of achieving the survival of the company as a going concern: Insolvency Act 1986, s.8(3)(a).

26. Cf. *Re Newdigate Colliery* [1912] 1 Ch. 468; *Parsons* v. *Sovereign Bank of Canada* [1913] AC 160.

27. Broadly, most agreements by which an individual (or partnership or other unincorporated body including at least one individual) is provided with credit not exceeding £25,000: Consumer Credit Act 1974, ss.8 and 189: SI 1998 No. 996.

28. Consumer Credit Act 1974, s.87(1): Consumer Credit (Enforcement, Default and Termination Notices) Regulations 1983, SI 1983 No. 1561, as amended by SI 1984 No. 1109.

29. *Bradford Old Bank* v. *Sutcliffe* [1918] 2 KB 833.

However, a demand upon the debtor will be required wherever the contract expressly so requires, and in any event in the following cases: (a) where the amount of the debt is uncertain,[30] (b) where the loan is repayable by instalments and it is sought to accelerate the debtor's liability,[31] and (c) (generally) where it is sought to enforce security held for the loan.[32]

3.16 The requirements of a valid demand will depend upon the purpose for which it is made. The contract of loan may itself impose requirements as to the form and manner of any demand. Where the making of a demand is required in order to permit the enforcement of security, the security may impose further requirements. Subject to those requirements, and to any particular requirements of the general law,[33] it seems that a valid demand can be made orally. The English courts[34] have accepted as "a fair, working definition" of a valid demand the formulation proffered by Walker J in the Australian case of *Re Colonial Finance, Mortgage, Investment & Guarantee Corpn Ltd*:[35]

> ... there must be a clear intimation that payment is required to constitute a demand; nothing more is necessary, and the word "demand" need not be used; neither is the validity of a demand lessened by its being clothed in the language of politeness; it must be of a peremptory character and unconditional, but the nature of the language is immaterial provided it has this effect ...

Of course, banks will generally make their demands formally and in writing.

3.17 Surprisingly, there is no unanimity among writers on banking matters as to whether a demand which *substantially* misstates the amount of the borrower's indebtedness can be effective. It is clear that a minor error in the amount due will not invalidate a demand.[36] However, James Lingard has expressed the view that if a bank demands materially more than is due to it,

30. *Brown* v. *Great Eastern Railway Co.* (1877) 2 QBD 406.

31. *Esso Petroleum Co. Ltd* v. *Alstonbridge Properties Ltd* [1975] 1 WLR 1474. A notice of acceleration under a contractual provision must be given strictly in accordance with the contract terms: see *Re Berker Sportcraft Ltd's Agreements, Hartnell* v. *Berker Sportcraft Ltd* (1947) 177 LT 420.

32. *Miller* v. *Cook* (1870) LR 10 Eq. 641 (and see the Law of Property Act 1925, ss.103(i) and 196) (power of sale under a mortgage); *Esso Petroleum Co. Ltd* v. *Alstonbridge Properties Ltd* [1975] 1 WLR 1474 (guarantee) (but see *M.S. Fashions Ltd* v. *Bank of Credit and Commerce International SA (in liquidation)* [1993] Ch. 425 for the effect of a "principal debtor" clause); Lingard, *Bank Security Documents* (3rd edn), para. 11.4.

33. For example, under the Law of Property Act 1925 (see note 33 above), the Consumer Credit Act 1974 (see note 28 above), or the Insolvency Act 1986, ss.123(1)(a) or 268(1)(a) (see note 37 below), and *Re a Debtor (No. 1 of 1987)* [1989] 1 WLR 271.

34. *Re a Company* [1985] BCLC 37, 41; *BCCI* v. *Blattner* (CA, 20 November 1986, unreported).

35. (1905) 6 SR NSW 6, 9.

36. See *Deverges* v. *Sandeman, Clark & Co.* [1902] 1 Ch. 579; *Stubbs* v. *Slater* [1910] 1 Ch. 632.

the borrower is justified in refuting the wrongful demand.[37] In reality it is the creditor, not the debtor, who will usually have the facilities for calculating the precise amount of compound interest due and who will, therefore, be the one who knows how much is owing. If the purpose of the demand is to give the debtor an opportunity, albeit brief,[38] of making payment before he is sued, or the security for the loan is enforced, he needs to be told how much he has to pay. Among the contrary arguments are these: that it is the debtor's duty to know how much he owes; that disputes over the amount due are so common that it is idle to impute to the parties an intention that a precisely correct demand should be a condition precedent to the debtor's liability; and that the calculation of the precise amount due as at the date of demand is, in most cases, an expensive waste of time, because there is no realistic prospect of the debtor paying anything. Where the debtor in fact needs to know how much to pay, he can always ask the creditor. These contrary arguments are supported by the decision of Walton J in *Bank of Baroda* v. *Panessar*[39] that a demand for "all monies due to us", without specifying the amount demanded, was a valid demand.

THE RIGHT TO COMBINE ACCOUNTS

3.18 Where the defaulting customer has two or more accounts with the same bank, one of which is in credit, English law gives the bank the right, subject to the limitations described below, to combine the two accounts and to apply the credit balance in reduction of the debt due from the customer to it.[40]

3.19 Except in insolvency, this right of combination may be excluded by express or implied agreement,[41] and such an agreement may be inferred from the mere fact that one of the accounts is described as a current account and one as a

37. *Bank Security Documents* (3rd edn), para. 11.5, citing *Pigot* v. *Cubley* (1864) 15 CBNS 701 (a pledge case, distinguished in *Deverges*), *Re a Company* [1985] BCLC 37, 41–43 (a case concerning the validity of a statutory demand under s.223(a) of the Companies Act 1948, now re-enacted in a materially amended form in s.123(1)(a) of the Insolvency Act 1986), and *Cryne* v. *Barclays Bank Plc* [1987] BCLC 548 (where the point does not seem to have been argued). Sir Gavin Lightman and Gabriel Moss QC, in *The Law of Receivers of Companies* (2nd edn), para. 4–11, take the contrary view.

38. See *Bank of Baroda* v. *Panessar* [1987] Ch. 335; *Sheppard & Cooper Ltd* v. *TSB Bank Plc* [1996] 2 All ER 654.

39. [1987] Ch. 335, following the Australian case of *Bunbury Foods Pty Ltd* v. *National Bank of Australasia Ltd* (1984) 51 ALR 609.

40. *Garnett* v. *McKewan* (1872) LR 8 Ex. 10; *Prince* v. *Oriental Bank Corp.* (1878) 3 App.Cas. 325.

41. See, for example, *Bradford Old Bank* v. *Sutcliffe* [1918] 2 KB 833, *Re E.J. Morel (1934) Ltd* [1962] Ch. 21, and *National Westminster Bank Ltd* v. *Halesowen Presswork and Assemblies Ltd* [1972] AC 785.

loan account, even if both are repayable on demand.[42] English law does not permit parties to increase[43] or to diminish[44] by contract the extent of the rights of set-off conferred in bankruptcy and liquidiation by statute.[45]

3.20 There can be no combination where the accounts are not held in the same right,[46] nor (it seems) where they are not held in the same name, even if the beneficial owner is the same.[47] Similarly, a banker may not combine moneys which to his knowledge are held by the customer on trust to use them for a particular purpose.[48] Accounts whose terms, for example as to time for payment,[49] are so materially different that they could not all be terms of one account may not be combined. So, in the absence of agreement, a bank may not combine the customer's contingent, future or unmatured liabilities to it with its present debts to the customer so as to excuse payment,[50] or achieve the same result by retaining money presently payable so as to combine accounts at a future date. As Sir Page Wood VC said in *Jeffryes* v. *Agra and Masterman's Bank*[51]: "... you cannot retain a sum of money which is actually due against a sum of money which is only becoming due at a future time ..."

3.21 It has not yet been judicially determined whether a bank may combine accounts maintained in different currencies.[52]

3.22 The precise theoretical analysis of this valuable right or remedy is surprisingly uncertain. One theory is that the matter is simply one of accounting, with the various accounts maintained by the bank being no more than sub-accounts of one overall account between the bank and its customer, under

42. *Ibid.* Such an agreement will normally be operative only for so long as the accounts are "alive", and will be determined by any event which terminates the relationship of banker and customer; see *British Guiana Bank* v. *Official Receiver* (1911) 27 TLR 454.

43. *British Eagle International Air Lines* v. *Compagnie Nationale Air France* [1975] 1 WLR 758.

44. *National Westminster Bank Ltd* v. *Halesowen Presswork and Assemblies Ltd* (*supra*).

45. Insolvency Act 1986, s.323; Insolvency Rules 1986, r. 4.90. See *Stein* v. *Blake* [1996] AC 243; *Re Bank of Credit and Commerce International SA (No. 8)* [1998] AC 214, 223D, *per* Lord Hoffmann.

46. *Re Gross* (1871) 6 Ch. App. 632; *Garnett* v. *McKewan* (1872) LR 8 Ex. 10; and cf. *Bank of Credit and Commerce International SA* v. *Al-Saud* [1997] 1 BCLC 457. However, where the customer has two accounts in his own name, one a purely private one, the other suggesting that someone else may have a proprietary interest in it, it would seem that a balance on the purely private account might be utilised to cover a debit on the other: cf. *Coutts & Co.* v. *Irish Exhibition in London* (1891) 7 TLR 313.

47. *Uttamchandami* v. *Central Bank of India* (1989) 139 NLJ 222. For dicta to the contrary, see *Barclays Bank Ltd* v. *Okenarhe* [1966] 2 Lloyd's Rep. 87; and *Bhogal* v. *Punjab National Bank* [1988] 2 All ER 296, 301.

48. *W.P. Greenhalgh & Sons* v. *Union Bank of Manchester* [1924] 2 KB 153; *Barclays Bank* v. *Quistclose Investments* [1970] AC 567.

49. Current account set-off depends upon the reciprocal claims being current. So accounts with different maturities cannot be the subject of combination; see Philip R. Wood, *English and International Set-Off* (1989), at para. 3–22.

50. *Jeffryes* v. *Agra and Masterman's Bank* (1866) LR 2 Eq. 674; *Bower* v. *Foreign and Colonial Gas Co. Ltd, Metropolitan Bank, Garnishees* (1874) 22 WW 740.

51. Above, at p. 680.

52. See *Paget's Law of Banking* (11th edn) at p. 537 for a discussion of the competing considerations.

which only the ultimate balance either way represents an enforceable debt. An alternative analysis is that the right is properly regarded as a right of set-off, or as an analogous right, which does not produce a single balance or debt until the bank actually exercises its right to combine.

3.23 The first theory is supported by a number of dicta in the authorities, the most famous of which is probably that of James LJ in *Re European Bank*:[53]

> In truth, as between banker and customer, whatever number of accounts are kept in the books, the whole is really but one account, and it is not open to the customer, in the absence of some special contract, to say that the securities he deposits are only applicble to one account.[54]

It is also supported by Rory Derham, who explains the right of combination in his book on *Set-Off*[55] in the following terms:

> . . . it is not so much a right to combine accounts, as a recognition that the balance of all the accounts represents the debt. Expressed more concisely, combination is a matter of account rather than of set-off. On this basis, a specific act of combination should not be required . . .[56]

3.24 By contrast, Philip Wood, in his monumental work *English and International Set-Off*,[57] rejects the "accounting" theory and prefers to regard the right as a right of current account set-off:

> . . . this idea that there is only one amount owing is no more than an expression of the fact that, in the absence of agreement to keep the accounts separate, the bank may instantly set off at any time without notice to the customer, so that at any point the bank can treat the divided accounts as being one single blended account. But two accounts are not one account and the real question is in what circumstances can the bank treat the account as a single account . . .

3.25 This seems to be the view of the majority of text-book writers,[58] who treat the bankers' right of combination as a species of set-off, and as a right

53. (1872) LR 8 Ch. App. 41, 44.

54. See also *Ex parte Pearce, in re Langmead* (1841) 2 Mount D & De G 142; *Bailey* v. *Finch* (1871) LR 7 QB 34; *Garnett* v. *McKewan* (1872) LR 8 Ex. Cas. 10; *Re Willis, Percival & Co., ex parte Morier* (1879) 12 Ch. D 491, *per* James LJ, at p. 498; *Greenwood Teale* v. *Williams* (1894) 11 TLR 56; *Mutton* v. *Peat* [1900] 2 Ch. 79; *Ex parte Douglas* [1930] 1 Ch. 342, 349, *per* Luxmoore J; *National Westminster Bank* v. *Halesowen Presswork and Assemblies* [1971] 1 QB 1, 19f, *per* Roskill J, and at p. 46, *per* Buckley LJ; and *Barclays Bank* v. *TOSG* [1984] BCLC 1, *per* Nourse J, at p. 22g, cited with approval by Millet J in *Re Charge Card Services* [1987] Ch. 150, 173–174.

55. 2nd edn, 1996, Ch. 11, where this passage in the first edition of this book is criticised in the course of a very detailed and illuminating discussion of this difficult area of the law.

56. *Ibid.* at p. 488.

57. 1989, para. 3–6.

58. Cresswell and Blair, *Encyclopaedia of Banking Law*, para. C631; Holden, *The Law and Practice of Banking* (5th edn) paras 2–55 to 2–72A; Ellinger and Lomnicka, *Modern Banking Law* (2nd edn), pp. 179–200; Goode, *Legal Problems of Credit and Security* (2nd edn), pp. 146–147. *Contra*, Penn, Shea and Arora, *The Law Relating to Domestic Banking* (1987), paras 13.31–13.36; McCracken, *The Banker's Remedy of Set-off* (2nd edn), Ch. 1; *Paget's Law of Banking* (11th edn), pp. 535–536; Cranston, *Principles of Banking Law* (1997), p. 176.

which requires some act of exercise by the bank. It also seems most nearly to reflect the commercial realities of the situation.[59]

3.26 As Wood points out, the idea that the accounts are always combined to produce a single debt is inconsistent with many of the features of distinct bank accounts prior to combination. For example, the bank will continue to charge interest on the full amount of an overdrawn bank account without netting out the credit balance. Where separate accounts are maintained, the *Clayton's Case*[60] appropriation rules are applied to the separate accounts, not to those accounts as combined. A debit balance may become statute-barred and hence ineligible for set-off against a credit balance. To this list may be added three further matters: the possibility that a bank might need to give notice before exercising its right of combination;[61] the "apparent anomaly"[62] that the bank may combine accounts at different branches, but the customer may not do so without specific agreement; and the greater anomaly that the bank may not even be obliged to combine accounts at the same branch in order to honour its customer's cheques.[63] All of these matters seem *prima facie* to be inconsistent with the idea that, prior to combination, the two or more accounts constitute a single debt.[64]

THE BANKER'S RIGHT OF LIEN

3.27 English law[65] gives a banker, in addition to the right of combination of accounts, a general lien[66] over securities deposited by the customer with the

59. The reasons why it would be commercially impracticable for the banker's right of combination to operate automatically (outside of insolvency) are cogently explained by Philip Wood (*op. cit.*) at p. 47.

60. *Devaynes* v. *Noble* (1816) 1 Mer. 572.

61. Contrast *Garnett* v. *McKewan* (1872) LR 8 Ex. 10 (where the Court of Exchequer unanimously held that no notice was required), with *Buckingham Co.* v. *London and Midland Bank* (1895) 12 TLR 70 (where Mathew J left to the jury the question of whether the customer was entitled to notice, and the jury found in the customer's favour). Derham (*op. cit.*) at pp. 501–2 accepts that notice might be necessary where there is an agreement between the parties to keep the accounts separate, which is terminable only on reasonable notice; and Ellinger (*op. cit.*) at p. 194 explains *Buckingham* as a case where there was such an agreement, made by the course of dealing.

62. *Per* Mocatta J in *Barclays Bank* v. *Okenarhe* [1966] 2 Lloyd's Rep. 87, 95.

63. Ellinger (*op. cit.*), at pp. 198–200, stating that there is no authority on the point to date.

64. It may also be said that the courts treat the banker's rights of combination as requiring an act of exercise, in the context of *Mareva* injunctions. However, the case which established the usual proviso permitting the continued exercise of those rights after service of an injunction, *Oceanica Castelana Armadora SA* v. *Mineralimportexport* [1983] 1 WLR 1294, did not concern ordinary current accounts but involved debits for interest on term loans. Contrast *Re K. (Restraint Order)* [1990] 2 QB 298, where Otton J sought to distinguish a bank's right to combine accounts from a right of set-off.

65. The banker's lien was recognised by the Court of King's Bench as early as 1794, in *Davis* v. *Bowsher* (1794) 5 Term. Rep. 488 and by 1846 was regarded as "undoubted" by the House of Lords in *Brandao* v. *Barnett* (1846) 12 Cl. & Fin. 787.

66. Arising by operation of law, and so not registerable as a bill of sale or under the Companies Act 1985, s.395.

bank to the extent of the customer's indebtedness to the bank. The right of lien extends to a banker acting as agent for a remitting banker,[67] and to the advising/confirming bank in a documentary credit transaction.[68]

3.28 In order to be subject to the lien, the securities must have come into the banker's hands in his capacity as banker in the course of his banking business. Curiously, although safe-custody is undoubtedly part of the modern business of banking, securities deposited merely for safe keeping are considered to be outside the scope of the banker's lien.[69]

3.29 The lien extends to "paper securities",[70] whether negotiable (such as cheques and bills of exchange[71] collected by the bank on its customer's behalf[72]) or not. So, for example, documents tendered under a letter of credit,[73] insurance policies,[74] deposit receipts,[75] orders for payment,[76] and share certificates[77] have all been held to be subject to the lien. It is unclear where it extends to documents of title to land.[78] It does not extend to goods, or (despite earlier dicta to the contrary) to the customer's credit balance with the bank,[79] and may be displaced by contrary agreement.

3.30 A banker's lien carries the right to sell the property subject to the lien,[80] after reasonable notice to the customer.[81]

67. *Re Parker, ex parte Froggatt* (1843) 3 Mont. D & DeG 322; *Prince* v. *Oriental Bank Corp.* (1878) 3 App. Cas. 325.

68. *Aschkenasy* v. *Midland Bank Ltd* (1934) 50 TLR 209; 51 TLR 34.

69. *Leese* v. *Martin* (1873) LR 17 Eq. 224; *Misa* v. *Currie* (1876) 1 App. Cas. 554.

70. *Davis* v. *Bowsher* (above); *Wylde* v. *Radford* (1863) 33 LJ Ch. 51.

71. *Davis* v. *Bowsher* (above); *Giles* v. *Perkins* (1807) 9 East 12; *Re Firth, ex parte Schofield* (1879) 12 Ch. D 337; *Dawson* v. *Isle* [1906] 1 Ch. 633.

72. *Barclays Bank Ltd* v. *Astley Industrial Trust Ltd* [1970] 2 QB 527. Cf. the Bills of Exchange Act 1882, s.27(3), which constitutes a collecting bank holder a holder for value to the extent of the sum for which it has a lien, and *Re Keever* [1967] Ch. 182.

73. *Sewell* v. *Burdick* (1884) 10 App. Cas. 74.

74. *Re Bowes, Earl of Strathmore* v. *Vane* (1886) 33 Ch. D 586.

75. *Jeffryes* v. *Agra and Masterman's Bank* (1866) LR 2 Eq. 674.

76. *Misa* v. *Currie* (above).

77. *Re United Service Co., Johnstone's Claim* (1870) 6 Ch. App. 212.

78. As explained by Buckley J in *Re London and Globe Finance Corporation* [1902] 2 Ch. 416, 420, *Wylde* v. *Radford* (above) (in which it was held that the bank was not entitled to a lien on a property, where its customer had deposited a deed of conveyance of that property and another, but had executed a memorandum charging only the other) was a decision on its own facts. Penn, Shea and Arora, *The law Relating to Domestic Banking* (1987) expresses the view that the banker's lien does extend to title deeds (at para. 13.07). *Paget's Law of Banking* (11th edn) takes the contrary view (at pp. 524–525).

79. *National Westminster Bank Ltd* v. *Halesowen Presswork and Assemblies*, in the Court of Appeal at [1971] 1 QB 1, 32 and 46, approved by the House of Lords at [1972] AC 785, 802 and 810.

80. Always assuming that the security is capable of sale by the bank: *Brandao* v. *Barnett* (1846) 3 CB 519; *Rosenburg* v. *International Banking Corpn* (1923) 14 Ll.L.Rep. 344, 347. This right is of most value where the security consists of negotiable instruments or transferable documents of title to goods.

81. Because it carries this right of sale, it is often described as an "implied pledge". Like a pledge, it depends upon possession. Unlike a pledge, however, the banker's lien is not created by agreement but arises by operation of law.

THE RIGHT TO CLOSE THE ACCOUNT

3.31 If the customer is operating his account unlawfully,[82] or commits a breach of a term which is a condition of the banker/customer contract, or commits a fundamental breach of an intermediate term of that contract, a bank may be entitled to close the account forthwith.[83] In the absence of such unlawful conduct or repudiatory breach by the customer,[84] a bank can only close a customer's credit account on reasonable notice.[85] Where a credit account is concerned, the period of notice must be long enough in the circumstances to enable the customer to make alternative banking arrangements.[86]

3.32 It is probable that there is a similar obligation upon a bank to give the customer sufficient notice to make other arrangements, even where the account is in debit, and even though no such notice would be necessary to call in the overdraft.

> A banker would be very imprudent if he called in an overdraft to close an account and then, prior to the expiry of a proper period of notice, he dishonoured cheques which the customer was prepared to cover by paying in cash. It is one thing to call in an overdraft; it is quite another matter to withdraw banking facilities without giving the customer sufficient notice to enable him to make other arrangements ...[87]

THE RIGHT TO ENFORCE SECURITY

3.33 The range of implied self-help remedies available to a bank is limited. Bank security documents usually seek to extend the range by express provision. They will often confer express powers of sale over items of security where none would be implied. To make those powers effective, they will often also appoint the bank, or a nominated bank official, as attorney for the owner of the security, to complete the sale in the owner's name. Provided that the necessary formalities have been observed, there is no reason in principle why provisions of this nature should not be effective.

3.34 Bank facility letters and security documents also often contain provisions entitling the bank to certify the existence of certain states of affairs, so that the bank's certificate is conclusive as between it and the borrower or giver of security. For example, a well-drawn Memorandum of Deposit by way of security will often provide that:

82. The law will not imply an obligation on the bank to allow its customer a reasonable time to make alternative banking arrangements if the purpose of making those alternative arrangements is to enable him to continue his unlawful conduct: see Holden, *The Law and Practice of Banking* (5th edn), para. 3–12.

83. Since the relationship is contractual, the ordinary rules as to termination of contract apply.

84. And in any event, for prudence.

85. *Joachimson* v. *Swiss Bank Corporation* [1921] 3 KB 110, 125, 127.

86. *Prosperity* v. *Lloyds Bank Limited* (1923) 39 TLR 372.

87. Holden (*op. cit.*) at para. 3–13; see also Cresswell and Blair, *Encyclopaedia of Banking Law*, at para. C345.

Upon any sale of [the security] ... which you may make ... under the provisions ... above, a statutory declaration made by any of your officers that the Customer has made default and that the power of sale has become exercisable shall be conclusive evidence of the fact in favour of any purchaser or other person to whom [the security] may be transferred ...[88]

3.35 The amount of the customer's indebtedness may also be the subject of certification by the bank. The validity of such clauses has been upheld by the High Court of Australia in *Dobbs* v. *The National Bank of Australia Ltd*,[89] and by the English Court of Appeal in *Bache & Co. (London) Ltd* v. *Banque Vernes et Commercial de Paris SA*,[90] where Lord Denning MR said:

This commercial practice (of inserting conclusive evidence clauses) is only acceptable because the bankers or brokers who insert them are known to be honest and reliable men of business who are most unlikely to make mistakes. Their standing is so high that their word is to be trusted. So much so that a notice of default given by a bank or broker must be honoured. It ranks as equivalent to, if not higher than, the certificate of an arbitrator or engineer in a building contract. As we have repeatedly held, such a certificate must be honoured, leaving any cross-claims to be settled later by an arbitrator. So if a bank or broker gives a notice of default in pursuance of a conclusive evidence clause, the guarantor must honour it, leaving any cross-claims by the customer to be adjusted in separate proceedings ...

This remark is difficult to justify, either in law[91] or in fact.[92]

3.36 It is often unattractive for a bank to rely on such clauses. If given full effect, a conclusive evidence clause buried in an ordinary guarantee could have the practical consequence of making that guarantee payable on first demand, irrespective of the principal debtor's true liability, as if it were a first-demand performance guarantee. *Dobbs* suggests that it will be possible to go behind the conclusive certificate in cases of established fraud. It is also possible that the inclusion of a conclusive evidence clause in a bank guarantee or other security

88. *Encyclopaedia of Forms and Precedents* (5th edn), Vol. 4, paras 236, 242, 249.

89. (1935) 53 CLR 643, which held that the clause was not void as an attempt to oust the jurisdiction of the court. It was a clause by which a party to a contract has vested a discretionary judgment in an ascertainable person. The clause was conclusive not only as to amount but also as to the legal existence of the customer's indebtedness. However, in special circumstances such as a clear case of fraud, the validity of the certificate could be challenged. It was said that the clause should not be interpreted as "covering all grounds which go to the validity of the debt". See also *A.N.Z. Banking Group (No. 2) Ltd* v. *Gibson* [1981] 2 NZLR 513.

90. [1973] 2 Lloyd's Rep. 437. The decision of the Privy Council in *Tai Hing Cotton Mill Ltd* v. *Liu Chong Hing Bank* [1986] AC 80 also provides indirect support for the validity of such clauses.

91. This high judicial trust in banks is, perhaps, the benefit they receive in return for the equally high judicial expectations of their conduct. See, for example, the comments of Woolf LJ in *Lloyds Bank* v. *Waterhouse* [1991] Fam. Law 23: "... the Bank's internal rules ... now provide that an intending guarantor *must* receive independent legal advice from a solicitor before executing the relevant document. *This is what I would expect of a responsible financial institution such as Lloyds Bank* ..."

92. Even the banks do not consider themselves infallible. There are, after all, several cases in the law reports in which banks have sought to recover payments made by them by mistake: see, e.g., *United Overseas Bank* v. *Jiwani* [1976] 1 WLR 964; *Barclays Bank* v. *W.J. Simms Son & Cooke (Southern) Ltd* [1980] QB 677; *Lloyds Bank Plc* v. *Independent Insurance Co. Ltd* [1999] 1 All ER (Comm.) 8.

could be challenged under sections 2 and/or 3 of the Unfair Contract Terms Act 1977 or under the Unfair Terms in Consumer Contracts Regulations 1994.[93] As there is a duty to give a correct account, a conclusive evidence clause might be siad to exclude or restrict liability for breach of the duty.[94]

3.37 In addition to conferring on the bank, wherever appropriate, the right to appoint a receiver to enforce the security, well-drawn bank security documents will also often seek to remove or attenuate many of the preconditions for the enforcement of that security which the law would otherwise imply. It is, for example, usual to exclude the restriction which would otherwise be imposed by section 103 of the Law of Property Act 1925 upon the bank's power of sale of mortgaged property. Some restrictions, however, cannot be excluded. Those imposed by the Consumer Credit Act 1974,[95] for example, are mandatory. It is also unusual for a bank to be able simply to take possession of mortgaged property for the purpose of exercising its power of sale. Where the tenancy is binding on the bank as mortgagee, the bank is an "owner" for the purpose of the restrictions on the eviction of a "residential occupier" without due process of law imposed by the Protection from Eviction Act 1977.[96] In any event, if violence is used to secure entry into any sort of property, the bank may be liable to prosecution under the criminal law.[97] "Violence" for these purposes includes violence in the manner of entry, for example by breaking open the doors of a house.[98]

3.38 Where the making of a demand is an express or implied condition precedent to the enforcement of the bank's security, the right must have accrued due at the date of enforcement.[99] If the right accrues later, this will not retrospectively validate the premature enforcement of the security, but merely justify fresh action.[100]

3.39 In Canada[101] and Australia[102] it has been held that the debtor is entitled (broadly) to a reasonable time to raise the money after the demand before the bank can become entitled to enforce its security. However, in England it appears to be the law that

93. SI 1994 No. 3159.

94. Cf. *Westpac Banking Corporation* v. *Sugden* (1988) NSW Conv. R 55–377 where, applying the Contracts Review Act, Brownlie J held that the conclusive evidence clause went far beyond what was reasonably necessary for the protection of the bank.

95. E.g., s.126.

96. See *Bolton Building Society* v. *Cobb* [1966] 1 WLR 1.

97. Criminal Law Act 1977, s.6(4). The offence is committed only when the accused knows that there is another person on the premises when he uses or threatens violence and knows that he is opposed to the entry: s.6(1)(a) and (b). The fact that the person has an interest or right in the property does not constitute lawful authority to use or threaten violence to secure entry: s.6(2). The Criminal Law Act 1977 repealed and replaced the Forcible Entry Acts.

98. *Hemmings* v. *Stoke Poges Golf Club* [1920] 1 KB 720.

99. *Cripps* v. *Wickenden* [1973] 1 WLR 944, 956–957 (a case involving the appointment of a receiver).

100. See generally Lightman & Moss, *The Law of Receivers of Companies* (2nd edn), para. 4–10.

101. See *Whonnock Industries Ltd* v. *National Bank of Canada* (1987) 42 DLR (4th) 1.

102. See *Bunbury Foods* v. *National Bank of Australasia* (1984) 51 ALR 609.

... a debtor who is required to pay money on demand ... must have it ready and is not entitled to further time in order to look for it ...[103]

3.40 This approach, which allows the debtor only enough time to operate the "mechanics of payment" and not the time needed to refinance his obligations, is understandably unpopular with debtors. The resistance by Sheppard & Cooper Ltd to the efforts of TSB Bank Plc to appoint a receiver over its assets and undertakings recently provided much-needed employment for lawyers and some clarification of the law in this area.

3.41 The company, at the instigation of the TSB, appointed Smith & Williamson, a firm of accountants, to investigate its financial affairs. The 1993 letter of appointment provided, *inter alia*:

So that there should not be any conflict of interest between the company, [Smith & Williamson] and the bank, and for the avoidance of doubt, [Smith & Williamson] will not undertake any responsibility for the management of the company's affairs, either now or in the future.

3.42 At 9.15 or 9.30 a.m. on 7 February 1996 TSB made demand on the company. At 10.15 a.m. that same day it purported to appoint two partners in Smith & Williamson as receivers. On 14 February 1996 the company issued a writ and obtained an *ex parte* injunction. On 16 February 1996 the company's application for interlocutory relief came before Harman J, *inter partes*. The company took two points. First, it claimed that the appointment broke the terms of the 1993 letter. Second, it asserted that the 30 minutes which had elapsed between demand and appointment was insufficient and that the appointment was therefore premature ("the timing point"). Harman J discharged the interlocutory injunction. On 26 February 1996 the Court of Appeal[104] restored the injunction, holding that the terms of the 1993 letter were clear and prevented the chosen receivers from acting.

3.43 The Court of Appeal, given the urgency of the matter, refused to decide the timing point. After a fresh demand and a fresh appointment had been made, that point came before Blackburne J under RSC O 14A.[105] He decided that where, as here, the debtor had made it clear that the required funds were not available, that admission established the necessary default and there was thus no need to allow any further time to elapse before treating the debtor as in default and appointing receivers.

103. *Brighty* v. *Norton* (1862) 3 B & S 305, 312, *per* Blackburn J; cited and applied in *Cripps* v. *Wickenden* [1973] 1 WLR 944 and in *Bank of Baroda* v. *Panessar* [1987] Ch. 335.
104. [1996] BCC 653.
105. [1996] 2 All ER 654.

THE RIGHT TO ASSIST IN A RESCUE

3.44 Banks have always realised that when a customer acknowledges his indebtedness but simply has insufficient funds, a rescue may offer the best chance not only of repayment but of future profit. The Insolvency Act 1986 contains provisions, some of which are entirely new to English law, designed to assist in such ventures.

3.45 Prior to 1985, an individual debtor who wanted to make an arrangement with his creditors to avoid the costs and other consequences of bankruptcy could seek to invoke the provisions of the Deeds of Arrangement Act 1914. But this procedure was little used.[106] The mere execution of a deed of arrangement was an act of bankruptcy, and the proposals could easily be frustrated by a dissenting creditor petitioning for bankruptcy. The Bankruptcy Act 1914 itself contained provisions for schemes of composition or arrangement, once bankruptcy proceedings were under way:[107] but, again, they were little used.

3.46 By contrast, the provisions for individual voluntary arrangements in the Insolvency Act 1986[108] have proved popular with debtors. The debtor may select a licensed insolvency practitioner to act as a trustee or otherwise to supervise the implementation of the proposals which he wishes to make to his creditors. A viable proposal cannot be destroyed by a selfish creditor, because the debtor can obtain a moratorium on proceedings against himself or his property by obtaining an interim order of the court.[109] While the application for an interim order is pending, the court may stay such proceedings. When it has been made, the stay is automatic. Such a procedure is, of course, open to abuse: but the debtor's attempt to use the interim order procedure to frustrate attempts to bring bankruptcy proceedings proved unsuccessful in *Re a Debtor (No. 83 of 1988)*.[110]

3.47 For a proposal to be implemented, it must be approved by a majority in excess of three-quarters in value of the creditors voting at a creditors' meeting summoned in accordance with the Insolvency Rules 1986.[111] The approved arrangement can be challenged by application to the court if it unfairly prejudices the interests of a creditor, or if there has been some material irregularity at or in relation to the meeting.[112] Subject to that, it binds every

106. There were only 51 in 1984: Sealy and Milman, *Annotated Guide to the 1986 Insolvency Legislation* (3rd edn), p. 294.

107. Ss.16, 17 and 21.

108. First enacted in the Insolvency Act 1985, ss.110 *et seq*. These provisions do not follow the specific proposals of the Cork Committee (Final Report of the Review Committee on Insolvency Law and Practice, Cmnd. 8558 (1982)).

109. Insolvency Act 1986, ss.252–263.

110. [1990] 1 WLR 708.

111. Insolvency Act 1986, s.258: Insolvency Rules 1986, r. 5.18. The provision that the majority is to be measured by the value of the debts of those actually voting, rather than of those entitled to vote, makes it much easier than formerly to obtain approval for a viable proposal.

112. Insolvency Act 1986, s.262. See *Re Naeem (A Bankrupt) (No. 18 of 1988)* [1990] 1 WLR 48.

person who had notice of and was entitled to vote at the meeting, as if he were a party to the arrangements.[113]

3.48 For companies in difficulties, there are similar provisions for voluntary arrangements,[114] although the moratorium achieved for an individual debtor by an interim order can only be achieved for a company in difficulties by the presentation of a petition for an administration order with a view to achieving approval of the voluntary arrangement. Both kinds of voluntary arrangement under the Insolvency Act 1986 have this in common: creditors have no standing to propose them.[115] The proposal must come from the individual debtor or from the directors of the debtor company. A creditor bank's only remedy, therefore, is to suggest and, if appropriate, to vote in favour of and participate in such an arrangement. In practice, however, the initiative for such arrangements may often come from the bank, either because it is the principal creditor, or because it is the debtor's most readily available source of financial advice.

3.49 By contrast, an application for an administration order[116] in relation to an insolvent company may be made by a creditor,[117] as well as by the company or the directors.[118] In that respect, therefore, a lending bank may take the initiative.

3.50 If an administration order is made, the company is given a statutory breathing-space during which it is substantially protected from its creditors. On the making of an administration order, any petition for the winding-up of the company must be dismissed, any administrative receiver must vacate office, and any receiver of part of the company's property must vacate office on being required to do so by the administrator.[119] During the period for which an administration order is in force, (a) the company cannot be wound up, (b) no administrative receiver may be appointed, (c) no other steps may be taken to enforce any security over the company's property, or to repossess goods on hire-purchase,[120] unless the administrator consents or the court gives leave, and (d) no other proceedings, execution, or distress against the company or its

113. Insolvency Act 1986, s.260.

114. Companies Act 1985, ss.425–427A: Insolvency Act 1986, ss.1–7.

115. Contrast, for example, the position under s.425(1) of the Companies Act 1985, where the application may be made by the company, or any creditor, member, liquidator or administrator of the company.

116. This procedure is often described as akin to the reorganisation procedure under Chapter 11 of the United States Federal Bankruptcy Code. In fact, it has closer similarities to the South African "judicial manager", and the Australian "official management" procedures. No application to the court is necesary under the Australian procedure, by which the conduct of the matter is placed entirely in the hands of the creditors. Singapore has recently introduced legislation on the UK model.

117. Including a contingent or prospective creditor Insolvency Act 1986, s.9(1).

118. That is, by all the directors, or by a majority acting on the basis of a properly passed resolution: *Re Instrumentation Electrical Services Ltd* (1988) 4 BCC 301. See also *Re Business Properties Ltd* (1988) 4 BCC 684; and *Re Equiticorp International plc* (1989) 5 BCC 599.

119. Insolvency Act 1986, s.11(1) and (2).

120. Defined to include conditional sale agreements, chattel leasing agreements and retention of title agreements: Insolvency Act 1986, s.10(4).

property may be begun or continued, again unless the administrator or the court permits.[121]

3.51 An administration order may only be made where the court is satisfied that the company is, or is likely to become, unable to pay its debts, and considers that the making of the order would be likely[122] to achieve one or more of the following purposes: (a) the survival of the company and the whole or any part of its undertaking as a going concern,[123] (b) the approval of a voluntary arrangement under the Insolvency Act 1986 or the Companies Act 1985,[124] or (c) a more advantageous realisation of the company's assets than would be effected on a winding-up.[125]

3.52 The role of the administrator[126] is crucial. The debtor company retains ownership and control of its assets. However, the management of the company[127] and its affairs, business and property[128] is placed in the hands of the administrator, who is deemed to act as agent for the company. The directors are not automatically removed from office: but the administrator may remove (and replace) them. Neither the directors nor the members of the company can do anything which would interfere with the exercise by the administrator of his powers, unless the administrator consents.[129] The administrator is given the same power as an administrative receiver, liquidator or supervisor of a voluntary arrangement to obtain supplies of gas, water, electricity and telephones on payment for the present supplies, irrespective of past debts.[130] He

121. *Ibid.* s.11. See *Air Ecosse* v. *Civil Aviation Authority* (1987) 3 BCC 492; *Re Meesan Investments Ltd* (1988) 4 BCC 788; *Re Barrow Borough Transport Ltd* [1990] Ch. 227; *Re Paramount Airways Ltd, Bristol Airport Plc* v. *Powdrill* [1990] Ch. 744; *Re Atlantic Computer Systems Plc* [1990] BCC 859; *Exchange Travel Agency Ltd* v. *Triton Property Trust Plc* [1991] BCC 341; *Barclays Mercantile Business Finance Ltd* v. *SIBEC Developments* [1992] 1 WLR 1253; *Re Atlantic Computer Systems Ltd* [1992] Ch. 505; *Re Olympia & York Canary Wharf Ltd* [1993] BCC 154; *Re Scottish Exhibition Centre Ltd* [1993] BCC 529; *Re David Meek Plant Ltd* [1994] 1 BCLC 680; *Re AGB Research Ltd* [1995] BCC 1091, for discussions of the difficulties to which these provisions give rise in balancing the rights of the individual creditor against those of the majority.

122. After some initial uncertainty, the weight of authority now seems to favour the view of Hoffman J in *Re Harris Simons Construction Ltd* [1989] 1 WLR 368, that the requirements of this section are satisfied if the court considers that there is a "real prospect" that one or more of the statutory purposes would be satisfied. This is a more "modest threshold of probability" than the "likely, on a balance of probabilities, to be achieved" test propounded by Peter Gibson J in *Re Consumer and Industrial Press Ltd* (1988) 4 BCC 68. See *per* Vinelott J in *Re Primlaks (UK) Ltd* (1989) 5 BCC 710; *per* Peter Gibson J in *Re SCL Building Services Ltd* (1989) 5 BCC 746; and *per* Harman J in *Re Rowbotham Baxter Ltd* [1990] BCC 113.

123. Mark Homan's research paper, "A Survey of Administrations Under the Insolvency Act 1986: The Result of Administration Orders made in 1987" (noted in Goode, *Principles of Corporate Insolvency*, at p. 112) shows that in 55 per cent of the administrations surveyed, the procedure enabled all or part of the business to survive.

124. See note 114 above.

125. Insolvency Act 1986, s.8.

126. Who must be a qualified insolvency practitioner: Insolvency Act 1986, s.230.

127. The administrator's powers do not extend to acts which the company itself is not competent to perform: *Re Home Treat Ltd* [1991] BCC 165.

128. Unlike a liquidator, an administrator has no statutory power of disclaimer.

129. Insolvency Act 1986, ss.14 and 17 and Sch. 1.

130. *Ibid.*, s.233.

is also given similar powers to get in the company's assets,[131] and to require co-operation and information from those concerned with the company and its dealings.[132] He may apply to the court for directions,[133] and his actions may be controlled by the court on the application of a creditor or member of the company, if his conduct of the company's affairs has been, or is, or will be, unfairly prejudicial to the interests of the creditors or members, or some part of the creditors or members.[134]

3.53 The administrator is given the unique power to override the rights of the holder of a security over the company's property,[135] and to dispose of the property in question as if the company owned it unencumbered. Unless the security is (or was when created) a floating charge, the administrator needs the leave of the court: and there are provisions designed to preserve the rights of the security holder in the proceeds of the disposal (or if the disposal is for less than full value, the full value). However, the power is a draconian one.[136]

3.54 As an office holder, an administrator is under a duty to report the conduct of the company's directors, if it appears to him that it makes them unfit to be concerned in the management of a company.[137] He may also apply to the court for orders restoring the company to the position it would have been in but for any relevant transaction with the company at an undervalue,[138] or voidable preference of one of the company's creditors or guarantors,[139] or transaction with intent to defeat creditors.[140]

3.55 Within three months (or such longer period as may be allowed by the court), the administrator must put forward a formal statement of his proposals for achieving the statutory purpose for which he was appointed, for approval by a creditors' meeting.[141] When the administration order will serve no further useful purpose, the order may be discharged. The creditors' former enforcement rights will then revive, except to the extent that they are bound by a voluntary arrangement reached as a consequence of the administration, or are discharged by a subsequent liquidation.

3.56 A lending bank which holds a floating charge over the company's assets

131. *Ibid.*, s.234.
132. *Ibid.*, ss.235–237.
133. *Ibid.*, s.14(3).
134. *Ibid.*, s.27.
135. Or the rights of the owners under a hire-purchase, conditional sale agreement, chattel lease agreement, or retention of title agreement: *Ibid.*, s.15(9).
136. *Ibid.*, s.15. See, generally, *Re Consumer and Industrial Press Ltd (No. 2)* (1988) 4 BCC 72; *Re AVR Aviation Ltd* (1988) 4 BCC 708; and *Re Newman Shopfitters (Cleveland) Ltd* [1991] BCLC 407.
137. Company Directors Disqualification Act 1986, s.6(3)(c).
138. Insolvency Act 1986, s.238(1).
139. *Ibid.*, ss.238(1) and 239.
140. *Ibid.*, ss.423 and 424(1)(a).
141. *Ibid.*, ss.23–26.

can prevent the making of an administration order.[142] The interim protection given to the company simply by the making of the application for an administration order does not prevent the appointment of an administrative receiver:[143] and a petition for an administration order must be dismissed if there is an administrative receiver of the company, unless the court is satisfied that the person who appointed the receiver consents to the making of the order, or his charge is liable to be set aside.[144] Because of the effective right of veto which a floating charge gives to a bank over the appointment of an administrator (who might deal with the charged property against their wishes), banks often now insist upon taking fixed and floating charges where in the past they would have been content with a straightforward fixed charge over specific property. However, experience suggests that lending banks are often content to allow the appointment of an administrator, even where it would be open to them to appoint an administrative receiver.

BANKRUPTCY AND LIQUIDATION

3.57 If all else has failed, a lending bank whose indebtedness has fallen due and not been repaid is likely to be able to rely upon its status as a creditor[145] to entitle it to petition the court for a bankruptcy or winding-up order against the debtor.

3.58 The costs of liquidation, and the principle of *pari passu* distribution of the insolvent's assets, make these formal procedures usually a last resort for the banker. At one time, it was the practice of the clearing banks never to seek a bankruptcy order against an individual debtor unless they considered that he had been guilty of sharp practice or fraud. Harder times make for harder attitudes: and not all banks are now so forbearing. In some cases, it may be the only way to have an effective investigation into what has become of the debtor's assets. If the debtor's assets have been diminished by transactions at an undervalue[146] or preferences,[147] there may be no option, if the case is unsuitable for an administration order. It may be the only way to obtain a proper enquiry into the directors' conduct, or to obtain possession of the bankrupt's house against his wife and children.[148] However, most bankers will feel a sense of failure if their customer ends up as one of the insolvency statistics.

142. Notice of the petition for the administration order must be given forthwith to any person who has appointed or may be entitled to appoint a receiver, and a copy of the petition and supporting affidavit and exhibits must be served on them (and on any receiver, provisional liquidator, or person petitioning for a winding-up order) not less than five clear days before the hearing: Insolvency Act 1986, s.9(4) and Insolvency Rules 1986, r. 2.6. The period for service can be, and often is, abridged.

143. Insolvency Act 1986, s.10.

144. *Ibid.*, s.9(3).

145. Under the Insolvency Act 1986, ss.123(1)(a) and (3) and 124(1) for winding-up, and under ss.264(1)(a), 267 and 268 for bankruptcy.

146. Insolvency Act 1986, ss.238 and 339.

147. Insolvency Act 1986, ss.239 and 340.

148. Insolvency Act 1986, ss.336–338.

THE REMEDY

3.59 If there were simple solutions for the problems which the banks in this country are now facing, no doubt the banks would have adopted them by now. The remedy for those problems, if there is one, lies outside the hands of mere lawyers. Even so, the range of remedies available to banks and their lawyers includes, as I have tried to show, many constructive elements. Before too long, our time may again be occupied setting transactions up, not merely doing our best to salvage planks in the shipwrecks.[149]

RICHARD SALTER

149. See *Brace* v. *Duchess of Marlborough* (1728) 2 P Wms. 491, where Jekyll MR ascribes to Hale CJ this graphic description of the pre-1926 seizure by a later equitable mortgagee of priority over an earlier equitable mortgagee by the acquisition of a legal mortgage with priority to both. It was said of this doctrine that it "could not happen in any other country but this": *Wortley* v. *Birkhead* (1754) 2 Ves. Sen. 571, 574, *per* Lord Hardwicke LC.

CHAPTER 4

DISCLOSURE OF DOCUMENTS*

INTRODUCTION

4.1 Dramatic changes took place on 26 April 1999 with the implementation of Lord Woolf's reforms which created a revolutionary change in the English civil justice system not seen for 100 years. They are encompassed in the new Civil Procedure Rules ("the CPR"). The overriding objective of the Rules will be to deal with all cases justly and this will inform every decision the Court makes.[1]

4.2 One of the main pillars of civil procedure affected by the change has been process of discovery, now known as disclosure.

4.3 This chapter deals with the process of disclosure from the point of view of a bank involved in litigation, whether as a direct party or otherwise, and deals with some of the problems banks are likely to experience. It is limited, therefore, to the disclosure process in the court and does not deal with tribunals, arbitration and the like.

DISCOVERY UNDER THE OLD RULES

4.4 Under the old rules (O 24 of the Rules of the Supreme Court) parties were obliged to disclose and mutually exchange all documents relating to matters in question in the action which were in the party's possession, custody or power. Discovery took place 14 days after close of pleadings. The parties could withhold from inspection those documents which attracted privilege, but otherwise the obligation was given a very wide definition.

4.5 The decision in *Compagnie Financière* v. *Peruvian Guano*[2] provided that a document was to be disclosed if it contained information which might either directly or indirectly advance one party's case or damage the other's or which might (not must) lead to a train of enquiry which might have either of these two consequences. Lord Woolf in *Access to Justice*, his interim report which

* This chapter is based on the chapter written by Anthony Pugh-Thomas which appeared in the first edition.

1. R. 1.1.
2. [1882] 11 QB 55, 63.

underpins the CPR, singled out this decision as the impetus for changing the rules of discovery. He commented that "the result of the *Peruvian Guano* decision was to make virtually unlimited the range of potentially relevant (and therefore discoverable) documents".[3] Discovery as a result became cumbersome, requiring large resources of time, money and personnel to be deployed in carrying it through; it caused long delays, significant expense and exposed inequalities between the parties. This was of particular concern to banks which often generate large numbers of documents internally, many of which, although of peripheral relevance, could have been considered to relate to the issues under *Peruvian Guano*.

DISCLOSURE UNDER THE CPR

4.6 Under the CPR, disclosure is a process that is available against all likely parties right from the very start of the dispute, even before proceedings have begun. It is most likely that in fast-track (claims between £5,000 and £15,000) and multi-track (claims over £15,000) cases a direction for disclosure will be made at the allocation hearing, if a direction is made at all.

4.7 Disclosure is a process by which parties search for and disclose relevant documents that are in their control. The increased scope for pre-action disclosure will in some cases help a party to establish whether it has a sufficiently solid case to justify instituting proceedings. Disclosure generally will allow parties to consider each other's case. Cases will be won and lost on disclosure, as they were on discovery, but the role played in disclosure is somewhat different and starts much earlier.

4.8 The courts are most likely to order "standard disclosure" which will considerably reduce the range of documents covered by the *Peruvian Guano* test and will limit the obligation of disclosure to documents on which a party relies or which adversely affect their own case or adversely affect or support another party's case.[4] However, the court may direct that, considering the financial standing of the parties and the nature of the case, no disclosure or more limited disclosure should take place. Banks, however, do need to be aware that where they are involved in litigation against less financially able parties, the courts, having regard to the overriding objective and the principle of proportionality, may require them to fulfil more onerous disclosure obligations.

4.9 In exceptional and more complex cases the court may order full disclosure. Under full disclosure a party will be expected to disclose relevant documents including those documents that may lead to a train of enquiry in keeping with *Peruvian Guano*. Full disclosure can be made in relation to one or more issues in the case or to the case as a whole. The court will, however,

3. Ch. 21, p. 167, para. 17.
4. R. 31.6.

exercise this power cautiously and the party requesting full disclosure will have to put forward strong and compelling arguments.

4.10 In the Commercial Court the position is slightly different. The court will consider whether standard disclosure should be ordered but that is subject to the overriding principle that the court will "seek to ensure so far as possible that the disclosure ordered in a particular case is tailored to the requirements of the particular case". A departure from standard disclosure either to limit or widen it will have to be justified.[5]

4.11 Part 31 will not apply to claims falling within the small claims track (claims under £5,000). Instead, the court when giving standard directions will order each party to serve on every other party 14 days before the hearing copies of all documents on which it relies.[6]

WHICH DOCUMENTS ARE TO BE DISCLOSED?

4.12 A party is only obliged to disclose documents which are or have been in their control. Control is defined as having physical possession, or a right to possession or a right to inspect or take copies of documents.[7]

4.13 The CPR requires each party to undertake a reasonable search for documents. Along with the overriding objective and the principle of proportionality there are four factors to be taken into account in deciding whether a search is reasonable: (a) the number of documents involved; (b) the nature and complexity of the proceedings; (c) the ease and expense of retrieval of any particular document; and (d) the significance of any document which is likely to be located during the search.[8]

4.14 A further welcome change is that a party need not disclose additional copies of a document[9] unless they have a material marking or other feature on them.

4.15 Banks, often embroiled in large-scale litigation, may at the end of the day be expected to provide full disclosure similar to that which was expected under the old rules. The differences will lie in the criteria for assessing which documents to disclose (i.e. those over which it has control) and the manner in which the documents will be obtained (the type and extent of the search).

5. R. E1.1 of the draft Commercial Court Guide as at 17 February 1999.
6. R. 27.4(3)(a)(i).
7. R. 31.8(2).
8. R. 31.7.
9. R. 31.9.

DISCLOSURE STATEMENT

4.16 A further and important provision under the CPR is that the list is to contain a disclosure statement.

4.17 The individual making the statement must state why he is considered the appropriate person to make the statement, that he knows and understands the duty to disclose and has carried out that duty to the best of his knowledge. He must also set out the extent of the search that has been made to locate documents which the party is required to disclose.

4.18 If the party has limited the search on the grounds that it would be unreasonable, the individual will be expected to state this and identify the respects in which the search was limited and any particular category or class of documents that was excluded from the search.

4.19 Two further matters may be addressed in the disclosure statement. First, and the only reason on which a party may object to disclosure, is on the ground of public policy. Whether a party may refuse to disclose documents can be decided by the court at a hearing without notice.[10] Second, if the party has disclosed a document but claims a right or duty to withhold inspection of the document, the individual must state that they have such a right and the grounds on which they claim that right. Grounds for withholding inspection will cover, for example, matters of legal privilege, without prejudice communications and self-incrimination.

WHO WILL MAKE THE DISCLOSURE STATEMENT?

4.20 A bank will now need to ensure that there is an appropriate member of its staff who will make the statement. The identity of the person is a matter for the bank and its solicitors to decide. It will be preferable that the person understands the issues in the litigation and participates in the decision-making process surrounding disclosure, i.e. what documents are to be disclosed and how extensive the search should be. That individual may be the in-house lawyer responsible for the litigation or a member of management with overall responsibility for the bringing or defending of proceedings, but generally it should not be someone who may be called as a witness in the case.

4.21 Solicitors along with their clients will have to give careful consideration to the extent of the search to be undertaken before the statement is prepared.

10. Known under the old rules as an *ex parte* hearing.

WHAT IS A DOCUMENT FOR THE PURPOSES OF DISCLOSURE?

4.22 Are the obligations of disclosure limited only to pieces of paper? This question has been reviewed in a great many cases and it is clear that the definition embraces, more or less—although there are some grey areas—any record of evidence or information. Photographs, film, tapes and records must be disclosed. A computer tape must be disclosed if the programme it contains or the data it stores is relevant (and it does not cease to be "a document" merely because equipment is necessary to render it intelligible—*Grant* v. *South Western and Country Properties*[11]) and film records taken at a festival in Windsor Great Park have been held to be a "document"—*Senior* v. *Holdsworth, ex parte ITN*.[12]

4.23 Mr Justice Vinelott in *Derby & Co and Others* v. *Weldon No. 9*[13] had to consider whether a computer database which might contain information capable of being retrieved and converted into reasonable form was a document within the meaning of Order 24 (the equivalent of Part 31). He had to decide not only whether he could order discovery but also whether he could direct one of the parties to transfer the database from their own computer to that of an independent expert—in his words:

> During the relevant period four systems were maintained for the money market, foreign exchange, terminal and physical trades, and they were processed each month. Back-up files at the month-end would be recorded on diskettes which were stored. Selected data was fed into the financial recording system and on to an on-line enquiry system. Month-end data files can be restored from the back-up diskettes though not all back-up diskettes can now be found and some have deteriorated to the point where restoration of the data damages the diskette reader. The restoration of this data gives rise to another problem. The IBM System 36 will only hold two months' restored back-up data in addition to current operational data, and recreating all the back-up data would accordingly take a considerable time. Moreover, often when a file has been recreated further time is needed to reprogramme the system so that current programs can access the recreated data file while continuing to access current data files.[14]

He had to decide whether the database was a document, and concluded that it was as he found that in "most businesses" tape or disk now takes the place of the carbon copy of outgoing letters which used to be retained in files. Then he had to decide in what circumstances a party seeking discovery was entitled to inspect and take copies of the database, but he recognised that there were very considerable problems arising out of new technology.

4.24 First, some means would have to be found of screening out irrelevant or privileged material when the tape was re-run. As the judge said, "the party

11. [1974] 2 All ER 465, 474.
12. [1976] QB 23.
13. [1991] 1 WLR 652; [1991] 2 All ER 901.
14. *Ibid*, p. 657.

seeking discovery cannot be allowed simply to seat himself at his opponent's computer console and be provided with all necessary access keys".

4.25 Second, the judge thought there might be material on the computer not accessible by current programs, but which could be retrieved by reprogramming; *prima facie*, in his view, the powers of the court would extend to requiring that the computer be reprogrammed so as to enable the relevant information to be retrieved.

4.26 Third, it might be necessary for the court to give directions as to when access to the computer should be granted. Acute problems will arise where a computer is in daily use.

4.27 The court's approach to the computer database in *Derby* v. *Weldon No. 9* was followed in *Alliance & Leicester Building Society* v. *Ghahremani*,[15] where a word-processing file was held to fall within the definition of a document for the purposes of an order to preserve documents relating to proceedings. The computer records of e-mails and voicemails will almost certainly be regarded as documents and a prudent banker will remind his staff to be as careful as to what they record in an e-mail as they would traditionally have been had they made a formal written file note. E-mail messages are often informal and candid and so can contain highly prejudicial material. In the USA, for example, evidence in the Rodney King trial included an e-mail from a Los Angeles police officer which said: "Oops, I haven't beaten anyone that bad in a long time."

4.28 Fourth, safeguards would have to be embodied in order to ensure that tapes or diskettes which might have deteriorated in storage would not be damaged by use and that the use of them would not damage the computer's reader.

4.29 Fifth, provision would have to be made for the results of any analysis of the computer print-outs, any print-outs made, and so on, to be available to the other party in good time so that he was not taken by surprise at trial.

WHEN MAY DISCLOSURE OCCUR?

4.30 Under the old rules pre-action discovery could only be sought against a likely party to litigation in personal injury and fatal injury cases and by way of *Anton Piller* orders and *Mareva* injunctions, now known as search orders and freezing injunctions. In limited exceptional cases discovery could be sought from non-parties by way of Norwich Pharmacal and Shapira orders. Discovery from non-parties after proceedings had commenced could only be obtained in personal injury and fatal injury cases.

4.31 Under the CPR there are now two definitive points at which disclosure can take place. It can take place before commencement of proceedings against likely parties to the litigation and in limited circumstances against non-parties.

15. [1992] 32 RVR 138.

After commencement of proceedings disclosure can be obtained both from parties and non-parties to the litigation, irrespective of the type of action that is brought. This is a fundamental change in the law.

PRE-ACTION DISCLOSURE AGAINST LIKELY PARTIES

4.32 The CPR has introduced pre-action disclosure against a party who is likely to become a party in future proceedings.[16] Under the CPR a likely party may apply on notice for an order seeking disclosure of specified documents or class of documents against another likely party. The concern of the legal profession and of any respondent facing such an application is that although the intention is that early disclosure might encourage parties to settle at an early stage without the need to institute proceedings, the risk is that this procedure may be abused and be used as a fishing expedition. One can only wait and trust that the judges will exercise caution when exercising their discretion in an applicant's favour.

4.33 The applicant must show that disclosure will be desirable in order to dispose fairly of the anticipated proceedings; or assist the dispute to be resolved without proceedings; or save costs. It is thought that the courts will concentrate on the latter two limbs, in particular the saving of costs. The applicant will be required to specify the documents or class of documents which the respondent must disclose.[17]

THE "MERE EVIDENCE RULE" AND ITS EXCEPTIONS

4.34 The effect of the CPR is to preserve in pre-action disclosure, the "mere evidence rule" and the exceptions to it. The mere evidence rule provides that a party cannot obtain disclosure against someone who has no connection with the potential litigation other than that he might be called as a witness either to testify or to produce documents.[18]

4.35 The exceptions to the rule are both statutory and common law based. It is not intended to deal with them except to mention one widely used method of obtaining a bank's papers, against a non-party prior to litigation, namely by way of a Norwich Pharmacal order.

4.36 In some cases a party may require documents urgently in order to freeze funds which have been misappropriated or make good a tracing claim, and in some cases he may not be able to identify the wrongdoer without first obtaining access to the bank's documents.

16. R. 31.16.
17. Part 31.
18. *Per* Lord Kilbrandon in *Norwich Pharmacal* v. *Customs & Excise Commissioners* [1974] AC 133.

4.37 Norwich Pharmacal relief remains as a means for the aggrieved party, pre-action, to obtain from an innocent non-party the name and identity and documentation relevant to the ascertainment of the identity of the wrongdoer where the non-party has unwittingly been caught up in the wrongdoing of another. This relief flows from the decision in the House of Lords in *Norwich Pharmacal* v. *Customs & Excise Commissioners*.[19] In that case, Norwich Pharmacal owned the patent for Furazolidone. They were aware of Furazolidone imitations being imported and wished to identify the importers. Customs & Excise knew the identity of the importers, because of documentation lodged with them, but declined to provide the names to Norwich Pharmacal on the grounds that it would be a breach of confidence to do so. The House of Lords directed them to disclose the names and supporting documentation. They drew a distinction between a person who had no involvement at all in the commission of a wrongdoing and was "merely a witness" and the person who, even without fault, had become involved in a wrongdoing. At page 175 of the report, Lord Reid enunciated the following principle:

> If through no fault of his own a person gets mixed up in the tortious acts of others so as to facilitate their wrongdoing he may incur no personal liability but he comes under a duty to assist the person who has been wronged by giving him full information and disclosing the identity of the wrongdoers.

4.38 That will often be the position of banks because of their money transfer functions. Norwich Pharmacal orders are often sought in conjunction with so-called Shapira orders (the name being taken from *Bankers Trust Company* v. *Shapira*[20]), search orders and freezing injunctions. This cocktail of orders enables claimants who believe they may have been defrauded to freeze assets within, and sometimes outside, the jurisdiction of the courts, to obtain access to a bank's documents even where the bank has been an innocent bystander, and to trace funds which have passed through a bank's accounts, so enabling a claimant to obtain further orders against the recipients. It is a very fortunate bank indeed who will never be in receipt of such an order—the only compensation for being drawn into other people's disputes is that it is reasonably well established that the bank is entitled to be fully compensated for the costs they will incur in complying with the orders.

DISCLOSURE AGAINST A NON-PARTY AFTER COMMENCEMENT OF PROCEEDINGS

4.39 A fundamental change is that the CPR now permits disclosure from non-parties after proceedings have commenced. An application under this rule requires supporting evidence to be produced. An applicant will have to show

19. [1974] AC 133.
20. [1980] 1 WLR 1274.

that specified documents are "likely" to support his case, or adversely affect an opponent's case, and such disclosure is necessary in order to dispose fairly of the claim or to save costs.[21] The test is thus fairly strict.

4.40 A party still retains the power to both compel a third party to attend trial and produce documents (by way of witness summons)[22] or to require a bank to produce its "books" for inspection and to take copies of any entries in those books if he can show "special cause" under the Bankers' Books Evidence Act 1879.

4.41 The provisions of the Act are quite restrictive. Although a party may seek disclosure of documents from non-parties under Part 31, the party will have to satisfy the court that the bank's duty of confidentiality should be subordinated to the overriding objective. It remains to be seen how the courts will deal with such applications given the special position a bank holds in relation to its customers. It may be that where a party wishes to obtain a bank's documents, where the bank is a non-party, it may find itself forced to rely on the provisions of the Act.

4.42 Under section 9(2) of the Act (as amended), bankers' books are defined as including

> ledgers, day books, cash books, account books and other records used in the ordinary business of the bank, whether those records are in written form or are kept on microfilm, magnetic tape or any other form of mechanical or electronic data retrieval mechanism.

Despite the apparent width of those words, they have been construed restrictively—they do not, for example, comprehend cheques and paying-in slips retained by a bank after the conclusion of the banking transaction to which they relate (*Williams* v. *Williams*[23]), nor do they include the bank's correspondence files, internal memoranda, summaries of dealings on the account and so on.

4.43 A party seeking production of a bank's documents under this Act applies by way of an application notice and a supporting affidavit. The circumstances in which the court will make an order were considered by the Court of Appeal in *D.B. Deniz Nakliyati* v. *Yugopetrol.*[24] The court must be satisfied that:

1. There are no reasons why it would be inappropriate to refuse inspection, and
2. The bank account of the third party is essentially the account of a party to the action, or
3. It is one with which the other party is so connected that items in it would be evidence against him at trial.

21. R. 31.17(b).
22. R. 34.2.
23. [1988] QB 161.
24. [1992] 1 All ER 205.

THE GROUNDS ON WHICH A PARTY MAY OBJECT TO INSPECTION

4.44 Under the CPR, there are three occasions on which a party giving disclosure has a right to object to their inspection. First, where the documents are no longer in their control, second, where a party considers that it would be disproportionate to the issues in the case to permit inspection (as on grounds of cost) and third, where the party has a right or a duty to withhold inspection. The latter category will be dealt with below.

PRIVILEGE

4.45 The rules relating to privilege remain essentially unchanged. There are various types of privilege; the best-known head of privilege is documents prepared for the purpose of obtaining legal advice: Jessel MR put the matter this way in *Wheeler* v. *Le Marchant*:[25]

> It must not be supposed that there is any principle which says that every confidential communication which it is necessary to make in order to carry on the ordinary business of life is protected. The protection is of a very limited character, and in this country is restricted to the obtaining [of] the assistance of lawyers, as regards the conduct of litigation or the rights to property. It has never gone beyond the obtaining of legal advice and assistance, and all things reasonably necessary in the shape of communication to the legal advisers are protected from production or discovery in order that legal advice may be obtained safely and sufficiently.

4.46 Jessel MR explained the justification for that rule in *Anderson* v. *Bank of British Columbia*:[26]

> The object and meaning of the rule is this: that as, by reason of the complexity and difficulty of our law, litigation can only be properly conducted by professional men, it is absolutely necessary that a man, in order to prosecute his rights or to defend himself from any proper claim, should have recourse to the assistance of professional lawyers, and it being so absolutely necessary, it is equally necessary, to use a vulgar phrase, that he should be able to make a clean breast of it to the gentleman whom he consults with a view to the prosecution of his claim, or the substantiating [of] his defence against the claim of others; that he should be able to place unrestricted and unbounded confidence in the professional agent, and that the communications he so makes to him should be kept secret, unless with his consent (for it is his privilege, and not the privilege of the confidential agent, that he should be enabled properly to conduct his litigation).

4.47 That being so, confidential communications between the lawyer and his client which come into existence for the purpose of giving or getting legal advice are privileged at all times—although it can sometimes be a nice question as to whether a document came into existence for the purpose of obtaining legal advice or merely as part of an administrative process.

25. (1881) 17 Ch. 675, 681.
26. (1876) 2 Ch. 644, 649.

4.48 Although one might think that this basis of privilege is so clear as not to give rise to problems, it can frequently be difficult to decide whether documents which come into existence for the purpose of disseminating legal advice—and this is an acute problem within large corporate entities—are privileged. Basically a document which merely passes on legal advice within the company is privileged, but if the communication goes further there is a danger that the documents will cease to be regarded as confidential and the privilege will be lost. This is a treacherous area and a prudent banker should look to his solicitors for guidance before disseminating legal advice too widely. An example of what can go wrong is provided by the case of *Nederlandse Reassurantie Groep Holding* v. *Bacon & Woodrow*.[27] NRG had been advised by merchant bankers and other professional advisers during the course of negotiations leading to the acquisition of a reinsurance company. NRG had also received advice from English and Dutch lawyers. Because the merchant bankers were co-ordinating the acquisition, numerous documents from those English and Dutch lawyers were sent to the merchant bankers. Subsequently, NRG sued their professional, actuarial and accountancy advisers as well as the merchant bank: NRG accepted they could not claim privilege in that case for documents emanating from the English or Dutch lawyers which had contemporaneously been sent to the merchant bankers but the judge did at least rule that it did not follow that the confidentiality was lost in other documents emanating from the English or Dutch lawyers which, although similar in nature, had not been disclosed to the merchant bankers or the other advisers and NRG were, therefore, entitled to maintain a claim for privilege in those documents.

4.49 A sub-species of legal professional privilege, litigation privilege arises only when litigation is in prospect or pending. And it can be much more difficult to decide whether a document, which on the face of it would not appear to be protected by legal advice privilege, is in fact protected by litigation privilege: there must, in the words of a leading textbook, "be some definite prospect of litigation and not a mere vague anticipation of it".[28] In the leading case of *Waugh* v. *British Railways Board*,[29] a widow claimed damages under the Fatal Accidents Act 1976 alleging that the death of her husband in a collision between two trains had been caused by the Board's negligence. The widow sought discovery of an internal inquiry report to the Railway Inspectorate incorporating statements of witnesses. The report was headed:

> For the information of the Board's solicitor: this form is to be used by every person reporting an occurrence when litigation by or against the BRB is anticipated. It is to be provided by the person making it to his immediate superior officer and has finally to be sent to the solicitor for the purpose of enabling him to advise the BRB in regard thereto.

Did the heading clothe the report with litigation privilege? The House of Lords

27. [1995] 1 All ER 976.
28. *Bray on Discovery* (1st edn, 1885), p. 408.
29. [1980] AC 521.

decided it did not, because it failed to pass what has become known as the "dominant purpose" test. In the words of Lord Wilberforce,

> the report was prepared for a dual purpose: for what may be called railway operation and safety purposes and for the purpose of obtaining legal advice in anticipation of litigation, the first being more immediate than the second, but both being described as of equal rank or weight.[30]

Applying that test, the House of Lords concluded that the report was not privileged.

4.50 Here are two more examples of how the courts deal with this problem. *Guinness Peat Properties* v. *Fitzroy Robinson Partnership*[31] concerned a letter written by architects to their professional indemnity brokers giving insurers notice of a claim against them. The Court of Appeal held the letter to be privileged on the basis that it owed its genesis to the dominant purpose that it should be used by insurers for the purpose of obtaining legal advice on the claim and in any ensuing litigation. The court ruled that the purpose had to be ascertained by an objective view of the evidence as a whole, looking at all the circumstances surrounding the writing of the letter, rather than confining the test to a narrow subjective examination of the purpose of the writers of the letter. It was, therefore, necessary to take into account in that case the purpose of insurers in including an obligation of notification in the policy. In *Price Waterhouse* v. *BCCI Holdings (Luxembourg)*,[32] the plaintiffs had conducted an investigation into problem loans made by a bank. Millett J (as he then was) held that the dominant purpose of their report was to establish the facts necessary to determine BCCI's financial position and so the reports were not privileged.

4.51 So, bankers need to take care. Inevitably, and because, as we have already seen, banks generate a great many documents, reports will undoubtedly be prepared and circulated when customers complain about the bank's activities. Traditionally, the bank's inspectors, or a special team, will investigate the complaint, interview the bank's officers, and then prepare a report for consideration by their principals. The report will express views on (a) the conduct of the bank's officers, (b) whether there should be disciplinary proceedings, and (c) the possible legal liability of the bank. When the bank rejects the complaint and the complainant sues, will that report be privileged from production: will it pass the "dominant purpose" test? Rather than run the risk of having to disclose the document, it would be much better, if feasible, to prepare separate documents, one dealing with the running of the bank and disciplinary recommendations, and the other being a report on the complaint and an assessment of the bank's liability.

4.52 The mere fact that a document is stamped "confidential—for use in legal proceedings" or "this report has been prepared in contemplation of legal

30. At p. 531.
31. [1987] 2 All ER 716.
32. [1992] BCLC 583.

proceedings and to enable the company to obtain advice from its lawyers" will not, therefore, be conclusive.

4.53 Incidentally, as Lord Jessel made plain in the passage quoted from *Anderson*, the privilege is that of the client, and he can, and in some cases will, be advised that it is expedient that he should waive that privilege and produce the document. Unfortunately, waiver can, on occasion, be accidental. A classic example is where parts of a document were read in court, as happened in *Great Atlantic Insurance Co.* v. *Home Insurance Co.*[33] The plaintiffs gave discovery of the first two paragraphs of a memorandum but claimed privilege from production in respect of the remainder. The first two paragraphs were read out in court at trial and the defendants claimed that amounted to a waiver of privilege in respect of the whole document. The Court of Appeal ruled that the whole memorandum was privileged and that as the plaintiffs "deliberately chose to read part of a document which dealt with one subject matter to the trial judge", they must disclose the whole. One consequence of that ruling is that solicitors, when giving disclosure, need to analyse each document with great care: if part is privileged the question arises whether the document is severable.

4.54 Banks will often find themselves involved in litigation relating to a particular customer but will find that their internal documents may relate to the affairs of a number of customers. Because the obligation to produce documents applies only to that part of a document which relates to a matter in issue in legal proceedings, a party has the right to seal or cover up parts of documents on the grounds, for example, that they do not relate to matters in issue in the action or they contain privileged material, and he can claim that right in his list of documents or, in contested cases, can apply for an appropriate order. Although the extent of the right to seal up was unclear for some time, the Court of Appeal in *GE Capital Corporate Finance* v. *Bankers Trust Company*[34] confirmed that irrelevant material can be covered up provided the sense of the remainder of the document is not destroyed and the document does not become misleading.

4.55 Before moving on from this difficult area, it should be stressed that the mere fact that a document may be addressed to an in-house lawyer in, say, the legal department of a bank will not, of itself, be sufficient to cloak it with privilege (as he may, for example, have received it in an executive and not a legal capacity, as in the *Waugh* case); and even where, according to English rules, such a document would be a privileged communication, in-house lawyers enjoy no privilege before the European Commission when, for example, the Commission is investigating breaches of Articles 85 and 86 of the Treaty of Rome.[35]

4.56 There is a caveat. There has been a surprising addition to the CPR. Rule 48.7, which deals with the personal liability of a legal representative for costs, provides that a court may direct that privileged documents be disclosed to the court or to the other party. This new rule raises questions well beyond the scope

33. [1981] 2 All ER 485.
34. [1995] 1 WLR 172.
35. *AM&S Europe* v. *Commissioners of the European Community* [1983] 3 WLR 17.

of this chapter but banks need to be aware that the area of privilege is not as impenetrable as was previously thought.

WITHOUT PREJUDICE CORRESPONDENCE

4.57 The resolution of disputes by the parties themselves would seriously be impeded if all letters and notes debating the rights and wrongs of their respective conduct, assessing the merits, and considering terms for settlement were to be disclosable and available for use in the litigation if the attempt to settle failed. The law encourages settlement by recognising that "without prejudice" negotiations can be disclosed by the parties without being disclosed to the court—but beware. Written or oral communications made for the purpose of a genuine attempt to compromise a dispute between the parties may generally not be admitted in evidence. But bear in mind that there does have to be (a) a dispute, and (b) an attempt to settle that dispute without resort to, or at least completing the process of, litigation.

4.58 Just as it is unsafe to assume that a document stamped "confidential—for use in legal proceedings" is necessarily privileged from production, so letters are often written "without prejudice" and bankers can be as guilty as insurance companies—who sprinkle that heading over all their letters—in assuming that it necessarily protects the letter from disclosure. That is not the case. Where there is a dispute, written (or oral) communications made as part of a genuine attempt to compromise the dispute will, generally speaking, not be admitted in evidence. In the words of Oliver LJ in *Cutts* v. *Head*:[36]

> . . . parties should be encouraged so far as possible to settle their disputes without resort to litigation and should not be discouraged by the knowledge that anything that is said in the course of such negotiations (and that includes, of course, as much the failure to reply to an offer as an actual reply) may be used to their prejudice in the course of proceedings. They should . . . be encouraged fully and frankly to put their cards on the table . . . the public policy justification, in truth, essentially rests on the desirability of preventing statements or offers made in the course of negotiations for settlement being brought before the court of trial as admissions on the question of liability.

4.59 Note that the "without prejudice" document would be privileged from production only if it was generated in the course of genuine negotiations. In *Re Daintrey*,[37] Vaughan-Williams J commented that the "rule has no application to a document which, in its nature, may prejudice the person to whom it is addressed" and on that basis a letter containing an admission of the writer's inability to pay his debts was admitted as evidence to prove an act of bankruptcy despite being marked "without prejudice".

4.60 If without prejudice negotiations result in a settlement then the whole course of the correspondence is open and the documents must normally be

36. [1984] Ch. 290, 306.
37. [1893] 2 QB 116, 120.

disclosed, where relevant, on discovery: that will not always be the case as the House of Lords decision in *Rush & Tompkins Limited* v. *GLC*[38] illustrates. The plaintiffs in that action reached a compromise with the first defendants, the GLC, following without prejudice negotiations. The second defendants were subcontractors of the plaintiffs and the litigation continued between them: the subcontractors sought production of the "without prejudice" correspondence which had led up to the settlement with the GLC. The House of Lords declined to order that it be produced and held that the public policy basis for the privilege would be weakened if a party negotiating with one defendant could not express his views openly for fear that, if he reached a compromise with that defendant, admissions made in those negotiations would be admissible in subsequent proceedings, either in the same action or in a subsequent action against another party.

A BANK'S DUTY OF SECRECY/CONFIDENTIALITY

4.61 The principle that the public interest in upholding the duty of confidentiality existing between banker and customer, as well as the duty that can exist in other contexts, is subject to being overridden by a greater public interest, was established in *Tournier* v. *National Provincial and Union Bank of England*.[39] Documents held by a bank on behalf of its client are confidential but not privileged in nature.

4.62 Millett J in *Price Waterhouse [a firm]* v. *BCCI Holdings [Luxembourg] SA*[40] stated the principle succinctly:

> The duty of confidentiality, whether contractual or equitable, is subject to a limiting principle. It is subject to the right, not merely a duty, to disclose information where there is a higher public interest in disclosure than in maintaining confidentiality.

4.63 There is little doubt that the ambit of disclosure will lead to an increase in applications against banks, as it will against all parties, but will not alter the substantive arguments a bank will advance to protect its duty to its customers. It is the procedural law that has been altered; the substantive law remains unchanged.

MONEY LAUNDERING AND THE NATIONAL CRIMINAL INTELLIGENCE SERVICE

4.64 An order for production of documents may be made against a bank where it is innocently involved (usually as a conduit) in the fraud or wrongdoing of

38. [1989] AC 1280.
39. [1923] All ER 550.
40. [1992] BCLC 583, 601.

another or when a liquidator or trustee in bankruptcy is seeking information about an insolvent company and the bank has documents which might assist his enquiries. A bank will be in contempt of court if it refuses to comply with a document production order. This may be punishable by imprisonment of an individual and would be commercially embarrassing.

4.65 Banks are often on the receiving end of production orders about accounts or customers in circumstances where the bank is suspicious about the movements on the accounts and has submitted money laundering reports to the NCIS. Once a bank has submitted a money laundering report it is bound by the provisions of the Criminal Justice Act 1988 and must ensure it does not commit an offence of "tipping off". If a bank knows or suspects that the police are conducting a laundering investigation and it discloses to anyone "information" or other matters which are likely to prejudice the investigation, it would constitute the offence of tipping off. A bank is placed in an invidious position, faced with a criminal sanction if it does comply with the court order and contempt of court if it does not.

4.66 The Court of Appeal has recently offered guidance to what banks and other financial institutions should do in these circumstances. In *C* v. *S*[41] the bank faced an order for disclosure of information and documents relating to accounts in respect of which laundering reports had been filed The bank applied *ex parte* that the discovery order be discharged. The case ended up in the Court of Appeal and an *amicus curiae* was appointed by the Attorney-General to assist the court in laying down guidelines on the future approach to such matters.

4.67 The Master of the Rolls recommended an eight-step approach which essentially required a bank, if aware of a document production order for documents which could prejudice an investigation, to inform the NCIS. The NCIS will consider which (if any) of the material should be disclosed and which (if any) of that will be subject to an undertaking from the applicant for the production or else to keep the information confidential. If the applicant is unhappy with partial or restricted disclosure, then directions from the court will have to be sought. The court must be warned in advance of the difficulties and the manner in which the matter is brought before the court. In *C* v. *S* only the court was provided with a skeleton argument setting out the background facts and issues and identifying the problem.

4.68 In deciding whether to make the order, the court will decide what evidence if any is required from the NCIS. It is for the NCIS to persuade the court that disclosure will prejudice the investigation. Where the applicant cannot be heard for reasons of confidentiality, the court recognises its responsibilities to protect the applicant's interests. Although the court's guidance does not solve the problem, it does offer a pragmatic way of dealing with it.

41. *The Times*, 5 November 1998.

COMMON LAW GROUNDS FOR LIMITING DISCLOSURE

4.69 *Baldock* v. *Addison*[42] was a copyright action where an order had been made for a split trial, with the issue of liability to be determined before any question of assessment of damages arose. On the hearing of a summons for directions, the plaintiffs sought an order for the exchange of lists of documents in the usual way but the defendants requested that discovery should be limited to the issue of liability. The court accepted that, whilst the ambit of its power to order discovery extended to "matters in question in the action" and was not limited to matters in question at the first or any other stage of a split trial, it should, in all ordinary cases of a split trial and in the absence of special circumstances, exercise its discretion in favour of limiting discovery to the issue of liability.

A PROCEDURAL DETERRENT—SUMMARY ASSESSMENT OF COSTS

4.70 There is one procedural sanction to eager claimants who abuse the rules. On 1 March 1999 summary assessment of costs was introduced for all interlocutory hearings lasting no more than a day. It is anticipated that this concept will be extended to all hearings (bar the trial itself). In applications for pre-action disclosure, the applicant will usually bear the costs. The effect of summary assessment is that the judge or master will now make an immediate assessment of the amount of costs which the applicant must pay within 14 days of the hearing. It would be a foolhardy litigant who ignored this factor when considering whether to seek an order for pre-action disclosure and it will hopefully deter those on a fishing expedition. The reality of actually having to dig deep into one's pockets within 14 days of the hearing is quite different from the costs order we have been accustomed to, which parties are only required to pay for at the end of the trial itself, and the benefit of which is all too often lost in a settlement before trial.

INSPECTION

4.71 After the lists have been exchanged, the parties have the right to inspect each other's documents: in practice, parties should always consider which categories should be inspected in original form. Copy documents do not always show what is to be found on the original; for example, it may be significant to know if any passages in the original have been highlighted; if they have been

42. [1995] 1 WLR 158.

annotated in any way (and sometimes a photocopier will not reproduce annotations on the back of a document); if they bear staple marks, the date, time and source on a fax, particularly as the older copy faxes tend to fade with time: also, and this may be very important, whether one's opponent has produced original documents, which he is obliged to do when they are in his possession. It may well be appropriate for the banker to accompany his solicitor when the documents are inspected, as his knowledge of banking practice may well lead him to suggest avenues of enquiry his solicitor should pursue.

4.72 The CPR also permit inspection of documents mentioned in statements of case,[43] a witness statement, a witness summary, an affidavit, even an expert's report.[44]

SPECIFIC DISCLOSURE

4.73 Under the CPR the court may order a party to disclose documents specified in the order, carry out a search to the extent stated in the order and disclose any documents located as a result of the search.[45]

CONTINUING OBLIGATION

4.74 The obligation of disclosure is ongoing and parties will be expected to disclose documents that arise after mutual exchange of lists.[46] It should be noted that where a party withholds disclosure it will be barred from relying on that document at trial.

RESTRICTIONS ON THE USE OF DISCLOSED DOCUMENTS

4.75 The disclosure process is an invasion of privacy: clients will undoubtedly be concerned that if another party gets hold of their documents they might be misused, either to his benefit or certainly to their prejudice: documents may contain financially sensitive information or trade secrets of commercial benefit to their rivals; details of internal structures might be leaked to the press; free and frank views of customers might be published, causing embarrassment even if they did not lead to defamation actions; concerns that conduct was short of the standard which all bankers would wish to observe might attract the attention of the Sunday press.

43. Statement of Claim or Defence under the old rules.
44. R. 31.14.
45. R. 31.12.
46. R. 31.11.

4.76 It is not, therefore, surprising that the court offers protection to parties who have to disclose their documentation. Rule 31.22 provides that a party to whom a document has been disclosed can use the document only for the purpose of the proceedings in which it is disclosed, except where the document has been read to or by the court, or referred to at the hearing which has been held in public, or where the party who discloses the document and the person to whom the document belongs agree. In practice all hearings under the CPR will be held in public and so the protection will be lost at a much earlier stage in the litigation than under the old regime. Notwithstanding this, the court still has an overriding discretion to prohibit or restrict the use of documents even where they have been read to or by the court or referred to at a public hearing.

4.77 Furthermore the court has a discretion, and where there are competing interests of disclosure as against confidentiality, the court may order that disclosure be subject to the proviso that the disclosure goes no further than is reasonably necessary to achieve that purpose of that public interest in disclosure.[47] An example of this is in *Church of Scientology* v. *DHSS*,[48] where the DHSS was concerned that the Church of Scientology might use documents disclosed on discovery for the purpose of harassing people who had complained about the activities of the church: a special order was made that documents be disclosed to the plaintiff's legal adviser only and not to the party itself. In *Davies* v. *Eli Lilly & Co*,[49] the court had to decide whether an investigative journalist who had in the past been critical of the defendant drug manufacturers should be allowed to inspect their documents in his capacity as a general adviser to the plaintiffs and co-ordinator of their experts: the court allowed the journalist to inspect the documents, but only on terms designed to protect their confidentiality.

HOW WILL DISCLOSURE WORK IN PRACTICE?

4.78 At the earliest possible opportunity, a solicitor must inform his client of its disclosure obligations. It is the practice of our firm to send clients a detailed note explaining the process of disclosure and, in the case of certain clients with whose operations we are very familiar, to include a checklist of the types of documents which we know from our experience are likely to be on their files.

4.79 Banks tend, in the ordinary course of their business, to generate a great many documents, of which there may well be more than one copy carrying annotations by different members of their staff: in order to contain a paper mountain, banks will often have established a destruction programme: there is nothing improper in that but it is essential that the programme should be

47. *Pharoan and others and Bank of Credit and Commerce International SA [In liquidation] (Price Waterhouse [a firm] intervening)* [1998] 4 All ER 455, 465.
48. [1979] 1 WLR 723.
49. [1987] 1 All ER 801.

interrupted when a dispute arises and special steps should be taken to preserve all documents relating to that dispute.

4.80 Although it is inconceivable that any reputable bank would deliberately destroy relevant documents, it is as well to bear in mind that a deliberate decision to do so, when proceedings are imminent or after they have started, could involve the criminal offence of obstructing or perverting the course of justice.[50] Even where there has been no deliberate attempt to destroy documents and the bank has done no more, in an attempt to be helpful, than limiting the volume of documents passed to their solicitors for the purpose of discovery by "weeding" them, a court will frown on such self-help, and where it becomes clear—and it often does because missing documents would be indicated in surviving ones—that there has been a "weeding" exercise, adverse inferences may well be drawn from their absence.

4.81 One further word of caution. A party must give proper disclosure. If he declines to follow his solicitor's advice and refuses to disclose documents which are relevant, his solicitor is under an obligation as an officer of the court to withdraw from the case. Furthermore, not only may the client and solicitor be embarrassed at trial and the client's commercial reputation harmed, but the client will be prevented from relying on the document at trial.

4.82 Once the documents have been obtained the solicitor has then to group them together in a sensible fashion; that is a matter for his judgement, but he will have to bear in mind, for example, that it can sometimes be significant to know precisely where in a file a document was found, what was stapled to it and so on.

4.83 The solicitor and client will then engage in a reasonable search, always bearing in mind that in most cases they only need to disclose those documents required under standard disclosure. A careful reading of the documents may show that the files are incomplete—memoranda may, for example, refer to documents enclosed with them, accounts, cashflow forecasts and the like—and they should be found or their absence explained, provided they are considered relevant. Letters will acknowledge other letters which are not in the file, or a document may show that a number of copies were made and distributed to different individuals: if those copies are considered to be relevant then a reasonable search will have to be undertaken to find them. The copies may be annotated and, if so, will need to be disclosed as separate documents.

WHAT IMPACT WILL THE RULES OF DISCLOSURE HAVE ON FUTURE LITIGATION?

4.84 Under the old rules parties tended to keep their cards close to their chests and were able to delay disclosure until well into the litigation. Litigants who had limitless resources could hold out against impecunious claimants; litigation was

50. *R* v. *Selvage* [1982] QB 372 and *R* v. *Rowell* [1978] 1 WLR 132.

prolonged. This will no longer be possible. The power of the court to order disclosure at an early stage coupled with further dramatic changes in the rules, such as permitting both claimants and defendants to bring summary judgment applications against a respondent who has no reasonable prospect of success at trial, will accelerate the process and will lead to an early end to a dispute.

4.85 Moreover, the availability of pre-action disclosure may increase summary judgment applications and Part 36 offers and payments into court, both of which are now available to claimants and defendants. Parties will now have the opportunity to consider the strengths and weaknesses of its own and its opponent's case on the basis of documents it acquired on pre-action disclosure.

4.86 In respect of disclosure against non-parties it is hoped that the court will take a cautious approach in applications brought against banks, weighing up the bank's duty of secrecy to its client against the public interest that justice be done and the advantages that disclosure might have in bringing an early end to the dispute. The court will inevitably be guided by case law and by the overriding objective and the principle of proportionality.

4.87 Ultimately the bank's success in defending disclosure applications will depend on the facts and merits of each individual application.

DAVID BAKER AND NICOLA ANSTEY

CHAPTER 5

CROSS-BORDER COURT ORDERS AND BANKS[1]

THE CONTEXT

5.1 There can be no doubt that today the need for cross-border co-operation between courts and enforcement agencies is greater than ever. Modern systems of communication, social mobility, the decline in business ethics and the revolution in electronic methods of settlement of international bank payments have all played their part in the increase of conduct which, both in its civil and criminal aspects, requires international remedies. If the traditional banking confidentiality rules applied as they have been understood since the decision in *Tournier*,[2] then the guilty, as well as the innocent, would be able to take advantage of banking secrecy in circumstances such as (and these are only examples) infringement of securities or revenue legislation; drug trafficking; fraud and breach of trust; the avoidance of execution of judgment debts. The freezing of foreign assets and the obtaining of evidence abroad have become ever more important. The US Securities and Exchange Commission has been in the forefront of efforts to obtain international co-operation in securities frauds, and has been successful in obtaining evidence abroad.

COURT ORDERS AND CONFIDENTIALITY

5.2 In the *Santa Fe* case,[3] the US Securities and Exchange Commission brought civil proceedings in New York alleging that insider trading had taken place prior to the announcement of a takeover of Santa Fe by Kuwait Petroleum Corporation. For the purposes of the New York proceedings, the Securities and Exchange Commission required evidence which was situated in England,

1. This paper draws on the following previously published papers: Collins, "Banking secrecy and the enforcement of securities legislation", in *Conflicts of Interest in the Changing Financial World*, ed. Goode 1986, pp. 81–90; "Problems of enforcement in the multinational securities market: A United Kingdom perspective" (1987) 9 Univ. Penn. J. Int. Bus. L. 487; "The territorial reach of Mareva injunctions" (1989) 105 LQR 262; "Fraudulent conduct in international law" [1989] Curr. L. Prob. 255; "The Siskina Again: An opportunity missed" (1996) 112 LQR 28.
2. *Tournier* v. *National Provincial and Union Bank of England* [1924] 1 KB 461 (CA).
3. 1985 ECC 187; (1984) 23 Int. LM 511.

documents and testimony from employees of a Luxembourg bank with a branch in England. Under the Hague Convention for the Taking of Evidence Abroad, to which both the UK and the US are parties, a judge in the US may request the English court to arrange for the evidence to be collected or taken in England, and pursuant to this procedure the English court made an order requiring examination of witnesses who had been employed in London by a Luxembourg bank, International Resources and Finance Bank SA, through whose London branch purchases of stock and options in Santa Fe had taken place. The employees sought to set aside the order requiring their examination on the ground, *inter alia*, that they were forbidden by Luxembourg law from revealing the identity of clients of the bank. In that case the relevant information related mainly to the operation of the London branch, and there was considerable doubt as to whether Luxembourg law did in fact forbid the disclosure of the information, but whether or not it did forbid it, it was held that there was no real or substantial risk of the applicants being charged with any criminal offence in Luxembourg. But Drake J accepted that there might be circumstances in which it would be against the public interest to order disclosure of confidential information, since there was:

> A public interest in maintaining the confidential relationship between banker and client, so that wherever a banker seeks to be excused from answering a question which would involve the breach of that confidentiality, it is proper ... for the court to consider such request and to judge it in the context of the circumstances in which it is made. There is ... also clearly a public interest, and a very strong one, in not permitting the confidential relationship between banker and client to be used as a cloak to conceal improper or fraudulent activities, evidence of which would otherwise be available to be used in legal proceedings, whether here or abroad.

5.3 In international securities fraud cases the decision of the House of Lords in *Re State of Norway's Application*[4] opened the door to more effective gathering of evidence in England (and other common law jurisdictions) in aid of foreign civil proceedings. The Hague Evidence Convention of 1970 provides for mutual assistance between countries for the purpose of evidence gathering in "civil or commercial" matters. The normal use of the Convention is for the execution of letters rogatory (or letters of request) issued by a court in one country for the taking of evidence in another country, usually under the supervision of the courts of the latter country. The Hague Evidence Convention of 1970 is given effect in the UK by the Evidence (Proceedings in Other Jurisdictions) Act 1975.

5.4 The decision in *Re State of Norway's Applications* concerned the question, *inter alia*, whether a letter of request from a Norwegian court to the English court to take evidence for the purposes of a tax claim pending in Norway was a "civil or commercial" matter. The evidence was sought from, *inter alios* the taxpayer's English bankers, Lazards. The doubt arose because in civil law countries (although not in Norway) a tax claim is regarded as part of public law

4. [1990] 1 AC 723.

and hence not part of civil or commercial law, whereas in England in general the expression "civil law" merely excludes criminal law, and tax proceedings which are not criminal in character would be regarded as civil. The question for decision was how to approach the classification of the expression "civil or commercial" in the 1975 Act. Two differently constituted divisions of the Court of Appeal in separate phases of the litigation had expressed different views. In the first decision[5] the Court of Appeal was unanimous in concluding that the appropriate approach was to classify the claim under the law of the requesting court, and accept this classification, provided that it was not in conflict with any fundamental principle recognised under English law; but Kerr LJ would have preferred to apply an internationally acceptable definition if there had been material before the court to supply the definition. In the second case[6] May and Balcombe LJJ held that the expression "civil or commercial" should be given a generally acceptable international interpretation based on that used in civil law countries, which would exclude fiscal matters. Woolf LJ thought there was no such internationally acceptable interpretation, but reached the same result by deciding that whatever the ambit of civil or commercial matters, fiscal matters did not fall within it.

But the House of Lords held that an application for assistance came within the scope of the 1975 Act if the foreign proceedings were "civil or commercial" by the law of the requesting state, and also if they were civil (i.e. not criminal) by English law. Accordingly, in the present case the application was within the 1975 Act because the proceedings were not criminal, and they were civil under Norwegian law.

5.5 So far as banking confidentiality was concerned, it was accepted by the parties that the question of confidentiality could only be answered by the court undertaking a balancing exercise, weighing on the one hand the public interest in preserving the confidentiality owed by the witnesses as bankers to their customers, and on the other hand the public interest in the English court assisting the Norwegian court in obtaining evidence in England. The judge had found that the crucial question was who was the settlor of a trust administered by the bank. The judge resolved the question by ordering the witnesses to reveal the identity of the settlor only if one of the witnesses said in evidence that the ultimate settlor was the taxpayer under investigation. This resolved the question of what might have happened if the true owner of the account was someone unconnected with the case (such as the Queen of England), whose confidentiality would thus be destroyed for no good reason. The Court of Appeal and the House of Lords refused to interfere with the exercise of this discretion by the judge.

5. [1987] QB 433.
6. [1988] 3 WLR 603.

ATTACHMENT OF ASSETS

5.6 It is not necessary to say much about the nature of *Mareva* injunctions.[6a] A *Mareva* injunction is, of course, an injunction restraining the disposal of assets pending trial, or pending execution of a judgment—although perhaps, as the Master of the Rolls observed in the *DST* case,[7] injunctions granted after judgment perhaps should not be treated as if they were *Mareva* injunctions.

5.7 Until 1988, it was generally thought that *Mareva* injunctions were limited to assets in England, and could not be granted in relation to assets abroad. In *Ashtiani* v. *Kashi*[8] the Court of Appeal held that the basis of the *Mareva* jurisdiction was "clearly limited to assets within the jurisdiction"[9] and the Court of Appeal refused to order disclosure (ancillary to the *Mareva* injunction) in relation to assets outside the jurisdiction. In Australia and Hong Kong, however, it was held that the *Mareva* jurisdiction did apply to foreign assets[10] and the English Court of Appeal held that disclosure orders relating to foreign assets could be made after judgment had been given against the defendant.[11]

5.8 In the first of the cases, *Babanaft International Co. SA* v. *Bassatne*,[12] judgment had been given in a civil fraud action against the judgment debtors in the sum of US$15 million. The judgment debtors were foreign nationals; one lived mainly in Switzerland and the other mainly in Greece, and they owned property in various countries through a network of companies which were incorporated in jurisdictions (Panama, Liberia and the Dutch Antilles) in which it was difficult for outsiders to obtain information about their ownership, control and assets. It was held that an injunction could be granted to restrain a person properly before the court from the disposal of assets abroad, and that the decision in *Ashtiani* v. *Kashi* was merely a decision on the practice in relation to the exercise of the discretion as it then was, and not a decision on the limits of the jurisdiction of the court. In *Republic of Haiti* v. *Duvalier*,[13] the defendants were "Baby Doc" Duvalier, who was President of Haiti from 1971 to 1986, and various members of his family. The Republic of Haiti alleged in proceedings in France that the Duvalier family had embezzled very large sums of money from the Republic of Haiti. The restraint was sought on the basis of the combined

6a. Under the Civil Procedure Rules 1998 they are to be known as "freezing injunctions": CPR 25.1(1)(f).

7. *DST* v. *Shell International Petroleum* [1990] 1 AC 295, rev'd on other grounds *ibid.*, p. 329.

8. [1987] QB 888 (CA).

9. At p. 899, *per* Dillon LJ.

10. See *Ballabil Holdings Pty Ltd* v. *Hospital Products Limited* [1984] 2 NSWLR 662, aff'd (1985) 1 NSWLR 155; *Coombs & Barei Construction Pty Ltd* v. *Dynasty Pty Ltd* (1986) 42 SASR 413; *Yandil Holdings Pty Ltd* v. *Insurance Co. of North America* (1987) 7 NSWLR 571; *Asean Resources Ltd* v. *Ka Wah International Merchant Finance Limited* [1987] LRC (Comm.) 835.

11. *Interpool Limited* v. *Galani* [1988] QB 738; *Maclaine Watson & Co. Ltd* v. *International Tin Council (No. 2)* [1989] Ch. 286.

12. [1990] Ch. 13.

13. [1990] 1 QB 202.

effect of section 25 of the Civil Jurisdiction and Judgments Act 1982 and Article 24 of the Brussels Convention on Jurisdiction and the Enforcement of Judgments in Civil and Commercial Matters of 1968, i.e. an ancillary proceeding in aid of proceedings which were pending in a foreign country on the substance. The Court of Appeal applied *Babanaft* by granting a pre-judgment injunction, the effect of which was to restrain English solicitors who had acted for the Duvalier family from dealing with assets which they held on its behalf abroad. In *Derby & Co. Ltd* v. *Weldon (No. 1)*,[14] the plaintiffs claimed that the defendants, through dishonest conduct, had been responsible for the insolvency of a group of companies which had caused huge losses to the plaintiffs. The Court of Appeal found, as a matter of fact, that there were grounds for supposing that the defendants had acted dishonestly and that they had the ability to lock away assets in inaccessible overseas companies, and that there was a very real risk that assets in England and abroad would remain hidden or be spirited away so as to render any future judgment useless. In those circumstances, the Court of Appeal applied the *Babanaft* principle to the ordinary pre-judgment case where the substantive proceedings were pending in England and granted a worldwide *Mareva* injunction. In the words of Kerr LJ in *Babanaft* "some situations, which are nowadays by no means uncommon, cry out—as a matter of justice to plaintiffs—for disclosure orders and Mareva-type injunctions, covering foreign assets of defendants".[15]

5.9 In a more recent case, *Crédit Suisse Fides Trust SA* v. *Cuoghi*,[16] the Court of Appeal was presented with the opportunity to consider the preconditions necessary for the grant of worldwide *Mareva* relief in aid of proceedings abroad. Crédit Suisse Fides Trust SA (CSFT) was seeking a worldwide *Mareva* injunction against an English domiciliary in connection with civil proceedings brought by CSFT in Switzerland alleging his complicity in the misappropriation of US$21.66 million by one of CSFT's employees. The relevant assets were not in England; the only connection with England was the domicile of the defendant. Acknowledging that had the action been commenced in England the English courts would have been entitled to grant a *Mareva* injunction of such scope, the defendant argued that the fact that the proceedings were in Switzerland made worldwide relief inexpedient and warranted exclusively domestic application of the *Mareva* injunction. The defendant submitted that only "very exceptional circumstances", which did not exist, would warrant the grant of a worldwide *Mareva* injunction having extraterritorial effect in aid of substantive proceedings being pursued abroad.

5.10 The Court of Appeal disagreed with the defendant's assertion and decided to uphold the global extension of *Mareva* relief. Millett LJ said[16a] that

14. [1990] Ch. 48.
15. [1990] Ch. 13, 33.
16. [1998] QB 818 (CA).
16a. At p. 827.

[w]here a defendant and his assets are located outside the jurisdiction of the court seised of the substantive proceedings, it is in my opinion most appropriate that protective measures should be granted by those courts best able to make their orders effective.

5.11 In many of these cases, however, the Court of Appeal had to grapple with a very serious question which arises in relation to injunctions covering foreign assets, namely the effect of such injunctions on third parties, particularly third parties who are abroad. A *Mareva* injunction in the normal case has a direct effect on third parties who are notified of it and who hold assets comprised in the order. This is because of the principle that a person who, knowing of an injunction, aids and abets the party enjoined in committing a breach of it, is guilty of a contempt of court tending to obstruct the course of justice.[17] The effect on third parties is crucial for the effectiveness of the *Mareva* jurisdiction. For a defendant (especially a foreign defendant) may not respect the terms of the injunction, and because a bank which allows the defendant to remove or dissipate assets in breach of a *Mareva* injunction is guilty of contempt, that is usually sufficient in the domestic context to freeze the money held by the bank. But in each of these cases relating to foreign assets the Court of Appeal limited the effect of the injunction as regards third parties, because it would be wrong for the English court to subject acts abroad to the principle that those who aid and abet a breach of an English injunction are guilty of contempt of court. The broad effect of the decisions was to exempt third parties in respect of acts abroad from compliance with the order unless and until the order had been rendered enforceable by the courts of the place where the assets were. In *Derby & Co. Ltd* v. *Weldon (Nos 3 and 4)*,[18] the Court of Appeal gave the order extraterritorial effect as regards third parties who were subject to the jurisdiction of the court and who had been given written notice of the order at their residence or place of business within the jurisdiction and who were "able to prevent acts or omissions outside the jurisdiction of this court which assist in the breach of the terms of the order".

5.12 In practice it is likely to be disclosure orders relating to foreign assets, which lead to the discovery of those assets, and subsequent attachment proceedings in the foreign countries, that are likely to be more effective than *Mareva* injunctions relating to assets abroad. It is only when the identity and location of the assets is known that the plaintiff is in a position to secure an effective order which binds third parties. In many foreign countries an attachment operates not only *in personam*, but also *in rem*, in the sense that if, for example, a bank account is involved it operates like a garnishee order, so that the bank repays the defendant at its peril, since it may be compelled to pay the plaintiffs again. In those circumstances a *Mareva* injunction would, in the words of Nicholls LJ in *Babanaft*, be a holding injunction, to give the plaintiff time to apply to the relevant foreign court for appropriate orders of attachment.[19]

17. See *Seaward* v. *Paterson* [1897] 1 Ch. 545; *Z Limited* v. *A–Z* [1982] QB 558 (CA).
18. [1989] 2 WLR 412. See also *Derby* v. *Weldon (No. 6)* [1990] 1 WLR 1139. See now CPR PD25, Annex; Commercial Court Guide, 1999, para. F19.10.
19. See [1990] Ch. 13, 43.

ATTACHMENT OF ENGLISH BANK ACCOUNTS IN SUPPORT OF FOREIGN PROCEEDINGS

5.13 Here the question is whether a plaintiff in proceedings abroad can freeze English accounts. In England, prior to 1982, it was not normally possible for a plaintiff in a foreign proceeding, who was pursuing his case abroad, to obtain the freezing of a foreign defendant's assets in England. The leading case was the unfortunate decision of the House of Lords in *The Siskina*.[20] The *Siskina* was carrying marble slabs originating in Italy and destined for Saudi Arabia. The *Siskina* was owned by a one-ship Panamanian company, but managed by Greeks in Piraeus. The ship owners, when the ship was near the entrance to the Suez Canal, alleged that the charterers had not paid the full freight due under the charterparty and ordered the master to turn back and go to Cyprus and unload the cargo, where the ship owners issued a writ *in rem* against the cargo. After discharge of the cargo, the vessel left Cyprus and sank on the way to Greece. The ship owners made a claim on London underwriters and were likely to receive US$750,000. The cargo owners were anxious about these moneys, since the ship owners had no other assets, and in particular the cargo owners were anxious that the money should not be paid to the ship owners because they would then be beyond reach of their claim for compensation for the storage charges etc., which had been caused by the wrongful arrest of the cargo in Cyprus. The cargo owners sought to have the insurance money of US$750,000 retained in England until their claim for damages was settled. The bills of lading contained a clause giving exclusive jurisdiction to the courts of Genoa. The only connection of the case with England was the location of the insurance money. The House of Lords held that it was not possible to obtain an injunction to hold money in the jurisdiction if there was no other cause of action over which the English court had jurisdiction.

5.14 Article 24, however, of the Brussels and Lugano Conventions provides that application may be made to the courts of a Contracting State for such provisional measures, including protective measures, as may be available under the law of that state, even if, under the Convention, the courts of another Contracting State have jurisdiction as to the substance of the matter. English law was altered by section 25 of the Civil Jurisdiction and Judgments Act 1982, the effect of which is that where proceedings are pending in another part of the UK or in another Contracting State, the English court may freeze a bank account here in support of the foreign proceedings.

5.15 In *Mercedes-Benz* v. *Leiduck*,[21] the Privy Council was presented the opportunity to revisit *The Siskina* under a substantially similar fact pattern where the only connection with the jurisdiction was that it was the *situs* of assets

20. [1979] AC 210.
21. [1996] AC 284.

of the defendant. In that case, Mercedes-Benz claimed to have been defrauded by Leiduck, a German citizen, alleging that he had misappropriated US$20 million advanced to him for expenses in connection with the purchase by him of 10,000 vehicles to be exported to Russia and secured by a promissory note for the whole amount of the advance. The transaction fell through, the advance was not repaid and the promissory note was dishonoured, and, as a result, Mercedes-Benz commenced civil proceedings agaisnt Leiduck in Monaco, where he was being held in custody pending criminal investigations. After the court in Monaco declined to extend an attachment order to a Hong Kong company controlled by Leiduck (which, it was alleged, had received some of the misappropriated funds), Mercedes-Benz sought a *Mareva* injunction in Hong Kong to prevent the transfer of shares in the company, and of other Hong Kong assets. After a deputy judge had granted Mercedes-Benz a worldwide *Mareva* injunction and leave to serve Leiduck in Monaco, the Hong Kong Court of Appeal overturned the decision on appeal by the defendant.

5.16 The plaintiff's appeal to the Privy Council involved two questions: (1) whether the court was entitled to permit service of proceedings on a foreigner outside the jurisdiction in such a case and (2) whether, irrespective of questions of service out of the jurisdiction, the court had the power to restrain disposal of assets within the jurisdiction to await the conclusion of the proceedings abroad, i.e. whether *The Siskina* was right in holding that the court had no power to grant a *Mareva* injunction otherwise than in support of a cause of action in respect of which the defendant was amenable to the jurisdiction. Answering the first question in the negative, the majority opinion determined that the second question (which would have raised directly the continued authority of wider propositions in *The Siskina*) did not therefore arise for decision.

5.17 The effect of the Privy Council's decision in *Mercedes-Benz* v. *Leiduck* was not only to deny English courts the ability to grant a *Mareva* injunction over English assets in cases where the defendant was abroad and the foreign litigation was not pending in a state which is a party to either the Brussels or Lugano Convention (a "Contracting State"), but it also threw into question the decisions in *Republic of Haiti* v. *Duvalier*, holding that an English court may grant interim relief where the defendant is abroad and the litigation is pending in a Contracting State, and *X* v. *Y*,[22] holding that service may be effected upon a defendant domiciled outside the Contracting States, as long as the proceedings are pending in another Contracting State.

5.18 The difficulties have, however, been removed with the introduction of new Order 11, rule 8A,[23] which effectively remedied the absence of jurisdiction highlighted in *Mercedes-Benz* v. *Leiduck* and *The Siskina*. Rule 8A provides that, with permission of the court, service may be effected out of the jurisdiction claiming interim relief under section 25(1) of the Civil Jurisdiction and

22. [1990] 1 QB 220.
23. Ord. 11, r. 8A is now in Schedule 1 to the Civil Procedure Rules.

Judgments Act 1982 (as extended by Order in Council made under section 25(3), which empowered the court to grant interim relief in aid of proceedings in countries which are not Contracting States). As a result, English courts have now been afforded broad latitude in providing interim relief in support of claims proceeding abroad.

RECOGNITION OF JUDGMENTS

5.19 In the *Babanaft* case Kerr LJ showed that, under the 1968 Convention, there might be circumstances in which a foreign attachment of an English bank account might have to be recognised in this country. In *Denilauler* v. *SNC Couchet Frères*,[24] a case before the European Court arising out of a reference by a German court, a French plaintiff had sued a German company in France, and in the course of the French proceedings the court made an order authorising the freezing of the German company's bank assets in the Frankfurt branch of a French banker's security. The order was made *ex parte* and the plaintiff sought to have it enforced in Germany. The basic thrust of the questions referred by the German court concerned the applicability of the various provisions in the Convention, which envisaged the giving of notice of proceedings to the judgment debtor before judgment is given against him by the original court or notice of the judgment itself prior to enforcement. The court concluded that although Article 24 did not preclude provisional or protective measures ordered in the state of origin from being the subject of recognition, this did not apply where the provisional or protective measures were ordered *ex parte* and were intended to be enforced without prior service.

TRACING OF ASSETS

5.20 In *Larkins* v. *NUM*[25] sequestrators were appointed by the English court over the property of the National Union of Mineworkers (NUM), following its failure to obey the orders of the English court in connection with the miners' strike in 1984. The order of sequestration authorised the sequestrators to prosecute proceedings in the Republic of Ireland to recover funds of the NUM on deposit with a bank. Subsequently, the English court appointed a receiver over the NUM's assets with authority to institute proceedings in any jurisdiction to recover assets belonging to the NUM. It was held that the claim by the sequestrators in the Republic of Ireland was not maintainable because the sequestration process was penal in effect, being a process of establishing the authority of the court against a recalcitrant litigant and punishing it for contempt. But the claim by the receiver was maintainable because there were

24. [1980] ECR 1553.
25. [1985] IR 671.

independent grounds for his appointment, and the receivership was not an indirect method of enforcing the sequestration and thereby enforcing the penal law or process of a foreign state.

SUBPOENAS AND EVIDENCE

5.21 This chapter has already mentioned evidence from banks in England in relation to proceedings pending abroad. It is only possible to touch upon some of the very difficult questions relating to subpoenas and evidence in connection with bank accounts held abroad.

5.22 In a sense *MacKinnon* v. *Donaldson Lufkin*[26] was a comparatively simple case. It was a civil fraud action pending in England in which the plaintiff sought documents from the defendant's New York bank, Citibank. The plaintiff obtained a subpoena requiring Citibank, which had a London branch, to produce by an officer evidence of the trial of the action, including all relevant documents relating to the defendant's account. The subpoena was directed to, and served on, the bank at its London branch. Hoffmann J held that even though Citibank had a branch in London and was present there:

> it does not follow from the fact that a person is within the jurisdiction and liable to be served with process that there is no territorial limit to the matters on which the court may properly apply its own rules or the things which it can order such a person to do ... The content of the subpoena and order is to require the production by a non-party of documents outside the jurisdiction concerning business which it has transacted outside the jurisdiction. In principle and on authority it seems to me that the court should not, save in exceptional circumstances, impose such a requirement on a foreigner and, in particular, a foreign bank. The principle is that the state should refrain from demanding obedience to its sovereign authority by foreigners in respect of their conduct outside the jurisdiction ... It seems to me that the subpoena and order in this case, taking effect in New York, are an infringement of the sovereignty of the United States. The need to exercise the court's jurisdiction with due regard to the sovereignty of others is particularly important in the case of banks. Banks are in a special position because their documents are concerned not only with their own business but with that of their customers. They will owe their customers a duty of confidence regulated by the law of the country where the account is kept... If every country where a bank happened to carry on business asserted a right to require that bank to produce documents relating to accounts kept in any other such country, banks would be in the unhappy position of being forced to submit to whichever sovereign was able to apply the greatest pressure.

5.23 Therefore, the solution in that case was to require the evidence to be obtained in New York. In some cases US courts have required branches of foreign banks in the US to produce details of accounts in foreign countries, even though they were forbidden by the criminal law of the relevant foreign country from producing the information. Thus, in the famous *Bank of Nova Scotia* case the Miami branch of the Bank of Nova Scotia (of course, a Canadian bank) was

26. [1986] Ch. 782.

ordered to produce information relating to its Cayman Islands branch, and when it refused because of the criminal sanctions which would be imposed in the Cayman Islands, the US court imposed substantial daily fines on it.

5.24 If the witness is within the jurisdiction and is not legitimately subject to a foreign secrecy law, then the court may compel the evidence. Thus, in *Spencer* v. *The Queen*,[27] the Supreme Court of Canada held that the Ontario court could subpoena a resident and citizen of Canada concerning information which he had acquired while being the manager of a Bahamas branch of the Royal Bank of Canada. The Supreme Court decided that foreign law could not exempt a witness, otherwise competent, compellable and present, from giving evidence within his knowledge in the Canadian courts. The judgment of the majority held that to allow the witness "to refuse to give evidence in the circumstances of the case would permit a foreign country to frustrate the administration of justice in Canada in respect of a Canadian citizen in relation to what is essentially a domestic situation". Such an approach could have serious repercussions on the operation of Canadian law generally.

5.25 In the *Marc Rich* case in England,[28] Mr Justice Leggatt was prepared to grant an injunction in favour of Citibank's Swiss customer, restraining Citibank from disclosing in New York confidential information held by it as banker in England for its Swiss customer. It will be recalled that the *Marc Rich* case involved an investigation into the crude oil trading of a US company which was the wholly-owned subsidiary of a Swiss company. In proceedings brought in the US by the Department of Justice, subpoenas were served on the Swiss company and its US subsidiary, and subsequently on Citibank in New York. The documents covered by the subpoena served on Citibank in the US were in fact kept at its London branch in its capacity as bankers to the Swiss company. The Swiss company brought proceedings in England against the London branch of Citibank to restrain it from disclosing confidential information held by it in its capacity as banker. Perhaps it is too cynical to suggest that the interests of both the bank and the customer were served by the English injunction, since the customer was preventing disclosure of its documents and the bank was obtaining the benefit of a potential "foreign governmental compulsion" defence. The case may be regarded as a somewhat artificial device both to prevent production of the material in the US and to relieve the bank from sanctions in the US. The artificiality of the device in that case is underlined by the fact that it would be inconceivable for a customer of a bank in England to obtain an injunction restraining production by the bank of documents which are the subject-matter of a subpoena in English proceedings. It is by no means easy to see why, in the US proceedings, it should make a great deal of difference whether the bank is under a duty of confidentiality in general (without an express court order in the foreign jurisdiction) and subject to an injunction (breach of which is punishable) brought in a suit by a customer to enforce that very same duty. It

27. [1985] 2 SCR 278.
28. *X* v. *A Bank* [1983] 2 All ER 464.

should also be noted that the operation of UK companies' legislation relating to disclosure is not affected by the fact that the person under a duty to disclose is a bank subject to banking secrecy in a foreign jurisdiction.

5.26 In *The Heidberg*[29] two French defendants sought the revocation of a discovery order on the basis that doing so would be in violation of French law and thereby expose them to criminal prosecution in their home jurisdiction. Article 1 bis of Law 80-538 of 16 July 1980 was enacted with the aim of putting an end, through the introduction of criminal consequences, to certain "*pratiques de tourisme juridique*", namely the American long-arm statutes extending the jurisdiction of US courts extraterritorially, particularly in respect to anti-trust matters. Although a strict reading of Article 1 bis of the 1980 Law would tend to indicate that no document could be produced in connection with an English trial without going through either the Bilateral Convention between the United Kingdom and France of 1922 or the Hague Evidence Convention of 1970, the court nonetheless upheld the order. Supported by affidavits from legal practitioners in both England and France and by confirmation from the Ministry of Justice in Paris that Article 1 bis of the 1980 Law was enacted not with the intention of prosecuting any French company but out of the interest of creating an operative "legal excuse" with which to protect French companies from foreign procedural abuses, the court concluded that there was no tangible risk that the French defendant companies would be charged with any criminal offence for abiding with the discovery order. Among other things, the court found to be important the fact that French companies had regularly given discovery in legal proceedings in England, that the defendants failed to offer even a single English decision where it was submitted that a court should not order discovery by a French company in light of this French law and that there was no evidence indicating that any French person had ever been prosecuted for breach of Article 1 bis.

LAWRENCE COLLINS *

29. [1993] 2 Lloyd's Rep. 324.
* This chapter has been brought up to date for this edition by Matthew Morgan.

CHAPTER 6

OFFICIAL REMEDIES: INQUIRIES UNDER SECTION 432(2) OF THE COMPANIES ACT 1985

INTRODUCTION

6.1 Section 432(2) of the Companies Act 1985 gives the Secretary of State for Trade and Industry the power to appoint one or more competent inspectors to investigate the affairs of a company[1] and to report to him on them in such manner as he directs if it appears to him that there are circumstances suggesting:

(a) that the company's affairs are being or have been conducted with intent to defraud its creditors or the creditors of any other person, or otherwise for a fraudulent or unlawful purpose, or in a manner which is unfairly prejudicial to some part of its members, or

(b) that any actual proposed act or omission of the company (including an act or omission on its behalf) is or would be so prejudicial, or that the company was formed for any fraudulent or unlawful purpose, or

(c) that persons concerned with the company's formation or the management of its affairs have in connection therewith been guilty of fraud, misfeasance or other misconduct towards it or towards its members, or

(d) that the company's members have not been given all the information with respect to its affairs which they might reasonably expect.

The Secretary of State may publish the report he receives from the inspectors,[2] although he is not obliged to do so. Inspectors can be appointed on the basis that their report is not for publication.[3]

6.2 There have been a number of high-profile inquiries under section 432(2). Those inquiries have often led to criminal prosecutions, to the disqualification of directors, to disciplinary action by regulators or to the making of winding-up

1. Company means a company formed and registered under the Companies Act ("CA") 1985 or various earlier Companies or Joint Stock Companies Acts: CA 1985, s.735. The Secretary of State's powers, however, extend to bodies corporate incorporated in and having a principal place of business in Great Britain (CA 1985, s.718 and Sch. 22) and to bodies corporate incorporated outside Great Britain but which carry on (or have at any time carried on) business there (CA 1985, s.453—but subject to certain limitations set out in s.453).

2. CA 1985, s.437(3).

3. CA 1985, s.432(2A).

orders.[4] Adverse criticism by inspectors in published reports has damaged or ended careers. The fairness of the process to the individuals involved in it has increasingly been questioned, although inevitably most vociferously by those most heavily criticised by inspectors. In 1990 the House of Commons Trade and Industry Committee reviewed and reported on company investigations, but their report led to very few changes to the law or practice relating to s.432(2) inquiries.[5]

6.3 The purpose of this chapter is to examine the powers of the inspectors, the manner in which inquiries are carried out and the fairness of the balance between the powers of the inspectors and the rights of the individual.

THE POWERS OF INSPECTORS AND THE CONDUCT OF INQUIRIES

6.4 Inspectors are appointed by the Secretary of State. A public announcement is made of any appointment in respect of a public company. The inspectors are given wide terms of reference (e.g. "to investigate and report on the affairs of X plc"). Although the appointment of inspectors can, of itself, cause significant damage to a company, the Secretary of State's decision to appoint inspectors is effectively unchallengeable. The Court of Appeal has held[6] that the Secretary of State's decision to appoint inspectors can only be challenged on the grounds that his decision was made in bad faith or for an improper purpose. The burden of proof is on the applicant. Since the Secretary of State cannot be compelled to give reasons for his decision to appoint inspectors and in practice does not do so, it is an impossible burden to discharge.

6.5 The DTI's practice in the case of an investigation into a large public company is to appoint two inspectors. One is usually a senior partner in a firm of accountants and the other a QC or leading solicitor. The accountant's or solicitor's staff provide the administrative support. The Secretary of State is, however, free to appoint anybody who is competent, and in smaller investigations it is usual for DTI officials to be appointed.

6.6 Inspectors are free to conduct the inquiry in the way which seems to them to be most appropriate, subject to an overriding, but limited, obligation to observe the rules of natural justice. This is considered in more detail below. Nevertheless, inquiries follow a broadly similar pattern:

(a) request for and review of documents;
(b) questioning of witnesses;

4. Memorandum submitted by the DTI to the House of Commons Trade and Industry Committee in October 1989.

5. See the Trade and Industry Committee Report dated 2 May 1990 and the government's response, dated August 1990.

6. *Norwest Holst Limited* v. *Secretary of State for Trade and Others* [1978] 1 Ch. 201.

(c) submission of proposed criticisms to witnesses; and
(d) submission of report to the Secretary of State.

DOCUMENTS

6.7 Inspectors are given powers to require production from any person of documents relating to matters which they believe to be relevant to their investigation.[7] Document requests are usually made in wide terms and it is often difficult for the recipient to ascertain from the request itself what lies behind it and in what matters the inspectors are really interested. The inspectors, if asked, will usually decline to say.

6.8 In addition to the power to request wide classes of documents, inspectors are given powers of entry and search. If the inspectors can satisfy a Justice of the Peace on information given on oath that there are reasonable grounds for believing that documents requested have not been produced, the inspectors can obtain a warrant to enter and search premises to find and remove the documents.[8] The inspectors can also obtain such a warrant[9] if they satisfy a Justice of the Peace on information given on oath:

(a) that there are reasonable grounds for believing an offence has been committed for which the penalty on conviction on indictment is imprisonment for a term of not less than two years and that there are on any premises documents relating to whether the offence has been committed;
(b) that the Secretary of State, or the person so appointed or authorised, has power to require the production of the documents under this Part; and
(c) that there are reasonable grounds for believing that if production was so required the document would not be produced but would be removed from the premises, hidden, tampered with or destroyed.

In this latter case the warrant can also authorise the removal of any other documents relevant to the investigation.[10] A police officer has to be present while the warrant is executed.[11] Any person named in the warrant can be required to provide an explanation of the documents or to state where they may be found.[12]

6.9 In addition to their powers of entry and search, the inspectors have the power to certify a refusal to produce documents to the court. The court may enquire into the refusal and, after hearing evidence and any statement which

7. CA 1985, s.434(2)(a).
8. CA 1985, s.448(1).
9. CA 1985, s.448(2).
10. CA 1985, s.448(4).
11. CA 1985, s.448(3).
12. CA 1985, s.448(3)(d).

may be offered in defence, may punish the person refusing to produce documents as though he were guilty of contempt of court.[13] This can involve heavy fines and imprisonment.

QUESTIONING OF WITNESSES

6.10 The inspectors have the power to compel individuals who may be in possession of information relating to a matter believed to be relevant to the investigation to testify before them on oath.[14] A refusal to answer questions can be certified to the court in the same way as a refusal to supply documents.[14a] An answer given to a question from the inspectors may be used in evidence against the person giving it.[15] The inspectors' practice as to the manner of conducting oral interviews varies. Some indicate to witnesses in advance those documents which they intend to put to the witnesses. Some indicate the areas, sometimes even the questions, which they intend to cover. Others do none of these things. Evidence is usually taken on oath and is recorded verbatim by a shorthand writer. The questions are primarily asked by the lawyer inspector. The witness is allowed to have his lawyer present, although the degree to which the lawyer is invited or permitted to intervene, or to address the inspectors or question the witness, varies. The witness is usually provided with a copy of his transcript of evidence and invited to correct it or to add to it. The practice varies as to whether the witness will be allowed to keep the transcripts. In some inquiries concern over confidentiality leads the inspectors to request the return of the transcripts. On occasions, the inspectors will ask witnesses to undertake not to discuss their evidence with other witnesses. Sometimes inspectors ask witnesses to sign a confidentiality agreement restraining them from disclosing the information put to them during questioning. The inspectors have, however, no right to demand such an undertaking.[15a] No witness has the right to see other witnesses' evidence or to cross-examine other witnesses.

6.11 The inspectors are not entitled to call for documents or information covered by legal professional privilege,[16] although it has been known for inspectors to exert considerable pressure on witnesses to waive that privilege. Nor can inspectors compel a person to produce documents or information in

13. CA 1985, s.436.
14. CA 1985, s.434(2) and (3).
14a. See *Re an Inquiry into Mirror Group Newspapers plc* [1999] 2 All ER 641 for an example of a case in which the court considered whether the proposed questioning by inspectors would be unfair and oppressive so that the individual should be excused for not answering.
15. CA 1985, s.434(5). This may be affected by the decision in *Saunders* v. *United Kingdom* (case 43/1994/490/572) and the forthcoming implementation of the Human Rights Act 1998. This is discussed in more detail below.
15a. *Re an Inquiry into Mirror Group Newspapers plc* [1999] 2 All ER 641.
16. CA 1985, s.452.

respect of which he owes an obligation of confidence by virtue of carrying on the business of banking unless:

(a) the person to whom the obligation of confidence is owed is the company or other body corporate under investigation;
(b) the person to whom the obligation of confidence is owed consents to the disclosure or production; or
(c) the making of the requirement is authorised by the Secretary of State.[17]

This exception does not apply where the bank owing the obligation of confidence is itself the company under investigation.[18]

SUBMISSION OF PROPOSED CRITICISM TO WITNESSES

6.12 The obligation of the inspectors to give a person whom they are minded to condemn or criticise an opportunity to meet the case against him is dealt with in more detail below. Although the inspectors are not, strictly speaking, obliged to do so, they often do give a witness a draft of their proposed criticism of him and invite the witness to make representations on it. Some even provide the relevant passages from their draft report.

THE MAKING OF THE REPORT

6.13 The inspectors may, and if directed to do so by the Secretary of State must, make interim reports to the Secretary of State. On the conclusion of their investigation they must make a final written report to him.[19] The inspectors may, and if directed to do so by the Secretary of State must, inform the Secretary of State of any matters coming to their knowledge as a result of their investigations.[20] Information which the inspectors pass to the Secretary of State can be used, or can be passed to others for them to use, for a number of defined purposes, including the institution or furtherance of criminal proceedings, disciplinary proceedings by regulators, proceedings for disqualification of directors and petitions by the Secretary of State to wind up companies.[21] Such information often is used for these purposes.

6.14 If the Secretary of State considers that matters have come to light in the course of the inspectors' investigation which suggest that a criminal offence has been committed, and those matters have been referred to the appropriate

17. CA 1985, s.452(1A).
18. CA 1985, s.452(1B).
19. CA 1985, s.437(1).
20. CA 1985, s.437(1A).
21. CA 1985, s.451A. However, in the case of criminal proceedings, this is likely to change following the decision in *Saunders* v. *United Kingdom* (case 43/1994/490/572). This is discussed below.

prosecuting authority, he may direct the inspectors to take no further steps in the investigation or to take only such further steps as he may specify.[22] If the Secretary of State makes such a direction, the inspectors only make a final report if and when the Secretary of State directs them to do so.[23]

6.15 The Secretary of State can publish the inspectors' report, but does not have to do so.[24] Reports on the affairs of a public company are usually published. Reports on the affairs of private companies are not, unless they raise some point of general public interest. If criminal proceedings are contemplated, the Secretary of State will only publish if he is satisfied that publication would not prejudice the criminal proceedings. There has been criticism of apparent inconsistency in the manner in which the Secretary of State has exercised this discretion. The County NatWest Report was published immediately, despite the fact that criminal proceedings followed. The House of Fraser Report, on the other hand, was held back from publication for a considerable time while the Serious Fraud Office and the police considered whether to bring charges. In the case of Guinness, an interim report was given to the Secretary of State two years into the investigation and publication of the final report was delayed for a further nine years, *inter alia*, because of extensive criminal trials and appeals.

6.16 Inspectors can be appointed on the basis that their reports are not for publication.[25] In these cases, the inspectors can, in theory, complete their work more speedily since they will not be obliged (see below) to put the substance of any adverse evidence to persons they are minded to criticise and give them the opportunity to deal with it. The DTI are particularly likely to appoint inspectors on this basis, where the purpose of the investigation is to ascertain as speedily as possible whether there are grounds for prosecution or regulatory action[26] and where there is no wider public interest which might be served by the publication of a report.

6.17 The length of time inquiries take varies. The County NatWest Report was published within seven months of the appointment. The Guinness plc Report was only completed eleven years after the appointment.

THE INSPECTORS' DUTY TO ACT IN ACCORDANCE WITH THE RULES OF NATURAL JUSTICE

6.18 The inspectors have very wide powers. Obviously, they cannot exceed those powers or exercise them for improper or collateral purposes. But are there any legal constraints on inspectors who remain within their statutory powers?

22. CA 1985, s.437(1B).
23. CA 1985, s.437(1C).
24. CA 1985, s.437(3)(c).
25. CA 1985, s.432(2A).
26. Memorandum submitted by the DTI to the House of Commons Trade and Industry Committee in October 1989.

Does the individual have any guarantee that the procedure adopted by the inspectors will be fair?

6.19 The law on procedural fairness in section 432(2) investigations is to be found in two Court of Appeal decisions.[27] The combined effect of those decisions is as follows.

1. An inquiry under section 432(2) of the Companies Act 1985 is *sui generis*. It is more than just an investigation (to which the rules of natural justice and procedural fairness would not apply), because the inspectors have a duty, having investigated, to produce a report which may be made public and may cause severe injury to an individual by its findings. On the other hand, the inquiry is something less than a judicial proceeding. There is no issue or question before the inspectors which they are called on to determine:

   > The inspectors' function is in essence to conduct an investigation designed to discover whether there are facts which may result in others taking action. It is no part of their function to take a decision whether action be taken, and *a fortiori*, it is not for them finally to determine such issues as may emerge if some action eventuates.[28]

2. Given the nature of section 432(2) inquiries, and in particular the fact that they may lead to the publication of a report which may be highly damaging to those criticised in it, the inspectors are under a duty to act fairly. That duty, however, means only that the inspectors must offer anybody they are minded to condemn or criticise in their report "a fair opportunity for correcting or contradicting what is said against him"[29] before the report is published.
3. The person whom the inspectors are minded to criticise must therefore be told sufficient of the case against him to enable him to have a fair opportunity of correcting or contradicting that case. Precisely what he needs to be told, and how, depends on the particular circumstances of each case and no detailed rules should be laid down.
4. An individual has no automatic right to see the inspector's proposed criticisms or conclusions in draft to comment on them (although inspectors in practice often permit this). Nor does he have the right to see the transcripts of evidence of other witnesses or to see documents adverse to him.
5. An individual has no right to cross-examine other witnesses.
6. Save for this, the inspectors are, and should be, masters of their own procedure.

6.20 The lack of information available to those involved in DTI inquiries

27. *Re Pergamon Press Ltd* [1971] Ch. 388 and *Maxwell* v. *Department of Trade and Industry & Ors* [1974] QB 523.

28. *Per* Sachs LJ in *Re Pergamon Press Ltd.*

29. *Per* Lord Denning MR in *Re Pergamon Press Ltd.*

means that there is, in practice, no real remedy against inspectors who infringe the limited controls on their wide powers. There is no right of appeal. It will be rare in practice that an individual is so confident that the inspectors are exceeding their powers, or exercising them for an improper purpose, that he will decline to answer questions or provide documents and challenge the inspectors' demands in court. Equally, especially if he is not given a draft of the relevant section in the inspectors' report, an individual will not usually know that the inspectors have failed to comply with the rules of natural justice or have reached "irrational" conclusions as far as he is concerned until he sees the published report. At that stage, he cannot seek an injunction to restrain publication. Publication has already taken place. Nor can he seek a declaration that the report is null and void.[30] Nor, save in the most exceptional circumstances, will he be granted a declaration that natural justice has not been observed:

> In my judgment a man who has been unfairly criticised in a report ... is in the same position as one who has been unfairly criticised in a speech made in Parliament. He has suffered "*damnum*" but not "*injuria*". Cases may occur (although they are unlikely to do so as long as the Minister appoints competent and experienced professional men as inspectors) in which the inspectors had behaved so unfairly that the public interest requires a court to say so.[31]

Nor can the inspectors be sued for making defamatory statements in their report unless the statements are irrelevant to their investigation or motivated by malice.[32]

PRIVILEGE AGAINST SELF-INCRIMINATION

6.21 The inspectors' report, or information passed by the inspectors to the DTI, often leads to criminal prosecutions. Indeed, one of the reasons for appointing inspectors under section 432(2) is to obtain evidence for use in possible future criminal proceedings:

> The effectiveness of the investigation process needs to be considered against the objectives it is designed to serve. An investigation may be said to be effective if it contributes to the reduction of commercial malpractice. It may achieve that if it leads to prosecution, winding-up or disqualification (of directors); or to regulatory or disciplinary action; or where the mere fact of the investigation acts as a deterrent.[33]

This raises two questions:

30. *Maxwell* v. *DTI*.
31. *Per* Lawton LJ in *Maxwell* v. *DTI*.
32. Although there is no authority directly in point, the inspectors' report must, as a matter of principle, be protected by qualified privilege. Lord Denning MR's *obiter* remark in *Re Pergamon Press Ltd* that the inspectors' report is protected by absolute privilege is unsupported by authority and seems contrary to principle.
33. Memorandum submitted by the DTI to the House of Commons Trade and Industry Committee in October 1989.

1. Can an individual refuse to answer the inspectors' questions on the grounds that his answers may incriminate him?
2. Can any answers be used against an individual in a subsequent criminal prosecution?

Can an individual refuse to answer questions on the grounds that his answers might incriminate him?

6.22 The right to decline to answer incriminating questions (a common law right now contained in section 14(1) of the Civil Evidence Act 1968) can be excluded by statute. Such an exclusion may be express.[34] It is not, however, necessary that the exclusion should be express:[35]

> Some statutes expressly provide that incriminating answers may be used against the person who gives them and some statutes expressly provide that they may not. Where... there is no such express provision the question whether such answers are admissible evidence must depend on the proper construction of the particular statute.[36]

It is a matter of construction of the individual statute whether the exclusion of the right to refuse to answer incriminating questions applies after the individual has been charged as well as before.[37]

6.23 In the case of section 432(2) inquiries the privilege against self-incrimination is not expressly excluded. On the proper construction of Part XIV of the Companies Act 1985, Parliament has, however, shown a clear intention that an individual should not have the right to refuse to answer incriminating questions, at any rate before he is charged:[38]

1. Inspectors are appointed in the circumstances set out in section 432(2). These circumstances include fraud and unlawful conduct. Section 432(2) therefore envisages in terms that the inspectors will investigate conduct which is criminal.
2. Various provisions of Part XIV of the Companies Act envisage that information obtained in the course of a DTI inquiry will lead to criminal proceedings.[39]

34. See Theft Act 1968, s.31; Supreme Court Act 1981, s.72.

35. *R* v. *Harz* [1967] 1 AC 760 (HL); see too *R* v. *Scott* (1856) 169 ER 909; *R* v. *Erdheim* [1896] 2 QB 260; *In re Atherton* [1912] 2 KB 251; *In re Paget* [1927] 2 Ch. 85 (CA): *DPP* v. *Ellis* [1973] 1 WLR 722; *EMI Records Ltd* v. *Spillane* [1986] 1 WLR 967.

36. *R* v. *Harz* [1967] 1 AC 760, *per* Lord Reid at p. 876.

37. *EMI Records Ltd* v. *Spillane* [1986] 1 WLR 967 (right excluded before and after charge); cf. *A.* v. *HM Treasury* [1979] 1 WLR 1056 (right excluded only before charge).

38. *Re London United Investments plc* [1992] Ch. 578; *R* v. *Seelig and Spens* [1992] 1 WLR 148; *R* v. *Harris* [1970] 1 WLR 1252; see too *London and County Securities Ltd* v. *Nicholson* [1980] 3 All ER 861 and *Sociedade Nacional de Combustiveis de Angola UEE* v. *Lunqvist* [1990] 3 All ER 283, 302.

39. CA 1985, ss.437(1B) and (1C), s.451A.

3. Individuals must answer questions put to them by the inspectors and must answer on oath.[40]
4. The answers can be passed to the prosecuting authorities "with a view to the institution of or otherwise for the purpose of criminal proceedings".[41]
5. The answers may be used in evidence against the individual.[42] Nothing in the wording of Part XIV of the Act suggests that the answers may only be used in evidence against the individual in *civil* proceedings. Nor is it at all likely that this is what Parliament intended. It is clear that at least one purpose of a section 432(2) inquiry is to facilitate the detection and punishment of commercial crime and of fraud in particular. To regard section 434(5) as limited to civil proceedings would be more likely to defeat than to further Parliament's intention.
6. Section 452 expressly preserves legal professional privilege and, to a limited degree, the banker's duty of confidentiality. Neither section 452 nor any other section of Part XIV, however, makes any mention of privilege against self-incrimination. If Parliament had intended that privilege to apply, it would have been logical for it to have been expressly mentioned in section 452.

There is no direct authority on the question of whether the exclusion of the privilege should be restricted to the period before an individual is charged, although authority in the area of Serious Fraud Office ("SFO") inquiries suggests that it should not be.[43]

Can any answers be used against an individual in a subsequent criminal prosecution?

6.24 In the prosecution of the former chairman of Guinness plc, Ernest Saunders, the transcripts of his DTI interviews were used extensively against him. Mr Saunders was convicted. He later, however, applied to the European Court of Human Rights, for a ruling that he had been deprived of his right to a fair hearing under Article 6 of the European Convention on Human Rights 1950, because of the use at his trial of evidence which he had been compelled to give in violation of the principle of privilege against self-incrimination. The European Court of Human Rights upheld his complaint. This ruling is not as yet part of English law[44] but will become so when the Human Rights Act 1998 is brought into force, which at present is anticipated by the Government to be in October 2000. At that point it will no longer be permissible to use incriminating

40. CA 1985, s.434(2) and (3).
41. CA 1985, s.451A.
42. CA 1985, s.434(5).
43. *R* v. *The Director of the Serious Fraud Office, ex parte Smith* (HL) [1993] AC 1.
44. *R* v. *Morrisey*, *The Times*, 1 May 1997.

evidence provided under compulsion in DTI inquiries against someone in a subsequent criminal prosecution.

6.25 On 3 February 1998, the Attorney General issued, as an interim measure, a guidance note for prosecutors concerning the use by the prosecution of answers obtained under compulsory powers in criminal proceedings. The prosecution are not to use such material either as part of its case, or in cross-examination, save where the defendant himself introduced such material in evidence, or where the prosecution is based on the defendant's failure to answer when he was under an obligation to do so, or his giving of an untruthful answer.

THE HYBRID NATURE OF SECTION 432(2) INQUIRIES: BALANCING THE POWERS OF THE INVESTIGATORS AGAINST THE RIGHTS OF THE INDIVIDUAL

6.26 Section 432(2) inquiries are hybrid. They are more than an investigation, since they may involve the publication of a report which will have damaging consequences to individuals criticised in it. They are less than a judicial hearing, since no charge is being tried and no issue being determined: but damaging conclusions are, nevertheless, reached and published. Such a hybrid system has inherent flaws:

1. The inspectors, however eminent, are investigators who have been given extremely wide powers. They are subject to the same temptations (e.g. to form theories and to gather, or be more receptive to, information which fits in with those theories) and the same risks of excess of zeal as all investigators. The evidence put before them is not reviewed or tested by those against whom the evidence is given and who may be condemned by it.
2. There is no corrective balance. Individuals are reluctant to challenge the inspectors, even with good cause, for fear of antagonising them. There is no right of appeal. The right to judicial review is of little practical help and the tendency of the courts (see *Pergamon* and *Maxwell*) has in the past been to trust the inspectors to police themselves.[45]
3. A report is published with little restraint on what may be said, save for the self-control of the inspectors and the DTI. Not surprisingly, that self-control is not always exercised. The media, given the eminence of the inspectors and the official nature of their appointment, tend to treat the inspectors' conclusions more as a result of a trial than a preliminary investigation. The effect of an adverse report on somebody's career can be devastating.

45. Although see *Re an inquiry into Mirror Group Newspapers plc* [1999] 2 All ER 641.

Is such a hybrid system, with its inherent flaws, necessary? Wide powers to investigate the affairs of companies are no doubt needed. Companies are economically powerful and the law gives them great privileges. The ownership and the management of the business are usually divorced and the controls on an entrenched secretive management are often lacking. To be effective, investigations must be thorough and fast. But must the report of the investigation be published? If so, must it contain criticisms or is it sufficient that it merely ascertain the facts, leaving others to draw conclusions and take any necessary action?

6.27 It is suggested that it is highly desirable, probably even necessary, that the Secretary of State be able to publish the report. First, such a power operates as a deterrent. Second, inspectors are often appointed in cases where the authorities or the public are concerned at the manner in which the affairs of public companies appear to have been conducted. In such a case the public have a legitimate interest in knowing what has happened, not least because they are actual or potential shareholders in the company. The publication of a report dispels rumours. It enables others to learn from it and it may provoke debate about legal or regulatory reform or changes in practice.

6.28 Moreover, it is inevitable—and desirable—that any report of an investigation contain some criticisms. At the most basic level, it is impossible to give any understandable account of complex factual situations without reaching conclusions which may, expressly or implicitly, be critical of certain individuals. If, for example, one witness's version of events is at complete variance with another's, the inspectors will have to decide which they prefer, even if it is quite apparent to the reader that that decision must have involved a conclusion on the part of the inspectors that one of the witnesses was deliberately not telling the truth. If criticisms or conclusions are not drawn, it will be hard for the outsider to understand the report, to determine how some of the acts described could have happened or sensibly to determine responsibility for those acts. He may wrongly ascribe blame in situations where the inspectors, with their greater knowledge of the facts and with the benefit of seeing the witnesses testify, would not have done so. Questions will be left unanswered and the value of the report in the public's eyes will be adversely affected, even to the point where its value and credibility is seriously damaged.

6.29 On the other hand, it is not necessary or desirable for the inspectors to make criticisms or reach conclusions which are not needed to enable the reader of the report properly to understand and appreciate what has taken place. The DTI indeed encourage inspectors only to make criticisms "to the extent necessary for a proper appreciation of their report".[46]

6.30 If wide powers of investigation must exist, and if it is appropriate that reports be published and contain criticisms, the hybrid and the flaws described earlier are inevitable. Complete protection for the interests of the individual

46. DTI Investigation Handbook (p. 44), published October 1990.

could probably only be obtained in some kind of judicial inquiry, with all interested parties having a right to be heard, to call evidence and to cross-examine. Such a lengthy and cumbersome process would frustrate the aim of a speedy investigation.

6.31 The search for a perfect balance between the needs of the investigator and the interests of the individual under investigation will, no doubt, always prove elusive. It is, nevertheless, noteworthy that although past inquiries have provoked substantial criticism of the present system, there has been no real change.[47] The question for the future is whether it is sufficient, as the government would wish, to rely on the professional standards and common sense of the inspectors to ensure an appropriate balance or whether it is necessary to impose more clearly defined legal restrictions on the manner in which section 432(2) inquiries are conducted.

IAN TAYLOR

47. See the Trade and Industry Committee Report dated 2 May 1990 and the government's response dated August 1990.

CHAPTER 7

BANKS AND EC REMEDIES

INTRODUCTION

7.1 European Community law has so far predominantly affected banking activities in the European Union through EC Directives principally concerned with public regulatory aspects of banks. These Directives have been primarily addressed to upholding the integrity of the banking system, and only indirectly to protecting the customer by ensuring that the institutions with which they contract today will still be able to meet their obligations tomorrow.[1] It is this body of EC law that may most easily be characterised as EC banking law.[2]

7.2 However, it is increasingly the case that EC law also directly affects the daily activities of banks in their transactions with customers, that is where banks act as suppliers of services, and increasingly as suppliers of cross-border services. The effect is primarily by way of European Community law of general application, rather than through legislative instruments specifically addressed to the banking sector, although this latter effect is growing. There are three areas of EC law of principal concern for banks in this regard: EC consumer protection law; EC competition law; and European law regulating jurisdictional and other procedural issues.

7.3 A detailed assessment of the impact of these growing areas is beyond the scope of this chapter. However, in this chapter we provide an overview of these areas, and a practical indication of areas of conduct where banks must pay an increasing regard to Community law. In so doing it is intended to raise the profile of Community law as it affects the operations of banks in dealings with their customers throughout the EU, and in particular the remedies available to banks in relation to defaulting debtors.

1. However, see the comments of the European Court of Justice in Case C–366/97 *Criminal Proceedings against Romanelli and Another* [1999] All ER (EC) 4738, discussed below.

2. See, for a discussion of the regulatory aspects of EC banking law, Dassesse, Isaacs & Penn, *EC Banking Law*, 2nd edn (LLP, 1994); Cresswell, Blair, Hill, Wood (eds), *Encyclopaedia of Banking Law* (Butterworths); Maitland-Walker (ed), *EC Banking Directives* (LLP).

EC CONSUMER PROTECTION LAW

7.4 Although the Treaty of Rome originally made no express provision for the adoption by the Community of consumer protection measures, consumer protection under the guise of "fair competition" underlies much Community legislation. The original omission was rectified by the Maastricht Treaty which added a new Title on Consumer Protection to the Treaty of Rome under Article 129a. Those provisions (now Title XIV) have been enhanced by the amendments made by the Amsterdam Treaty.[3]

7.5 Article 153 (which supersedes Article 129a) now provides, as material, that:

> 1. In order to promote the interests of consumers and to ensure a high level of consumer protection, the Community shall contribute to protecting the ... economic interests of consumers, as well as promoting their right to information, ... and to organise themselves to safeguard their interests.
> 2. Consumer protection requirements shall be taken into account in defining and implementing other Community policies and activities.[4]

A central element of this concern has been the need to protect consumers in the retail financial services market as part of the Community's encouragement of a single market for financial services. The central role of consumer protection in the banking sector has been underlined again in a recent case from the European Court of Justice[5] ("ECJ"), building on earlier case law,[6] where the ECJ stated:

> ... the banking sector is a particularly sensitive area from the point of view of consumer protection. Consumers must be protected against the harm which they could suffer through banking transactions effected by credit institutions disregarding the requirements relating to their solvency or whose managers do not have the necessary professional qualifications or integrity.

7.6 Four areas of intervention have particular relevance for banks: consumer credit; electronic payment systems; cross-border transfers; and unfair contract terms. However, of the four, by far the most important for banks seeking to enforce their contracts with debtors have been the provisions relating to unfair contract terms.[7]

3. The Amsterdam Treaty has effected significant amendments to and a re-ordering of the Treaty on European Union, as well as to the underlying Treaties of the European Communities, including the Treaty of Rome (the European Community Treaty). The Amsterdam Treaty came into force on 1 May 1999. References therein to Treaty Articles are, unless otherwise indicated, to Articles of the EC Treaty, as amended by the Amsterdam Treaty.

4. And see Art. 94(3) (ex 100a(3)) specifically on this aspect in relation to the adoption of measures for the establishment and functioning of the internal market.

5. Case C–366/97, *Criminal Proceedings against Romanelli and Another* [1999] All ER (EC) 4783, at para. 11.

6. Case C–22/95 *Société Civile Immobilière Parodi* v. *Banque H. Albert de Bary et Cie* [1997] ECR I–3914 (see para. 22).

7. See the Unfair Terms in Consumer Contracts Directive 93/13/EEC, (1993) OJ L95/29 and see further below.

7.7 The Community has intervened in the field of consumer protection either by means of Recommendations or Directives. Such instruments (as compared with certain Treaty provisions and Commission or Council Regulations) do not directly create rights for individuals which are directly enforceable against private parties. Recommendations (which used to be the main Community instrument used to address the protection of consumer economic interests) do not have any binding force.[8] Their role is intended to be persuasive only, although, if not acted on, as a matter of practice they often lead to legislation.

7.8 Directives are binding only on the Member States to which they are addressed. The Member States are obliged to implement them in national legislation by Articles 10 and 249 (ex Articles 5 and 189) of the EC Treaty and by the Directives themselves. As the case law of the ECJ has indicated, Directives may have direct effect against the State or emanations of the State once their time limit for implementation has passed and the provision relied upon is clear, precise and unconditional, and intended to create rights for individuals.[9] Further, national courts are under an obligation so far as possible to interpret national legislation in the light of the wording and purpose of any relevant EC Directive, whether implemented or not.[10]

7.9 A toughening of the Community's stance with regard to protecting consumers' economic interests can be seen not only in the increased scope of the Community's policy on consumer protection under Article 153, but also in the recent (11 June 1998) European Parliament and Council Directive on injunctions for the protection of consumer interests.[11] This will require the UK to make provision in national law for "qualified entities" to have rapid recourse to the courts for injunctions against bodies which infringe certain listed Directives aimed at protecting the consumer. Orders that the courts can make include ordering an unsuccessful defendant to make payments to the public purse or to a designated beneficiary, as well as to make penalty payments (for example on a daily basis) for failing to comply with an order to rectify the infringement in question. The list of Directives includes Council Directive 87/102/EEC concerning consumer credit, and Council Directive 93/13/EEC on unfair terms in consumer contracts.

8. Art. 249 (ex Art. 189) of the Treaty of Rome. However, they are not without legal effect: national courts are bound to take them into consideration when deciding disputes submitted to them: *Salvatore Grimaldi* v. *Fonds des Maladies Professionnelles* [1989] ECR 4407, paras 16–19.

9. See, by way of example, Cases C–6/90 and C–9/90 *Francovich and Bonifaci* v. *Italy* [1991] ECR I-5357.

10. See, for example, Case C–106/89 *Marleasing SA* v. *La Comercial Internacional de Alimentation SA* [1990] ECR I–4135.

11. OJ L166 of 11 June 1998, to be implemented into national law by 21 December 2000. See also 98/257/EC, Commission Recommendation of 30 March 1998 on the principles applicable to the bodies responsible for out-of-court settlement of consumer disputes (Text with EEA relevance) OJ L115/31 of 17 April 1998; and Decision 283/199/EC of the European Parliament and of the Council of 25 January 1999 establishing a general framework for Community activities in favour of consumers, OJ L34/1 of 9 February 1999.

Consumer credit

7.10 In terms of its impact on banks, the Consumer Credit Directive[12] is probably the least important of the Community's consumer measures in the four areas referred to above. It imposes requirements on credit institutions when dealing with consumers to disclose certain information, principally relating to the cost of credit, but also to the creditor's rights on default. It does not provide any remedies where a creditor fails to comply with these measures, although it does require such persons to be subject to official authorisation and inspection. It also imposes certain requirements as to the formalities of consumer credit agreements. However, by and large its implementation did not change the way in which banks did business in the UK since they were in any event, before the Directive came into force, subject to the Consumer Credit Act 1974 which generally imposes on them more stringent requirements in respect of such matters.

Electronic payment systems

7.11 In the field of electronic payment systems the European Commission has so far proceeded by way of Recommendations only.[13] In 1987 it recommended a code of conduct governing, *inter alia*, relations between financial institutions and consumers, and in the following year it issued a Recommendation to payment card issuers establishing minimum standards.[14] Both Recommendations form part of the Commission's programme for the development of the internal market. Of the two, the 1988 Recommendation is principally concerned with the protection of consumers. It has been given effect in the UK by means of the United Kingdom's code of banking practice[15] which affords consumers similar protection to that conferred by the Consumer Credit Act 1974. The Commission has, however, now proposed a Directive to bring electronic money institutions within the same regulatory regime as credit institutions.[15a]

12. Directive 87/102/EEC, (1987) OJ L42/48 as amended by Directive 90/88/EEC, (1990) OJ L6/114; and by Directive 98/7 of the European Parliament and the Council (1998) OJ L101/17 of 1 April 1998.

13. But see the proposal for a European Parliament and Council Directive on the taking up, the pursuit and the procedural supervision of the business of electronic money institutions, 1998, OJ C317/7; and, on a more general basis, the proposal for a European Parliament and Council Directive on Certain Legal Aspects of Electronic Commerce in the Internal Market, OJ (1999) C30/4.

14. EC Commission Recommendation on a European Code of Conduct relating to Electronic Payment, 87/598/EEC (1987) OJ L365/72; EC Commission Recommendation Concerning Payment Systems and in particular the Relationship between Cardholder and Card Issuer, 88/590/EEC (1988) OJ L317/55.

15. See Part C of "Good Banking—code of practice to be observed by banks, building societies and card issuers in their relations with personal customers", March 1994; see the *Encyclopaedia of Banking Law*, pp. H8–H11.

15a. IP/98/727.

Cross-border transfers

7.12 The failure of banks to follow a Commission Recommendation on cross-border transfers[16] led to the Commision proposing a Directive to govern credit transfers. An amended version[17] was passed by the Council of Ministers on 21 January 1997[18] and is required to be implementd by 14 August 1999 (see Art. 11).[19] The Directive is primarily for the benefit of individuals and small and medium-sized businesses: hence the restriction on the application of the Directive to amounts of less than ECU 50,000 (Art. 1).[20] It is intended to facilitate the use of cross-border transfers by promoting transparency of charging, and hence competition.

7.13 The Directive sets out the minimum information that institutions are to make available to customers both before and after cross-border credit transfers (Arts 3 and 4) and minimum obligations regarding the time both for the execution of the transfer by the originator's institution and for making the funds available to the beneficiary (Art. 6). Article 7 expressly imposes an obligation on the institutions to execute the cross-border transfer in accordance with the customer's instructions, in particular without deduction of costs unless the originator has specified that the beneficiary is wholly or partly to bear them. The Directive also sets out who is to pay compensatory interest in the event of late transfers/availability of funds (Art. 6), namely the originating institution in the case of late execution and the beneficiary's institution in the case of late availability of the transferred funds. Article 8, in the event of the non-execution of transfers, imposes an obligation on institutions to credit the originator within 14 banking business days, without prejudice to any other claim which may be made, with up to ECU 12,500 plus interest and the charges paid by the originator, subject to certain derogations and a *force majeure* exception (in Art. 9). It also requires Member States to ensure that there are effective complaints and redress procedures for dissatisfied customers (Art. 10).

Unfair contract terms

7.14 The aim of the Unfair Terms in Consumer Contacts Directive, which was implemented in the United Kingdom by the Unfair Contract Terms in Consumer

16. EC Commission Recommendation on the Transparency of Banking Conditions Relating to Cross-border Financial Transactions 90/109/EEC, (1990) OJ L67/39.

17. Amended Proposal for a European Parliament and Council Directive on EU Credit Transfers, (95/C199/07) COM(95) 264 final.

18. Directive 97/5/EC, (1997) OJ L43/25.

19. HM Treasury has produced draft Cross Border Credit Transfer Regulations 1999, but these are not in force as at the date of writing.

20. Note that by Art. 2 of Council Regulation 1103/97 ((1997) OJ L162/1) on Certain Provisions relating to the Euro, all references to ECUs in this, as in all the Directives mentioned in this section, are replaced by a reference to a euro at a rate of one to one with effect from 1 January 1999.

Contracts Regulations 1994 (SI 1994 No. 3159)[21] and applies to contracts entered into between a seller or supplier of goods or services and a consumer,[22] is to assist in the progressive establishment of the internal market.[23]

7.15 The Directive is based on the premise that, generally speaking, consumers do not know the rules of law of other Member States which govern consumer contracts, with the result that they are deterred from entering into "direct transactions for the purchase of goods and services" in those Member States. The removal of unfair terms from consumer contracts, which the Directive seeks to effect, is an attempt to equalise the safeguards available in Member States, and so promote these direct transactions (see paras 5 and 7 of the preamble). Notwithstanding the aim of encouraging cross-border sales, the Directive also applies to such transactions concluded between sellers and purchasers located within the same Member State.

7.16 The contractual terms covered by the Directive are those "not individually negotiated".[24] However, the Directive will not apply in any event to terms incorporated in the contract in order to comply with UK mandatory (statutory or regulatory) provisions or international Conventions to which Member States or the Community are party.[25] However, the fact that a certain term is individually negotiated does not exclude application of the Directive to the rest of a contract where the overall assessment of the contract indicates that it is nevertheless a pre-formulated standard agreement (see Arts 3(1) and (2)).

21. Note that Art. 10 of the Directive provides that the Directive is to apply to all contracts concluded after 31 December 1994, whereas the UK Regulations, which did not come into force until 1 July 1995, do not expressly apply only to contracts entered into, if not at least in the six months prior to that date, then on or after a specific date, be it 1 July 1995 or thereafter. It is arguable that, notwithstanding normal UK principles of construction against the "restrospective" application of legislation, as a matter of Community law, in fulfilment of the UK's obligation to implement the Directive, the Regulations are to be construed so as to apply to contracts concluded in this six-month period. In any event, it is submitted that the *Marleasing* principles should apply to such contracts with regard to the Directive, and where the supplier is the State or an emanation of the State, the Directive itself should apply, a situation envisaged by the Directive: see Art. 2. However, there are no decided cases in point.

22. Both the seller and supplier, whether a natural or legal person, in making the contract have to be "acting for purposes relating to his business" and the consumer, who can only be a "natural person", has to be "acting for purposes outside his business": Reg. 2(1) and Art. 2 of the Directive. By analogy with Case C–269/95 *Benincasa* v. *Dentalkit* [1997] ECR I–3767, a person will not be a "consumer" in relation to a contract if that person has concluded the contract in question with a view to pursuing a trade or profession in the future pursuant to that contract (the contract in question was a franchising agreement).

23. See also above on the European Parliament and Council Directive on Injunctions for the protection of consumer interests of 11 June 1998.

24. Certain contracts are excluded *in toto*: those relating to employment, succession rights, rights under family law and to the incorporation and organisation of companies or partnerships: see Sched. 1 to the Regulations and the Directive, Preamble, 10th recital.

25. The latter provision, however, is somewhat problematic as there is a potential conflict between Sched. 1 to the Regulations, which disapplies the Regulations to terms reflecting the provisions and principles of international Conventions (e.g. an applicable law clause reflecting the Rome Convention), and Reg. 7, which applies the Regulations "notwithstanding any contract term which applies or purports to apply the law of a non-member State". On further problems regarding the application of Reg. 7, see below.

7.17 A contractual term which has not been individually negotiated is to be regarded as unfair if, contrary to the requirement of good faith, it causes a significant imbalance in the other party's rights and obligations arising under the contract, to the detriment of the consumer (see Art. 3(1)).

7.18 It is sometimes said that the concept of "good faith" (in the sense of fair dealing between contracting parties) is alien to English law. But this is to overstate the case, and in particular ignores the well-established line of cases in English law where transactions have been set aside on the ground of "unconscionability".[26] Schedule 2 to the Regulations specifies four matters to be taken into account in assessing good faith: the strength of the bargaining positions of the parties; the provision of inducements; whether the services/goods were supplied to special order; whether the consumer was dealt with "fairly or equitably". The term appears to have a subjective element (in effect, arguably, whether the supplier has acted honestly) but also to impose an objective standard, possibly along the lines suggested by Lord Steyn: "The observance of reasonable commercial standards of fair dealing in the conclusion and performance of the transaction concerned".[27] Understood in this light, as Lord Steyn has commented, "it [the concept of good faith] is entirely practical and workable".[28]

7.19 The "unfairness" of a term is to be assessed by taking into account the nature of the goods or services for which the contract was concluded, and with reference, at the time the contract was concluded, to all the circumstances attending its conclusion, and to all of the terms of the contract or related contract on which it is dependent (see Art. 4(1)). This assessment does not relate to any term which defines the "main subject matter" of the contract, nor to the adequacy of the price and remuneration, on the one hand, as against the services or goods in exchange, on the other, insofar as these terms are in plain and intelligible language[29] (see Art. 4(2) and Reg. 3(2)).[30] Annexed to the Directive is an indicative, non-exhaustive list of terms which may be regarded as unfair.

7.20 Where a term is unfair, then, as provided for under national law, that term is not binding on a consumer, but the contract continues to bind the parties upon such terms as remain if it is capable of continuing in existence on those terms (see Art. 6(1)). In addition Member States are required to take measures to

26. See, for a more recent example, the judgment of Millet LJ in *Crédit Lyonnais Bank Nederland NV* v. *Burch* [1997] 1 All ER 144.

27. Lord Steyn, "Contract Law: Expectations of Honest Men" (1997) 113 LQR 433, 438–439.

28. *Ibid.*

29. By Art. 5, where all or certain terms offered to the consumer are in writing, they must be drafted in plain and intelligible language, and in the event of ambiguity, the interpretation most favourable to the consumer is to prevail.

30. This approach seems rather curious. The "fairness" of terms other than the main subject-matter and the adequacy of the price would arguably, and reasonably, seem to turn on what was in fact being purchased by way of the main subject-matter together with the price and remuneration. Further, if this is so, a supplier would appear to be in potentially a more advantageous position if the term defining the "main subject matter" is not in fact in "plain and intelligible language".

ensure that the consumer does not lose the protection under the Directive by virtue of the choice of law of a non-member country as the law applicable to the contract where the contract has a close connection with the territory of the Member States (see Art. 6(2)).[31]

7.21 Banks are clearly within the definition of suppliers of services. Hence, the provision of normal banking services to non-business customers, including account facilities, loans, banking references and so forth, fall within the Directive and the Regulations. Services not ordinarily supplied to those regarded as consumers, for example derivatives trading, may also fall within the Directive and Regulations where the customer, however sophisticated, is acting for a purpose outside his trade or business.

7.22 However, where the contract for the provision of services requires the conclusion of contracts for or the provision of security, the contract of security for example the provision of a third-party guarantee to the bank may well fall outside the Directive. This is probably also the case where the third party does not give the guarantee in the course of his business but the person whose debt is guaranteed is acting within the course of his trade or profession in relation to the lending services provided—see, by analogy, the judgment of the European Court of Justice in *Bayerische Hypotheken- und Wechselbank AG* v. *Dietzinger*[32] in respect of a guarantee provided by the son for the liability of the father acting for the latter's business activities for the purposes of the "Doorstep-selling Directive".[33]

7.23 It should be noted, however, that the Court here held that a contract benefiting a third party, such as a contract of guarantee, could not be excluded from the protection (and so was within the scope) of the Directive on the sole ground that the goods or services purchased were intended for a third party outside the contractual relationship.[34] In so doing, the Court rejected the

31. There are two further problems with this Article and Reg. 7 which implements it in addition to the potential conflict between Reg. 7 and Sched. 1 to the Regulations identified above. They are: (1) it is unclear which law is to apply in determining whether the contract has a "close connection" with Member States (Community law, which is to be preferred; the *lex fori*; or the otherwise applicable law of the contract); (2) it is likewise unclear which law is to apply to determine, if an "unfair" term is excised, whether the contract is capable of continuing in existence (the *lex fori* or the applicable law of the contract). Note also that Reg. 2 defines "Member States" by reference to contracting parties to the Agreement on the European Economic Area of 2 May 1992 (and so including all EFTA states) rather than, simply, by reference to states acceding to the Treaty of Rome.

32. Case C–45/96, [1998] ECR I–1199. In the light of this judgment it is submitted that the view expressed by R. Harrison in *Good Faith in Sales* (Sweet & Maxwell, 1997), para. 19.16, namely, that a guarantee taken from a wife in respect of her husband's debts by a bank lender is caught by the Directive and Regulations, is no longer able to hold good, at least where the debts guaranteed are the husband's business debts. Note also that a company director giving a guarantee in respect of his company's liabilities to a bank is not a consumer for the purpose of the Directive and Regulations, but would be, it is submitted, if the guarantee was, for example, in respect of his son's debts if the son's debts were incurred in the course of the son acting other than for the purpose of the son's own trade or business.

33. Directive 85/577/EEC, (1985) OJ L372/31.

34. Case C–45/96 *Bayerische Hypotheken- und Wechselbank AG* v. *Dietzinger*, [1998] ECR I–1199, para. 19.

argument of various governments which had submitted observations to the Court to the effect that *no* guarantee was covered by the Directive on the basis that a guarantee was not a contract "under which a trader supplies goods or services to a consumer" as provided by Article 1(1) of the Directive.

7.24 There has been little, if any, practical guidance by the courts as to the sort of terms in banking contracts that are "unfair" for the purposes of the Directive. However, by analogy with the Annex to the Directive, the following might be regarded as unfair:

- a term "inappropriately" entitling a bank to offset debts owed to it by the consumer so as to diminish a claim that the consumer might have against it (para. 1(b) of the Annex); it is unclear what forms of off-setting would be "inappropriate", but a contractual right to offset the liabilities of a company owned by a consumer against the liabilities of the bank to the consumer personally may fall into this category;[34a]
- a term entitling a bank to terminate a loan without reasonable notice and without a valid reason (paras 1(g) and 2(a));
- a term entitling the bank to raise interest rates without a valid reason (paras 1(j) and (l), and 2(b) and (c)); but indexation clauses or payments by reference to exchange rates are permitted as are variations to contracts of indeterminate duration provided the consumer is informed with reasonable notice and is entitled to "dissolve" the contract; again it is unclear what terms would be regarded as "unfair", but a term entitling a credit institution to raise interest rates to an excessive level as a result of default in payments is likely to be regarded as "unfair".[35]

EC COMPETITION LAW: ARTICLES 81 AND 82[36] AND BANK/ CUSTOMER AGREEMENTS

7.25 The EC competition rules (Arts 81 and 82 of the EC Treaty[37]) are the means by which the Community regulates distortions of the market caused by unfair trade practices, as well as promoting the creation of the single market.

34a. Query if such an "entitlement" not actually used would be relevant here.

35. Note that such an agreement might also be regarded as an extortionate credit bargain within the meaning of the Consumer Credit Act 1974: it is not clear, however, whether the test for "unfairness" is lower than the test for "extortionate" for these purposes. See also the Report of the Office of Fair Trading recording that City Mortgage Corporation had agreed to remove "unfair" penalties (dual interest rates and expensive early repayment calculations) from its loan agreements: *Consumer Law Bulletin* No. 138 (March 1998) p. 7.

36. Under the Amsterdam Treaty Arts 81 and 82 replace Arts 85 and 86.

37. Note that there is a considerable body of case law on [ex] Arts 85 and 86. This section is only intended to highlight those areas in which EC competition law may affect banking transactions with individual customers. For a fuller discussion of these provisions, such works as *Butterworths Competition Law*; Bellamy and Child, *Common Market Law of Competition*, 4th edn (Sweet & Maxwell, 1993); Whish, *Competition Law*, 3rd edn (Butterworths, 1993) may usefully be consulted.

They apply to banks as to other undertakings and trade associations.[38] As the Commission indicated, in a 1995 Decision giving conditional approval to proposed state aid to support Crédit Lyonnais, "[t]he liberalization of financial services and the integration of financial markets are making intra-Community trade more and more sensitive to distortions of competition".[39]

7.26 Article 81 of the EC Treaty prohibits agreements and concerted practices which have as their object or effect the distortion of competition within the common market or a substantial part thereof, provided there is also an appreciable effect on trade between Member States. Article 82 prohibits abusive behaviour by undertakings in a dominant position, again provided inter-state trade and competition are affected. Both Articles 81 and 82 have direct effect,[40] which is to say that they may be relied upon both as a shield and as a sword by persons in disputes with banks in national courts. It is also generally accepted that breaches of Articles 81 and 82 by undertakings give rise to a claim for damages both under English and under Community law, although this has not been expressly decided.[41]

7.27 However, in the recent case of *Crehan* v. *Courage Ltd*,[42] the Court of Appeal referred to the ECJ the question whether, assuming that a party to an agreement prohibited by [ex] Article 85 might be someone who was given rights against the other party by virtue of Article 85, the national court was obliged as a matter of Community law to award damages to that injured party to the extent that he was injured by the actions of the other party under the agreement. In so doing, the Court of Appeal appeared implicitly to accept that damages were able (if not required) to be awarded for breach of Article 85. It asked the further specific questions whether, in given instances, an "injured" party to the agreement, itself contrary to Article 85, was also able to claim damages against the "injuring" party.

38. See Case 172/80 *Zuchner* v. *Bayerische Vereinsbank* [1981] ECR 2021.

39. Commission Decision 95/547/EC of 26 July 1997 giving conditional approval to the aid granted by France to the bank Crédit Lyonnais (Text with EEA relevance) OJ L308/92 of 21 December 1995, para. 6.5, subsequently approved, as an amended proposal, by Commission Decision 98/490/EC of 20 May 1998 OJ L221/28 of 8 August 1998.

40. Case 127/73 *BRT* v. *SABAM* [1974] ECR 51, [1974] 2 CMLR 238.

41. But see Case C–128/92 *Banks* [1994] ECR I–1209, *per* Advocate General Van Gerven, albeit in relation to the ECSC, but in terms considering the availability as a Community law obligation of damages for breach of EC competition rules; and *Society of Lloyd's* v. *Clementson* [1995] LRLR 307 at 329 *per* Lord Bingham MR for a view inclining towards the right to damages. Other dicta to the same effect may be found in *Bourgoin SA* v. *Ministry of Agriculture, Fisheries and Food* [1986] 1 QB 716 at 787D *per* Parker LJ ([ex] Art. 86); *Plessey Co. plc* v. *General Electric Co. plc and Siemens* [1990] ECC 384 at 393, 394 *per* Morritt J ([ex] Art. 85). See also Commission Notice on Cooperation Between National Courts and the Commission in Applying Articles 85 and 86 of the EEC Treaty, (1993) OJ C39/6, para. 11: "It is the right of parties subject to Community law . . . that compensation should be awarded for the damage suffered as a result of infringements, where such damages are available in proceedings relating to similar national law", and see the *Crehan* case below.

42. Joined with *Byrne* v. *Inntrepreneur Beer Supply Co. Ltd*; *Langton* v. *Inntrepreneur Beer Supply Co. Ltd*; *Smith* v. *Greenhalls Management Ltd*; and *McGaughey* v. *Walker Cain*, CA, decision of 27 May 1999, NewLaw 199055201.

7.28 Competition law so far has had limited direct impact on the terms of agreements that individual banks may enter into with their customers, and thus on the contractual remedies available to customers.[43] Case law so far has principally been concerned with agreements between banks regarding standard terms and conditions in dealing with customers and their collective imposition by banks. Absent a collective arrangement, there has been little direct guidance either by the courts or the Commission on an individual bank's standard terms, although in the recent case of *Bagnasco* (see further below) the ECJ did examine the likely competitive effect of standard terms for the operations of current account facilities and guarantees for the same.

7.29 The *Zuchner* case[44] (which confirmed the applicability of competition law to banks) was concerned with the collusive fixing of commission for the transfer of money abroad. Other cases have concerned such matters as an agreement on the conditions on which automatic bank teller machines could operate in Italy,[45] a series of twelve Conventions, two agreements and eight recommendations of the Association of Belgium Banks relating to the commissions charged by banks,[46] and an agreement concerning the commission that French banks charged for the use of Eurocheques.[47]

7.30 In principle, however, and as the *Bagnasco* case illustrates, there is no reason why European competition law should not be applied to an individual bank's standard terms and conditions in the same way that it may be applied to, for example, standard brewery leases.[48] This may be particularly pertinent given that the Unfair Terms in Consumer Contracts Directive only applies to contracts with consumers who are defined as "any natural person who, in contracts covered by the Directive, is acting for purposes outside his trade, business or profession".[49] That is to say, bank loans to, for example, small businesses fall outside the consumer protection granted by the Directive.

7.31 If a standard term were regarded as anti-competitive, by Article 81(2) it would be void (save if exempted under Article 81(3)). The effect of this on the agreement as a whole is a matter of national law, and in England is to be determined in particular by the application of the English doctrine relating to

43. But see below the growing case law in this area, which in our submission is bound to increase as more Community measures address the relationship between banks and their customers.

44. [1981] ECR 2021.

45. *Re Associazione Bancaria Italiana* [1989] 4 CMLR 238.

46. *Re The Belgian Association of Banks* [1989] 4 CMLR 141. See also *Re The GSA Agreement 1991* [1997] 5 CMLR 550 (Commission Notice regarding a collective agreement between Dutch banks on, *inter alia*, interbank settlement charges).

47. *Eurocheque Helsinki Agreement* (1992) OJ L95 (9.4.1992).

48. But note that such leases, where the overall benefits of the agreement may outweigh any anti-competitive effect, may be exempted by the European Commission under Art. 81(3) from the application of Art. 81(1). See, for example, the Commission's indication that it intends to exempt the standard form tenancy agreements used by Spring Inns Ltd: (1998) OJ C61/3, and Commission Decision 1999/230 of 24 February 1999 regarding the standard form 20-year leases of Whitbread, OJ L88/26 of 24 February 1999.

49. Art. 1(1).

severance.[50] It is also possible (although, as indicated above, yet to be decided definitively) that a party to such a contract could sue the bank for damages for any loss suffered as a result of the inclusion of the offending provision in the loan agreement. It should be noted that there is no equivalent provision for an exemption under Article 82 which simply prohibits provisions falling within its terms where their inclusion amounts to an abuse of a dominant position in a relevant market.

7.32 It would appear nonetheless that, in practice, banks may have little fear from any actions of discontented borrowers based on Articles 81 and 82. A likely outcome in the event of a challenge to a bank's terms and conditions in connection with a particular banking transaction is that indicated by *Oakdale (Richmond) Ltd* v. *National Westminster Bank plc*, a 1996 case in which a company sought to argue in support of its summons seeking an injunction to restrain National Westminster Bank plc from making demand for payment that the standard form all monies debenture under which it had been lent money was prohibited and void under Articles 81 and 82.[51] Under the terms of the debenture, the company's book debts were charged to the bank, and the company was obliged to pay the proceeds of its debts into the company's account with the bank and not to charge or assign the book debts without the prior written consent of the bank. The company argued that these provisions were anti-competitive and prevented lending by a third party.

7.33 Upholding the first instance judge, Chadwick J's, dismissal of this claim, the Court of Appeal held[52] that these provisions were essential for the bank's security and were such as any sensible lender would consider necessary to protect its security. In these circumstances, the provisions fell outside [ex] Article 85(1) altogether. Millett LJ, giving the leading judgment, cited[53] the opinion of the Advocate General in *Gottrup-Klim* v. *Dansk Landbrugs Grovvareselskab Amba*[54] to the effect that

> the Court normally concludes that no anti-competitive object is contained in clauses which are found in the abstract to be necessary to ensure that a contract, which is not itself harmful to competition, can fully discharge the legal and economic functions which it pursues.

7.34 In *Citibank International plc* v. *Kessler and Another*[55] a similar argument was raised that a provision in a standard legal charge that the mortgagor not lease or agree to lease the mortgaged premises in whole or part without the prior written agreement of the mortgagee was contrary to Community law, in this case because alleged to be contrary to Article 48[56] (the current Article 39). The court ruled that the standard clause was not contrary to

50. See *Chemidus Wavin Ltd* v. *Société pour la Transformation CA* [1978] 3 CMLR 514.
51. [1997] ECC 130.
52. [1997] 3 CMLR 815.
53. [1997] 3 CMLR 815 at 820.
54. Case C-250/92, [1994] ECR I-5641.
55. Decision of the Court of Appeal of 10 March 1999. NewLaw Case 199032201.
56. [Ex] Art. 48 provides the right of free movement of persons.

Article 48 as the clause was not "a rule aimed at regulating employment", nor part of a collective arrangement as to employment.[57] In addition, the clause was not "the sort of obstacles to which Article 48 was directed". In any event, there was nothing in the clause itself which amounted to a restriction on movement between Member States as it did not hinder the defendant from moving to another Member State for any purpose.

7.35 The ECJ has itself dealt with a case challenging the validity under Article 81(1) and/or 82 of various standard conditions applied by two Italian banks in accordance with the requirements of the Italian Banking Association to both the variation of interest rates on current accounts, and the provision of "general guarantees" to secure the provision of current account facilities.[58] The ECJ did not rule that Articles 81 and 82 could not have any application to the operation of such standard clauses or conditions. However, in the case of the standard clauses applying to the variation of interest rates on current accounts the Court held that they did not have as their object or effect a restriction on competition within Article 81 insofar as they enabled the banks to change the interest rates at any time by reason of changes occurring in the money market, and to do so by way of a notice displayed on their premises or such other manner as they considered appropriate (para. 37). With regard to the standard conditions applied to the provision of "general guarantees" to secure the provision of current account facilities, the Court considered that such rules (including the requirement that a guarantor repay liabilities which had increased from the date when the guarantee was given) were not, taken as a whole, liable to affect trade between Member States within [ex] Article 85(1).[59]

7.36 A challenge that the application by the Italian Banking Association of those standard conditions infringed [ex] Article 86 as an abuse of a dominant position was also rejected. This was because it was held that changes in an interest rate based on changes in the money markets would, in any event, be changes based on objective factors, and hence would not constitute an abuse.

7.37 As the above cases illustrate, it is likely that many, if not most, restrictions contained in loan agreements and other standard bank documents will survive scrutiny under Article 81 on the basis either that they fall outside Article 81 altogether or are merely ancillary restraints, or are objectively justified (in the case of Article 82), albeit that each restriction has to be considered on a case-by-case basis.

7.38 English courts traditionally appear reluctant to interfere and undo an otherwise uncontroversial commercial bargain. This may be seen in the case of *Marchant & Eliott (Underwriting) Limited* v. *Higgins*[60] where the first instance

57. The court drew this conclusion as to the test to apply from Case 36/74 *Walgrave & Koch* v. *Association Union Cycliste Internationale and Others* [1974] ECR 1405, and Case C–415/93 *Union Royale Belge des Sociétés de Football Association ASBL and others* v. *Bosman* [1995] ECR I–4921.

58. Joined Cases C–215/96 and C–216/96 *Bagnasco and others* v. *Banca Populare de Novara Soc. Coop. Arl (BPN)* and *Cassa di Risparmio de Genova e Imperia SpA (Carige)* [1999] 4 CMLR 624.

59. Para. 53.

60. [1996] 1 Lloyd's Rep. 313; [1996] 2 Lloyd's Rep. 31 (CA).

judge, Rix J, dismissed the defence to an application for summary judgment which asserted that certain terms of the Lloyd's standard Managing Agent's Agreement as set out in the Schedule to a Lloyd's byelaw of 1988 were contrary to [ex] Article 85. This judgment was also subsequently upheld by the Court of Appeal which commented, "in our judgment the attempt to invoke art. 85 is a pretext for non-payment" and maintained "that through the ingenuity of his lawyers he [Dr Higgins] relies upon the Article to evade payment of his debts."[61] In the absence of an obviously anti-competitive provision,[62] courts may well look sceptically on the invocation of European competition law as a means of relieving a debtor from liability where his contractual obligation is otherwise clear and unimpeachable.

EC COMPETITION LAW AND BANK RESCUES

7.39 When a customer acknowledges his indebtedness to a bank, but has insufficient funds to repay in accordance with the contract terms, a rescue may offer a better chance of repayment than suing for the debt and risking the debtor's insolvency. However, such rescues, especially where a debtor company concerned is substantial, may risk encountering the hurdles of EC competition law.

7.40 The possibility of agreements falling within the prohibitions set out in Articles 81 and 82 has already been discussed briefly above. These Articles, equally applicable in principle to bank rescues, are not discussed further here, although in principle an agreement between a number of competitor banks in respect of an ailing debtor might be caught by them.

7.41 The EC competition regime also extends to controlling government assistance or aid to ailing businesses and, if certain threshold tests are satisfied, mergers. It is possible that bank rescues of insolvent debtors may be subject to either or both controls.

State aids[63]

7.42 By Article 87 (ex Article 92) of the Treaty of Rome aids given by a Member State which favour certain undertakings or the production of certain goods and

61. [1996] 2 Lloyd's Rep. 31, at respectively 36 and 39.

62. For example, some brewery leases include what is arguably a classic form of anti-competitive provision in the form of an exclusive purchasing obligation imposed by brewers on a link, i.e. the public house, in the distribution chain to the end-user, i.e. the consumer.

63. This section is intended only to highlight those aspects of what is a complex area of law as it may affect banks and their remedies. For a fuller discussion, see further *Butterworths Competition Law*; Bellamy & Child, *op. cit. supra*. However, this area generally is in a state of flux. The Commission now has competence in Art. 89 to adopt regulations on the application of Art. 87 (and Art. 88), and adopted one such regulation—994/98 ((1998) OJ L142/1). It has since adopted three draft regulations on: aid to SOLEs, training aid and *de minimis* aid (IP/99/584). Whether credit institutions might benefit from a general exemption here is the subject of a review by the Commission submitted to the Council of Ministers of 17 June 1998.

thereby distort or threaten to distort competition are declared incompatible with the common market unless they fall within one of the exceptions provided by Articles 87(2) or 87(3).[64] By Article 88 (ex Article 93) such aids may be ordered to be abolished or amended, and they may be suspended pending a decision by the Commission on compatibility.[65] They may also be ordered to be repaid, and if so, the Member State in question will be under an obligation to take all necessary steps to recover the aid from individuals and companies which have benefited.[66] Article 88(3) requires a Member State to notify the Commission of any aid before it has been granted or altered.[67] This latter provision has direct effect, that is to say it is enforceable by an individual in a national court.[68]

7.43 The concept of a state aid is broad:[69] it includes not only investment grants,[70] subsidies[71] and loans at prefential rates,[72] but also such matters as debt write-offs,[73] guarantees[74] and counter-guarantees.[75] It may be given by any level

64. Art. 87(2) provides that aid (a) having a social character granted to individual consumers, (b) to make good damage caused by natural disasters or other exceptional occurrences and (c) aid granted to certain areas of the Federal Republic of Germany affected by the division of Germany *shall* be compatible with the common market; and by Art. 87(3) aid (a) to promote economic development, (b) to promote the execution of an important European project or to remedy a serious disturbance in the economy of a Member State, (c) to facilitate the development of certain economic activities or areas and (d) such other categories as may be specified by the Council *may* be compatible with the common market (emphasis added).

65. Art. 11 of Council Regulation 659/1999, OJ L83 of 27 March 1999, laying down detailed rules for the application of Art. 88.

66. Case C–6/97 *Italian Republic* v. *EC Commission*, not yet reported. Decision of the ECJ of 19 May 1999. If the aid is ordered to be recovered, the repayment shall include interest at a rate fixed by the Commission (see Art. 14(2) of Council Regulation 659/1999). Provisional repayment may be ordered pending a final determination by the Commission (see Art. 11). However, repayment is subject to a limitation period of 10 years beginning on the day on which the unlawful aid is awarded to the beneficiary (see Art. 15).

67. As to the procedure to be followed on notification, see Chapter II of Council Regulation 659/1999, *supra*, fn. 65.

68. See, in this context, Case C–354/90 *FNCEPA* v. *France* [1991] ECR I–5505.

69. See *XXVI Report on Competition Policy* (1997) point 167: "The Court and the Commission have consistently held that the concept of aid to a firm must be viewed in the broadest possible sense."

70. See, for example, Case 730/79 *Philip Morris* v. *Commission* [1980] ECR 2671.

71. For example, aids to the shipbuilding industry under Directive 90/684/EEC, (1990) OJ L380/27 as amended.

72. See, for example, Case 328/82 *Intermills* v. *Commission* [1984] ECR 3809.

73. See, for example, Case 294/90 *British Aerospace and Rover* v. *Commission* [1992] ECR I–493; and the assumption of debt risk: see Commission Decision 95/547/EC of 26 July 1995 giving conditional approval to aid granted by France to the bank Crédit Lyonnais (text with EEA relevance) OJ L308/92 of 21 December 1995; subsequently approved, as an amended proposal, by Commission Decision 98/490/EC of 20 May 1998 OJ L221/28 of 8 August 1998.

74. See, for example, *EFIM* (1993) OJ C267/11. The difficulties that can arise for banks from non-notified state aid guarantees have been usefully set out in a number of Financial Law Panel papers—the latest of which is from July 1999 on "Unapproved State Guarantees for Bank Loans and Other Borrowings".

75. Commission Decision 98/276/EC of 18 November 1997 covering counter-guarantees given by the German Federal State of Sachsen-Anhalt to cover guarantees of the Bürgenshaftsbank Sachsen-Anhalt GmbH in favour of companies in difficulties (Text with EEA relevance) OJ L126/32 of 28 April 1998.

of government, central or local,[76] and by public undertakings.[77] Banks are most likely to encounter them as part of a rescue or restructuring package in which they participate as third-party lenders to an ailing business.[78] Such aid by definition tends to distort competition, and unless *de minimis* (below ECU 100,000 [approximately £70,000] over three years)[79] will require exemption under Article 87(3)(c) on the basis that it is not "contrary to the common interest".

7.44 The Commission has recently indicated what conditions are to be satisfied if it is to regard this criterion as being fulfilled.[80] In the case of rescue aid, it must be a one-off operation, be restricted to the form of loan guarantees or loans bearing normal commercial interest rates and to the amount needed to keep the firm in business, be paid only for the time needed to devise a recovery plan (generally not more than six months) and be warranted on the ground of serious social difficulties. In the case of restructuring aid, it must be linked to a viable recovery programme, involve measures to off-set adverse effects on competitors (for example, involve a proportionate reduction in capacity in cases of structural excess production capacity in the relevant market), be limited to the minimum necessary to enable restructuring to be undertaken, and be subject to monitoring by the Commission by means of annual reports.

7.45 The publication by the Commission of the 1994 Notice, together with other Notices and communications by the Commission on state aids,[81] heralded its intention to take an increasingly active role in ensuring that state aids do not distort competition in the Community. Indeed, in its *XXV Report on Competition Policy* (1995) at p. 64 the Commission refers to its approach aimed "at ensuring that Member States comply more strictly with Article 93(3) of the EC Treaty and . . . at encouraging economic operators to be more vigilant about the lawfulness of the aid granted to them".

7.46 This has culminated in Council Regulation 659/1999 of 22 March 1999[82] laying down detailed rules for the application of Article 88 (ex Article 93) of the EC Treaty. This Regulation sets out the powers of the Commission and the procedure to be followed regarding both notified and unlawful state aids, and as regards the continuing review of existing aid schemes.

7.47 As part of its 1995 movement, in June 1995 the Commission sent to all Member States a detailed questionnaire on state guarantees. Although its

76. See, for example, Case 323/82 *Intermills* v. *Commission* [1984] ECR 3809.

77. See, for example, Case 177/78 *Pigs and Bacon Commission* v. *McCarren* [1979] ECR 2161.

78. For example, *EFIM* (1993) OJ C267/11.

79. See the Commission Notice on the *de minimis* rule for state aid (1996) OJ C68/9.

80. Community Guidelines on State Aid for Rescuing and Re-structuring Firms in Difficulty (94/C 368/05) (1994) OJ C368/12.

81. See further Commission Notice on Co-operation between National Courts and the Commission in the State Aid Field (C–95 2436 final) (1995) OJ C312/8; Commission Communication to Member States concerning procedures for notification of aid plans and procedures applicable when aid is provided in breach of the rules of Article 93(3) of the EC Treaty, (1995) OJ C156/5.

82. OJ L83 of 27 March 1999.

discussions in this area have not yet directly borne fruit in the form of clear policy guidance,[83] it is clear that state aids from which banks benefit in the form of state guarantees are increasingly in the Commission's firing line. For example, in 1993 the Commission concluded that a guarantee given to banks by the Freie Hansestadt Bremen in favour of the Hanseatische Beteiligungen GmbH to enable it to acquire indirectly another undertaking was a state aid, although the actual decision itself was subsequently overturned by the Court of First Instance on appeal, principally on the basis that the Commission failed to take account of all relevant factors when assessing whether the guarantee was one that a substantial private investor might have given.[84] In February 1995 the Commission decided to initiate the procedure under [ex] Article 93(2) of the Treaty with respect to a state guarantee to an Italian company, Breda Fucine Meridonali, which enabled it to raise loans of ECU 49.3 million (approximately £36 million) from private banks.[85] In 1996[86] the Commission ruled that the guarantee was illegal, as it was not notified in advance to the Commission in accordance with Article 93(3) of the EC Treaty. The aid was also incompatible with the common market within the meaning of [ex] Article 92 of the Treaty. Italy was ordered to recover the aid from BPM.

7.48 The difficulty that banks have faced, and still face at present, in this area,[87] in the absence of guidance from the Commission, is that it is unclear how the state aids provisions of the Treaty will affect the rescue transactions that they may enter into where the Treaty rules relating to state aids have not been followed by the relevant government. However, it is likely that where banks lend money to ailing companies on the basis of state guarantees or similar arrangements they will encounter two principal difficulties. The first is that the obligations of the state arising from contractual arrangements entered into between the bank and the state, insofar as they constitute a state aid, are

83. See further its *XXV Report on Competition Policy* (1996), p. 63. However, a Commission draft notice is currently being circulated for comments.

84. (1993) OJ L185/43; Joined Cases C–329/93, C–62/95 and C–63/95, *Federal Republic of Germany* v. *Commission* [1996] ECR I–5151. Other recent Commission Decisions include: *Bestwood E.F. Kynder GmbH* v. *GV*, (1997) OJ L194/32 (decision, *inter alia*, that a guarantee by the Land Mecklenburg-Vorpommern for a loan by Nord LB, a state-owned bank, to Bestwood, a company that subsequently went into liquidation, was a state aid; note the Commission's statement at L194/35 that the aid element in such a guarantee is generally equal to the difference between the rate of interest on a loan raised on normal market terms and the actual rate secured by virtue of the guarantee, but that when, absent the guarantee, no credit institution would have agreed to lend, the entire amount of the loan is to be regarded as the aid); *EPAC*, (1997) OJ L186/25 (interim decision requiring Portuguese government to suspend aid in form of a state guarantee of loans from a group of banks to EPAC, one of a number of operators in the cereals market).

85. European Commission *XXV Report on Competition Policy* (1996) p. 229.

86. Commission Decision 96/614/EC of 29 May 1996 concerning certain measures granted by Italy in favour of Breda Fucine Meridionali SpA (only the Italian text is authentic) (text with EEA relevance) OJ L272/46, of 25 October 1996.

87. See a full and helpful discussion in Financial Law Panel Discussion Paper, *State Guarantees and the State Aid Rules* (October 1997). For a particularly alarmist view of the impact of the European state aids regime on the banking sector, see M. Dassesse, "State Aid and Banking Activities: the Impact of European Community Law", [1997] BJIBFL 99–102.

unenforceable by English courts on the ground of illegality where (but arguably only for so long as) that arrangement has been put in place without notification to and authorisation from the Commission as required by Article 88(3).[88] The second is that the Commission in theory might, in exercising its power under Article 88(2) to order the abolition of the unlawful aid,[89] be able to order a Member State not to honour any such contractual arrangement. In principle it is also possible for the Commission to order the bank to repay any money received under a state guarantee where the bank can properly be characterised as a recipient of state aid.[90] However, the Commission indicated (without further explanation) in its June 1995 questionnaire on state guarantees that banks are unlikely to be regarded as beneficiaries unless they have derived an "undue advantage".[91] It is not clear what this means.

7.49 In view of these uncertainties, banks should be particularly vigilant when participating in rescues. It may be appropriate for banks involved in such activities to obtain prior confirmation from the European Commission that any government aid to the debtor-borrower is compatible with EC rules on state aid, and/or obtain prior information as to whether an aid has been notified to the Commission and, if so, with what results. Banks may also consider it desirable to include in any loan documentation a condition precedent to the effect that the relevant measure had been notified to the Commission and declared compatible with EC rules on state aids or a warranty that the relevant measure is not an aid requiring prior notification to the European Commission. Whilst the prospect of a government-backed rescue may be an attractive alternative to pursuing claims under loan documents against debtor companies, banks need to be aware that in pursuing this remedy they may face EC law problems of this nature.

88. Note, however, that the aid itself is not unlawful by reason of the Member State's failure to notify: see Case C–303/87 *Boussac* [1990] ECR I–307. What is unlawful is the Member State's implementation of the aid prior to a decision having been reached by the Commission under its examination procedure. This is expressly provided for by Art. 3 of Council Regulation 659/1999 which states that: "Aid notifiable pursuant to Article 2(1) shall not be put into effect before the Commission has taken, or is deemed to have taken, a decision authorising such aid."

89. This is on the assumption that such a direction is ancillary to the Commission's powers to order the abolition of the aid under Art. 88(2). However, there is no decided case in point and the Commission has not indicated whether it considers that it has the power to make such a direction.

90. Note in this regard that an institution benefiting from state aid cannot rely on a legitimate expectation that the aid is lawful and granted in compliance with Community procedures. "A diligent businessman should normally be able to determine whether that procedure has been followed": Case C–24/95 *Land Rheinland-Pfalz* v. *Alcan Deutschland CmbH* [1997] ECR I–1591.

91. Financial Law Panel Discussion Paper, *State Guarantees and the State Aid Rules* (October 1997) p. 16.

Mergers[92]

7.50 Mergers which have a Community dimension[93] fall under the exclusive jurisdiction of the European Commission. The test is a simple threshold test without reference to any potential anti-competitive effects of the merger. What matters is simply the size of the turnovers of the undertakings concerned. Where this is the case, prior notification has to be given to the European Commission which then decides whether it is compatible with the common market.

7.51 A merger exists (in Community parlance a "concentration"[94]) where one undertaking acquires control (which includes the acquisition of "decisive influence"[95]) over another.[96] "Decisive influence" may exist not only as a result of the acquisition of a shareholding, but also, for example, as a result of a management agreement concerning the business policy of the undertaking.[97] *Prima facie*, therefore, a bank involved in a rescue that involves restructuring a business, or a capital injection by a bank or some other direct bank involvement, may either directly or indirectly find itself acquiring control over the business of its debtor within the meaning of the Merger Regulation and thus be subject both to the potentially burdensome notification requirements of the Regulation and to an investigation by the European Commission.

92. There is now a substantial secondary literature on the EC Merger Regulation to which reference should be made for a fuller consideration of this area of law. See, for example, Cooke and Kerse, *EC Merger Control*, 2nd edn (Sweet & Maxwell, 1996); Jones and Gonzalez-Diaz, *EEC Merger Regulation* (Sweet & Maxwell, 1992); Portwood, *Mergers under EEC Competition Law* (The Athlone Press, 1994). See, too, the Commission's Summary of Merger Control Law in the European Union, Situation as at March 1998, published by the Official Publications of the EC.

93. A merger is caught by the EC Merger Regulation (No. 4064/89), as amended, ((1990) OJ L257/14) where (a) the combined worldwide turnover of the undertakings concerned is in excess of ECU 5,000 million; and (b) at least two of the undertakings have a Community turnover of more than ECU 250 million; provided: (c) that more than two-thirds of the Community turnover of each of the undertakings concerned does not take place within one and the same Member State. From 1 March 1998, by amending Regulation No. 1310/97 ((1997) OJ L180/1), a merger is additionally caught where (a) the combined worldwide turnover is more than ECU 2,500 million and (b) in each of at least three Member States the combined turnover of all of the undertakings concerned is more than ECU 100 million where (c) in each such state the turnover of each of at least two of the undertakings concerned is more than ECU 25 million and (d) at least two of the undertakings concerned has a Community-wide turnover of more than ECU 100 million provided (e) that more than two-thirds of the Community-wide turnover of each of the undertakings concerned does not take place within one and the same Member State. Special provisions exist for the calculation of the turnover of credit and other financial institutions which, from 1 March 1998 by reason of the new amending regulation, is calculated by reference to specified items of income (rather than, as before, by reference to assets). As to the calculation of turnover, see Commission Notice on the Calculation of Turnover under Council Regulation (EEC) 4064/89 on the Control of Concentrations between Undertakings (1998) OJ C66/25.

94. Art. 1(1) of Regulation (EEC) No. 4064/89, hereinafter "the Merger Regulation".

95. Art. 3(1) of the Merger Regulation.

96. Note also that by reason of the amending Regulation 1310/97 the Merger Regulation now also applies to all full function joint ventures. See further Commission Notice on the Concept of Full-Function Joint Ventures under Council Regulation 4064/89 on the Control of Concentrations Between Undertakings (1998) OJ C66/1.

97. This follows from Art. 3(1) which provides that "decisive influence" may be acquired "by purchase of securities or assets, by contract or by any other means, direct or indirect".

7.52 To a limited extent this problem has been recognised by the Merger Regulation itself. This provides in Article 3(5)(a) that a concentration shall not be deemed to arise where a financial institution holds securities in an undertaking on a temporary basis with a view to reselling them, provided no voting rights are exercised with a view to determining the competitive behaviour of the undertaking other than with a view to the disposal of all or part of the undertaking and the resale takes place within a year. But, as will readily be apparent, this exemption fails to cover many if not most bank rescues which often involve the conversion of existing debt into equity in a company jointly owned by the lending banks and which in its turn owns the rescued company. The Commission in its Notice on the meaning of a concentration[98] indeed expressly excludes such a rescue from the exemption in Article 3 and states that it will normally be considered a concentration notwithstanding that the primary intention of the banks is subsequently to resell the undertaking concerned. This is principally on the basis that the controlling banks are likely to determine the strategic commercial behaviour of the rescued undertaking. This was the case in *Kelt/American Express*[99] where an international syndicate of eight banks led by American Express rescued a company involved in the oil and natural gas markets in order to prevent its going into receivership.

7.53 In such cases, however, it is possible to obtain some relief from the more onerous requirements of the Merger Regulation. Indeed, the recital to the implementing regulation[100] specifically provides that the Commission will give notifying parties an opportunity to discuss an intended concentration on an informal, but confidential, basis. Further, Article 3(2) of that Regulation empowers the Commission to dispense with the obligation to provide particular information where it considers it is unnecessary for the examination of the case. Banks should therefore first approach the Commission on an informal basis with a view to obtaining a derogation from some of the notification requirements. It is also possible to obtain a derogation from some of the other requirements that follow from a rescue being a "concentration" within the meaning of the Merger Regulation. In particular, it is possible under Article 7(4) of the Merger Regulation to obtain a derogation from the obligation not to implement a concentration within the first three weeks following its notification. This may be particularly important in bank rescues where time is often of the essence in order to prevent the financial collapse of the debtor. Indeed, in the *Kelt/American Express* case an Article 7(4) derogation was obtained.

7.54 When taking shareholdings in non-banking companies, banks should also bear in mind the restrictions that they are under that limit their exposure to such risks. Although these are primarily matters for the national supervisory

98. Commission Notice on the Concept of Concentration under Council Regulation (EEC) 4064/89 on the Control of Concentrations between Undertakings, (1998) OJ C66/5.

99. Case IV/M.116. Decision of 20 August 1991.

100. Recital 10 to Commission Regulation (EC) 447/98, (1998) OJ L61 replacing Commission Regulation (EC) No. 3384/94, (1994) OJ L377/1.

regime, they also derive from Article 12 of the Second Banking Directive.[101] This provides that no credit institution may have a qualifying holding the amount of which exceeds 15 per cent of capital qualifying for the purposes of its solvency ratio in an undertaking which is neither a credit nor a financial institution, nor an undertaking whose business is a direct extension of banking or is limited to services ancillary to banking. It also imposes a limit on the total amount of a credit institution's qualifying holdings in undertakings other than credit and related institutions. Shares held "temporarily" during a financial reconstruction or rescue operation are excluded from the relevant calculations.[102] However, no indication is given as to what is meant by "temporary", unlike the rule under the Merger Regulation where a one-year period is specified.

JURISDICTIONAL ISSUES: THE BRUSSELS, SAN SEBASTIAN AND LUGANO CONVENTIONS[103]

7.55 The Brussels Convention 1968, as amended, and the San Sebastian Convention 1989 provide for procedural remedies regarding the allocation of jurisdiction in civil and commercial matters[104] and for the recognition and enforcement of foreign judgments. They apply as between Member States of the European Union which have ratified and brought them into force within their own states. The Brussels Convention, as amended, applies as between 12 Member States,[105] the San Sebastian Convention, whereby Spain and Portugal acceded to an amended Brussels Convention, applies as between all 15 Member States.[106] There is a parallel Convention, which is to apply as between the 18 European Union and the (present and former) EFTA States, called the Lugano Convention.[107] This, with some variations, replicates the essential elements of

101. Directive 89/646, (1989) OJ L368/1.

102. Art. 12(4).

103. This section is intended to highlight some of the main issues that may affect the enforcement of rights a bank may have against a customer, and vice versa, in relation to the provision of banking services within the European Union and EFTA States. On what is an increasingly complex and complicated area, further reference may usefully be made to fuller works on this area such as Briggs and Rees, *Civil Jurisdiction and Judgments*, 2nd edn, (LLP, 1997); O'Malley and Layton, *European Civil Practice* (Sweet & Maxwell, 1989); and Dicey and Morris, *The Conflict of Laws*, 12th edn, (Sweet & Maxwell, 1993).

104. But not, for example, applying to insolvency matters (see Art. 1, second indent, (1)) and see further below as to the Insolvency Convention; nor to arbitrations (see Art. 1, second indent (4)).

105. Namely, Belgium, Denmark, France, Germany, Greece, Ireland, Italy, Luxembourg, the Netherlands, United Kingdom. Note, however, that a 1996 Accession Convention, bringing in Austria, Finland and Sweden into this Convention regime applies, as at July 1999, between the latter three States and Denmark, Germany, Italy, the Netherlands and Spain.

106. Namely, Austria, Belgium, Denmark, Finland, France, Germany, Greece, Ireland, Italy, Luxembourg, the Netherlands, Portugal, Spain, Sweden and the United Kingdom.

107. It applies, as at July 1999, between the following States: Austria, Belgium, Denmark, Finland, France, Germany, Greece, Ireland, Italy, Luxembourg, the Netherlands, Portugal, Spain, Sweden and United Kingdom (being European Union Member States) and Iceland, Norway and Switzerland (being EFTA States).

the Brussels Convention.[108] In 1997 the Commission put forward a proposal for a Council Act designed to improve and accelerate the circulation between Member States of judgments in civil and commercial matters, and to that end, to simplify the formalities to which the recognition and provisional enforcement of judicial decisions are subject (the 1997 Commission proposal).[109] The main discussion below concentrates on the current text of the Convention.

7.56 For banks, these Conventions determine matters such as where a bank is required as a primary or exclusive obligation to sue a defendant (or likewise is required to be sued), or the circumstances when and as to where the options to sue (or likewise as to being sued) apply; the ancillary relief available in another Contracting State for the protection of assets said to be the target of litigation in a first Contracting State, and the ability and mechanisms for obtaining enforcement of judgments obtained in one Contracting State in other Contracting States. Of these three areas of application, this section is principally concerned with the first, namely the allocation of jurisdiction.

7.57 The Brussels Convention is given effect in the United Kingdom by the Civil Jurisdiction and Judgments Act 1982 ("CJJA"), in force in the United Kingdom on 1 January 1987. An amended text following the accession of Greece entered into force in the United Kingdom on 1 October 1989. The San Sebastian Convention entered into force with respect to the United Kingdom on 1 December 1991. The Lugano Convention entered into force with respect to the United Kingdom on 1 May 1991.[110]

7.58 The Brussels Convention does not alter the substantive law affecting any disputes before the courts (see *Sanicentral GmbH* v. *Collin*[111]). The law applicable to a given dispute is to be determined according to the conflicts of laws rules of the forum seised of the dispute, which may require reference to be made to the Rome Convention.[112]

7.59 The determination of the applicable law may itself also determine whether a UK court sought to be seised by way of election by a bank[113] actually has jurisdiction in accordance with the Brussels Convention. For example, the

108. In each case it is necessary to consider the relevant text of the applicable Convention in order to apply exactly the provisions of the text applicable as regards the particular dispute involving the particular Contracting States. The relevant date for these purposes is the date when a court is seised of the dispute (subject to the point in fn. 110 below): Art. 54 of the Brussels Convention (and see also Briggs and Rees, para. 2.21 *et seq.*). Interpretation of the Conventions is assisted by various Reports written to explain the effects of their Articles, and named after the co-ordinating Rapporteurs for the Reports. In the United Kingdom the courts are entitled to consider the Reports and give such weight to them as they consider appropriate in the circumstances—see s.3(3) of the Civil Jurisdiction and Judgments Act 1982.

109. COM/97/0609 Final, OJ C33/20 of 31 January 1998.

110. It is important to bear in mind that each of the relevant Conventions (or amendments) comes into force as between the United Kingdom and another Contracting State as from when the Convention in question came into force in both States.

111. Case 25/79 [1979] ECR 3423, 3492, para. 5.

112. See further below.

113. As to the principal provision regarding the matter of election by parties as to jurisdiction, see Art. 5 and see further below.

applicable law may determine the place of performance of an obligation at issue in the proceedings (for example where the obligation to repay a loan to a bank arises) which in turn may determine jurisdiction.[114]

7.60 The primary rule under the Brussels Convention as to allocation of jurisdiction between Contracting States is set out under Article 2.[115] This provides that a plaintiff should sue a defendant, regardless of the nationality of the defendant,[116] in the courts of the State in which the defendant is domiciled.[117]

7.61 This primary rule can be displaced in a number of different ways. The first is by a "mandatory obligatory" provision such as Article 16, which requires disputes as to immovable property to be litigated in the courts of the place where the property is located;[118] second by Articles 7–12 (specific provisions in the case of insurance matters); or, third, by the rules set out in Articles 13–15 regarding consumer contracts.[119] Note that under Article 16 a bank cannot allocate by a choice of jurisdiction clause an alternative jurisdiction,[120] nor could a defendant grant jurisdiction by entering an appearance[120a] before a court wrongly seised or purportedly seised of jurisdiction in such a case by a bank.[121] Entering an appearance otherwise generally gives jurisdiction to the court before which proceedings are initiated (see Art. 18).[122]

7.62 Whether a claim falls within Article 16 is of obvious importance to banks when enforcing secured lending agreements. However, the ECJ has adopted a narrow interpretation of the scope of Article 16 as the leading case of *Webb* v. *Webb*[123] illustrates. Here a father sought a declaration in the United Kingdom that his son held property located in France on trust for the father. No

114. As to the obligation to pay, see further below.

115. And similarly with the Lugano Convention, Art. 2. Save where otherwise indicated, reference to Articles in this section of the chapter are to Articles in the Brussels Convention, as amended, in force in the UK as at the date of going into print.

116. See Art. 2, first indent.

117. Domicile is to be determined by the internal law of the court seised of the dispute (see Art. 52, first indent) to see, first, if that person is domiciled in that state. If not so domiciled, the courts then seised of the dispute shall determine the place of domicile of the defendant in accordance with the internal law of such other Contracting State (Art. 52, second indent). A similar provision applies within the UK, as between respective jurisdictions in, for example, England and Wales, Scotland and Northern Ireland—see s.41 CJJA. Under the 1997 Commission proposal, "domicile" would be replaced with a test for "habitual residence".

118. However, for Art. 16 to apply, there must be a dispute as to a right *in rem* in the property enforceable against the whole world, rather than for example rights *in personam* in relation to the property, save where the rights in question involve tenancies—see Case C–294/92 *Webb* v. *Webb* [1994] ECR I–1717, paras 14 and 15. See also Case 115/88 *Reichert* v. *Dresdner Bank AG* [1990] ECR I–27 and *Jarrett* v. *Barclays Bank* [1997] ILPr 531 and the discussion below.

119. Such contracts can cover, for example, a contract for a loan repayable by instalments made to finance the sale of goods.

120. See Art. 17, third indent.

120a. See Art. 18.

121. In fact, in the event that a judgment was entered in error where Art. 16 would apply, a court asked to recognise the judgment would be obliged to refuse recognition—see Art. 28.

122. Not, however, if the appearance is entered solely to contest jurisdiction; or, if jurisdiction is disputed first in any defence, notwithstanding that a substantive defence is thereafter pleaded: see Case 150/90 *Elefanten Schuh* v. *Jacqmain* [1981] ECR 1671.

123. Case 294/92 [1994] ECR I–1717.

relief was sought in respect of the property itself: the father did not seek a transfer of ownership. On the basis that the father's action was not based on a right *in rem* but on an equitable right that operates *in personam*, the ECJ rejected the son's submission that only the courts of France had jurisdiction. Although this judgment has been criticised,[124] the narrow construction of Article 16 has been followed by the Court of Appeal in England and Wales in the time-share case of *Jarrett* v. *Barclays Bank*[125] in which claims brought in England by time-share owners of foreign properties against lenders under sections 56(2) and 75 of the Consumer Credit Act 1974 were held to fall outside Article 16 on the basis that the actions were founded on the relevant debtor-creditor-supplier agreements and not the time-share agreements, notwithstanding the "connection" or "link" with the latter.[126] Note, however, that a claim in England by a trustee in bankruptcy to recover from a third party a beneficial interest in a villa in Minorca that belonged to the bankrupt was a claim falling within Article 16;[127] it was a claim falling outside the bankruptcy jurisdiction and, as a matter of Spanish law, a beneficial half-share was also a legal interest in the property.

7.63 On this understanding of Article 16, a bank's claim for a declaration that a property stands as security for a liability, where that is the sole issue before the court, is, it is submitted, likely to fall outside Article 16. It may also be the case that a claim for an order pursuant to a contract for secured lending that a person transfer the property to the lender also falls outside Article 16. This is on the basis that the foundation of the claim is a personal contractual right, not a property right (an action to enforce a contract for sale of a property does not fall within Article 16).[128] However, a bank's claim to possession arising under a mortgage or legal charge will fall within Article 16. A lender within the European Union, therefore, should be careful when taking properties located abroad as security for a loan to ensure that the rules of the jurisdiction in which the property is situated regarding the enforcement of the security are adequate to meet its requirements.

7.64 Of more concern to banks will be the rules as to allocation of jurisdiction where the bank is dealing with a person as a "consumer". These rules deal primarily with contracts for the sale of goods (and to a more limited extent, for the supply of services) on instalment or other forms of credit terms. As indicated above, Articles 13–15 of the Convention govern jurisdiction where a bank sues a person dealing as a consumer.

7.65 The concepts set out in these Articles are designed to create their own

124. See Briggs and Rees op. cit. p. 43: "The reasoning is almost wholly spurious".

125. [1997] ILPr 531.

126. Under the 1997 Commission proposal, "contracts for the acquisition of a time-share of immoveable property" would be expressly within Art. 13.

127. *In re Hayward, decd.* [1997] Ch. 45.

128. See the Schlosser Report on the Brussels Convention, at para. 171.

code, and have their own independent interpretation.[129] A person is not acting as a consumer within these Articles where the claim is in respect of a contract under which he will engage in a trade or profession in the future.[130] Nor, by analogy, will a person be acting as a consumer where he provides a guarantee for another where the latter is acting in the course of his own business.[131] Nor will a contract be within these Articles merely because the contract provides for payment by instalments.[132]

7.66 The primary rule as to the allocation of jurisdiction may also be displaced by an "elective mandatory" rule such as Article 17 whereby parties attribute exclusive jurisdiction to the courts of a particular State by written or other form of agreement established between them; or, in international trade or commerce, where the agreement is in a form which accords with practices in that trade or commerce of which the parties were aware or ought to have been aware. It can also be displaced by a choice made by a plaintiff as to another jurisdiction such as under Article 5, provided that is accepted by the other party.

7.67 Of the exceptions to the allocation of jurisdiction under Article 2, however, the most important in practical terms are in Article 5. The principal relevant provisions are Article 5(1): which permits the plaintiff to sue in matters relating to the performance of an obligation in the courts of the place of performance of that obligation;[133] Article 5(3): which provides that in matters relating to tort, delict or quasi-delict, a plaintiff can choose to sue in the courts of the place where the "harmful event took place";[134] and Article 5(5): regarding disputes arising out of the operation of a branch, agency or other establishment, where a plaintiff may sue in the courts of the place where the branch, agency or establishment is situated.[135]

7.68 As to Article 5(1), the contractual obligation in question is to be determined by reference to the scope of the dispute with which the court is seised.[136] The danger that banks and other plaintiffs face when electing jurisdiction under Article 5(1) (or indeed under Article 5 generally) is that by

129. See Case 150/77 *Bertrand* v. *Ott* [1978] ECR 1431, paras 14–16 and 19; Case C–89/91 *Shearson Lehman Hutton* v. *TVB* [1993] ECR I–139, para. 13; Case C–269/95 *Benincasa* v. *Dentalkit* [1997] ECR I–3767, para. 12; and Case C–99/96 *Hans-Hermann Mietz* v. *Intership Yachting Sneek BV*, not yet reported, Decision of the ECJ of 27 April 1999, para. 26.

130. See the *Benincasa* case, *supra*, fn. 129.

131. See Case C–45/96 *Bayerische Hypotheken- und Wechselbank AG* v. *Dietzinger*, [1998] ECR I–1199.

132. See the *Intership Yachting* case, *supra*, fn. 129.

133. Under the 1997 Commission proposal, Art. 5(1) would read "in matters relating to a contract for the sale of goods, in the courts of the place where the goods were delivered, or where the delivery was or should have been carried out, except in cases where the goods were delivered, or deliverable, to more than one place".

134. Under the 1997 Commission proposal, Art. 5(3) would read "in matters relating to tort, delict or quasi-delict, in the courts of the place where the event giving rise to the damage occurred, or in the courts for the place where the damage or part thereof was sustained".

135. Unchanged in the 1997 Commission proposal.

136. Provided at all times that there is a particular close relationship between the dispute and the court which may most conveniently be called upon to take cognisance of the matter—see Case 12/76 *Tessili* v. *Dunlop* [1976] ECR 1473, para. 13.

widening the scope of any claim, they may find that they have deprived themselves of their jurisdiction of choice.[137]

7.69 For example, an action whereby a bank claims payment of commission in respect of money transfer services supplied at a predetermined level for a period of years to a foreign domiciled party would probably be categorised under the law applicable within the Contracting States to the Brussels Convention as an action on a debt. Under the law of some countries, for example England, Ireland, Greece and Italy, the place of performance of the obligation (other specific provisions affecting this aspect of the contract, contractual or otherwise, aside) is at the place of the creditor.[138] However, if the bank's claim is widened to include a claim for damages for wrongful early termination of that contract, the scope of the "dispute" before the court will have been extended to one relating to damages for breach of the obligation to call on the bank to arrange for transfers for the remainder of the contract. This obligation might be one which was to have been performed in the state of the debtor.

7.70 In cases where there is more than one obligation in issue, a bank is entitled to sue in the courts of the place for the performance of the primary obligation (that is the "contractual obligation forming the actual basis of the legal proceedings": see, for example, the case of *de Bloos* v. *Bouyer*[139]). This element requires of the court that it identifies that obligation in accordance with the applicable law of the contract in question,[140] even if this is itself identified as the law applicable under an international Convention.[141]

7.71 As to Article 5(3), the phrase "matters relating to tort, delict or quasi-delict" has a Community or autonomous meaning.[142] That is to say, such matters are wider than those which a national court might recognise as, say, a tort, although the precise content of this term under Article 5(3) is controversial.

137. They should also be wary (where there is any doubt as to the effectiveness of the election under Art. 5) of concentrating on a claim in a jurisdiction elected under Art. 5 at the risk of a limitation period expiring that is applicable in a jurisdiction allocated under Art. 2.

138. In English law, this was determined in *The Eider* [1893] P 119. However, this may, obviously, be subject to specific rules for place of payment in a commercial contract with a bank, and in the specific case of payment as between a customer and his bank relating to the operation of a current account, in the absence of specific provision, a customer must demand payment at the branch where the account is kept—see further *Royal Bank of Scotland* v. *Cassa di Risparmio delle Provincie Lombardi and others* [1991] ILPr 411. Note that under French, Spanish and German law the place of performance appears to be at the place of the debtor; see further Briggs and Rees, p. 107.

139. Case 14/76 [1976] ECR 1497; and see, too, Case 266/85 *Shenavai* v. *Kreischer* [1987] ECR 239; and Case C–288/92 *Custom Made Commercial Ltd* v. *Stawa Metalbau GmbH* [1994] ECR I–2913.

140. The question of whether the place of performance is to be determined by the applicable law of the contract or by some other means is now the subject of a reference to the ECJ. See Case C–440/97 *Cie Groupe Concorde and others* v. *The Master of the Vessel "Suhadiwarno Panjan" and others* [1997] ILPr 207. The opinion of the Advocate-General, M. Ruiz-Jarabo Colomer (of 16 March 1999) favours abandoning the simple reference to the applicable law of the contract, in apparent favour of some "closest connection" factor.

141. On the basis that that Convention is able to take effect on the domestic plane in that Contracting State—see Case C–288/92 *Custom Made Commercial Ltd* v. *Stawa Metalbau GmbH*, *supra*, fn. 139.

142. Case 189/87 *Kafelis* v. *Schroeder* [1988] ECR 5565.

The place where the harmful event occurred is either the place where the source of the harm arose, or the place where harm was occasioned—see, for example, *Bier* v. *Mines de Potasse*.[143] In banking terms, it is likely that claims falling within Article 5(3) include such causes of action as breach of a duty of care owed between banker and customer; and possibly (but less clearly) breach of trust and alleged constructive trusts, at least where there is no underlying agreement governing the relations between the bank and the other party. Attempts have been made to extend the scope of Article 5(3) beyond that indicated in *Mines de Potasse* to allow for recovery of the "indirect" or "downstream" consequences of a tort, such as the collapse of a business. However, the ECJ has rejected these attempts: for recourse to be made to Article 5(3) both the harm and the victim must be "direct".[144]

7.72 The provisions of Article 24 are a further exception to the primary rule of Article 2 and are of considerable practical importance, if perhaps under-used within the scheme of the Brussels Convention, in terms of protecting effective enforcement.[145]

7.73 Article 24 allows for ancillary interlocutory relief to be granted in one Member State even if under the Brussels Convention the courts of another Member State have jurisdiction over the substantive proceedings,[146] provided the substantive claim falls within the Convention *ratione materiae*.[147] Where the courts of a Member State would in any event be able to have jurisdiction over the case under the Convention, it is not necessary for them to have recourse to Article 24 if national rules would permit the grant of the provisional measures sought.[148] Conversely, Article 24 cannot be used to bring within the scope of the Convention provisional or protective measures relating to matters which are themselves excluded from the scope of the Convention.[149]

143. Case 21/76 [1976] ECR 1735.

144. See, respectively, Case C–220/88 *Dumez France* v. *Hessiche Landesbank* [1990] ECR I–49, and Case C–364/93 *Marinari* v. *Lloyds Bank* [1995] ECR I–2719.

145. Under the 1997 Commission proposal, Art. 24 would be deleted, with some partial substitution under a new Art. 27 reading as follows: "Judgments given in a Contracting State shall, where a final order is issued, generate an entitlement on the grounds of which provisional protective measures may be ordered in accordance with the law of the State applied to, even where they are not enforceable or have not been declared enforceable in the State applied to for the purposes of Article 31."

146. Before the coming into force of s.25 of the Civil Jurisdiction and Judgments Act 1982, interlocutory relief could not be granted by a UK court where there were no substantive proceedings within the jurisdiction: *The Siskina* [1979] AC 210.

147. Case C–391/95 *Van Uden* v. *Deco Line* [1998] ECR I–7091. In this case, it was also held that Art. 24 can be used for the grant of provisional measures notwithstanding that the dispute is subject to an arbitration clause; arbitration is outside the scope of the Brussels Convention in any event (see its Art. 1, second indent, para. 4). The place of Art. 24 interim measures in the scope of the Convention is determined, not by their own nature, but by the nature of the rights those measures seek to protect, *ibid.* para. 33; and see, too, Case C–261/90 *Reichert* v. *Dresdner Bank AG* [1992] ECR I–2149, para. 32.

148. Case C–391/95 *Van Uden* v. *Deco Line* [1998] ECR I–7091, para. 19; and Case C–9/96 *Hans-Hermann Mietz* v. *Intership Yachting Sneek BV*, not yet reported, Decision of the ECJ of 27 April 1999, para. 40.

149. See Case 143/78 *De Cavel* v. *De Cavel* [1979] ECR 1055, para. 9.

7.74 In order to obtain the benefit of Article 24 provisional or protective measures, which can in principle be enforced in another Member State,[150] it is necessary, *inter alia*, that there be a real connecting factor between the subject-matter of the measures sought and the territorial jurisdiction of the Contracting State of the court before which the measures are sought.[151] Article 24 measures can include an interim order for payment of a contractual consideration. However, as such an order can by its nature be such that it may pre-empt the decision on the substance of the case,[152] the ECJ has ruled that, to qualify as an Article 24 measure, such an interim payment order must ensure, first, that repayment to the defendant of the sum awarded is guaranteed if the plaintiff is unsuccessful as regards the substance of the claim, and second, that the measure sought relates only to specific assets of the defendant located or to be located within the confines of the territorial jurisdiction of the court to which the application is made.[153]

7.75 Article 24 was employed to useful effect in the United Kingdom in the *Duvalier* case[154] where the substantive proceedings were taking place in France and no substantive relief was being sought in England. The effect of the judgment in that case was to grant *Mareva*-like orders to freeze assets in the United Kingdom to the "potential" benefit of the proceedings in France. In exceptional cases assets outside the jurisdiction may also be frozen.[155] In the light of the *Van Uden* and the *Intership Yachting* cases, it is arguable whether such "extra-territorial" orders, or such elements of such orders, would constitute measures within Article 25.[156] It remains to be seen whether a *Mareva* order which ordered a defendant, who was thus amenable to the UK court's jurisdiction, to bring within the "territorial" jurisdiction of the UK court certain assets would thereby mean that such assets would constitute assets "to be located within" the territorial jurisdiction of the court.

7.76 With regard to the recognition and enforcement of judgments,[157] it is

150. See Articles 25 and 26, but see the cautionary note in fn. 155 below.

151. Case C-391/95 *Van Uden* v. *Deco Line* [1998] ECR I-7091, para. 40.

152. *Ibid.*, para. 46.

153. *Ibid.*, para. 47; and Case C-9/96 *Hans-Hermann Mietz* v. *Intership Yachting Sneek BV*, not yet reported, Decision of the ECJ of 27 April 1999, para. 42.

154. *Republic of Haiti* v. *Duvalier* [1990] 1 QB 202. See more recently *Crédit Suisse Fides Trust SA* v. *Cuoghi* [1998] ILPr 41, CA.

155. *Republic of Haiti* v. *Duvalier* [1990] 1 QB 202. But note that if such an injunction is obtained *ex parte* without notice it will not be enforceable in the other state under the Brussels Convention either because it lacks the quality of a "judgment" or because it was obtained in default of the defendant having had an opportunity to be heard. See further Briggs and Rees, para. 6.17.

156. However, see, in this regard the case of *Normaco Ltd and Norilsk Nickel* v. *Lundman* [1999] ILPr 381, and the observations of Carnwath J.

157. "Judgment" means "any judgment given by a court or tribunal of a Contracting State, whatever the judgment may be called, including a decree, order or writ of execution, as well as the determination of costs or expenses by an officer of the court" (Art. 25). See, however, in apparent contrast to this approach, the recent case of *Barney's Inc.* v. *C.M.C.S.A.* [1999] ILPr 386, where the French Court of Appeal (Paris) considered that no enforcement of an "instrument" would follow under its enforcement of judgments provisions [art. 509 NCPC] in respect of an "order" from the Bankruptcy Court of the South District of New York where the "instrument" did not indicate that

important to bear in mind the difference the ECJ has drawn between "enforcement" and "execution". The Convention enforcement procedure constitutes an autonomous and complete system in itself.[158] "Enforcement" for these purposes means only "enforceability, in formal terms".[159] Execution in one Member State of a judgment given in another Member State remains subject to the domestic law of the court of the latter State.[160]

7.77 That apart, little will be said here on recognition and enforcement, save to highlight the potential difficulty created by Article 27(1) which provides that a judgment shall not be recognised where such recognition is contrary to the public policy of the state in which recognition is sought.[161] Some states in the past, relying on the public policy exemption, have refused to recognise a judgment given without reasons, such as is likely to be the case with summary or default judgments obtained in English courts.[162] However, it may be thought that with similarities of economic, political and social circumstances in the Member States growing ever closer, the protection of difference that the public policy exception represents may no longer be required. Cases like *Hengst Import BV* v. *Campese*[163] may in fact point this way.[164] In this case a summary, *ex parte*, procedure available under Italian law for the enforcement of debt was

the judge had been able to proceed to verify the infringement or respect of a legal rule, and thus that he had exercised a control over the issues submitted to him. In Case C–260/97 *Unibank A/S* v. *Flemming G. Christensen*, not yet reported decision of ECJ of 17 June 1999, it was held that acknowledgement of indebtedness, whose authenticity has not been established by a public authority or other authority empowered for that purpose, was not a "judgment" for these purposes, notwithstanding that on their face, as permitted by national law, they expressly stated that they could be used as a basis of execution to be levied.

158. Case 148/84 *Deutsche Genossenschaftsbank* v. *Brasserie du Pêcheur* [1985] ECR 1981, para. 17; Case C–172/91 *Sonntag* v. *Waidmann* [1993] ECR I–1963, para. 32–33; and Case C–267/97 *Éric Coursier* v. *Fortis Bank SA, Martine Coursier, née Bellami*, not yet reported, Decision of the ECJ of 29 April 1999, para. 25.

159. Case C–267/97 *Éric Coursier* v. *Fortis Bank SA, Martine Coursier, née Bellami*, not yet reported, Decision of the ECJ of 29 April 1999, para. 29.

160. Case 148/84 *Deutsche Genossenschaftsbank* v. *Brasserie du Pêcheur* [1985] ECR 1981, para. 18; Case 145/86 *Hoffman* v. *Krieg* [1988] ECR 645, para. 27; and Case C–267/97 *Éric Coursier* v. *Fortis Bank SA, Martine Coursier, née Bellami*, not yet reported, Decision of the ECJ of 29 April 1999, para. 28.

161. Under the 1997 Commission proposal, Art. 27 (and Art. 28—other grounds for refusing recognition) would be deleted in full as regards the specific reference to "public policy", although other provisions within these Articles would be reproduced under later Articles dealing with enforcement and protection against enforcement orders made in another Member State. Such a deletion may remove an important safeguard against abuse of the rights of defendants where national rules preclude representation before them in cases where the defendant itself does not appear—see, by way of illustration, Case IX ZB 23/97 *Krombach* v. *Bamberski* [1998] ILPr 681 (a reference for clarification as to the scope of public policy in such cases was made to the ECJ).

162. However, it is submitted that public policy under Art. 27(1) will have no application to a situation the regulation of which, for the purpose of the recognition and enforcement of a judgment, is dealt with ultimately under the Convention, for example under Art. 27(2) (certain cases of judgment in default of appearance). See, too, Briggs and Rees, para. 7.15 and O'Malley and Layton, paras 27.14–27.20.

163. Case C–474/93 [1995] ECR I–2113.

164. The 1997 Commission proposal itself reflects such thinking in that the current Arts 27 and 28 would be deleted. See *supra*, fn. 161.

held by the ECJ to be compatible with the scheme of the Brussels Convention and did not offend against the particular rule of the Brussels Convention (itself possibly to be considered as a public policy rule of the Brussels Convention) that had been invoked as the basis for non-recognition, namely Article 27(2), which requires that a defendant should have notice of the proceedings so as to be able to allow him to defend himself.

THE ROME CONVENTION[165] AND CHOICE OF LAW ISSUES

7.78 The comments on the Rome Convention are made briefly as it is not considered that this Convention is likely to be of significant practical effect for banks in the UK. It is, of course, important that such banks are aware of its provisions, because, in the absence of a choice of law clause, they may find themselves with difficulties on the issue of applicable law where they are dealing with consumers, with nationals from other Member States or with financial transactions involving the provision of facilities in another Member State or the taking of security in another Member State.

7.79 The purpose of the Rome Convention on the Law Applicable to Contractual Obligations, which was concluded on 19 June 1980, is to establish rules to determine the proper law of contracts in situations where there is a choice to be made between the laws of different countries (Article 1), including between the laws of Scotland and England and Wales.[166] The Convention is a harmonising instrument designed to eliminate differences between national conflicts rules, and so promote the creation of a single market. It entered into force in the United Kingdom by virtue of the Contracts (Applicable Law) Act 1990 on 1 April 1991.[167]

7.80 Specifically in connection with financial institutions, it should be noted that the Convention does not apply to obligations arising under bills of exchange, cheques, promissory notes and other negotiable instruments to the extent that the obligations under such negotiable instruments arise out of their negotiable character (see Art. 2(c)). So far as the United Kingdom is concerned, the rules for the determination of the rights and liabilities of the parties in relation to a bill of exchange drawn in one country but to be negotiated, accepted or paid in another are as provided under section 72 of the Bills of

165. The Rome Convention is, as at July 1999, applicable as between Belgium, Denmark, France, Germany, Greece, Ireland, Italy, Luxembourg, the Netherlands, United Kingdom. Note that a 1992 Accession Convention, bringing Portugal and Spain into this Convention regime applies, as at July 1999, between the latter two States and all the mentioned ten States save for Denmark and Ireland; and that a 1996 Accession Convention, bringing in Austria, Finland and Sweden into the Rome Convention regime applies, as at July 1999, between the latter three States and Germany, Greece, the Netherlands and Spain.

166. This follows from the definition of country as a "territorial unit" with its "own rules of law": see Art. 19 and s.2(3) of the Contracts (Applicable Law) Act 1990.

167. S.7 of the 1990 Act, and the Contracts (Applicable Law) Commencement (No. 1) Order 1991 (SI 1991 No. 707).

Exchange Act 1882, as amended. According to the Giuliano-Lagarde Report[168] national law also determines whether an instrument is properly to be characterised as negotiable, although this is not a question that has been finally determined.[169]

7.81 The dominant rule of the Convention is that a contract shall be governed by the law chosen by the parties (Art. 3(1)), subject to certain exceptions. Of principal concern for banks is the exception relating to contracts for the provision of credit for the purposes of a contract for the supply of goods or services to a "consumer" (see Art. 5).[170] This is because by Article 5(2), notwithstanding an express or implied choice of law, in certain circumstances such a choice cannot deprive the consumer of the protection afforded him by the laws of the country in which he has his habitual residence. The specified circumstances are: where the trader has marketed his goods or services in the country where the consumer resides; where the trader has received the order in that country; where the consumer placed his order outside his country of residence, but the consumer's journey to effect the purchase was arranged by the seller (this being a phenomenon common on mainland Europe as an inducement to purchase). In these cases a consumer cannot "contract out" of his national law rights.

7.82 In the absence of a choice effected by the parties, the Convention provides that the contract shall be governed by the law of the country (as opposed to the legal system) with which it is most closely connected (see Art. 4(1)).[171] By Article 4(2) it is presumed that the contract is most closely connected with the country:

> . . . where the party who is to effect the performance which is characteristic of the contract has, at the time of the conclusion of the contract, his habitual residence, or, in the case of a body corporate, its central administration. However, if the contract is entered into in the course of that party's trade or profession, that country shall be the country in which the principal place of business is situated, or, where under the terms of the contract the performance is to be effected through a place of business other than the principal place of business, the country in which that other place of business is situated.

7.83 As a consequence, where banking services are provided to a customer (and not caught by the rules relating to "consumers") and the service is to be effected through an overseas branch, caution should be exercised to try and ensure that that provision is subject to an agreed applicable law. This is because by the application of Article 4 an applicable law may be determined that is

168. Giuliano and Lagarde, *Report on the Convention on the Law Applicable to Contractual Obligations* (1980) OJ C282/1 at 11. By s.3(3)(a) of the Contracts (Applicable Law) Act 1990 courts in the UK are to have regard to this Report when construing the Convention.

169. See Plender, *The European Contracts Convention* (Sweet & Maxwell, 1991), para. 4.16.

170. A consumer is a person who is the recipient of those goods or services for a purpose which can be regarded as outside his trade or profession (Art. 5(1)).

171. To the extent, however, that the subject-matter of the contract is a right in or to use immovable property, there is a presumption that the contract is most closely connected with the country where the immovable property is situated (see Art. 4(3)).

suitable for neither party's interests. For example (on the assumption that the lending is "the performance which is characteristic of the contract"), where a UK bank through an overseas branch in Spain lends to a German national for the purchase of buying a property in Spain, in the absence of an express provision the applicable law is arguably the law of Spain.

THE INSOLVENCY CONVENTION[172]

7.84 Disputes stemming directly from the insolvency of a party, other than from a voluntary winding-up, lie outside the jurisdiction of the Brussels Convention of 1968.[173] The consequence is that an English bank faced with a debtor with assets in a number of jurisdictions should consider very carefully if and where to bring insolvency proceedings with a view to recovering its debt. In particular, it will have to consider not only whether an English court has jurisdiction over the debtor, but also whether the court of a foreign jurisdiction where relevant assets are located will recognise and enforce any insolvency judgments of an English court; whether it may institute proceedings in a foreign jurisdiction where assets are located; and whether, if there is a race to establish control over those assets, proceedings should be commenced in that jurisdiction or in England, a question which may in part depend on differing rules of priority as they apply to creditors in the various jurisdictions. It can be seen that English banks faced with cross-border insolvencies have to negotiate a maze of domestic insolvency law and private international law.

7.85 The reason why insolvency was left outside the scope of the Brussels Convention was the need perceived at the time of the Brussels Convention to avoid duplication as the Community had, since 1960, been engaged in a project to draft an insolvency Convention. However, it was only on 25 September 1995 that the governments of all Member States of the EU approved the text of a European Union Convention on Insolvency Proceedings. It was agreed that it would be open for signature for a six-month period ending on 23 May 1996, and provided all Member States signed it by that date, it would be validly adopted. All but the UK government signed it. Accordingly, the Convention lapsed, despite the UK government's prior approval of its content. It is nonetheless likely that eventually the Convention will be adopted and ratified.[174] In any event,

172. For commentaries on the Convention, see Johnson, "The European Union Convention on Insolvency Proceedings" [1996] *INSOL International Insolvency Review* 80; Turing, "The European Convention on Insolvency Proceedings" [1996] *Butterworths Journal of International Banking and Finance Law* 56.

173. A claim arising under general law, for example an action on a debt due to a company, does come within the jurisdiction of the Brussels Convention notwithstanding that the claim is brought by a liquidator. The test to determine whether the claim falls outside the Brussels Convention is whether it relates to a legal provision specifically applicable to insolvency. See further Case C–214/89 *Powell Duffryn plc* v. *Petereit* [1992] ECR I–1745 and Briggs and Rees, para. 2.25.

174. The House of Lords Select Committee Report supported it in 1997.

since the draft Convention is intended to operate in parallel with the Brussels Convention, an understanding of the proceedings that it is intended to cover is a helpful guide when determining the jurisdiction of the Brussels Convention itself.[175] For these reasons it is considered here.

7.86 The Convention is akin to the Brussels Convention in that it contains binding rules of jurisdiction which must be complied with by the courts of the Member States in relation to matters falling within the Convention's scope. It is also akin to the Brussels Convention in that it is concerned with jurisdictional and applicable law issues, and the enforcement of judgments, and not with substantive insolvency law. Its interpretation is a matter for the European Court of Justice (Article 43) to which references may be made for preliminary rulings by specified courts of Member States (Article 44). Insolvency proceedings concerning insurance undertakings, credit institutions (e.g. banks) and investment undertakings are excluded from its scope (Article 1(2)).[176] Also excluded from the definition of insolvency proceedings is the appointment of administrative receivers, although the appointment of administrators and voluntary arrangements are included (Art. 2 and Annex A). The Convention does not apply to undertakings which have their centre of main interests (on which see below) outside the European Union.

7.87 At the heart of the Convention is the distinction between primary, or main, and secondary insolvency proceedings. Main proceedings may only be commenced in the courts of the state within the territory of which the centre of a debtor's main interests is situated (Art. 3). It is unclear what the "centre of main interests" means for this purpose, although there is a rebuttable presumption in the case of a company that it is the place of its registered office (Art. 3(1)). The law of such proceedings is, except where the Convention specifies otherwise, the law of the state where the proceedings have been commenced (Art. 4).

7.88 Proceedings may be commenced in another Contracting State (and which are termed "territorial proceedings") only if the debtor possesses an establishment within that state, and the effects of those proceedings are limited to the assets of the debtor within the territory of that state (Art. 3(2)). "Establishment" is defined as "any place of operations where the debtor carries out a non-transitory economic activity with human means and goods". It is unclear what this means, other than that something more than assets is required.[177] The applicable law of the territorial proceedings is again, save where the Convention provides otherwise, the law of the state where they have been

175. See, for example, the approach adopted in *Norsk Hydro and Hydro Aluminium AS* v. *Alumix SPA* [1998] ILPr 83 (judgment of the Norwegian Supreme Court).

176. Note that Directive 98/26 of the European Parliament and the Council of 19 May 1998 (L166/45 of 11 June 1998) lays down particular insolvency rules governing the rights and obligations of insolvent participants in cross-border payment and securities settlement systems in relation to their participation in such systems.

177. No doubt some guidance can be obtained from Community case law relating to the right to establishment under Art. 52, albeit that the meaning of "establishment" for the purposes of Art. 52 is also somewhat vague.

commenced (Arts 4 and 28). Where these proceedings are begun after the opening of main proceedings, they are termed secondary proceedings (Art. 3(3)). The significance of this is that they must be confined to winding-up proceedings (Art. 3(3)), which excludes voluntary arrangements. They are subordinated to the main proceedings in that the court which opened the secondary proceedings is obliged to stay them (subject to certain conditions being satisfied) at the request of the liquidator in the main proceedings (Art. 33). Where these proceedings have been opened prior to the main proceedings (in which case they are not confined to winding-up proceedings), the court is also obliged to stay them following a request from the liquidator, but only "in so far as the progress of those proceedings so permits" (Art. 36). It is unclear what this latter provision means.

7.89 Banks will understandably be concerned as to how this mandatory resolution of jurisdictional and applicable law conflicts affects their position as creditors. As creditors, they may begin either main proceedings or territorial proceedings, but the latter may only be opened prior to main proceedings if the bank either has its registered office in the territory where the establishment is situated or its claim arises from the operation of that establishment (Art. 4(b)). There are no such restrictions on the opening of secondary proceedings (Art. 29), provided the bank otherwise has locus under local insolvency law. However, if the bank's aim is ultimately a rescue, secondary proceedings will be inappropriate.

7.90 The bank as creditor (irrespective of whether it has initiated proceedings) may lodge its claims in both the main and secondary proceedings, and may do so in writing (Art. 39), supported by relevant documentation (Arts 32(1) and 41). All known creditors also have a right to be informed both of the commencement of insolvency proceedings where they have their registered offices in Contracting States, and of certain procedural requirements in connection with the making of claims (Art. 40). Any judgment opening proceedings in one Contracting State is, subject to a public policy exception,[178] to be recognised by all other Contracting States and, without further formalities, is to produce the same effects in those other states as under the law of the state where insolvency proceedings were commenced. This is provided that the Convention does not provide otherwise and no territorial or secondary proceedings have been commenced in that state (Arts 16 and 17). Thus, depending on the extra-territorial effect of the insolvency law of any particular Contracting State, in the absence of secondary proceedings, the disposition of a debtor's assets is likely to be frozen. In any event, by Article 20, a creditor who, by whatever means, obtains total or partial satisfaction of his claims through realisation of the debtor's assets in another Contracting State is obliged to return

178. Art. 26. Note that the Contracting State can only refuse to recognise such a judgment where the "effects" of such a recognition "would be *manifestly* contrary to the State's public policy" (emphasis added); cf. Art. 27(1) of the Brussels Convention where a judgment shall not be recognised, "If such recognition is contrary to public policy".

any benefit obtained after the commencement of proceedings to the liquidator, subject to any rights *in rem* or deriving from a reservation in title clause that the creditor might have in relation to those assets.

7.91 However, a legal right to set-off is preserved where the applicable law of the insolvency proceedings recognises it, as is a contractual right where the law applicable to the insolvent debtor's claim permits it (Art. 6). The latter is one of the exceptions to the principal applicable law rules of the Convention.

7.92 Other exceptions concern secured creditors. Article 5 specifically provides that creditors' (and all third parties') rights *in rem* are not affected by the opening of insolvency proceedings. A non-exhaustive list of rights *in rem* is provided in sub-Article 2 which includes rights to dispose of assets arising by virtue of a mortgage or lien. However, it is not clear from the list whether the right to appoint an administrative receiver for the purpose of realising the assets of the debtor is included as a right *in rem*, nor whether quasi-security rights (such as rights arising under title finance arrangements such as ready forward or repurchase contracts) fall within the definition of rights *in rem*. Of the other exceptions (which include reservation of title clauses, employment contracts, registered rights to immovable property and Community intellectual property rights), Article 7 is most likely to be of interest to banks. This provides that the rights of parties to a payment or settlement system or to a financial market are to be governed solely by the law of the Contracting State applicable to that system or market.

7.93 It will be apparent from this brief overview that the Insolvency Convention, while attempting to substitute multiple complex territorial jurisdictional and applicable law rules by a single system, does so in a way which itself is complex, involves untried and unclear legal concepts, and does not itself exclude multiple proceedings. No doubt some of this confusion will be ended by the publication of the Explanatory Report. Nonetheless it is likely that this Convention, as with the Brussels Convention, will provoke new case law and new strategems as parties attempt to maximise their position under the new rules. One fruitful area will be the interplay between main and territorial proceedings as creditors, insofar as they are able, go jurisdiction shopping for the most advantageous realisation of assets.

CONCLUSION

7.94 From this survey it will be apparent that Community law has already had a considerable effect on the contracts that banks are able to conclude with their customers and on steps for their enforcement. As UK banks provide more cross-border retail services, Community law will increasingly affect their day-to-day activities.

7.95 However, Community law has so far fallen short of harmonising remedies. This is illustrated by the, perhaps, extreme case of *Société Generale*

Alsacienne de Banque v. *Koestler*.[179] The facts were that a German national when resident in France had run up an overdraft with a French bank as a result of speculations in contracts for differences. The French bank sued for the debt in Germany to where the defendant had moved. It was accepted that the transaction giving rise to the debt was governed by French law and that the underlying transactions were lawful in France. However, under German private international law contracts for differences, although entered into abroad, were illegal, and this illegality tainted the debt, rendering it unactionable in Germany. The European Court of Justice had to decide whether the German law was contrary to [ex] Articles 59 and 60 (now Articles 49 and 50) of the Treaty of Rome which provide for the progressive abolition of restrictions on the freedom to provide services. It was held that it did not on the basis that it was non-discriminatory: it applied equally to German and non-German nationals. As a consequence the French bank was denied a remedy in Germany that would have been open to it in France.

7.96 Nonetheless the general trend is against such inequalities. Although the Second Banking Directive[180] permits a "host" state's rules to be applied to banks operating under another Member State's authorisation where such rules are "in the general good" (what this means is unclear),[181] both the Commission and the European Court have imposed limitations on this concept.[182] It is likely with the onset of a single European currency and the creation of a European Central Bank that the trend towards an increasingly integrated banking system will bring with it a set of Europe-wide remedies for banks. Indeed, as banks increasingly operate in a genuine cross-border market, commercial pressures are likely to lead to a demand for closer harmonisation of remedies in addition to the harmonisation of the regulatory framework that presently exists.

MAURICE SHERIDAN AND RICHARD BRENT

179. Case 15/78 [1978] ECR 1971.

180. (1989) OJ L368/1.

181. See, for example, Katz, "The general good and the Second Banking Directive: a major loophole" [1993] *Butterworths Journal of International Banking and Finance Law* 166–169; Bernitz and Mohamed, "National prudential rules override capital freedom" [1996] 6 JIBL 235. See now also Commission Interpretation Communication, "Freedom to provide services in the interest of the general good in the Second Banking Directive" [1997] OJ C209/6.

182. See Case C–76/90 *Saeger* v. *Dennemeyer & Co. Ltd* [1991] ECR I–4221. See now also Commission Interpretation Communication, "Freedom to provide services in the interest of the general good in the Second Banking Directive" [1997] OJ C209/6.

CHAPTER 8

PRE-TRIAL PROCEEDINGS IN US COURTS

BASIC PRINCIPLES OF US FEDERALISM

Divided legislative authority

8.1 The United States is a federal republic: legal authority is divided between a single national (or federal) government and the governments of the 50 states and the District of Columbia. Under the US Constitution, the federal government is vested with authority to make and enforce laws concerning a wide range of issues of national concern. Most significantly, the federal government is granted the power to regulate both interstate and foreign commerce;[1] this authority has been construed to extend to virtually every subject that the federal government wishes to reach, except those of the most local character.[2]

8.2 Exercising its constitutional authority, Congress has enacted a wide range of federal legislation in areas of national import. Federal law governs subjects such as banking, transportation, employment discrimination and labour relations, employee benefit and welfare plans, the environment, communications and securities. These federal statutes override, or "pre-empt", all state laws that are inconsistent with federal objectives.[3]

8.3 There are, however, a number of extremely important areas in which Congress has not chosen to exercise its legislative authority, and which are therefore governed by state law. These include basic contract law, tort law, corporation statutes, agency law and a wide range of local matters. The several states are almost entirely free to adopt whatever rules they deem advisable in areas where Congress has not acted; although all states (except perhaps

1. US Const. Art. I, §8.

2. G. Born, *International Civil Litigation in United States Courts* 8–9 (3rd edn, 1996). See *South Carolina* v. *Baker*, 485 US 505 (1988); *Garcia* v. *San Antonio Metropolitan Transit Authority*, 469 US 528 (1985) (Tenth Amendment limits on Congress's authority to regulate states is structural not substantive); *Heart of Atlanta Motel, Inc.* v. *United States*, 379 US 241 (1964) (Congress's authority to regulate interstate commerce extends to purely local activity that in the aggregate may affect interstate commerce).

3. US Const. Art. VI, cl. 2; *Hines* v. *Davidowitz*, 312 US 52 (1941); *Silkwood* v. *Kerr-McGee Corp.*, 464 US 238 (1984).

Louisiana) share the Anglo-American common law tradition, significant differences exist among the laws in different states.

Dual judicial system

8.4 Two largely parallel judicial systems exist in the US: (a) a federal court system and (b) a system of state courts. The federal court system covers the entire US and consists of trial courts (the US District Courts), appellate courts (the US Courts of Appeals), and the US Supreme Court. Each of the 50 states (plus the District of Columbia) also has an independent judicial system, typically with trial courts, intermediate appellate courts and a state supreme court.

8.5 A US federal court may only hear a case over which it has been granted both "personal jurisdiction" (discussed below at paras 8.24–8.53) and "subject-matter jurisdiction" (discussed below at paras 8.9–8.11). Congress has granted the federal courts subject-matter jurisdiction—or the power to decide the type of dispute in question—over only limited categories of cases. The most significant category of case decided in federal courts is that involving substantive federal law.

8.6 In contrast, state courts are generally courts of general jurisdiction that are empowered to decide any claim brought before them. In the ordinary course, each state court system deals principally with cases involving claims based on that state's law; as noted above, state law covers almost every conceivable subject-matter, including commercial transactions, product liability, corporations and property rights. State courts also have subject-matter jurisdiction over all federal claims, except those relatively few that have been placed within the exclusive jurisdiction of the federal courts.

8.7 Procedural matters in all civil cases in federal district courts are generally governed by the Federal Rules of Civil Procedure. Among other things, the Federal Rules govern such issues as service of process, personal jurisdiction, time for answering complaints, discovery, procedures for counterclaims and cross-claims, class actions and the procedures for pre-trial and trial dispositions of cases. "Local rules", adopted in particular federal judicial districts, elaborate on the provisions of the Federal Rules, sometimes adding significant requirements.

8.8 Procedural matters in state courts are governed by state procedural rules. In many cases, these rules are similar to the Federal Rules. Federal and state appellate courts also have their own procedural rules. Criminal cases are governed by separate sets of rules.

Limited federal subject-matter jurisdiction

8.9 Unlike state courts, the federal courts are courts of limited jurisdiction: federal courts may decide disputes only where Congress (or the Constitution in certain limited cases applicable to the Supreme Court) has granted them subject-matter jurisdiction.[4] Congress has established a number of significant areas of federal subject-matter jurisdiction.

8.10 First, federal courts enjoy jurisdiction over cases "arising under" federal law; this includes statutes enacted by Congress, such as antitrust and securities laws, as well as US treaties and the US Constitution.[5] Second, a federal court also enjoys so-called "diversity jurisdiction" over cases arising under state (or foreign) law if the amount in controversy exceeds US$75,000 and the case is between citizens of different states.[6] Third, federal courts possess "alienage jurisdiction" over suits between US and non-US citizens, provided again that the dispute involves more than US$75,000.[7] Finally, federal courts also have subject-matter jurisdiction over a number of other types of specialised disputes defined by federal law.[8]

8.11 Congress has the authority to grant the federal courts exclusive jurisdiction, thereby eliminating the jurisdiction of state courts, and it has done so for a number of categories of cases, including bankruptcy proceedings,[9] cases arising under the Securities Exchange Act,[10] and federal antitrust actions.[11] Unless Congress expressly grants federal courts exclusive jurisdiction, state courts retain concurrent jurisdiction over federal causes of action.

The "Erie" problem

8.12 One of the most complex aspects of US law, for both US and foreign counsel, concerns the so-called "*Erie*" problem:[12] What law—state or federal—does a federal court apply when it decides a dispute? When a federal court

4. *Owen Equipment & Erection Co.* v. *Kroger*, 437 US 365 (1978).

5. See 28 USC §1331 (1993). In addition to this general conferral of "federal question" jurisdiction, many federal statutes contain their own jurisdictional provisions. See e.g., 15 USC §1 *et seq.* (1993) (Sherman Antitrust Act); 15 USC §78a *et seq.* (1993) (Securities Exchange Act of 1934); 28 USC §1337 (1993) (antitrust generally).

6. See 28 USC §1332 (1993).

7. See 28 USC §1332(a)(2) (1998).

8. This includes actions against foreign states; admiralty and maritime cases; patent, copyright, and trade mark matters; and cases in which the US government is a party. See 28 USC §§1330–1364 (1993).

9. 28 USC §1334 (1993).

10. 15 USC §78a.

11. 25 USC §15. See also 28 USC §1338(a) (patent and copyright cases); 28 USC §1355 (actions for the recovery or enforcement of civil fines, penalties, or forfeitures incurred under federal statute); 18 USC §3231 (crimes against the US).

12. In *Erie R.R. Co.* v. *Thompson*, 304 US 64 (1938), the Supreme Court addressed the issue of what substantive law a federal court should apply when the case is not governed by the Constitution or a federal statute. The court reversed the long-standing practice by federal courts of developing their own body of case law and applying this so-called "general federal common law" to cases brought pursuant to diversity jurisdiction. Instead, the court ruled, a federal court sitting in diversity jurisdiction should apply the state's common law as well as its statutes. Thus, under *Erie*, a federal court hearing a diversity case must decide the case with reference to state, not federal, law. The year *Erie* was decided, the Federal Rules of Civil Procedure also went into effect; this reversed the traditional rule of federal courts applying state procedural law in diversity cases. See C. Wright and A. Miller, *Federal Practice and Procedure* §§4503–4510 (1996).

decides federal question cases—cases arising under substantive federal statutes like the antitrust laws—it will of course apply federal law. In doing so, the court will look both to positive federal statutes and to federal judicial interpretations thereof. When a federal court decides a diversity or alienage case, however, it ordinarily will apply the substantive law of a state or foreign country. To determine which jurisdiction's law to apply, a court will employ the conflict of laws rules of the state in which the particular federal court is located.[13] For example, when a federal district court in Virginia hears a contract dispute between diverse citizens, it will apply Virginia's conflict of laws rules to determine the applicable law—in this case, the law of the jurisdiction where the contract was made.[14] On matters of state law, the federal courts must defer to state supreme courts and their interpretation of local law; in contrast, where interpretation of federal law is at issue, both state and federal lower courts may rule, with the federal Supreme Court providing the ultimate authority as to the content of federal law.

Removal

8.13 Many types of claims may be filed in the United States by a plaintiff in either federal or state court. Thus, many federal claims can be brought in state courts, as well as in federal courts; conversely, some state law claims may be brought in federal courts under diversity or alienage jurisdiction. Although plaintiffs ordinarily have the option of choosing to file a complaint in either state or federal court, defendants may seek to alter the plaintiff's choice. Most significantly, a defendant may "remove" an action to federal court in certain cases. In particular, removal is available either (a) if the action arises under federal law, or (b) if a federal court otherwise has diversity or alienage jurisdiction and none of the defendants are citizens of the state where the action was brought.[15] A petition for removal must ordinarily be filed by the defendant within 30 days of the receipt of the pleading commencing the state court action.[16] Removal is a matter of right and cannot be refused by either the federal or state court.

8.14 If at any time before final judgment the district court determines that it lacks subject-matter jurisdiction, it may remand the case back to state court.[17] With the exception of civil rights cases, an order of a district court remanding a

13. *Klaxon* v. *Stentor*, 313 US 487 (1941).

14. Different states have different conflict of laws rules; it is entirely possible that the same case brought in federal court in different states could lead to the application of different substantive laws and conflict of laws rules.

15. 28 USC §1441(a) and (b) (1994). Limited classes of state court actions are not removable. See 28 USC §1445 (1994).

16. 28 USC §1446(b) (1994).

17. 28 USC §1447(b) (1994).

case improperly removed to it from a state court is not generally reviewable on appeal.[18]

PRE-TRIAL PLEADINGS UNDER THE FEDERAL RULES OF CIVIL PROCEDURE

Complaint

8.15 In order to commence a lawsuit in a US court, the plaintiff files a complaint in a particular court.[19] Most US complaints provide relatively limited information about the details of the plaintiff's claims. Under the Federal Rules, a complaint must provide nothing more than a "short and plain statement" concerning the court's subject-matter jurisdiction, the plaintiff's entitlement to relief, and the relief sought.[20] As a practical matter, complaints usually contain limited factual allegations and a conclusory statement of the plaintiff's legal claims. A plaintiff is generally not obliged to specify the amount of the damages desired, but is free to do so if they so choose. In practice, US complaints often contain substantially more factual and legal detail than English writs or most notices of arbitration, but somewhat less information than a fully-pleaded statement of claim. The plaintiff ordinarily will have considerable latitude (subject to judicial approval) in amending his complaint during the course of litigation.

8.16 All pleadings, motions and other papers filed in federal district court (except for those filed by an individual appearing *pro se*) require the signature of an attorney admitted to practise in that court. Rule 11(b) of the Federal Rules provides that the attorney's signature certifies that the filing:

> (1) [. . .] is not being presented for any improper purpose, such as to harass or to cause unnecessary delay or needless increase in the cost of litigation;
> (2) the claims, defenses, and other legal contentions therein are warranted by existing law or by a nonfrivolous argument for the extension, modification, or reversal of existing law or the establishment of new law;
> (3) the allegations and other factual contentions have evidentiary support or, if specifically so identified, are likely to have evidentiary support after a reasonable opportunity for further investigation or discovery; and
> (4) the denials of factual contentions are warranted on the evidence or, if specifically so identified, are reasonably based on a lack of information or belief.

18. 28 USC §1447(d) (1994).

19. Simultaneously, or soon thereafter, the plaintiff will cause the complaint to be "served" upon the defendant, together with a "summons" that requires the defendant to respond to the compaint. Service is discussed below at paras 8.54–8.65.

20. Fed. R. Civ. P. 8(a). A defendant may file a motion for more definite statement of the plaintiff's claims, but such motions are disfavoured except in limited circumstances where pleading with particularity is required. See Fed. R. Civ. P. 9(b) (fraud or mistake); 9(c) (denial of performance or occurrence); 9(g) (items of special damages).

If the court determines, upon another party's or the court's motion, that the filing does not meet the Rule 11 standards, the attorney who signed the complaint is subject to appropriate sanctions.[21] The sanctions may include payment of the opponents' expenses, including attorneys' fees, incurred in opposing the objectionable conduct, and additional monetary sanctions. Because of its broad applicability to nearly every paper filed in a case and its potential for punishing various forms of poor conduct and slipshod practices, Rule 11 motions have become a widely used, and often abused, tactic; parties have been known to file and win Rule 11 motions directed at an opposing party's Rule 11 motion.

Answer

8.17 Defendants in federal court will ordinarily respond to a complaint with either an "answer" or a "motion to dismiss" (discussed below at paras 8.19–8.20). An answer must admit, deny, or state lack of sufficient information to respond to each of the factual allegations and legal claims of the complaint.[22] In addition, an answer must assert certain affirmative defences, specified in the Federal Rules, or they are waived,[23] unless the court permits the defendant to amend its answer to assert later.[24]

8.18 Under the Federal Rules, most private defendants have 20 days from the date on which process is served upon them to file an "answer" to the complaint.[25] (As a practical matter, extensions of time can usually be obtained fairly readily from the plaintiff or the trial court.) Unlike private litigants, foreign states, including their "agencies and instrumentalities", have 60 days to answer a complaint.[26]

Motion to dismiss

8.19 Rather than answering the complaint, a defendant may present certain defences by "motion". Unlike an answer, a motion does not respond directly to the complaint's basic substantive allegations, but instead asserts some legal bar to the claims. Defences that are most commonly raised by way of motion include lack of subject-matter or personal jurisdiction, insufficiency of service of

21. Fed. R. Civ. P. 11(c).
22. Fed. R. Civ. P. 8(b).
23. Fed. R. Civ. P. 8(c).
24. Fed. R. Civ. P. 15(a).
25. See Fed. R. Civ. P. 12(a).
26. See 28 USC §1608(d) (1998). Under the US Foreign Sovereign Immunities Act, a foreign state's agencies and instrumentalities are defined to include companies that are more than 50 per cent owned by the foreign state: 28 USC §1603(b)(2). See G. Born, *International Civil Litigation in United States Courts*, Ch. 3 (3rd edn, 1996).

process, improper venue, and failure to state a claim on which relief can be granted.[27]

8.20 A motion must be filed within 20 days after service of a complaint on the defendant. If the defendant's motion is subsequently denied, an answer must generally be filed within ten days of the decision.[28]

Counterclaims, cross-claims and third-party complaints

8.21 To avoid unnecessary multiplicity of suits, defendants are permitted to assert claims against the plaintiff, co-defendants or third parties. Under the Federal Rules, a claim by the original defendant against the plaintiff is denominated a counterclaim;[29] a defendant's claim against co-defendants (or a plaintiff's claim against a co-plaintiff) is termed a cross-claim;[30] a defendant's claim against a third party is called a third-party claim.[31] If a claim by the defendant arises out of the subject-matter of the complaint, then the defendant must assert that claim as a counterclaim or cross-claim or it will lose the chance to assert the claim elsewhere in the US.[32]

8.22 Unlike counterclaims, a cross-claim *must* arise out of the subject-matter of the original suit or counterclaim, or relate to property that is the subject of the original suit. The availability of cross-claims is of particular significance to joint tortfeasors, which may cross-claim against each other for contribution in the event liability is assessed in the original suit.[33] In contrast to compulsory counterclaims, there is no fixed time within which a party must present a cross-claim; the decision whether to allow a cross-claim is within the court's discretion.

8.23 Finally, under a procedural device known as impleader, the defendant may file claims against additional parties that the defendant alleges are liable to it for all or part of the plaintiff's claims.[34] The defendant may file its claim against the third party without leave of the court if it does so within ten days after filing the answer; otherwise it must file a motion seeking the court's permission. Unlike compulsory counterclaims, impleader is not mandatory; the defendant may choose to assert its claim in an independent action.

27. Fed. R. Civ. P. 12(b). A motion to dismiss for failure to state a claim asserts that, even assuming that the facts alleged by plaintiff are true, the law provides no basis for relief against the defendant.
28. Fed. R. Civ. P. 12(a).
29. Fed. R. Civ. P. 13(a)–(f).
30. Fed. R. Civ. P. 13(g).
31. Fed. R. Civ. P. 14.
32. Fed. R. Civ. P. 13(a) (compulsory counterclaim).
33. Fed. R. Civ. P. 13(g).
34. Fed. R. Civ. P. 14. Plaintiffs against whom counterclaims have been raised may also implead third parties.

PERSONAL JURISDICTION

8.24 A critical issue in many US pre-trial proceedings—particularly in international cases—is that of personal jurisdiction. A US court must have personal (or *in personam*) jurisdiction over the defendant in order to adjudicate claims against the defendant.[35] Two conditions must be satisfied before a US court may exercise personal jurisdiction: (a) there must be some statutory grant of jurisdiction; and (b) the Due Process Clause of the US Constitution must not prohibit the assertion of jurisdiction. Unless both of these requirements are satisfied, claims against the defendant may not proceed.

Long-arm statutes

8.25 All 50 states have enacted statutes (or court rules) that define the personal jurisdiction of local courts over non-resident defendants, including foreign defendants.[36] Like Order 11 of the Rules of the Supreme Court of England, these so-called "long-arm" statutes set forth the circumstances in which personal jurisdiction may be asserted and service abroad effected.

8.26 As with other laws, state long-term statutes vary significantly from state to state. Nonetheless, two general statutory approaches can be identified. First, a number of states have adopted detailed statutory definitions (similar to Order 11) of personal jurisdiction over non-resident defendants. For example, state long-arm statutes will often authorise local courts to adjudicate claims arising from "transact[ing] any business within the state" or "commit[ting] a tortious act within the state".[37]

8.27 Second, some states have simply incorporated the Due Process Clause by asserting jurisdiction to the limits permitted by that clause. For example, California's long-arm statute provides that "[a] court of this state may exercise jurisdiction on any basis not inconsistent with the constitution of this state or of the United States".[38]

8.28 The decisions of state courts are controlling as to the reach of a state long-arm statute. State courts have often interpreted state long-arm statutes

35. When a US court renders an *in personam* judgment, it may be satisfied out of any of the judgment debtor's assets, wherever located. The judgment is only binding, however, upon the defendant and not upon third parties. *Shaffer* v. *Heitner*, 433 US 186 (1977). Alternatives to personal jurisdiction are *in rem* and *quasi in rem* jurisdiction, which can be exercised to determine the defendant's rights in property within the court's power or to adjucicate other claims that can be satisfied in whole or in part from such property, even if the court lacks personal jurisdiction over the defendant.

36. See G. Born, *International Civil Litigation in United States Courts* 67–70 (3rd edn, 1996); R. Casad, *Jurisdiction in Civil Actions*, §4.01 (2nd edn, 1990). By statute, federal courts have personal jurisdiction over a foreign state, and any agency or instrumentality of a foreign state, that is properly served with process and that is not entitled to foreign sovereign immunity. 28 USC §§1330(b) (1991).

37. See e.g. N.Y. Civ. Prac. Law and Rules §302(a) (McKinney 1998).

38. Cal. Code Civ. Pro. §410.10 (1998).

quite broadly, often reading such laws to authorise jurisdiction to the full limits of the Due Process Clause; this has occurred even as to "laundry-list" style statutes that make no reference to the Due Process Clause. When this happens, most courts have concluded that only a single jurisdictional issue remains—namely, whether a "trial court's exercise of jurisdiction . . . is consistent with the requirements of due process of law under the Constitution of the United States".[39]

Due Process Clause

8.29 As noted above, the Due Process Clause of the US Constitution has been interpreted as limiting the personal jurisdiction of both state and federal courts.[40] In broad outline, the Due Process Clause requires that a defendant have sufficient "minimum contacts" with the forum state so that "maintenance of the suit does not offend 'traditional notions of fair play and substantial justice' ".[41] Whether a defendant has "minimum contacts" often depends on many factual considerations, such as the ownership of property in the forum; representation by an agent in the forum; solicitation of business by mail or telephone in the forum; advertisements in the forum; shipment of products into the forum; or sending officers or employees into the forum. As discussed below, there is a fairly elaborate body of case law that considers whether the "minimum contacts" requirements of the Due Process Clause are satisfied in particular circumstances.

General jurisdiction

8.30 In considering Due Process Clause limits on personal jurisdiction, it is vitally important to ditinguish between "general" and "specific" jurisdiction. "General jurisdiction" is an extremely broad form of personal jurisdiction: it subjects the defendant to suit in the forum's courts on *any claim*. If general jurisdiction exists, it is irrelevant that the claims against the defendant lack any relation to or connection with the forum.[42] As the Supreme Court has explained, general jurisdiction will lie even if the cause of action is not related to the defendant's activities in the state.[43]

39. *Hall* v. *Helicopteros Nacionales de Colombia, SA*, 638 SW2d 870, 871 (Tex. 1982).

40. The Due Process Clause makes no express reference to jurisdictional limits: it provides simply that "No person shall . . . be deprived of life, liberty, or property, without due process of law . . .", US Const. amend. V and XIV. The jurisdictional constraints that have evolved from the Clause are entirely the product of judicial common law.

41. *International Shoe Co.* v. *State of Washington*, 326 US 310, 316 (1945).

42. *Helicopteros Nacionales de Colombia* v. *Hall*, 466 US 408, 414 (1983).

43. *Ibid.* at 414 (citing *Perkins* v. *Benguet Consolidated Mining Co.*, 342 US 437, 446–447 (1952)).

CONTINUOUS AND SYSTEMATIC BUSINESS CONTACTS

8.31 Because the scope of general jurisdiction is so broad, the requirements for establishing this form of jurisdiction are fairly rigorous. The most common basis for establishing general jurisdiction is the continuous and systematic engagement in business activities within the forum state.[44] This standard requires a fairly substantial, ongoing level of business activities, usually involving some physical presence, within the forum. For example, the presence of a branch office or other unincorporated facilities in the forum ordinarily provides a basis for general jurisdiction.[45]

8.32 Contacts falling short of a substantial physical presence seldom provide an adequate basis for general jurisdiction. For example, in *Complaint of Damodar Bulk Carriers, Ltd*, the Ninth Circuit held that the plaintiffs had not satisfied the "stringent standard" of general jurisdiction, even though vessels belonging to the Chilean defendants had made repeated calls to a port within the forum.[46] Although at least one lower court has been willing to assert general jurisdiction based on a non-resident's sales of products to forum residents,[47] sales of unrelated products generally are deemed insufficient to establish general jurisdiction.[48]

CITIZENSHIP, DOMICILE AND INCORPORATION

8.33 General jurisdiction may also be asserted over both citizens and domiciliaries of the forum. "Domicile in the state is alone sufficient to bring an absent defendant within the reach of the state's jurisdiction . . ."[49] Thus, an individual is subject to general jurisdiction at his domicile: for example, an individual residing in New York is subject to personal jurisdiction in New York with respect to claims arising out of his business dealings in California or an automobile accident in London. Similarly, a corporation is subject to general jurisdiction in the state in which it is incorporated.[50]

"TAG SERVICE"

8.34 Some US courts will also assert general jurisdiction over non-resident defendants simply because they are served with process while physically present

44. *Perkins* v. *Benguet Consol. Mining Co.*, 342 US 437, 446–447 (1952); *Complaint of Damodar Bulk Carriers, Ltd*, 903 F.2d 675 (9th Cir. 1990).
45. See e.g. *Ciprari* v. *Servicos Aereos Cruzeiro do Sul, SA*, 232 F. Supp. 433 (DCNY 1964).
46. *Complaint of Damodar* 903 F.2d 675. See also *Shute* v. *Carnival Cruise Lines*, 863 F.2d 1437, 1440 (9th Cir. 1990), *rev'd on other grounds*, 499 US 585 (1991); *Congoleum Corp.* v. *DLW AG*, 729 F.2d 1210, 1242–1243 (9th Cir. 1984).
47. *Eason* v. *Linden Avionics, Inc.*, 706 F.Supp. 311 (DNJ 1989).
48. *Keeton* v. *Hustler Magazine, Inc.*, 465 US 770, 779 (1984) (in dicta suggesting sales of goods may be insufficient to support general jurisdiction); *Scott* v. *Breeland*, 792 F.2d 925 (9th Cir. 1986) (sale of record albums insufficient basis for jurisdiction over band member accused of committing tort).
49. *Milliken* v. *Meyer*, 311 US 457 (1940); Restatement (Second) Conflict of Laws §29 (1971).
50. R. Casad, *Jurisdiction in Civil Actions* §3.02 (2nd edn).

within the forum. Thus, in *Burnham* v. *Superior Court*, a divided Supreme Court held that the Due Process Clause was not violated when the California long-arm statute was iterpreted to permit personal jurisdiction over an individual non-resident defendant *solely* because he was served with process while he was physically present within the forum.[51] Moreover, the court permitted so-called "tag" service to establish jurisdiction even as to claims having no relationship to the forum.

8.35 It is not clear that the *Burnham* case would allow so-called "tag service" over a company based upon service on its officers or directors. A number of lower courts have refused to permit general jurisdiction over a corporate defendant based on tag service upon a corporate representative.[52]

Specific jurisdiction

8.36 Even if a defendant's forum contacts do not justify general jurisdiction, the defendant may nonetheless be subject to jurisdiction with respect to claims that are related to or arise out of the defendant's activities in the forum. "[W]hen a State exercises personal jurisdiction over a defendant in a suit arising out of or related to the defendant's contacts with the forum, the State is exercising 'specific jurisdiction' over the defendant."[53] Due Process standards for specific jurisdiction require a showing that the non-resident defendant purposefully availed itself of the privilege of conducting activities in the forum, that the plaintiff's claim arose from that forum-related activity, and that assertion of jurisdiction is reasonable.[54]

PURPOSEFUL AVAILMENT

8.37 A non-resident defendant can satisfy the purposeful availment requirement even if it does not (and its employees do not) ever physically enter the forum. Instead, the question is whether the defendant deliberately engaged in business activities that had substantial connections with the forum: "It is essential in each case that there be some act by which the defendant purposefully avails itself of the privilege of conducting activities within the forum State, thus invoking the benefits and protections of its laws."[55]

8.38 There is considerable uncertainty over precisely what is required to satisfy the "purposeful availment" test. According to a recent Ninth Circuit decision, "[p]urposeful availment requires that the defendant engage in some form of affirmative conduct allowing or promoting the transaction of business

51. *Burnham*, 495 US 604 (1990).

52. *Amusement Equipment Inc.* v. *Mordelt*, 779 F.2d 264 (5th Cir. 1985); *Scholz Research and Development, Inc.* v. *Kurzke*, 720 F.Supp. 710 (ND Ill. 1989); *Easterling* v. *Cooper Motors, Inc.*, 26 FRD 1 (MDNC, 1960).

53. *Helicopteros*, 466 US at 414, n. 8.

54. See e.g. *T.M. Hylwa, M.D., Inc.* v. *Palka*, 823 F.2d 310 (9th Cir. 1987).

55. *Hanson* v. *Denckla*, 357 US 235, 253 (1957).

within the forum state".[56] "[A] non-resident defendant's act of soliciting business in the forum state will generally be considered purposeful availment if that solicitation results in contract negotiations or the transaction of business."[57]

8.39 It is well settled that the mere foreseeability that a non-resident's products will make their way into the forum is insufficient to satisfy the purposeful availment test. Thus, in *World-Wide Volkswagen Corp.* v. *Woodson*, the Supreme Court declined to permit an Oklahoma court to assert jurisdiction over an East Coast automobile dealer; although it was conceded that the dealer could have foreseen that its mobile products would end up throughout the continental US, the court demanded greater evidence of a deliberate contact with the forum. "[F]oreseeability alone has never been a sufficient benchmark for personal jurisdiction under the Due Process Clause."[58]

8.40 Similarly, in *Asahi Metal Indus.* v. *Superior Court*, the court held that a Japanese manufacturer of motorcycle tyre tube assemblies was not subject to California jurisdiction in an action arising from the alleged malfunction of such an assembly. The Japanese defendant had sold the assemblies to a Taiwanese motorcycle tyre maker, which used the assemblies in tyres, some of which were shipped to California. In a split opinion, four members of the court held that "purposeful availment" did not include merely placing a product into the "stream of commerce", even where it is foreseeable that the products will be distributed in the forum state. Rather, "purposeful availment" requires

> ... designing the product for the market in the forum state, establishing channels for providing regular advice to customers in the forum state, advertising in the forum state, or marketing the products through a distributor who has agreed to serve as the sales agent in the forum state.[59]

"ARISING FROM"

8.41 Specific jurisdiction can only be exercised over claims against the defendant that "arise from" the defendant's contacts with the forum state. For example, a company that distributes only Product A in the forum cannot ordinarily be subject to specific jurisdiction there in a case involving Product B (which it distributes only elsewhere).

8.42 There is some uncertainty as to the precise scope of the "arising from" requirement. In *Carnival Cruise Lines* v. *Shute*, the Ninth Circuit expressly adopted a "but for" test for determining when a claim arises from the defendant's forum contacts: if the plaintiff's claims exist because of the

56. *Shute*, 863 F.2d at 1441.

57. *Ibid.* (citing *Decker Coal Co.* v. *Commonwealth Edison Co.*, 805 F.2d 834, 840 (9th Cir. 1986) and *Sinatra* v. *National Enquirer, Inc.*, 854 F.2d 1191, 1195 (9th Circ. 1988)).

58. *World-Wide Volkswagen Corp.* v. *Woodson*, 444 US 286, 295 (1980).

59. *Asahi*, 480 US 102, 112 (1987). In *Asahi*, Justice Brennan and three other justices defined purposeful availment even less strictly and would include placing products in the "stream of commerce" with knowledge that they will reach the forum state, plus deriving economic benefit from this.

defendant's forum contacts, then the claims are deemed to arise from those contacts.[60] Other Courts of Appeal have adopted more restrictive tests, especially where a tort claim is alleged to "arise from" a contract made in the forum.[61]

REASONABLENESS

8.43 Finally, any assertion of specific jurisdiction must also be "reasonable".[62] According to the Supreme Court, a number of factors bear on the reasonableness of exercising jurisdiction, including the degree of the defendant's purposeful interjection in the forum state's affairs; the burden to the defendant of defending the suit; conflict with the sovereignty of the defendant's state; the forum state's interest in adjudicating the dispute; the interstate judicial system's interest in obtaining the most efficient resolution of disputes; the importance of the chosen forum to the plaintiff's interest in obtaining convenient and effective relief; and the existence of an alternative forum.[63]

8.44 The Supreme Court has emphasised that, where jurisdiction over a *non-US* defendant is involved, particular caution must be exercised: "The unique burdens placed upon one who must defend onself in a foreign legal system should have significant weight in assessing the reasonableness of stretching the long arm of personal jurisdiction over national borders."[64] Nonetheless, it is often difficult successfully to defeat jurisdiction based solely on the reasonableness test. Reasonableness is generally presumed where there are minimum contacts; the defendant must present "a compelling case to rebut it".[65]

8.45 One important recent application of the reasonableness requirement was the *Asahi Metal Indus.* case, discussed above. There, the Supreme Court also held that it was unreasonable for the California courts to assert jurisdiction over a Japanese defendant in an indemnity action by a Taiwanese plaintiff.[66] The court reasoned that California had relatively little interest in resolving a dispute between two foreign parties, and that "great care and reserve should be exercised when extending our notions of personal jurisdiction into the international field".[67]

60. 863 F.2d 1437 (9th Cir. 1990), *rev'd on other grounds*, 499 US 585 (1991). See also *Lanier* v. *American Bd. of Endodontics*, 843 F.2d 901 (6th Cir. 1988) (adopting "but for" test); *Prejean* v. *Sonatrack, Inc.*, 625 F.2d 1260 (5th Cir. 1981).

61. See e.g. *Marino* v. *Hyatt Corp.*, 793 F.2d 427 (1st Cir. 1986).

62. *World-Wide Volkswagen* v. *Woodson*, 444 US 386 (1980).

63. *Ibid.*

64. *Asahi Metal Indus.* v. *Superior Court*, 480 US 102, 114–115 (1987).

65. *Shute*, 863 F.2d at 1445; *Meyers*, 711 F.Supp. at 1007 (district court held that assertion of jurisdiction over non-US defendant in patent case was reasonable).

66. The dispute arose when a California resident was killed because of a malfunctioning tyre jointly manufactured by the Japanese and Taiwanese parties. The California plaintiff's direct claims against the foreign parties settled, leaving only the Taiwanese defendant's indemnity action.

67. 480 US at 115 (quoting *United States* v. *First National City Bank*, 379 US 378, 404 (Harlan J., dissenting)). See G. Born, "Reflections on judicial jurisdiction in international cases", 17 Ga. J. Int'l & Comp. L. 1, 24–25 (1987).

National contacts

8.46 The preceding discussion has considered the level or quantum of contacts that a defendant must have with the forum in order to satisfy the Due Process Clause. Nearly as important is whether the forum is defined as the entire US (a "national contacts" test), or merely an individual state of the union (a "state contacts" test). This distinction can be of considerable practical significance.

8.47 To determine whether or not to apply a national contacts test, the court must first enquire whether there is statutory authority for the court to issue either nationwide or worldwide service of process.[68] Second, the exercise of jurisdiction based on an aggregation of national contacts must comport with the Due Process Clause.[69]

8.48 A number of federal statutes contain provisions explicitly authorising worldwide or nationwide service of process.[70] Thus, virtually all Courts of Appeal have held that where a federal statute permits nationwide service of process on defendants, the question becomes whether the party has sufficient contacts with the United States, not any particular state.[71] Additionally, the Federal Rules of Civil Procedure were recently amended to authorise application of a national contacts standard in federal courts in any case involving claims based on federal substantive law.[72]

8.49 A few courts have also held that a state long-arm statute may supply the necessary statutory authority for applying the national contacts test. For

68. See Fed. R. Civ. P. 4(k)(1)(D).

69. See Fed. R. Civ. P. 4(k)(2).

70. See J. Moore, J. Lucas, H. Fink and C. Thompson, *Moore's Federal Practice* ¶4.33 (2nd edn, 1988) (listing statutes).

The Supreme Court has rejected the argument that R. 4 of the Federal Rules of Civil Procedure should be interpreted as establishing a general federal long-arm standard in federal question cases. In *Omni Cap. Int'l* v. *Rudolf Wolff & Co.*, 484 US 97 (1987), British defendants moved to dismiss the claims against them for lack of personal jurisdiction. The plaintiff conceded that the state long-arm statute did not encompass defendants' contacts with the state, and the court construed the relevant federal statute as neither explicitly nor implicitly providing for nationwide service of process. The court declined to fill in the interstices of federal statutory law by creating a rule to authorise service on an alien in a federal question case where the alien is not amenable to service under the applicable state long-arm statute. Although the court recognised that such a narrowly tailored service of process provision might serve statutory purposes, it concluded that it is for Congress or those who propose the Federal Rules of Civil Procedure, rather than the federal courts, to create such a rule. *Ibid.* at 97.

71. G. Born, *International Civil Litigation in United States Courts*, 173–182 (3rd edn, 1996). See *Securities Investor Protection Corp.* v. *Vigman*, 764 F.2d 1309, 1315 (9th Cir. 1985) (aggregating nationwide contacts in Securities Exchange Act suit) (citation omitted); *Fitzsimmons* v. *Barton*, 589 F.2d 330, 333 (7th Cir. 1979) (same); *Go-Video, Inc.* v. *Akai Elec. Co.*, 885 F.2d 1406 (9th Cir. 1989) (antitrust laws); *Meadows* v. *Dominican Republic*, 628 F.Supp. 599 (ND Cal. 1986) (Federal Sovereign Immunities Act suit); *United States* v. *Toyota Motor Corp.*, 561 F.Supp. 351 (CD Cal. 1983) (federal tax statute).

72. Fed. R. Civ. P. 4(k)(2). R. 4(k)(2) provides: "If the exercise of jurisdiction is consistent with the Constitution and laws of the United States, serving a summons or filing a waiver of service is also effective, with respect to claims arising under federal law, to establish personal jurisdiction over the person of any defendant who is not subject to the jurisdiction of the courts of general jurisdiction of any state."

example, in *Cryomedics, Inc.* v. *Spembly, Ltd*, the district court applied a national contacts test in a federal patent case after borrowing an expansive state long-arm statute.[73] Other courts, however, have refused to rely upon a state long-arm statute to aggregate the foreign defendant's contacts with the entire US for the purpose of asserting personal jurisdiction, even in cases based upon substantive federal law.[74] It appears that no court has sought to use a national contacts test where both a state's substantive law and its long-arm statute are involved.[75]

8.50 Virtually all lower courts have held that the Due Process Clause permits the use of a national contacts test in cases where a federal long-arm statute specifically authorises a federal court to aggregate the defendant's contracts.[76] Indeed, most lower courts have concluded that the Due Process Clause is not offended when a federal court relies upon an expansive state long-arm statute in applying a national contacts test.[77] It is doubtful, however, whether a state court could constitutionally apply a national contacts test.

Consent to jurisdiction

8.51 US courts will also accept personal jurisdiction based upon a defendant's consent to litigate in the forum.[78] In *National Equipment Rental, Ltd* v. *Szukhent*, the Supreme Court held that the Due Process Clause does not prevent a party from knowingly consenting to suit in a specified forum.[79] Some lower courts will strain, particularly in consumer contracts, to overturn consent-to-jurisdiction clauses on grounds of unconscionability, lack of notice and the like.[80] But where sophisticated commercial entities are involved, such results are unlikely.

Jurisdiction based upon corporate affiliation

8.52 In limited circumstances, a US court may also assert personal jurisdiction over a non-US parent corporation based solely upon the fact that the defendant owns a US subsidiary. Courts have held that a non-US parent is not subject to jurisdiction solely on the basis of the local activities of a US subsidiary—even a 100 per cent owned subsidiary—if the subsidiary is carrying on its own business

73. 397 F.Supp. 287 (D. Conn. 1975). See also *In re United Rope Distributors, Inc.* v. *Seatriumph Marine Corp.*, 930 F.2d 532 (7th Cir. 1991) (dicta).

74. *Johnson Creative Arts, Inc.* v. *Wool Masters, Inc.*, 743 F.2d 947, 950 (1st Cir. 1984); *Max Duetwyler Corp.* v. *R. Meyer*, 762 F.2d 290, 295–297 (3d Cir. 1985).

75. *Wells Fargo & Co.* v. *Wells Fargo Express Co.*, 556 F.2d 406, 416–419 (9th Cir. 1977).

76. *Securities Investor Protection Corp.*, above.

77. *Wells Fargo, supra.*

78. However, a litigant generally may not consent to subject-matter jurisdiction.

79. 375 US 311 (1964). *Accord Carnival Cruise Lines, Inc.* v. *Shute*, 499 US 585 (1991); *The Bremen* v. *Zapata Off-Shore Co.*, 407 US 1 (1972).

80. *Colonial Leasing Co.* v. *Pugh Bros. Garage*, 735 F.2d 380 (9th Cir. 1984). But see *Carnival Cruise Lines*, 499 US 585 (1991), and *Spradlin* v. *Leursiegler Management Services Co., Inc.*, 926 F.2d 865 (9th Cir. 1991).

and has a measure of independence from the parent. On the other hand, if the local subsidiary is a "mere department" or "alter ego" of its foreign parent—determined with respect to common ownership and personnel, financial and operational control, and disregard for corporate formalities—a court will exercise jurisdiction over the parent.[81]

8.53 Particularly in antitrust cases, the trend in the US has been in the direction of greater jurisdictional reach. Any significant showing that the subsidiary's business is closely integrated with the parent's may well result in a finding that the parent is doing business in the US.[82] In the absence of an alter ego relationship, some courts will exercise jurisdiction over a foreign parent on an agency theory if the local subsidiary conducts all of the business in the forum that the parent would conduct if it were present.[83]

SERVICE OF PROCESS

Service under federal rules

8.54 Service of process is another common area of pre-trial dispute, especially in international cases. In the federal courts, original "process" is a summons identifying the court and the parties, and specifying the time within which the defendant must respond and the consequences of failing to do so.[84] Service of process itelf does not confer personal jurisdiction (except arguably in the case of tag jurisdiction), subject-matter jurisdiction or proper venue. Conversely, even when jurisdiction exists and venue is proper, a plaintiff's failure to comply with applicable service of process rules will lead to dismissal of the complaint.[85] An objection to improper service of process will be waived unless asserted in a defendant's answer or motion to dismiss.[86]

8.55 In federal court, service must be made in the manner prescribed by the Federal Rules. Service may be made on most individual or corporate defendants by personal delivery, registered mail, or in any manner prescribed by the law of the state in which the court sits.[87]

8.56 For service outside the United States, service under the Federal Rules shall be made by any internationally agreed means "reasonably calculated to

81. *Volkswagenwerk AG* v. *Beech Aircraft Corporation*, 751 F.2d 117, 120–122 (2d Cir. 1984).

82. G. Born, *International Civil Litigation in United States Courts*, 151–170 (3rd edn, 1996).

83. *Frummer* v. *Hilton Hotel, Int'l, Inc.*, 19 NY2d 533 (1967). See *Wells Fargo*, 556 F.2d at 422–424.

84. Fed. R. Civ. P. 4(a) and (b). When service is made pursuant to state rules, process may consist of a summons, notice or order in lieu of summons. See Fed. R. Civ. P. 4(b).

85. See Fed. R. Civ. P. 12(b)(4) and (5). Dismissal will ordinarily be "without prejudice" to plaintiff's right to file the suit again and to seek to effect proper service. But if the plaintiff is unable to serve the defendant in the manner prescribed, or if the limitation period for the action has expired in the mean time, dismissal can mean the end of the action.

86. See Fed. R. Civ. P. 12(h)(1).

87. Fed R. Civ. P. 4(e) and 4(h).

give notice", such as the Convention on Service Abroad of Judicial and Extrajudicial Documents in Civil or Commercial Matters ("Hague Service Convention") or other applicable treaty, provided that the applicable treaty prescribes the exclusive means of service.[88] If an "internationally agreed means" of service is not available, or if such a means is non-exclusive, then service may be effected

(a) in the manner permitted by foreign law in the place where service must be effected;
(b) as directed by a foreign authority;
(c) by personal delivery to an individual (but not a corporation), unless prohibited by foreign law;
(d) by return receipt mail, unless prohibited by foreign law; or
(e) by other means "not prohibited by international agreement" as directed by the district court.[89]

Revised Rule 4(d) also sets forth "waiver of service" provisions, which provide the foreign defendant with an extended period to answer if it agrees to waive formal service of process.[90]

Hague Service Convention

Background

8.57 Service of process in international matters is often affected by the Hague Service Convention.[91] The Hague Service Convention came into force for the US in 1979. The UK and most other EC Member States are signatories to the Convention. The Convention applies only to "civil or commercial matters" and to "judicial or extrajudicial documents".[92]

8.58 The Hague Service Convention establishes a mechanism for service of US civil process on persons within the territory of other signatories to the Convention. Under the Convention, service usually begins with a written request by the plaintiff's attorney, who is a "judicial officer" within the meaning

88. Fed. R. Civ. P. 4(f)(1).

89. Fed. R. Civ. P. 4(f)(2) and (f)(3). It is generally held that the Hague Service Convention is exclusive, where service within a state that has ratified the Convention is concerned. Of course, the Convention itself may permit a wide range of service mechanisms, depending upon the reservations and local law of the state of destination.

90. Fed. R. Civ. P. 4(d); see G. Born and A. Vollmer, "The effect of the revised Federal Rules of Civil Procedure on personal jurisdiction", *Service and Discovery in International Cases*, 150 FRD 221 (1993).

91. 20 USC 361, TIAS No. 6638.

92. Hague Service Convention, Art. 1. There is some debate in the US over the precise scope of the Convention. It is clear that criminal proceedings are not civil or commercial matters within the meaning of the Convention. It also seems clear that the Convention applies principally to service of documents that initiate (e.g. complaints) or terminate (e.g. judgments) a lawsuit. Other documents are commonly served on the US lawyers representing the party in the case.

of the Convention.[93] The letter of request is prepared in the form prescribed by the Convention and attaches the US summons and complaint; these documens must be submitted to the "central authority" of the nation in which service is to be made. The central authority is required to review the letter of request for compliance with the Convention and promptly inform the applicant of any defect.[94] If the letter of request is in proper form, the foreign central authority will either effect service itself or through the appropriate local court[95] and will transmit a certificate of service to the plaintiff's attorney.[96]

8.59 A foreign central authority may refuse a request for service if it fails to meet the formal requirements of the Convention[97] or if "compliance would infringe [the requested state's] sovereignty or security".[98] Service will be refused if the letter of request and underlying documents are not in the appropriate language or accompanied by an accurate translation as required by the foreign state. Service may also be refused if the letter of request concerns matters that are not "civil or commercial" or seeks service of documents that are not "judicial or extrajudicial" within the Convention's meaning.

8.60 The Hague Service Convention provides several alternatives to the use of the central authority to effect service. Provided that a signatory state does not object, Article 10(c) permits service "by postal channels", and Article 10(b) and 10(c) permits "judicial officers, officials or other competent persons of the foreign state to effect service". Article 8 permits diplomatic and consular agents to make service abroad on their own nationals, and, if a signatory state does not object, to others located in that state.

Exclusivity of Hague Service Convention

8.61 As noted above, US courts generally have held that service of process within the territory of a signatory of the Hague Service Convention must comply with the procedures of the Convention, unless the other country has agreed to permit service by other means. The US Supreme Court has expressly held that the Hague Service Convention is the exclusive mechanism for serving process *into* nations that are party to the Convention.[99] Because the Convention is a treaty of the US, it is the "supreme law of the land", and therefore pre-empts—or overrides—inconsistent state and federal service rules. In the words of the Supreme Court, "By virtue of the Supremacy Clause, US Const. Art. VI, the Convention pre-empts inconsistent methods of service prescribed by state law in

93. Hague Service Convention, Art. 3.
94. *Ibid.*, Art. 4.
95. *Ibid.*, Art. 5.
96. *Ibid.*, Art. 6.
97. *Ibid.*, Art. 4.
98. *Ibid.*, Art. 13.
99. *Volkswagenwerk AG* v. *Schlunk*, 486 US 694 (1988).

all cases to which it applies".[100] Thus, a foreign defendant may only be served in a signatory state in a manner that is consistent with the Hague Service Convention; service that is inconsistent with the Convention is invalid as a matter of US law, even if it was effected pursuant to a rule of local US law.

Service by mail under Article 10(a)

8.62 An issue involving service in countries that are parties to the Hague Convention is whether service by mail is permitted. A number of lower courts have held that the Hague Service Convention permits service of process by registered mail. These courts have relied on Article 10(a) of the Convention, which reads in relevant part as follows:

> Provided that the state of destination does not object, the present Convention shall not interefere with—
>
> (a) the freedom to *send judicial documents*, by postal channels, directly to persons abroad ...
>
> (emphasis supplied)

A number of signatories to the Convention have not objected to the provisions of Article 10(a) concerning "the freedom to send judicial documents by postal channels".

8.63 There is a significant division of authority among the lower US courts concerning Article 10(a). A number of courts have held that, where no objection by the receiving state exists, service by mail is effective under Article 10(a). These decisions have generally reasoned that a nation's failure to object to the provisions of Article 10(a) indicates a willingness to permit service by mail.

8.64 On the other hand, a number of other courts have held that Article 10(a) is not a service of process provision. These courts have emphasised that the language of Article 10(a) does not authorise "service" or process, as several other sections of the Convention do, but instead refers only to the "sending" of other judicial documents. The lower courts that adopt this position also have emphasised that the service mechanisms of the Hague Service Convention are straightforward and expeditious, and that when the central authority mechanisms are followed, US courts respect the sovereignty of foreign nations.[101]

100. *Ibid.* p. 2108. See *Vorhees* v. *Fischer & Krecke*, 697 F.2d 574 (4th Cir. 1983); *Harris* v. *Browning-Ferris Indus. Chem. Serv.*, 100 FRD 775 (MD La. 1984); *Kadota* v. *Hosogai*, 608 P.2d 68 (Az. App. 1980).

101. *Bankston* v. *Toyota Motor Corp*, 889 F.2d 172 (8th Cir. 1989); *Mommsen* v. *Toro Co.*, 108 FRD 444, 446 (SD Iowa 1985); *Reynolds* v. *Koh*, 109 AD 2d 97, 490 NYS 2d 295 (1985); *Ormandy* v. *Lynn*, 122 Misc.2d 954, 472 NYS 2d 274 (NYS Ct 1984); *Cooper* v. *Makita*, 117 FRD 16 (D Me. 1987).

Schlunk: circumventing the Convention

8.65 In *Volkswagenwerk AG* v. *Schlunk*, the Supreme Court held that the Hague Service Convention did not apply to service effected within the US upon a foreign defendant.[102] Moreover, the court held that local law defined when service was fully effected within the US. The court affirmed a lower court decision permitting service upon Volkswagen AG (a German company) by means of serving Volkswagen AG's US subsidiary, reasoning that local Illinois law permits substituted service upon a foreign parent by means of serving its US subsidiary, when the subsidiary is shown to be merely the "alter ego" of the parent. The court held that, because service could be effected entirely within the US, there was no need for service "abroad"—and thus that the Hague Service Convention was simply not implicated. One lower court has extended *Schlunk* to permit substituted service within the US on a foreign company by means of service on a local secretary of state.[103]

FORUM SELECTION: VENUE, *FORUM NON CONVENIENS* AND REMOVAL

Venue

8.66 Under US law, venue refers to the place where an action may properly be brought. Venue rules are designed to ensure that litigation will generally proceed in the most convenient forum, particularly for defendants. Because of its federal system, US venue rules are often complex. Nonetheless, the Alien Venue Act (discussed below) usually prevents venue from being a significant issue in international litigation.

8.67 In the federal courts, a federal question case may be brought only where all the defendants reside, where the claim arose, or as otherwise provided by law.[104] A diversity case may be brought where all the plaintiffs or all the defendants reside or where the claim arose;[105] in addition, a corporation may be sued where it is incorporated, licensed to do business or doing business.[106] These restrictions can create significant obstacles and complexities in domestic US litigation.

8.68 Under the Alien Venue Act, however, a non-US citizen ("an alien") may be sued in any district.[107] The Supreme Court has held that this venue provision overrides more restrictive venue rules contained in specific statutes like the

102. 486 US 694.
103. *Melia* v. *Les Grands Chais de France*, 135 FRD 28 (DRI 1991).
104. 28 USC §1391(b) (West Supp. 1998).
105. 28 USC §1391(a) (West Supp. 1998).
106. 28 USC §1391(c) (1993).
107. 28 USC §1391(d) (1993). Special provisions govern venue over a foreign state or any agency or instrumentality of a foreign state. See 28 USC §1391(f) (1982).

patent laws.[108] As a consequence, venue is typically not a significant issue in cases against non-US defendants.

8.69 A federal court may dismiss an action if venue is improper in the plaintiff's chosen forum. More commonly, however, the court will transfer the case to a proper federal forum. Even if venue is proper, a federal court may transfer the case to another more convenient federal forum.[109] Federal trial judges have very broad discretion in granting or denying such transfers. As with personal jurisdiction, improper venue will be waived if no objection is included in the defendant's answer to the complaint or filed before an answer in the defendant's motion to dismiss.[110]

Forum non conveniens

8.70 A foreign defendant sued in a US forum may sometimes be able to dismiss the complaint on grounds of "*forum non conveniens*". The common law doctrine of *forum non conveniens* gives the trial court discretion to evaluate the practical inconveniences posed to the litigants of litigating in one forum rather than another.[111] The court seeks to determine not only the inconvenience to the defendant of plaintiff's forum choice, but the relative advantages and disadvantages to all parties of each available forum. In making its determination, the court will consider factors relating both to the private interests of the litigants and to the public interest. These factors include the residence and nationality of the parties; the convenience to the parties and witnesses of ligitating in one forum or another; the location of the evidence; the benefits of local determination of localised controversies; and the potential for avoiding unnecessary problems in interpreting and applying foreign law.[112]

8.71 The classic *forum non conveniens* case is *Piper Aircraft & Co.* v. *Reyno*,[113] where the Supreme Court upheld a *forum non conveniens* dismissal of an action arising from an aeroplane crash in Scotland. The plaintiffs—the survivors of several Scottish citizens and residents killed in the crash—filed suit in US federal court against the US manufacturers of the aircraft. The trial court dismissed the case because of the close connections between the action and Scotland: the decedents' heirs were Scottish; the crash occurred in Scotland; the pilot was Scottish; and a large portion of the relevant evidence was located in the

108. *Brunette Machine Works* v. *Kockum Indus. Inc.*, 406 US 706 (1972).

109. A federal statute specifically authorises federal courts to transfer cases to other federal courts in the interest of justice and convenience: 28 USC §1404(a) (1993).

110. See Fed. R. Civ. P. 12(b)(3), 12(h)(1).

111. The discussion in this section deals with *forum non conveniens* in the federal court. Most, but not all, states have *forum non conveniens* doctrines, but they may differ somewhat from the federal doctrine.

112. See *Gulf Oil Corp.* v. *Gilbert*, 330 US 501, 508–509 (1947). The *forum non conveniens* doctrine does not permit the defendant entirely to escape the burden of litigating, since a prerequisite to dismissal is the existence of an adequate alternative forum. Rather, the doctrine compels the plaintiff to pursue its action in a forum that may be more favourable to the defendant.

113. 454 US 235 (1981).

UK. The Supreme Court agreed, concluding that the US nationality of the aircraft manufacturers was insufficient to justify permitting a case with such extensive connections with the UK to proceed in the US, the forum preferred by the plaintiffs because of its more favourable law.[114]

8.72 The *forum non conveniens* doctrine rests largely on the discretion of the trial judge. "The *forum non conveniens* determination is committed to the sound discretion of the trial court. It may be reversed only where there has been a clear abuse of discretion."[115] There are, however, a number of important guidelines that govern *forum non conveniens* analysis.

8.73 First, a defendant has a much better chance of obtaining *forum non conveniens* dismissal if the plaintiff is not a US citizen or company. A US plaintiff's choice of forum is ordinarily entitled to considerable deference: "a plaintiff's choice of forum should rarely be disturbed ... [Only] when trial in the chosen forum would establish ... oppressiveness and vexation to a defendant ... out of all proportion to plaintiff's convenience" is dismissal appropriate.[116] In contrast, however, no deference is afforded to the plaintiff's choice of forum if the plaintiff is not an American.[117] (A few courts have suggested that a foreign plaintiff can "win" a measure of deference if it shows that its choice of a US forum was motivated solely by reasons of convenience.[118])

8.74 Second, *forum non conveniens* analysis devotes virtually no attention to the substantive laws applicable in different fora. In *Piper*, for example, the court granted a *forum non conveniens* dismissal, notwithstanding the fact that Scottish law was far less favourable to the plaintiffs than the applicable US law. "The possibility of a change in substantive law should ordinarily not be given conclusive or even substantial weight in the *forum non conveniens* inquiry."[119] Only if the alternative foreign forum provides "no remedy at all", are changes in substantive law relevant.[120]

8.75 Third, even if the balance of convenience weighs in favour of dismissal, a trial court cannot dismiss a case on *forum non conveniens* grounds unless the plaintiff can obtain relief in another forum. As noted above, the alternative forum requirement will only bar dismissal if the plaintiff will be effectively deprived of any remedy. For example, if the alternative forum will not permit the plaintiff's claim to be raised or the remedy available is so inadequate as to

114. *Ibid.*, at 260–261. Similarly, in *Pain* v. *United Technologies Corp.*, 637 F.2d 775 (DC Cir. 1980), the court upheld dismissal on *forum non conveniens* grounds of a suit by French, Norwegian, British, American and Canadian plaintiffs arising out of a crash in the North Sea of a helicopter manufactured in the US, but owned and operated in Norway. See also *In re Union Carbide Corporation Gas Plant Disaster at Bhopal*, 634 F.Supp. 842 (SDNY 1986).

115. *Piper Aircraft Co.* v. *Reyno*, 454 US 235, 256, 257 (1981).

116. *Ibid.*, at 241 (quoting *Koster* v. *Lumbermens Mut. Cas. Co.*, 330 US at 524 (1947).

117. See *ibid.*, at 251–252; *Pain* v. *United Technologies Corp*, 637 F.2d 775, 795–796 (DC Cir. 1980).

118. *Nieminen* v. *Breeze-Eastern*, 736 F.Supp. 580 (DNJ 1990); *Cliffs-Neddrill Turnkey Int'l Organjestad* v. *M/T Rich Duke*, 734 F.Supp. 142 (D Del. 1990).

119. *Piper Aircraft*, 454 US at 247.

120. *Ibid.*, at 254–255.

amount to no remedy at all, then the alternative forum requirement will not be satisfied.[121] But a reduced likelihood of recovery or less favourable measure of damages will not prevent dismissal.

Raising and proving issues of foreign law

8.76 Rule 44.1 governs the procedure for raising the applicability of, and the method of proving, foreign law. Rule 44.1 requires that a party that contends, by virtue of applicable conflict of laws rules, that a cause of action be determined by foreign law must "give notice by pleadings or other reasonable written notice" to this effect. This notice requirement will be satisfied by a simple statement that foreign law is applicable. That statement may be included in the complaint, a responsive pleading (the matter often will be raised as one of the public interest factors in a *forum non conveniens* motion) or, to leave no doubt of the adequacy of the form of notice, in a separate document filed with the court and served on the other parties.[122]

8.77 Although there is no hard and fast rule concerning the timeliness of a Rule 44.1 notice, it is advisable for a litigant to file one fairly early in the case—as soon as it has decided on its theory of the case and what substantive law it wants the court to apply. A litigant that waits to raise an issue of foreign law, especially to the eve of trial, runs the risk that the court will find the notice untimely and refuse to apply foreign law.

8.78 Questions of foreign law are considered to be issues of law, to be decided by the court and reviewable *de novo* on appeal. Rule 44.1 authorises the judge to ascertain the content of foreign law in any way he or she determines is appropriate, including affidavits, live expert testimony, and independent research.

PRE-TRIAL PROCEEDINGS: THE SPECTRE OF DISCOVERY

Introduction and scope of discovery

8.79 US procedural rules permit a litigant to obtain "discovery" both from its adversary and from third-party witnesses (i.e. persons that are not plaintiffs or defendants in the lawsuit). As is well known, discovery under the Federal Rules is extremely broad. Indeed, the breadth of US discovery accounts in significant part for the deep concern with which most foreign parties view US litigation.

8.80 The Federal Rules entitle a party to discover any "non-privileged"

121. *Ibid.*, at 254. In the *Laker* antitrust suit, the US trial court took the view that the doctrine of *forum non conveniens* was inapplicable because the British courts have no power to adjudicate a claim under the US antitrust laws. See *Laker Airways Ltd.* v. *Pan American World Airways*, 568 F.Supp. 811 (DDC 1983).

122. C. Wright and A. Miller, *Federal Practice and Procedure*, §2443 (1995 and 1998 Supp.). Other, more informal methods of notice often are also acceptable. *Ibid.*

information that is relevant to the subject matter of the lawsuit.[123] Discovery may relate to any claim or defence of the party seeking discovery (or any other party), or may be designed merely to ascertain the existence or location of relevant documents or "persons having knowledge of any discoverable matter".[124] The Federal Rules of Civil Procedure expressly provide that "[t]he information sought need not be admissible at the trial if the information sought appears reasonably calculated to lead to the discovery of admissible evidence".[125] Even the trial preparation materials of a party or his or her lawyer may be discovered, but only on a showing of special need. State discovery procedures are generally similar.

8.81 Under 1993 amendments to the Federal Rules, the parties must, without awaiting a discovery request, meet and then disclose all potential witnesses and documents which may be "relevant to disputed facts alleged with particularity in the pleadings ... based on the information then reasonably available" to them.[126] Similarly, the parties must produce a computation of damages, applicable insurance contracts and the names of potential expert witnesses. These "initial disclosures" may be altered (within certain limits) by local district court rules, order of the individual judges or by the parties' stipulation.

Discovery mechanisms

8.82 The principal discovery methods available under US procedure are written interrogatories, requests for production of documents, requests for admission and depositions upon oral examination.[127] All of these procedures are available to obtain discovery from parties; third parties can only be required to produce documents and submit to depositions. A party ordinarily initiates discovery by seeking answers to interrogatories and document production, then takes depositions, and concludes with requests for admission. The procedures can be used, however, in any sequence the party chooses. With the exception of interrogatories, unless the court orders or the local rules of the judicial district stipulate otherwise, the number of discovery requests made by a party is unlimited.[128]

8.83 Federal discovery rules provide only limited time for responding to

123. "Parties may obtain discovery regarding any matter, not privileged, which is relevant to the subject matter involved in the pending action ..." Fed. R. Civ. P. 26(b)(1). The most frequently asserted privilege is the attorney–client privilege, which shields from discovery certain communications between lawyers and their clients. Other privileges recognised in many US jurisdictions protect confidential communications between physicians and their patients, between spouses, and between accountants and their clients.

124. Fed. R. Civ. P. 26(b)(1).

125. Fed. R. Civ. P. 26(b)(1).

126. Fed. R. Civ. P. 26(a)(1), 26(f).

127. Fed. R. Civ. P. 30, 33, 34 and 36. Other available discovery methods are requests for permission to enter on land or other property; requests for physical or mental examination of a party; and depositions on written questions. Fed. R. Civ. P. 31, 34 and 35.

128. Fed. R. Civ. P. 26(b)(2) and 33.

discovery requests. Unless the court otherwise orders, the time for responding to interrogatories, document requests, and requests for admission is only 30 days or, in the case of defendants, 45 days after service of the complaint, whichever is longer;[129] depositions may be scheduled on any "reasonable" notice.[130] As a practical matter, however, courts routinely grant extensions of time to respond to discovery requests. Although parties should not necessarily count on receiving more than one 30-day extension, 60 or even 90-day extensions are not uncommon. Courts can also be persuaded to defer all discovery (or all discovery except that relating to specified issues) pending determination of jurisdictional and other threshold dispositive motions.[131]

8.84 Access to discovery provided in US litigation ordinarily is not restricted to the parties and court personnel. Absent a confidentiality agreement among the parties or entry of a "protective order" by the court, any member of the public (including representatives of government agencies, competitors or newspaper reporters) can inspect and obtain copies of responses to discovery from court files or from any party, witness or lawyer for a party or witness who is willing to provide it. Ordinarily documents produced in discovery will not be filed with the court, unless used to support a motion or offered into evidence at trial. In addition, courts will sometimes dispense with filing of responses to discovery and deposition transcripts to save filing space.[132] But again, absent a protective order, parties, witnesses and their lawyers are free to make information obtained in discovery publicly available.

Interrogatories

8.85 The discovery mechanism that litigants typically utilise first is interrogatories. Indeed, a plaintiff will often serve interrogatories together with the complaint. Interrogatories are written questions to which a party must respond in writing under oath. Interrogatories often seek identification of documents and witnesses. When the answer to an interrogatory can be obtained from business records of a party, and the burden of obtaining an answer from the records is substantially the same for either party, it is a sufficient answer for a party to make the relevant records available for inspection and copying. Answers to interrogatories are ordinarily admissible in evidence against the responding party at trial as admissions.[133] Accordingly, as a practical matter, answers, although responsive, are usually brief and as noncommittal as possible.

129. Fed. R. Civ. P. 33(b), 34(b) and 36(a).
130. Fed. R. Civ. P. 30(b).
131. C. Wright and A. Miller, *Federal Practice and Procedure*, at §§2009, 2040 n. 6–12.
132. Fed. R. Civ. P. 5(d).
133. Fed. R. Civ. P. 33.

Document requests

8.86 Perhaps the single most important discovery mechanism under US procedural rules is the document request. Under the Federal Rules, a litigant can require either parties or non-parties to produce for inspection and copying all non-privileged documents relating to the litigation.

8.87 Requests for production of documents are often, but not invariably, served together with interrogatories. Although the rules require that a request for production describe "each item and category" of documents requested "with reasonable particularity", US courts routinely approve far broader requests than those permitted, for example, under English procedure. A request for "all documents relating to the special audit of X date" would be unobjectionable so long as the subject-matter of the audit is relevant to the lawsuit. When accompanying interrogatories, document requests often simply demand production of "all documents identified in, used in the preparation of, or relating to" the interrogatory answers. Documents must be produced either in the form kept in the ordinary course of business or organised and labelled to correspond to the request.[134]

Depositions

8.88 The Federal Rules permit litigants in civil suits to take depositions of any party or non-party witness. A deposition is the oral questioning of an individual (the "deponent") by the lawyers of the other parties. The deponent is sworn to tell the truth and the deposition generally is transcribed verbatim by a stenographer or is videotaped. If it is otherwise admissible under general evidentiary rules, a deposition transcript may be used at trial.

8.89 A deposition typically is initiated by a notice from one party to all other parties setting forth the name and address of the witness and the time and place of the examination.[135] A deposition can be scheduled on any "reasonable" notice and at any place specified by the requesting party. In practice, time and place are usually negotiated between the parties before or shortly after the notice is served.

8.90 The deposition of a party, an officer, director, managing agent or designee of a party, or any witness not available to testify in person[136] may be used at trial or at an interlocutory hearing against parties with reasonable notice of the deposition. Statements made in a deposition can be used to contradict or

134. Fed. R. Civ. P. 34(b).

135. If a party does not know the identity of the employees of a corporation or other entity with knowledge of a particular subject, it may, in the notice or subpoena, name the corporation or entity as the deponent. The corporation or entity must then designate one or more witnesses who consent to testify on its behalf concerning the subject in question. Fed. R. Civ. P. 30(b)(6).

136. In addition to unavailability by reason of death, injury, illness or imprisonment, a witness is considered unavailable if he or she is more than 100 miles from the place of trial or hearing or is outside the US, and if the absence was not procured by the party offering the deposition: Fed. R. Civ. P. 32(a)(3).

impeach the deponent's testimony as a witness (or in any other manner permitted by the rules of evidence). Certain objections to using a deposition as evidence at trial may be made on any ground that would permit excluding evidence given by a trial witness.[137]

Admissions

8.91 Under the Federal Rules, a party may serve other parties with written requests for the admission of any relevant matters. Each matter whose admission is requested is deemed admitted, unless the requested party answers or objects. An answer must either deny the matter or detail the reasons why the answering party cannot truthfully admit or deny it. Any matter admitted is deemed conclusively established for purposes of the pending action (but not for any other purpose).[138]

Non-party discovery

8.92 Much pre-trial discovery is directed at, and obtained from, other litigants in the lawsuit in question. Nonetheless, under the Federal Rules, a party may also take discovery from non-party witnesses—that is, persons not named as parties to the action. The principal mechanism for accomplishing this is by "subpoena", which is served on the person or company from whom discovery is sought. A subpoena may require the witness to appear at a deposition and testify, produce documents, or both. Failure to comply with a subpoena, without seeking relief from the court, is punishable as contempt of court.

8.93 Although subpoenas are technically issued under the seal of the court, they are usually issued in blank by the court, and are completed and served by litigants without judicial approval. Unlike discovery requests directed against parties, a subpoena must be served by hand or mail on the witness himself. In the federal courts, a subpoena may only be issued by the court in the district where the deposition is to be taken. Absent a special court order, a subpoena may only require the witness to attend a deposition within 100 miles of the place where the witness resides, is employed or transacts business, or is served.[139]

8.94 Although a subpoena will direct a witness to appear at a particular place and time, the actual place and time of the appearance of the witness is often negotiated in advance of issuance of the subpoena between counsel for the party issuing the subpoena and the witness. Unlike parties, third-party witnesses cannot be required to answer written interrogatories or respond to requests for admission.

137. Fed. R. Civ. P. 32.

138. Fed. R. Civ. P. 36(b). A party may seek the leave of court to withdraw or amend an admission.

139. Fed. R. Civ. P. 45(c)(3).

RESISTING DISCOVERY

8.95 Pre-trial discovery is often highly contentious. Parties seeking discovery typically make the broadest requests conceivable, and persons from whom discovery is sought often resist nearly all the adverse parties' demands. These disagreements are usually settled by negotiations between the parties' counsel, but on occasion the trial judge (or a magistrate) will become involved.

8.96 A party can refuse to respond to interrogatories, document requests or requests for admission by delivering a statement of objections to the requesting party.[140] Objections can be based on relevance, burdensomeness or privilege, as well as on several grounds of particular interest to foreign litigants, as discussed below. However, a party cannot properly avoid appearing to testify without filing a motion for a protective order requesting such relief with the court.[141]

8.97 A non-party witness (as opposed to a party) may resist compliance with a subpoena by serving objections within 14 days of service.[142] A witness may file a motion to "quash" or modify the subpoena on the grounds that it fails to allow reasonable time for compliance, requires a non-party to travel more than 100 miles, requires disclosure of privileged or other protected matter or subjects a person to undue burden.[143] Ordinarily, the recipient of a subpoena will proceed via the objection route, which forces the adverse party to seek a court order compelling compliance.

8.98 As noted above, a number of grounds are available for resisting discovery. A person from whom discovery is sought may seek a protective order against "annoyance, embarrassment, oppression, or undue burden or expense".[144] The application of these terms is left largely to the trial court's discretion; it is safe to say, however, that many discovery demands that foreign litigants regard as "annoying" or "oppressive" will routinely be approved by US judges. For "good cause shown", the court may order that discovery not take place or that discovery take place only on specified terms and conditions, including a designation of the time, place, form or scope. A protective order may also require that discovery take place with no one present, except persons designated by the court, that a deposition be sealed, or that a trade secret or other confidential information must not be disclosed, or be disclosed only in a designated way.[145]

140. Fed. R. Civ. P. 33(b) (interrogatories), 34(b) (document requests), 36(a) (requests for admission).

141. See Fed. R. Civ. P. 26(c). The same requirement applies to a deponent who wishes to limit or terminate questioning at a deposition. Fed. R. Civ. P. 30(d).

142. Fed. R. Civ. P. 45(c)(2)(B).

143. Fed. R. Civ. P. 45(c)(3)(A). In international cases, territorial principles may significantly limit the power of a court to compel attendence of a witness or production of documents under Federal Rule 45. See G. Born, *International Civil Litigation in United States Courts*, 864–66 (3rd edn, 1996). These territorial limitations, however, do not generally apply to US citizens or residents located abroad. 28 USC §1783.

144. Fed. R. Civ. P. 26(c).

145. Fed. R. Civ. P. 26(c).

8.99 If a person fails to provide requested discovery, the requesting party may move for an order compelling discovery.[146] If a party then fails to comply with an order compelling discovery, the court may "make such orders in regard to the failure as are just".[147] The trial court has broad discretion in rendering such orders. Among other things, a court may order that particular facts be deemed established in favour of the party seeking discovery; that the disobedient party not be permitted to support or oppose designated claims or defences or to introduce designated matters in evidence; that certain pleadings or parts of pleadings be stricken; that further proceedings by stayed until the order is obeyed; that the action (or defence) be dismissed; that a default judgment be entered; that the failure to comply be treated as contempt of court (and punished by monetary fine); or that the disobedient party or its attorney pay the reasonable expenses, including attorneys' fees, incurred as a result of the failure to comply.[148]

8.100 A third-party witness who fails "without adequate excuse" to obey a subpoena may be held in contempt of court.[149] The penalty for contempt is imprisonment, fine or both.[150]

EXTRATERRITORIAL DISCOVERY

8.101 In principle, the Federal Rules authorise the discovery of materials located outside US territory, just as they authorise discovery within the US. As one Court of Appeal has observed, "[i]t is no longer open to doubt that a federal court has the power to require the production of documents located in foreign countries if the court has *in personam* jurisdiction of the person in possession or control of the material".[151] Countless lower US courts have used this authority to order extraterritorial discovery from foreign companies.[152]

8.102 Two requirements must be satisfied before a US court will order direct extraterritorial discovery from a foreign party under the Federal Rules of Civil Procedure. First, the party from whom discovery is sought must be subject to the

146. Under the Federal Rules, the district court can require the party or witness who loses the motion, as well as the advising lawyer, to pay the reasonable expenses incurred in connection with the motion, including attorneys' fees, unless the court finds that the making of or opposition to the motion "was substantially justified, or that other circumstances make an award of expenses unjust" Fed. R. Civ. P. 37(a)(4).

147. Fed. R. Civ. P. 37(b)(2)

148. Fed. R. Civ. P. 37(b).

149. Fed. R. Civ. P. 45(e).

150. 18 USC §§401–402 (West Supp. 1998).

151. *United States* v. *First National City Bank*, 396 F.2d 897, 900–901 (2d Cir. 1968). See Restatement (Third) Foreign Relations Law of the United States §442(1)(a) (1987) ("A court ... in the United States, when authorised by statute or rule of court, may order a person subject to its jurisdiction to produce documents, objects, or other informatiion relevant to an action ... even if the information or the person in possession of the information is outside of the United States.").

152. *United States* v. *Vetco, Inc.*, 691 F.2d 1281 (9th Cir. 1981); see G. Born, *International Civil Litigation in United States Courts* 856–870 (3rd edn, 1996).

personal jurisdiction of the forum court. Second, if the discovery of documents is requested, the foreign party must "control" those documents,[153] while if depositions are sought, then the deponents must be "officers, directors or managing agents" of the foreign corporate party.[154] Similar, but more rigorous, requirements apply to non-party witnesses.

Document discovery outside the US

8.103 With one important exception, discovery may not be compelled from either a party or a non-party witness unless that person is subject to the personal jurisdiction of the forum court.[155] The standards of jurisdiction applicable to parties are those set forth above (paras 8.24–8.53), while those applicable to non-parties are solely those set forth in case law interpreting and applying the Due Process Clause.

8.104 The Federal Rules permit broad discovery of documents located outside the US from both parties[156] and non-party witnesses[157] subject to US jurisdiction. A party that is subject to the court's jurisdiction must provide discovery of documents that are within its "possession, custody or control".[158] A corporation is presumed to control all corporate documents and records, whether they are located inside or outside the US.[159] Corporations with unincorporated offices or branches both within and outside the US will ordinarily be required to produce documents located in both their US and non-US offices.[160]

8.105 United States corporations can be compelled to produce documents held by their subsidiaries, including both US and foreign subsidiaries. The

153. *United States* v. *Vetco, Inc.*, 691 F.2d 1281 (9th cir. 1981); see G. Born, *International Civil Litigation in US Courts* 856, 858–859 (3rd edn, 1996).

154. See C. Wright and A. Miller, *Federal Practice and Procedure*, at §2103. Lower-level employees are treated as non-party witnesses, whose depositions can be compelled only if they are independently subject to the jurisdiction and subpoena service of the District Court. *Ibid.* Nonetheless, as a practical matter, it is often difficult to avoid "voluntary" production of important fact witnesses even if they are lower-level employees.

155. *In re Sealed Case*, 832 F.2d 1268 (DC Cir. 1987); *United States* v. *First National City Bank*, 396 F.2d 898 (2d Cir. 1968); *In re Uranium Antitrust Litigation* 480 F.Supp. 1138 (ND Ill. 1979). This requirement that personal jurisdiction exists does not apply to jurisdictional discovery, as discussed below.

156. Fed. R. Civ. P. 34(a).

157. Fed. R. Civ. P. 45; see C. Wright and A. Miller, *Federal Practice and Procedure*, §2454, (1995).

158. Fed. R. Civ. P. 34(a).

159. *In re Grand Jury Subpoena Addressed to Canadian International Paper Company*, 72 F.Supp. 1013 (SDNY 1947) ("The fact that a corporation's records and documents are physically located beyond the confines of the United States does not excuse it from producing them if they are in its possession and the court has jurisdiction of the corporation."); *United States* v. *First National City Bank*, 396 F.2d 897 (2d. Cir. 1968); *First National City Bank* v. *IRS*, 271 F.2D 616, 618 (2d Cir. 1959); *Elder-Beerman Stores Corp.* v. *Federated Dept. Stores, Inc.*, 45 FRD 515 (SDNY 1968).

160. See C. Wright and A. Miller, *Federal Practice and Procedure*, §2210, at 401 (1994). Cf. *In re Grand Jury, 81–2*, 550 F.Supp. 24 (WD Mich. 1982) (Deutsche Bank ordered to comply with subpoena served on New York branch requesting production of documents from Frankfurt offices).

rationale is that a corporation controls its subsidiaries, and hence their documents.[161] In contrast, foreign corporations with no links to the US generally may not be required to produce documents held abroad solely because a US subsidiary of the parent is subject to the US court's personal jurisdiction. Nonetheless, discovery probably can be obtained from a foreign parent if the US subsidiary and foreign parent have substantially overlapping officers or directors, and the documents relate to the activities of the subsidiary as well as the parent.[162]

8.106 Non-party witnesses can also be required to produce documents that are within their possession, custody and control. In order to obtain document discovery from non-party witnesses, however, those persons must be subject both to the personal jurisdiction and the subpoena power of the court. For foreign entities, the latter requirement generally means that service must be effected within the judicial district where the district court is located.[163] Even where service can be effected, US courts are sometimes reluctant to order non-party discovery of evidence located in foreign offices of a foreign company, even if the company also has offices or branches in the US.[164]

Depositions of corporate personnel located abroad

8.107 Under the Federal Rules, a corporate party can be required to produce for deposition any "officers, directors, or managing agents" with knowledge of the dispute.[165] This obligation extends to persons outside, as well as within, the US.[166] In contrast, as noted above, a corporation cannot be compelled to produce lower-level employees for deposition; corporate employees are treated as non-party witnesses and a party desiring to depose an employee must proceed by way of subpoena.[167]

161. *United States* v. *Vetco*, 644 F.2d 1324 (9th Cir. 1981); *In re Investigatioin of World Arrangements*, 13 FRD 280, 285 (DDC 1952).

162. *In re Uranim Antitrust Litigation*, 480 F.Supp. 1138, 1144 (ND Ill. 1979). See also *Société Internationale* v. *McGremery*, 111 F.Supp. 435, 440–442 (DDC 1953) (requiring production because of "interlocked web of corporate organisation, management and finance"), *aff'd*, *Société Internationale* v. *Brownwell*, 225 F.2d 532, 536 (DC Cir. 1955), *rev'd on other grounds*, *Société Internationale* v. *Rogers*, 357 US 197, 204 (1958).

163. Fed. R. Civ. P. 45. As described below, the so-called Walsh Act permits service of a subpoena outside of the territorial jurisdiction of the district court, and indeed, outside of the US, in specified circumstances. 28 USC §1783.

164. See e.g. *Laker Airways Ltd* v. *Pan American World Airways*, 607 F.Supp. 324 (SDNY 1985). In *Laker*, the District Court quashed subpoenas *duces tecum* served on the New York offices of Midland Bank and Samuel Montague & Co. The subpoenas demanded production of documents located in the British offices of both companies. The District Court held that it would be "inappropriate" to order discovery of the documents because they were regularly maintained in Britain and because the US offices of the two companies had no involvement in the subject-matter of the litigation.

165. Fed. R. Civ. P. 30(b)(6).

166. See *In re Anschuetz & Co.*, 754 F.2d 602, 617 (5th Cir. 1985) (US district court has power to order depositions within the US of persons located outside the US).

167. C. Wright and A. Miller, *Federal Practice and Procedure*, §2103 (1994).

8.108 The attendance of a non-party witness at a deposition requires service of a subpoena on the witness.[168] If the witness is a corporation subject to the court's jurisdiction and to service, it can be required to produce its officers, directors, and managing agents for deposition—even if they are located overseas. Failure to produce corporate officers, directors or managing agents (but not employees) for deposition will result in sanctions against the corporation.

8.109 Finally, the so-called Walsh Act authorises US courts to issue subpoenas to US nationals or "resident[s] of the United States who are in a foreign country".[169] In civil cases, a subpoena may issue only if "necessary in the interest of justice" and if there is no other way to obtain the documents or testimony.[170] The Walsh Act ordinarily will not permit discovery from foreign companies or their personnel, if discovery is not otherwise available under the Federal Rules.

Compelled discovery from third parties not subject to US jurisdiction

8.110 The Federal Rules only permit a federal court to compel discovery from non-party witnesses when they are subject to the federal court's jurisdiction and to subpoena service. In all other cases, the Hague Evidence Convention or customary letters rogatory provide the only mechanism for obtaining compelled discovery abroad.

8.111 The Hague Convention on the Taking of Evidence Abroad in Civil or Commercial Matters ("Hague Evidence Convention"),[171] came into force for the US in 1979. The Convention was intended to provide an internationally acceptable framework for litigants to obtain evidence abroad in civil or commercial litigation. The UK and most other European nations are also party to the Convention.

8.112 The Convention's basic mechanism for evidence-taking is the "Letter of Request" procedure of Articles 1–14. Under these provisions, Convention signatories are obliged to establish "central authorities"—governmental departments responsible for receiving incoming letters of request from foreign nations and arranging for them to be executed. A litigant may request the dometic court in which its suit is pending to send a letter of request—seeking production of specified materials or other evidence—to the central authority in the country where the sought-after evidence is located. The foreign central authority is then obliged to forward the letter of request to the foreign court where the witness is located; that court then conducts an evidentiary proceeding and returns the completed letter of request to the requesting court. In executing a letter of

168. Fed. R. Civ. P. 30(a), 45.
169. 28 USC §1783 (1994).
170. 28 USC §1783(a), (1994).
171. 23 USC 2555, TIAS No. 744.

request, the receiving court will ordinarily follow its own rules of procedure and practice.[172]

8.113 In general, the Convention *requires* signatory states to fulfil all properly completed letters of request. The Convention establishes only limited exceptions to this obligation. First, a signatory country may refuse to execute letters of request in the very limited circumstances in which its "sovereignty or security are threatened".[173] Second, and more importantly for litigants in US courts, a signatory country may declare under Art. 23 that it "will not execute letters of request issued for the purpose of obtaining pre-trial discovery of documents as known in common law countries".[174] Most signatories to the Convention have issued some sort of declaration under Art. 23.

Relationship between Hague Evidence Convention and Federal Rules

The Aerospatiale decision

8.114 Until 1987, US courts were sharply divided over the effect of the Hague Evidence Convention on the discovery methods of the Federal Rules that are available where the court possesses personal jurisdiction over the witness. In *Société Nationale Industrielle Aerospatiale* v. *US District Court*,[175] the Supreme Court ended this disagreement. First, the court rejected the suggestion that the Convention is wholly inapplicable to discovery from abroad where the recipient of the discovery request is subject to US personal jurisdiction and could be required under the Federal Rules to produce materials in the US; the court specifically held that the Convention was available for both party and non-party discovery. Second, the court held that the Convention was *not* the exclusive means of discovering evidence located in the territory of a foreign signatory nation and "did not deprive the District Court of the jurisdiction it otherwise possessed" under the Federal Rules.[176] The court emphasised that the Convention provided merely "optional procedures" and did not "require any contracting state to use" those procedures. Finally, the court concluded that the Convention *must* be used in certain circumstances, which are defined by the doctrine of international comity.[177]

8.115 The court divided over what comity requires. A five-justice majority concluded that comity calls for a case-by-case weighing of foreign and US "interests", and certain other factors, to ascertain when first use of the Convention is mandated. This comity analysis required lower courts to consider a variety of factors to determine whether extraterritorial discovery pursuant to the Convention should be required, including:

172. Art. 9.
173. Art. 12.
174. Art. 23.
175. 482 US 522 (1987).
176. *Ibid.*, p. 540.
177. *Ibid.*, pp. 543–546.

(a) the sovereign interests of the US;
(b) the sovereign interests of the concerned foreign nation;
(c) the scope and intrusiveness of the requested discovery;
(d) the likelihood that resort to the Convention's procedures would be effective in a given case; and
(e) the difficulties that a foreign party would encounter if forced to comply with US-style discovery.[178]

The court specifically refused to provide guidance for the application of these factors in specific cases: "We do not articulate specific rules to guide this delicate task of adjudication."[179]

Post-Aerospatiale decisions

8.116 Recent lower-court decisions applying *Aerospatiale* have provided a measure of additional guidance as to when the Convention, rather than the Federal Rules, must be used to obtain extraterritorial discovery.[180] A number of lower courts have held that the party that urges first use of the Convention bears the burden of demonstrating that comity requires this. At least one lower court has reached the opposite conclusion.[181]

8.117 The majority of post-*Aerospatiale* decisions have *not* required first use of the Convention.[182] These decisions have relied on the perception that discovery under the Federal Rules is quicker and more effective than Convention discovery.[183] Lower courts have also tended to place a relatively low value upon foreign sovereign interests.[184]

8.118 Despite this, foreign litigants have obtained some benefits from raising the Convention as a defence to US-style direct discovery. Thus, lower US courts have usually ordered direct discovery under the Federal Rules *only after*

178. *Ibid.*, pp. 545–546.
179. *Ibid.*, p. 546.
180. See Born and Hoing, "Comity and the Lower Courts: Post-Aerospatiale Applications of the Hague Evidence Convention", 24 Int'l Law. 393 (1990).
181. *Hudson* v. *Hermann Pfauter GmbH & Co.*, 117 FRD 33 (NDNY 1987).
182. *Bedford Computer Corp.* v. *Israel Aircraft Indus., Ltd*, 1990 Bank LEXIS 964 (US Bankr. NH 15 Feb 1990) (documents from Israel); *Great Lakes Dredge & Dock Co.* v. *Harnischfeger Corp.*, 1990 US Dist. LEXIS 12843 (ND Ill. 1990) (depositions from Germany); *Haynes* v. *Kleinwefers*, 119 FRD 335 (EDNY 1988) (interrogatories and document requests from Germany); *Rich* v. *KIS Cal., Inc.*, 121 FRD 254 (MDNC 1988) (interrogatories from France); *Benton* v. *Uddeholm Corp.*, 118 FRD 386 (DNJ 1987) (interrogatories and document requests from Sweden); *Scarminach* v. *Goldwell GmbH*, 531 NYS 2d 188 (NY Sup. Ct 1988) (interrogatories and document requests from Germany); *Sandsend Financial Consultants* v. *Wood*, 743 SW 2d 364 (Tex. App. Houston 1988) (deposition and document request from Channel Islands). But see *Hudson* v. *Hermann Pfauter GmbH & Co.*, 127 FRD 33 (NDNY 1987).
183. *Benton*, 118 FRD at 391.
184. *Rich*, 121 FRD at 258; *Benton* 118 FRD at 391.

requiring a narrowing of the breadth, intrusiveness and burdensomeness of the relevant discovery requests.[185] As one lower court has declared,

> expansive discovery without concomitant relevance is not what the court envisioned when it handed down the *Aerospatiale* decision . . . I believe that a number of the requests are not "simple" [as required by *Aerospatiale*] and may require streamlining if we are to proceed under the federal rules.[186]

Impact of "blocking" and bank secrecy laws on discovery outside the US

8.119 A number of countries have enacted so-called "blocking" statutes to forbid US courts access to evidence on foreign soil.[187] In general, these statutes make it a crime to disclose certain information or documents to third parties, including foreign government authorities or litigants. Some such statutes are self-executing, while others (like the Protection of Trading Interests Act) apply only if a foreign government enters specific orders concerning particular discovery disputes. Many countries also have bank secrecy laws which forbid banks or bank officials from disclosing client records or information without their customers' consent.

8.120 It goes without saying that the target of a US discovery request that conflicts with another country's blocking statute is in a difficult situation. Violation of the blocking statute may result in serious penalties, while non-compliance with a US discovery order may result in equally harsh sanctions, including fines or imprisonment for contempt, dismissal of the complaint or entry of a default judgment.

8.121 United States courts are not entirely insensitive to the harshness that results from conflicting legal obligations. In determining whether to order discovery or impose sanctions for non-compliance with a discovery request, courts usually will consider constraints imposed by blocking statutes.[188] A representative lower-court decision is *United States* v. *Vetco Inc.*,[189] a case involving enforcement of an IRS subpoena seeking documents in Switzerland. In *Vetco*, the court held that it "must balance competing interests" in deciding

185. *Benton*, 118 FRD at 390; *Rich*, 121 FRD at 260; *Scarminach*, 531 NY 2d at 191; *Bedford Computer Corp.*, 1990 Bankr. LEXIS 964.

186. *Benton*, 118 FRD at 390.

187. Examples of countries with bank secrecy laws which could affect discovery include: Australia (1979 Banking Statute of Australia, §23); Bahamas (Banks and Trust Companies Regulation Act 1965, §10, 1965 Bah. Act No. 64, as amended by the Banks and Trust Companies Regulation (Amendment) Act 1980,§10, 1980 Bah. Act No. 3); Bermuda (Evidence Act 1905 §59); Cayman Islands (The Confidential Relationships (Preservation) (Amendment) Law 1979); Liechtenstein (Banks and Savings Law of December 21, 1960); Panama (Banking Law of Panama, Rep. of Panama); Singapore (Banking Act, §42); Switzerland (Swiss Penal Code, Art. 273 (1971); Law on Banks and Savings Associations, Art. 47, 8 November 1934)).

188. See Restatement (Second) of Foreign Relations Law of the United States, §40 (1965); Restatement (Third) of Foreign Relations Law of the United States, §442 (1986).

189. 691 F.2d 1281, 1286–1291 (9th Cir. 1981); see *United States* v. *First Nat'l. Bank of Chicago*, 699 F.2d 341 (7th Cir. 1983) (US interest in collecting taxes must be balanced against Greece's bank secrecy law; remanding to district court for determination).

whether to order extraterritorial discovery in violation of foreign law. The factors balanced by the court included the "vital national interests" of the US and Switzerland, the "extent of hardship" suffered by the defendant, the "location" of the documents, the defendant's nationality, the "importance of the documents" and the "availability of alternative means of compliance". Weighing these various factors, the court ordered discovery. It emphasised that any IRS summons reflects a strong governmental interest, that the Swiss defendants were owned by a US company and that Switzerland had expressed no particular interest in the case.

8.122 Courts enjoy broad discretion to impose sanctions, notwithstanding a blocking statute. As a practical matter, trial judges show no sympathy for litigants that fail to make every reasonable effort to comply with discovery orders. At a minimum, a litigant seeking to avoid sanctions must produce all relevant information and documents consistent with the blocking statute's restrictions and must make reasonable efforts to obtain a waiver of blocking restrictions.[190] A litigant that solicits imposition of a blocking order or that removes documents to a jurisdiction with blocking restrictions will likely face severe sanctions.[191]

Jurisdictional discovery

8.123 There is one important exception to the general rule that a person must be subject to the forum's personal jurisdiction before the court may order discovery. This exception relates to so-called jurisdictional discovery, which is directed solely at obtaining facts needed to determine whether a defendant is subject to the court's jurisdiction.

8.124 Disputes over personal jurisdiction are often decided solely on the basis of the parties' pleadings and written affidavits concerning jurisdictional facts. Nonetheless, district courts possess broad discretion to order discovery into facts relevant to personal jurisdiction over the defendant.[192] After allowing such discovery, the district judge may permit additional written submissions or conduct an evidentiary hearing on jurisdiction.

8.125 The decision whether or not to allow jurisdictional discovery generally lies within the discretion of the trial court. Plaintiffs ordinarily are entitled to conduct discovery on the issue of personal jurisdiction, provided that they have

190. See *Société Internationale pour Participations Industrielles et Commerciales, SA* v. *Rogers*, 357 US 197 (1958) (upholding order for production of documents but rejecting sanction of dismissal against plaintiff who attempted in good faith to obtain waiver of Swiss bank secrecy law).

191. *In re Marc Rich & Co., AG* 707 F.2d 663 (2d Cir. 1983); see also *United States* v. *Bank of Nova Scotia ("Bank of Nova Scotia II")*, 740 F.2d 817 (11th Cir. 1984); *United States* v. *Bank of Nova Scotia ("Bank of Nova Scotia I")*, 691 F.2d 1384 (11th Cir. 1982); *United States* v. *Vetco*, 644 F.2d 1324 (9th Cir. 1981); *SEC* v. *Banca della Svizzeria Italiana*, 92 FRD 111 (SDNY 1981).

192. For example, in *Oppenheimer Fund, Inc.* v. *Sanders*, 437 US 340, 351 n. 13 (1978), the Supreme Court observed that "where issues arise as to jurisdiction or venue, discovery is available to ascertain the facts bearing on such issues". See also *United States* v. *United Mine Workers*, 330 US 258, 292 n. 57 (1947); C. Wright and A. Miller, *Federal Practice and Procedure*, §2009 (1994).

alleged a plausible basis for jurisdiction over the defendant, and there are disputed issues of fact. One Court of Appeal has held that, "[d]iscovery may appropriately be granted where pertinent facts bearing on the question of jurisdiction are controverted or where a more satisfactory showing of the facts is necessary".[193] Courts typically will grant leave to conduct jurisdictional discovery if a *prima facie* showing of jurisdiction has been made—that is, if the plaintiff alleges facts that would support a colourable basis for jurisdiction.[194]

8.126 Jurisdictional discovery will be denied if the plaintiff has failed to allege a credible basis for jurisdiction, or if there is no reason to believe the plaintiff will succeed in establishing jurisdiction.[195] Additional criteria relevant to the availability of jurisdictional discovery are the complexity of the facts, the extent to which facts are within the defendant's control, the extent to which the plaintiff has availed itself of opportunities to establish jurisdictional facts, and the degree to which the defendant has submitted evidence of no US contacts.[196]

8.127 Finally, although the plaintiff ordinarily must show affirmatively that the defendant is subject to personal jurisdiction,[197] the precise weight of this burden depends upon the plaintiff's opportunity to conduct jurisdictional discovery. If jurisdictional discovery has been conducted, then the plaintiff must generally show by a preponderance of the evidence that the defendant is subject to personal jurisdiction; if no such discovery is made available, then only a *prima facie* showing of jurisdictional facts is required.[198]

Effects of jurisdictional discovery on general discovery

8.128 The presence of an unresolved, dispositive jurisdictional issue does not necessarily bar general discovery on other issues, but trial courts have discretion to stay discovery on the merits until the jurisdictional question is resolved.[199] In the words of one leading commentator,

> ... the court has discretion to stay discovery on other issues until [a] critical issue [that is in dispute] has been decided. In accordance with this principle ... a court may decide that in a particular case it would be wise to stay discovery on the merits until challenges to jurisdiction have been resolved.[200]

193. *Data Disc*, 557 F.2d 1280, 1285 n. 1 (9th Cir. 1977).

194. *In re Marc Rich & Co.*, 707 F.2d 663, 670 (2d. Cir. 1983) (party seeking jurisdictional discovery must demonstrate "a reasonable probability that ultimately it will succeed in establishing the facts necessary for the exercise of jurisdiction"); *Insurance Company of the State of Pennsylvania* v. *Centaur*, 590 F.Supp. 1187, 1189 (SDNY 1984).

195. See, e.g. *Compagnie des Bauxites de Guinée* v. *L'Union*, 723 F.2d 357, 362 (3d Cir. 1983); *Shaw* v. *Boyd*, 658 F.Supp. 89 (ED Pa. 1987).

196. See *Kamen* v. *American Tel. & Tel. Co.*, 791 F.2d 1006 (2d Cir. 1986) (error to deny plaintiff jurisdictional discovery based upon conclusory and hearsay statements offered by defendant); "Use of Discovery to Obtain Jurisdictional Facts", 59 Va. L. Rev. 533 (1973).

197. *Data Disc*, 557 F.2d at 1285; *Pena*, 563 F.Supp. at 746.

198. *Data Disc*, 557 F.2d at 1285.

199. C. Wright and A. Miller, *Federal Practice and Procedure*, at §§2009 n. 25, 2040 n. 76 (1994).

200. Wright and Miller, at §2040.

PRE-TRIAL CONFERENCES AND SCHEDULING ORDERS

8.129 During the pre-trial phase of a case, the judge will ordinarily convene one or more pre-trial conferences. The purposes of pre-trial conferences are to expedite disposition of the case, establish early and continuing control of the case by the judge, discourage wasteful pre-trial activities, improve the quality of trial and facilitate settlement.[201] Within 120 days after filing of the complaint, the court will consult with counsel for the parties and enter a scheduling order setting time limits for joining additional parties, amending pleadings, filing motions and completing discovery.[202] Thereafter, one or more pre-trial conferences may be held to formulate and simplify the issues in the case; to avoid unnecessary proof (such as proof of the authenticity of documents); to rule in advance on the admissibility of evidence; to explore settlement possibilities; to schedule exchange of any pre-trial briefs; and to deal with other matters that may expedite disposition of the action.[203] A final pre-trial conference will be held close to the time of trial to devise a plan for the trial and a programme for facilitating the admission of evidence.[204]

8.130 After any pre-trial conference, a scheduling or pre-trial order will be entered reciting the actions taken and governing the subsequent proceedings.[205] Failure to comply with a scheduling or pre-trial order will subject a party or its lawyer to the same sanctions as failure to comply with a discovery order.[206] The final pre-trial order will sometimes include a recitation of stipulated facts, issues in dispute, and witnesses and documents to be presented at trial. Efforts to dispute stipulated facts, raise new issues, or present additional witnesses or documents at trial will be rejected, absent a showing of extraordinary circumstances.

GARY B. BORN
JOSEPH R. PROFAIZER

201. Fed. R. Civ. P. 16(a).
202. Fed. R. Civ. P. 16(b).
203. Fed. R. Civ. P. 16(c).
204. Fed. R. Civ. P. 16(d).
205. Fed. R. Civ. P. 16(e).
206. Fed. R. Civ. P. 16(f).

CHAPTER 9

ARBITRATION IN BANKING AND FINANCE

INTRODUCTION

9.1 Not long ago, many bankers and lawyers considered arbitration of financial disputes as somewhat of a non-subject. In contrast to commercial transactions[1] and insurance agreements,[2] where arbitration clauses have long been used to reduce litigation costs and the risk of "hometown justice" in the other side's courts, international credit agreements generally provide that disputes will be subject to the jurisdiction of courts in the lender's country.

9.2 The banker's traditional preference for judges over arbitrators should not be surprising. First, a debtor's default usually results from simple inability or unwillingness to pay, rather than any honest divergence in the interpretation of complex or ambiguous contract terms. Arbitration therefore may appear as an unnecessary invitation to a "split the difference" award, reminiscent of King Solomon's famous threat to cut the baby in two.[3] Second, financial institutions with a security interest over a debtor's assets will usually find it easiest to bring a court action where the pledged property is located. Finally, going to court may also give the lender the benefit of summary procedures for the enforcement of promissory notes and other commercial paper obligations.[4]

9.3 Herd mentality and respect for custom provide other clues to understanding the banker's hesitation with respect to private adjudication. Not without good reason, the financial sector has tended to be conservative, wary of rapid change. If suing borrowers before judges rather than arbitrators has worked

1. See generally W. Laurence Craig, William W. Park & Jan Paulsson, *International Chamber of Commerce Arbitration.*

2. See, e.g., *Quackenbush* v. *Allstate Ins. Co.*, 116 S.Ct. 1712 (1996) (motion to compel arbitration in federal court; abstention in favour of state court not appropriate); *US Fire Insurance Co.* v. *National Gypsum*, 101 F.3d 813 (2d Cir. 1996) (arbitration of insurance coverage of bodily injury claims against asbestos producers; issue preclusive effect of court decision must be arbitrated).

3. Of course, when Solomon called for a sword to divide the infant, he was rendering only an interim award, designed to discover the real mother. See I Kings 3:24–25.

4. See, e.g., French Nouveau Code de Procédure Civile, Art. 1405(2) (formerly Code de Commerce, Art. 641) providing the courts with power to order an *injonction de payer* with respect to promissory notes.

well enough in the past, few bankers will buck the trend without a very good reason.[5]

9.4 More and more, however, the financial community is finding benefits in arbitration, particularly in connection with securities transactions, guarantees, documentary credits, consumer loans, and public sector lending.

9.5 Several factors explain the increase in financial arbitration, particularly among American financial institutions:

(i) the multilateral treaty network for the enforcement of arbitral awards;
(ii) the arbitrator's ability to ignore "Act of State" defences arising from foreign exchange controls; and
(iii) the risk of excessive American jury awards with respect to both punitive damages and "lender liability" claims.[6]

The interaction of these factors with other elements of financial transactions will determine when and how arbitration may (or may not) be appropriate to the resolution of banking and securities controversies.

9.6 To the extent that arbitration promotes respect for bargains between creditor and debtor, it commends itself not only to the bankers' self interest, but also as a matter of sound international economic policy. The greater the risk in loan recovery, the higher the interest rate. Because loans are loans, not gifts, untrustworthy enforcement mechanisms will tend to chill cross-border economic cooperation to the detriment of those countries that depend most on foreign capital for development.

LOAN ENFORCEMENT

9.7 At the outset, arbitration should be distinguished from other non-judicial forms of alternative dispute resolution currently in vogue. Arbitration implies not only the consent of the parties to settle their dispute out of court, but also bindingness of result. On the strength of an arbitral award, assets can be attached and competing litigation precluded. By contrast, neither mediation

5. One is reminded of Winston Churchill's warning, "We must beware of needless innovation, especially when guided by logic", House of Commons, 17 December 1942, replying to a suggested renaming of certain cabinet positions on the ground that their titles were not logical. For an analysis of factors that explain deference to the past even when it may be inefficient, See Mark J. Roe, "Chaos and evolution in law and economics", 109 *Harvard Law Review* 641 (1996).

6. Samuel Johnson commented on the salutary effects of looming catastrophe: "Depend upon it, Sir, when a man knows he is to be hanged in a fortnight, it concentrates his mind wonderfully." (Letter to Boswell of 19 September 1777, cited in Boswell's *Life of Johnson*, p. 167).

nor conciliation is legally binding, and may end up being little more than foreplay to litigation.[7]

Treaties

9.8 Bankers sometimes must enforce judgments in their favour against assets located outside the country where the judgment was rendered. For example, an American bank that obtained a favourable judgment in New York against a foreign borrower might have to seek its enforcement against property in Europe, Asia or Latin America.

9.9 Unfortunately, not all banks will benefit from an adequate treaty network for the recognition of foreign judgments. Although the Brussels and Lugano Conventions bless many European nations with a sound mechanism to enforce each other's court judgments,[8] these treaties will be of no avail in recovering loans against assets in non-treaty countries. Moreover, no treaties at all exist for the enforcement of American judgments abroad.[9] While the domestic law of some countries might as a matter of "comity" enforce a foreign judgment,[10] not all legal systems will be so generous.[11]

9.10 On the other hand, a worldwide network of bilateral[12] and multilateral[13] treaties provides for the enforcement of arbitral awards. The most

7. Dispute resolution possessing a moral force only will be more effective in a closely knit, ethnically homogeneous community with repeat dealings among community members, rather than among culturally diverse and mutually suspicious (or even hostile) commercial actors. See Jerold Auerbach, *Justice Without Law* (1983); Lisa Bernstein, "Opting out of the legal system: Extralegal contractual relations in the diamond industry", 21 J. Leg. Stud. 115 (1992).

8. See, e.g., Arts 13–17, Brussels Convention on Jurisdiction and Enforcement of Judgments in Civil and Commercial Matters, 27 September 1968, as amended, 1990 OJ (C189) 1, and Lugano Convention on Jurisdiction and Enforcement of Judgments in Civil and Commercial Matters, 16 September 1988, 1988 OJ (L319) 9.

9. The United States' failure to conclude any judgments treaty derives in part from our trading partners' apprehension over punitive damages, civil juries, contingency fees and other quaint aspects of the American judicial system. See generally William W. Park, *International Forum Selection*, 46–49 (1995).

10. See, e.g., A.V. Dicey & J.H.C. Morris, *The Conflict of Laws*, 418–508, Rules 35–53 (Lawrence Collins (ed.), 11th edn, 1987); Uniform Foreign Money Judgments Act 13 ULA 261 (1962); Restatement (Third) of Foreign Relations Law, §481 (1987); Restatement (Second) of Conflict of Laws, §98 (1988).

11. See, e.g., Wetboek van Burgerlijke Rechtsvordering [Code Civ. Proc.] Art. 431(1) (Netherlands) ("Except for provisions of Articles 985–94 [concerning treaties] decisions rendered by foreign judges or public deeds executed outside the Netherlands cannot be enforced in the Netherlands.") (Translation by Albert Jan van den Berg). See also Danish Code of Civil Procedure §223–a. Chinese procedure apparently conditions judgment enforcement on an explicit "judicial entrustment" of the judgment by a foreign court to a People's Republic of China tribunal. See Zhonghua Renmin Gongheguo Guowuyuan Gongbao [Foreign Economic Contract Law] Art. 204, published in 6 *People's Republic of State Council Gazette* 207 (1982) (discussed in Andrew Coy-Nung Cheng, "Enforcement of foreign arbitral awards in the People's Republic of China", 34 *American Journal of Comparative Law*, 295, 317 (1986)).

12. See Rudolf Dolzer & Margrete Stevens, *Bilateral Investment Treaties* (1995).

13. See discussion below of New York, Panama and Washington Conventions.

important of these treaties is the New York Arbitration Convention,[14] which requires courts of 120 Contracting States to enforce written arbitration agreements[15] and the resulting awards,[16] subject only to a limited litany of defences related to procedural matters such as the validity of the arbitration agreement, the opportunity to be heard, and the limits of the arbitral jurisdiction.[17]

9.11 Many Latin American countries have also adopted the Inter-American Arbitration Convention, often referred to as the Panama Convention. The Inter-American Convention mirrors much of the New York Arbitration Convention, albeit with a more limited enforcement scheme.[18]

9.12 In addition, the Washington Convention has established an arbitration procedure under the auspices of the World Bank's International Centre for the Settlement of Investment Disputes ("ICSID"),[19] covering disputes arising out of investment contracts between a host state and a foreign national.[20] Investment treaties frequently contain submissions to ICSID jurisdiction, and many define investment to include "all categories of assets" including claims to money.[21]

14. United Nations Convention on the Recognition and Enforcement of Foreign Arbitral Awards, 10 June 1958, 21 UST 2518, 330 UNTS 3. The operation of the New York Convention is supplemented by the European Convention of 1961, but only as between residents of European Convention countries. European Convention on International Commercial Arbitration, Geneva, 9 February 1968, 484 UNTS 349.

15. New York Convention, Art. II.

16. New York Convention, Art. III. The Convention requires that a foreign award be enforced as would be a domestic award.

17. New York Convention, Art. V.

18. The Panama Convention is silent on orders to compel arbitration, stating only that an agreement to arbitrate is "valid". Moreover, the Panama Convention provides that execution and recognition of an award "may" be ordered, as contrasted with the New York Arbitration Convention's mandatory "shall". Finally, the Panama Convention's enforcement obligation applies only to awards that are "not appealable"; no similar limitation is found in the New York Convention.

19. Convention on the Settlement of Disputes Between States and Nationals of Other States, 575 UNTS 159. See generally Moshe Hirsch, *The Arbitration Mechanisms of the International Centre for the Settlement of Investment Disputes* (1993); W. Michael Reisman, *Systems of Control in International Arbitration*, 46–106 (1992); Georges Delaume, "ICSID and the courts", 77 *American Journal Int'l Law* 784 (1983).

20. Washington Convention, Art. 25.

21. See Rudolf Dolzer & Margrete Stevens, *Bilateral Investment Treaties* (1995), at 25–31 and 130–146. See also Jan Paulsson, "Arbitration Without Privity", 10 *ICSID Review* 232 (1995). Consent to ICSID jurisdiction may be given in an individual investment agreement, host state legislation or treaty obligations, but may not be withdrawn unilaterally. The North American Free Trade Agreement (NAFTA) gives investors a right to bring claims for expropriation under the arbitration rules of ICSID, the ICSID "Additional Facility" or UNCITRAL. See NAFTA, Art. 1120.

Lender liability[22]

Claims by debtors

9.13 A chameleon-like catch-word with several meanings, the term "lender liability" has been pressed into service by non-performing debtors in the United States seeking damages for a bank's alleged failure to fulfil an implicit obligation of "good faith" in dealings with a customer.[23] Analogous regimes have been imposed in some Continental legal systems.[24]

9.14 The "lender liability" label has been affixed to duties owed by a creditor to a debtor under theories of breach of contract, fraud and bad faith in precontractual negotiation. Such claims typically arise on termination of a line of credit, upon acceleration of payment under a note, or at foreclosure on collateral.[25] Bankers have been held liable even when exercising an explicit

22. See generally Helen Chaitman, *The Law of Lender Liability* (1990); Gerald L. Blanchard, *Lender Liability Loan Practice and Prevention* (1989); A. Brooke Oveby, "Bondage, domination and the art of the deal: An assessment of judicial strategies in lender liability good faith litigation", 61 *Fordham Law Review* 963 (1993); Daniel Fischel, "The economics of lender liability", 99 *Yale Law Journal* 131 (1989); Dennis Patterson, "Good faith, lender liability and discretionary acceleration: Of Llewellyn, Wittgenstein and the U.C.C.", 68 *Texas Law Review* 169 (1989); Werner Ebke & James Griffin, "Good faith and fair dealing in commercial lending transactions: From covenant to duty and beyond", 49 *Ohio State Law Journal* 1237 (1989).

23. On good faith in contract performance, see generally Steven J. Burton & Eric G. Andersen, *Contractual Good Faith* (1995); Steven J. Burton, *Judging in Good Faith* (1992); E. Allen Farnsworth, *Contracts*, at 550–559 (2nd edn 1990); E. Allan Farnsworth, "Good faith performance and commercial reasonableness under the Uniform Commercial Code", 30 *University of Chicago Law Review* 666 (1963); Steven J. Burton, "Breach of contract and the common law duty to perform in good faith", 94 *Harvard Law Review* 369 (1980); Clayton P. Gillette, "Limitations on the obligation of good faith", 1981 *Duke Law Journal* 619 (1981); "Symposium on good faith in the law", 16 *William Mitchell Law Review* 1105 (1990).

24. Art. 60 of France's Loi No. 84-46, 27 January 1984, provides: "*Tout concours à durée indeterminée, autre qu'occasionnel, qu'un établissement de crédit consent à une entreprise, ne peut être réduit ou interrompu que sur notification écrite et à l'expiration d'un délai de préavis fixé lors de l'octroi du concours.*" ("Any assistance with an indeterminate limit, other than occasional, that a credit institution grants to an enterprise cannot be reduced or interrupted except with written notice, effective at the end of a period fixed at the time the credit was granted.") The Cour de Cassation has held that renewal of a fixed-term loan may create an indeterminate credit. Cour de Cassation, 3 December 1991, *Revue Banque* (1992), p. 842, commentary by Rives Lange. If a loan does not contain a specific term, then the courts may deem a "reasonable" term to be implied, which might extend the time required to find substitute financing. See e.g. decision of Cour d'Appel d'Agen, D. 87, Jur., p. 59, note by Derrida. See generally Stéphane Astruc, *La Responsabilité Bancaire dans l'Octroi du Crédit aux Entreprises* (1994).

25. See, e.g., *Reid* v. *Key Bank*, 821 F.2d 9 (1st Cir. 1987); *KMC* v. *Irving Trust*, 757 F.2d 752 (6th Cir. 1985); *Martin Specialty Vehicles* v. *Bank of Boston*, 87 *Bankruptcy Reporter* 752 (Bankruptcy Ct. D. Mass 1988), *reversed on other grounds*, 97 *Bankruptcy Reporter* 721 (D. Mass. 1989); *Duffield* v. *First Interstate Bank of Denver*, 13 F.3d 1403 (10th Cir. 1993), *cert. denied*, 13 June 1994. For a case rejecting a borrower's claim, see *Roberts* v. *Wells Fargo AG Credit Corp.*, 990 F.2d 1169 (10th Cir. 1993) (duty of good faith imposed by Oklahoma's "acceleration at will" statute did not cover refusal to renew line of credit).

power under the loan agreement.[26] The duty of good faith can arise under common law[27] or commercial statute.[28] Bankers can get into trouble for being too generous with credit, as well as for being too closefisted.[29]

9.15 To discourage what they consider to be excessive and unpredictable awards by juries in such litigation, several American financial institutions now provide for arbitration in credit agreements.[30] An arbitral panel presumably will be less swayed by solicitude for the borrower than will members of a civil jury, whose own credit problems may cause them to empathise with the debtor.

Claims by third parties

9.16 Another incarnation of lender liability relates to a banker's duty toward the borrower's other creditors. Bankers have sometimes been asked to pay their debtors' bills, under the theory that the lenders were *de facto* partners in the borrowers' ventures.[31] The plausibility of such claims usually turns on the

26. Many states have now added credit agreements to statutes of frauds in order to preclude lender liability claims based on alleged oral contract terms. See Todd C. Pearson, "Limiting lender liability: The trend toward written credit agreement statutes", 76 *Minnesota Law Review* 295 (1991).

27. In the United States, the duty of "good faith" usually arises under state rather than federal law. Restatement (Second) of Contracts, §205 provides: "Every contract imposes upon each party a duty of good faith and fair dealing in its performance and its enforcement."

28. See Uniform Commercial Code §1–203: "Every contract or duty within this Act imposes an obligation of good faith in its performance and its enforcement." The Code defines good faith generally as "honesty in fact" §1–201(19). For certain portions of the Code the definition is extended to include the "observance of reasonable commercial standards of fair dealings". See §2–103(1)(b), §2A–103(3), §3–103(a)(4), §4–104(c), §4A–105(a)(6). Although the Code governs security agreements under its Art. 9 (Secured Transactions), it is uncertain whether the Code also covers other aspects of secured loans themselves.

29. Several American banks have recently come under attack for allegedly making excessive loans on overpriced houses to low-income borrowers, thereby bringing on foreclosure and bankruptcy. See, e.g., "Bad credit in Dorchester", *Boston Globe*, 28 October 1996, page A–14. Banks in the United States have also been subject to allegations of insufficient lending in poorer communities, leading to remedial legislation in the form of the Community Reinvestment Act. The complexity of mortgage lending to less affluent borrowers is explored in Levine and Lawrence Harmon, *The Death of an American Jewish Community* (1992).

30. See, e.g., model clauses adopted by Bank of California and Bank of America, reprinted in James R. Butler, *Arbitration in Banking* (RMA 1988). See generally Michael L. Weissman, *Lender Liability: How to Protect Yourself Against Unwarranted Suits* (1988). In June 1992, the Bank of America announced that it would require all deposit and bankcard agreements to be submitted to binding arbitration under the rules of the American Arbitration Association. See statement of Winslow Christien (Senior VP and Director of Litigation), reported in *BNA World Arbitration and Mediation Report* 135 (July 1992).

31. See, e.g., *United States* v. *Fleet Factors Corp.*, 901 F.2d 1550 (11th Cir. 1990), *cert. denied*, 111 S.Ct. 752 (1991) (security interest and role in borrower's management created liability for hazardous waste clean-up costs). For French analogues, see Art. 180 of Loi 85-98, 25 January 1985 ("*redressement judiciaire*"), permitting a court to impose liability on a "*dirigeant de fait*" of a bankrupt company. Third-party lender liability may also be based on general tort responsibility under Arts 1382 and 1383 of the French Code Civil, requiring payment of damages for any harm caused to another by intentional fault or negligence.

amount of control exercised by the financier over the management of the borrower's business.

9.17 Lenders will not always be able to impose arbitration of such third-party claims, for the simple reason that a borrower's other creditors will not necessarily have agreed to arbitration. Nevertheless, arbitrators sometimes do end up hearing third-party claims, and their commercial sophistication has on occasion led to reasonable solutions.[32]

Exchange controls

9.18 Borrowers sometimes invoke exchange controls as defences to loan recovery,[33] on the theory that such controls constitute a foreign "Act of State" to which courts must defer. Although principally an American obsession, the Act of State doctrine exercises an influence well beyond common law countries, given the large number of cross-border financial transactions routinely subjected to the law of New York or to the jurisdiction of New York courts.

9.19 The Act of State doctrine generally prohibits courts from calling into question a foreign government's behaviour concerning assets within its territory.[34] Sometimes explained as a limit on judicial interference with the conduct of foreign affairs,[35] the doctrine might best be understood as a conflict-of-laws rule that imposes foreign law even if such law is contrary to the public policy of the forum.[36]

9.20 Creditors sometimes avoid application of the Act of State doctrine by virtue of judicial manipulation of the *situs* of the debt in question. Courts may

32. See arbitration award in *Schlumberger* v. *Duferco*, ICC Case 8465, reported in 11 *Mealey's International Arbitration Report* (No. 3) at C–1. In connection with an oil-drilling contract in Iran, Company No. 1 owed Company No. 2 for services performed. Company No. 2 attempted to recover this amount from Company No. 3 (the "deep pocket") which, through a separate contract, had helped finance the project. The arbitrators rejected the claim against Company No. 3 in an award confirmed by the United States District Court for the Southern District of Texas on 8 March 1996, Civil Action H–94–2409.

33. See, e.g., *Allied Bank* v. *Banco Credito Agricola*, 566 F.Supp. 1440 (SDNY 1983), *confirmed*, 733 F.2d 23 (2d Cir. 1984), *annulled on rehearing* 757 F.2d 516 (2d Cir. 1985); *Wells Fargo Asia Ltd* v. *Citibank*, 852 F.2d 657 (2d Cir. 1988), *confirming*, 695 F.Supp. 1450 (SDNY 1988), *vacated and remanded by the Supreme Ct.*, 495 US 660 (1990), *confirmed*, 936 F.2d 723 (2d Cir. 1991), *cert. denied*, 505 US 1204 (1992); *Perez* v. *Chase Manhattan*, 474 NYS2d 689 (1984); *Garcia* v. *Chase Manhattan*, 735 F.2d 645 (2d Cir. 1984).

34. See the Restatement of Foreign Relations Law of the United States in s.443.

35. See generally *Banco Nacional de Cuba* v. *Sabbatino*, 376 US 398 (1964).

36. An alternative rationale sees the Act of State doctrine as promoting security of transactions, an explanation that works best when tangibles are concerned. For example, without the Act of State doctrine, one who buys wood or sugar from a revolutionary government might later be subject to a claim brought by the original owner seeking to recover the goods.

deem the debt to be located outside the territory of the country imposing the exchange controls.[37] Favourable characterisation of the debt *situs*, however, may come only after years of costly litigation.[38]

9.21 The United States has eliminated the Act of State defence in actions to enforce arbitration agreements and awards. The Federal Arbitration Act provides: "The enforcement of arbitral agreements, and the confirmation of arbitral awards, shall not be refused on the basis of the act of state doctrine."[39] The scope of this remarkably succinct bit of legislation, however, has never been extended to court litigation. Thus an arbitration clause in a cross-border loan agreement can on occasion enhance the creditor's prospect of loan recovery.

Sovereign immunity

9.22 To avoid repayment of loan obligations, government debtors often invoke principles of "sovereign immunity", which operate to prevent one country from hauling another country into its courts. The modern rationale for sovereign immunity mirrors the justification sometimes given for the Act of State doctrine, to the effect that judges should not risk interfering with the executive branch of government in its conduct of foreign relations.

9.23 Most nations now grant immunity to foreign governments and their agencies subject to several exceptions, the most notable of which relates to the nature of the act in question. Immunity generally covers "public" rather than

37. See discussion of the *Allied Bank* case, above. Such *situs* manipulation works best when the place of payment and/or applicable law are other than the country of the debtor's residence. For alternative ways to analyse the legitimate extent of exchange controls, see P.S. Smedresman and Andreas Lowenfeld, "Eurodollars, multinational banks, and national laws", 64 *New York University Law Review* 733 (1989).

38. For example, the saga of Wells Fargo's deposit at Citibank's Manilla branch involved a half dozen separate federal court decisions concerning whether Wells Fargo could look to Citibank's New York assets for recovery of a deposit that had been blocked under Philippine law. See *Wells Fargo* v. *Citibank*, 660 F.Supp. 946 (SDNY 1987) (recovery allowed); *remanded by Second Circuit for clarification*, 847 F.2d 837 (2d Cir. 1988); *recovery again ordered*, 695 F.Supp. 1450, *aff'd*, 852 F.2d 657 (2d Cir. 1988); *vacated & remanded*, 110 S.Ct. 2034 (1990); *reaffirmed on remand*, 936 F.2d 723 (2nd Cir. 1991); *cert. denied*, 505 US 1204 (1992). Subsequent legislation provides that banks which are members of the Federal Reserve are not required to repay foreign branch deposits blocked by foreign government action, absent an express agreement to the contrary. See §25C, Federal Reserve Act, 12 USC §633.

39. See 9 USC §15, enacted following a frustrating attempt to enforce an arbitration award against Libya in American courts. See *Libyan American Oil Company (LIAMCO)* v. *Libya*, 482 F.Supp. 1175 (DDC 1980), *vacated as moot*, 684 F.2d 1032 (1981).

"commercial" acts.[40] The character of an act will be determined by its nature rather than its purpose.[41]

9.24 Immunity from suit is further restricted if a creditor benefits from an arbitration clause. Many national legal systems deny a foreign state jurisdictional immunity in an action to enforce an arbitration agreement or to confirm an arbitral award.[42]

9.25 Arbitration can be of special benefit to a lender when an award must be enforced against a sovereign debtor's assets in the United States. Normally, a functional connection is required between the property to be attached and the activity that gave rise to the claim. A judgment against a foreign state can be executed only against property used in the same commercial activity upon which the claim is based.[43] In the case of a loan, this "same activity" requirement can limit attachment of assets to funds earmarked for debt reimbursement, which may be scarce when the debtor defaults.

9.26 The Foreign Sovereign Immunities Act, however, removes this requirement of a functional nexus with respect to arbitral awards. The statute provides that property of a foreign state used for a commercial activity in the United States shall not be immune from attachment in aid of execution if judgment is based on an order confirming an arbitral award.[44]

9.27 An arbitration clause in a loan agreement can also be helpful when the borrower is an international organisation. In Britain a dispute between the International Tin Council ("ITC") and its creditors ended up before the House of Lords, which interpreted the ITC Headquarters Agreement with the United Kingdom as granting the ITC sovereign immunity.[45] The same Headquarters Agreement, however, had also provided that the ITC would *not* benefit from immunity in the enforcement of arbitration awards. The metal exchanges were thereby protected, since their trading contracts contained arbitration clauses.

40. See, e.g., US Foreign Sovereign Immunities Act 1976, 28 USC §§1601–1611. UK State Immunity Act 1978, Ch. 33. A Swiss wrinkle to sovereign immunity requires a link ("internal connection"—*Binnenbeziehung*) between the sovereign act and Switzerland before Swiss courts will accept jurisdiction over the sovereign or its assets.

41. For the United States, see 28 USC §1603(d). Legislative history indicates that "both a foreign government sale of bonds and a loan from a commercial bank to a foreign government are to be considered activities of a commercial nature." See HR Rep. No. 1487, 94th Cong., 2d Sess., at 10 (1976). The British statute defines a commercial transaction to include "any loan or other transaction for the provision of finance and any guarantee or indemnity in respect of any such transaction or of any other financial obligation". See State Immunity Act, 1978, s.3(3)(b).

42. In the United States see 28 USC §1605(a). Compare Great Britain's State Immunity Act 1978, s.9. The limit on jurisdictional immunity in the United States has both a territorial and a treaty link. An arbitration agreement or award will be enforceable notwithstanding a claim for sovereign immunity if (i) the arbitration takes place in the United States, or (ii) the agreement or award is or may be governed by a treaty calling for the recognition and enforcement of arbitral awards. The latter would include the 1958 New York Convention.

43. Some property, such as central bank funds (absent an explicit waiver of immunity), is always immune, unless perhaps the central bank functions as a commercial bank in a particular transaction.

44. 28 USC §1610(a)(6).

45. *J.H. Rayner Ltd* v. *Department of Trade*, [1989] 3 All ER 523 (HL).

Banks were in a different situation, however, since few lenders had the foresight to incorporate arbitration clauses in their loan agreements.

Interbank disputes

Court selection clauses

9.28 Not all jurisdictions are user-friendly in matters of court selection. If two banks wish an unbiased judge in a neutral third country to resolve a controversy between them, the contractually selected neutral court may not always have enough links to the parties or the controverted event to justify hearing the case.

9.29 While some countries require their judges to hear cases pursuant to court selection clauses,[46] others do not. In particular, no American jurisdiction except New York mandates recognition of court selection clauses;[47] neither federal statute nor treaty enforces choice-of-court clauses in the way that the Federal Arbitration Act and the New York Arbitration Convention enforce arbitration agreements.[48]

9.30 United States Supreme Court decisions are often cited for the proposition that court selection clauses will be recognised.[49] Yet what the cases actually say is that jurisdiction agreements will be respected if "reasonable" by reference to a multiplicity of factors (place of contract execution, place of performance, location of witnesses and documents, remedies available in the alternate forum, and public policy) all of which vary from case to case.[50] Moreover, unless a controversy implicates a question of federal law, one foreigner normally may not sue another in federal court, regardless of how eager the litigants are to thrust jurisdiction on the designated tribunal.[51]

46. See, e.g., Article 5 of the Swiss Loi fédérale sur le droit international privé, which mandates respect for court-selection clauses as long as Swiss law applies to the dispute.

47. See NY General Obligations Law §5–1402 (McKinney 1989) and NYCPLR §327. For a New York choice of forum to be dispositive, the transaction must cover no less than $1 million, and the parties must have elected application of New York law. Without this statute, two foreign banks might have considerable difficulty getting a New York court to hear their case. See NY Banking Law §200–b (McKinney 1990) and NY Bus. Corp. Law §1314(b)(1)–(5) (McKinney 1987).

48. For a recent US federal case citing absence of a court selection statute as a factor justifying refusal to enforce a jurisdiction clause, see *Richards* v. *Lloyd's*, 107 F.3d 1422 (9th Cir. 1997) ("[The Court in *Scherk*] chose to apply the Arbitration Act. It did not weigh reasonableness or pit amorphous policy against an act of Congress.")

49. See *Bremen* v. *Zapata Off-Shore Co.*, 407 US 1 (1972); *Carnival Cruise Lines* v. *Shute*, 499 US 585 (1991); *Stewart Organization Inc.* v. *Ricoh Corp.*, 487 US 22 (1988).

50. One decision set forth nine factors relevant to the reasonableness of a jurisdiction clause, emphasising "the totality of the circumstances measured in the interests of justice". See *D'Antuono* v. *CCH Computax Sys.*, 570 F.Supp. 708 (DRI 1983).

51. Federal court power is limited to cases arising on the basis of a federal question or diversity of citizenship. The latter requires litigation between citizens of different states or between a US citizen and a foreigner. For a recent case discussing the complexity of "diversity jurisdiction," see *Dresser Industries* v. *Lloyd's*, 106 F.3d 494 (3d Cir. 1997).

9.31 The situation is even more complex when one looks at state law,[52] which may refuse to enforce court selection clauses either in general or with respect to particular types of contracts.[53] Even when acknowledging the validity of court selection clauses in theory, state courts may in practice give such clauses a restrictive reading that vitiates their effect. State decisions have construed court selection clauses narrowly, either as non-exclusive (therefore allowing actions in competing fora),[54] or as excluding actions based on extra-contractual wrongs such as deceit and unfair business practices.[55]

9.32 A court may also decline to hear a case on *forum non conveniens* grounds, because of the location of witnesses and documents, or the drain on public resources. While one overworked judge might enforce a jurisdiction clause to clear a crowded docket, an equally overworked judge in the contractually selected jurisdiction may decline to hear the dispute on the basis that a more convenient forum may be found elsewhere.[56] This risk is particularly significant in a transaction between two foreign entities, when the controversy lacks sufficient connection with the state.[57]

Arbitration clauses

9.33 Unlike judges, arbitrators rarely (if ever) refuse to hear a dispute because of *forum non conveniens*, the parties' lack of diversity of citizenship, or any of the other above-described problems that often plague the enforcement of court selection clauses. If the parties can provide an adequate deposit to cover costs, professors around the world can usually be found eager to serve as arbitrators, thereby supplementing meagre academic stipends.

9.34 Arbitration, of course, suffers from its own forms of uncertainty. Particularly when consolidation of related claims becomes desirable, there will

52. State law may apply not only in state courts, but also in federal courts where jurisdiction is based on diversity of citizenship between the parties. Some federal courts see enforcement of a jurisdiction clause as a matter of substantive law, requiring application of state norms in diversity cases under the principle of *Erie* v. *Tompkins*. Other courts have assumed (often with little discussion) that the matter is procedural, and that federal law applies.

53. See cases surveyed in William W. Park, *International Forum Selection*, at 35–36 (1995). For a recent illustration of restrictive state law, see *Kubis & Perszyk Associates* v. *Sun Microsystems*, NJ Sup. Ct., A–104, 23 July 1996, 65 LW 2076, arising under New Jersey Franchise Practices Act; the ill-fated jurisdiction clause would have sent parties to Santa Clara, California.

54. See, e.g, *Brooke Group* v. *JCH Syndicate*, 663 NE2d 635 (NY 1996) (Jurisdiction clause permissive rather than mandatory, therefore allowing dismissal on *forum non conveniens* grounds of action by American insured against foreign underwriter). See also *Blanco* v. *Banco Industrial de Venezuela*, 997 F.2d 974 (2d Cir. 1993).

55. In one case, the trial judge was instructed by the state supreme court to determine whether the "principal focus" of the plaintiff's claims was for breach of contract or for extra-contractual wrongs, with the result that to the date of this writing the case has not been sent to the contractually selected forum. See *Jacobson* v. *Mailboxes Etc.*, 419 Mass. 572 (1995).

56. At least one Circuit, however, has held that signature of a valid court selection clause constitutes a "waiver of the right to move for a change of venue on the ground of inconvenience to the moving party." *Northwestern Nat'l Ins. Co.* v. *Donovan*, 916 F.2d 372, 378 (7th Cir. 1990).

57. See *United Adjustment* v. *Midland Bank*, 281 Mass. 303 (1933).

be many disputes better litigated before courts than dealt with by arbitrators. These drawbacks of arbitration are discussed more fully later in the chapter.

SECURITIES

Broker misbehaviour

9.35 Securities-related disputes involving broker-dealers now provide one of the most frequent occasions for arbitration in the financial services industry.[58] The explosion of securities arbitration in the United States dates from 1989, when the United States Supreme Court finally permitted arbitration of securities disputes in domestic transactions.[59] In Britain, by contrast, courts never displayed the same hostility toward arbitration of securities claims,[60] probably because awards in domestic cases could traditionally be challenged on their legal merits.[61]

9.36 Claims against brokerage firms usually relate to misbehaviour such as "churning" (needless buying and selling to generate commissions), unauthorised or unsuitable trading, and misrepresentations. Occasionally brokers are accused of outright theft, euphemistically referred to as misappropriation.[62]

9.37 In the United States, arbitration reduces the cost and delay in dealing with such disputes, as well as reducing the prospect of punitive damages awarded by pro-customer juries. American brokerage firms' customer account agreements usually provide that any disputes will be settled by arbitration. The customer often has the right to elect among several sets of rules, including those

58. For 1994, the NASD reported 5,570 new arbitration claims filed under its Code of Arbitration Procedure, up from 318 in 1980. See discussion in Deborah Masucci, "Securities arbitration: A success story: What does the future hold?", 31 *Wake Forest Law Review* 183 (1996).

59. See *Rodriguez de Quijas* v. *Shearson/American Express, Inc.*, 490 US 477 (1989) (Securities Act of 1933) and *Shearson/American Express* v. *McMahon*, 482 US 220 (1987) (Securities Exchange Act of 1934). Earlier court decisions had allowed arbitration of securities disputes in international transactions. See *Scherk* v. *Alberto Culver Co.*, 417 US 506 (1974).

60. See generally John J. Kerr, "Arbitrability of securities law claims in common law countries", 12 *Arbitration International* 171 (1996).

61. Before 1979 the "case stated" procedure permitted *de facto* challenge for error of law. A more limited non-waivable right of appeal existed under the 1979 Arbitration Act, but exclusion of appeal on points of law could not be made in domestic cases until after the dispute had arisen. The 1996 Arbitration Act permits exclusion of appeal on points of law. Although the Act prohibited pre-dispute exclusion of such appeal in domestic cases, this provision never entered into force, due to a perceived conflict of nationality based distinctions with the non-discrimination regime of the European Union; see *Philip Alexander Securities* v. *Bamberger, Theele, Kefer et al.*, Queen's Bench Division, 12 July 1996, reported in [1977] ILPr. 73.

62. See generally David E. Robbins, *Securities Arbitration Procedure Manual* (1990); David E. Robbins, "Seven deadly sins that lead to arbitration disaster", *PLI Corporate Law and Practice Course Handbook*, B4–7036 (July–August 1993); Shelly James, "Arbitration in the securities field: Does the present system of arbitration between small investors and brokerage firms really protect anyone?", *Journal of Corporation Law* 363 (Winter 1996).

of the American Arbitration Association (AAA), the New York Stock Exchange (NYSE) and the National Association of Securities Dealers (NASD).[63]

Punitive damages

9.38 When a wrong is aggravated by defendant's malice, fraud or wanton conduct, civil juries in the United States often award punitive damages for amounts over and above the plaintiff's actual loss.[64] Arbitration provides a vehicle to reduce the risk of such damages, at least if the arbitration clause explicitly excludes or limits punitive damages.[65]

9.39 The United States Supreme Court has recently obscured analysis of punitive damages in a decision upholding an award that included $400,000 to punish a brokerage house, in addition to $159,000 in actual customer loss.[66] In *Mastrobuono* v. *Shearson Lehman Hutton* the customer agreement was governed by New York, which allowed only courts to award punitive damages.[67] The Supreme Court read the relevant choice-of-law clause to refer only to substantive contract law, to the exclusion of state arbitration principles.

9.40 The decision in *Mastrobuono* is hard to square with previous Supreme Court pronouncements on choice of law in arbitration. A few years earlier, the Court had upheld a stay of arbitration on the basis of a choice-of-law clause deemed to incorporate state law into the agreement to arbitrate.[68]

9.41 Court decisions since *Mastrobuono* have sometimes distinguished that

63. Under some rules arbitrators are classified as either "public" (i.e., customer) or "industry" arbitrators, with the latter category including broker-dealers and their employees, as well as attorneys, accountants and other professionals with close ties to the securities industry. See §19 of NASD Code of Arbitration Procedure (1995), which excludes from the public arbitrator category professionals who have worked 20 per cent or more for the securities industry during the previous two years. A study done by the US General Accounting Office has found no evidence of pro-industry bias in such arbitration. See US General Accounting Office, *Securities Arbitration: How Investors Fare* (1992).

64. On the Biblical origins of punitive damages, see Exodus 22:1, requiring multiple payments for theft.

65. In January 1997 the NASD Board of Governors approved a cap that will limit punitive damages to $750,000 or twice compensatory damages, whichever is less. See *Report of the Arbitration Policy Task Force to the Board of Governors National Association of Securities Dealers* ("Ruder Report", so named for Task Force Chairman David Ruder), Fed. Sec. L. Rep. (CCH) ¶85, 735, s.V(B).

66. *Mastrobuono* v. *Shearson Lehman Hutton*, 115 S.Ct. 1212 (1995). For a pre-*Mastrobuono* survey of the subject, see E. Allen Farnsworth, "Punitive damages in arbitration", 7 *Arbitration International* 3 (1991).

67. See *Garrity* v. *Lyle Stuart, Inc.*, 40 NY2d 354 (1976). Recently, however, at least one New York decision has allowed arbitrators to award punitive damages unless the parties have unequivocally agreed otherwise. See *Mulder* v. *Donaldson, Lufkin & Jenrette* (No. 59192N, Appellate Division 1st Dept.), 1996 NY App. Div. Lexis 9920 (8 Oct. 1996), which considered the *Garrity* by the *Mastrobuono* decision.

68. *Volt* v. *Stanford*, 489 US 468 (1989). In *Volt*, the US Supreme Court relied on a decision of the California state Court of Appeals, which had interpreted the choice-of-law clause to cover California arbitration rules. By contrast, in *Mastrobuono* the US Supreme Court interpreted the choice-of-law clause *de novo*.

decision on the basis of forum public policy or the drafting of the choice-of-law clause, so as to reject the arbitrators' power to grant punitive damages.[69] The path of prudence for financial institutions therefore lies in explicit exclusions of punitive damages, rather than reliance on unpredictable choice of law clauses.

Time bars

9.42 Certain securities arbitration rules provide for disputes to be brought within a fixed term after the controverted events.[70] No consensus yet exists, however, on whether courts or arbitrators should determine whether time limits have been met.[71] Some decisions have held time bars to be a matter for arbitrators,[72] while others have held interpretation of these limits to be for courts.[73]

9.43 Courts have also struggled with analogous issues related to statutes of limitations. Some decisions have held that statute-of-limitations questions are for judges in the context of a motion to compel arbitration, but for arbitrators hearing the underlying claim.[74] This approach assumes that there are two separate time limits: one applicable to the principal agreement (to buy, sell, license, lease or lend) and one applicable to the agreement to arbitrate the dispute. The main agreement is covered by the statute of limitations contained in its applicable law clause, or in the law otherwise governing its interpretation. On the other hand, a motion to compel arbitration implicates the relevant arbitration statute.[75]

69. See, e.g., decision of Judge Jane Solomon, Supreme Court of New York State, in *Dean Witter Reynolds* v. *Trimble*, 631 NYS2d 215 (1995). Compare *Merrill Lynch* v. *Levine*, New York State Supreme Court, 5 July 1995.

70. See r. 10304 (formerly s.15) National Association of Securities Dealers Code of Arbitration, providing that "no dispute, claim or controversy shall be eligible for submission to arbitration under this Code where six (6) years have elapsed from the occurrence or event giving rise to the act or dispute, claim or controversy". See generally David Rivkin, "Courts differ on arbitrability of time limitations", *ADR Currents* (ABA, Autumn 1996) 21; Sean Costello, "Time limits under rule 10304 of the NASD Code of Arbitration Procedure: Making arbitrators more like judges or judges more like arbitrators", 52 *Business Lawyer* 283 (1996). Under a recently proposed change in the NASD rules the six-year eligibility rule will be suspended for a three-year period. See Ruder Report, Fed. Sec. L. Rep. (CCH) ¶85, 735, s.V(B).

71. The Third, Sixth, Seventh, Tenth and Eleventh Circuits have considered time limits contained in arbitration rules to constitute a jurisdictional prerequisite to arbitration, to be determined by courts. The First, Second, Fifth, Eighth and Ninth Circuits have held the matter to be for the arbitrator. See cases summarised in *PaineWebber* v. *Elahi*, 87 F.3d 589 (1st Cir. 1996).

72. See, e.g., *PaineWebber* v. *Elahi*, 87 F.3d 589 (1st Cir. 1996), citing language in s.35 of the NASD Code of Arbitration Procedure providing for arbitrators to "interpret and determine the applicability of all provisions under this Code". *Id.* at 601. Contrast the result in *Merrill Lynch* v. *Cohen*, 62 F.2d 381 (11th Cir. 1995) (time bars for courts).

73. See, e.g., *Merrill Lynch* v. *Cohen*, 62 F.2d 381 (11th Cir. 1995).

74. See *National Iranian Oil* v. *Mapco Int'l*, 983 F.2d 485 (3d Cir. 1992); *Avant Petroleum* v. *Pecten Arabian Ltd*, 696 F.Supp. 42 (SDNY 1988).

75. See discussion in *National Iranian Oil* v. Mapco, 983 F.2d 485 (3d Cir. 1992), looking to the Federal Arbitration Act. Since the FAA does not specify a statute of limitations, the court reasoned that it must borrow the most closely analogous one from state law under the conflict of laws principles of the state in which the court sits.

9.44 Some courts have held that a choice of law clause covers statute-of-limitations matters as well as the merits of the dispute.[76] Others have interpreted the US Supreme Court's analysis in *Mastrobuono* to exclude time limits from the scope of choice-of-law clauses.[77]

9.45 The parties' intent remains the polar star for analysis of who determines whether preconditions to arbitration have been satisfied. To enforce the contract as drafted, judges must examine whether a time bar was explicitly or implicitly incorporated into the arbitration clause as a restraint on the arbitrators' power. If so, only courts should have the last word on the matter.

SELECTED FINANCIAL TRANSACTIONS

Guarantees

9.46 Issuers of first demand guarantees often find themselves bound by the dispute resolution clause in the principal contract.[78] For example, a guarantee issued in favour of Company Y might incorporate by reference the arbitration clause in the contract between Company Y and Company Z.[79]

9.47 Principles of contract interpretation that subject a guarantee to the forum selection mechanism in the primary obligation have developed from cases in the areas of reinsurance, charter-parties and construction. Whether the guarantor will be bound by the arbitration clause in the principal agreement depends on the parties' intent, as determined by the language of the guarantee, the relationship between the guarantor and the principal obligor, and the reasonableness of characterising several documents as a single transaction.[80] Conflict-of-laws doctrine in some countries favours submission of suretyships

76. See *Smith Barney* v. *Luckie*, 85 NY2d 193 (1995) (NYCPLR §7502 permits statute-of-limitations issues to be decided by courts).

77. See *PaineWebber* v. *Bybyk*, 81 F.3d 1193 (2d Cir. 1996), holding that the *Mastrobuono* reasoning requires the choice of New York law to be interpreted so as to exclude New York law limiting the authority of arbitrators. *Id.* at 1200.

78. See generally Bertrand Chambreuil, "Arbitrage international et garanties bancaires", 1991 *Revue de l'arbitrage* 33; Bernard Hanotiau, "La pratique de l'arbitrage international en matière bancaire", in *Les Modes Nonjudiciaires de Règlement des conflits* (Brussels, 1995).

79. See *Compania Espanol de Petroleos* v. *Nereus Shipping*, 527 F.2d 966, 969–73 (2d Cir. 1975), *cert. denied*, 426 US 936 (1976).

80. See, e.g., *Ameritrust* v. *Chanslor*, 803 F.Supp. 893 (SDNY 1992) (creditors of partnership can compel arbitration by guarantor of partner's obligations); *United States Fidelity* v. *West Point Construction*, 837 F.2d 1507 (11th Cir. 1988) (performance bond incorporated subcontract terms by reference.); *Hoffman* v. *Fidelity and Deposit Company*, 734 F.Supp. 192 (DNJ 1990) (arbitration provision in construction contract incorporated into performance bond); *O & Y Landmark Associates* v. *Nordheimer*, 725 F.Supp. 578 (DDC 1989) (individuals who guaranteed obligations of

and other "accessory" agreements to the same law governing the principal obligation, in order to promote uniformity of contract interpretation.[81]

Documentary credits

The context

9.48 A typical documentary credit transaction can implicate controversies between issuing and confirming banks, as well as bank–customer relationships. Complications might arise out of alleged fraud by the seller; use of buyer's funds to offset indebtedness to the issuing bank, or simple disagreement about how to interpret the terms of the letter of credit. For example, a seller in Boston might be the beneficiary of a letter of credit issued by the buyer's bank in France and confirmed by the seller's bank in Massachusetts. If the issuing bank refused to make payment on the ground that the documents presented by the seller were not in conformity with the documentary credit (e.g., the bill of lading lacked the mention "Clean on Board"), the confirming bank might argue that no such requirement existed under the Uniform Customs and Practices for Documentary Credits ("UCP").[82]

A cautionary tale

9.49 If scholars had tried to construct a hypothetical example of the hazards of going to court over a documentary credit dispute, it would have been hard to

one partnership bound to join arbitration with second partnership); *Lemme* v. *Wine of Japan Import*, 631 F.Supp. 456 (EDNY 1986) (New York distributor sues New York importer and Japanese alcohol producer that guaranteed obligations of importer; Japanese producer deemed to have consented to New York jurisdiction by virtue of consent-to-jurisdiction clause in contract between importer and distributor). For cases *contra*, see *General Electric* v. *Toups*, 644 F.Supp. 11 (SDNY 1985) (guarantors held not to have consented to jurisdiction of courts selected in loan agreement); *Grundstad* v. *Ritt*, US Court of Appeals, 7th Cir., 1997, reported in Vol. 12 *Mealey's International Arbitration Reports*, s.F (February 1997) (reversing summary judgment compelling Norwegian guarantor to arbitrate dispute arising from guarantee of non-competition and payment obligation relative to cruise ship gambling concession; court distinguished cases where guarantee in separate document from case in which guarantee included beneath signature line of principle agreement); *Progressive Casualty Insurance* v. *CA Reaseguradora Nacional de Venezuela*, 802 F.Supp. 1069 (SDNY 1992).

81. See generally Restatement (Second) Conflict of Laws, s.194; cases cited in Eugene Scoles & Peter Hay, *Conflict of Laws*, s.18.27; Bernard Audit, *Droit International Privé*, s.797, at 633. Audit notes however that this general rule presumes no contrary agreement by the parties.

82. Cases in which the arbitrator is called to decide only on the basis of the UCP provide an interesting example of application of what has come to be called "international law merchant", or *lex mercatoria*. On *lex mercatoria* see generally essay contributed to *Lex Mercatoria and Arbitration* (Thomas E. Carbonneau, ed., 1990); W. Laurence Craig, William W. Park and Jan Paulsson, *International Chamber of Commerce Arbitration*, Ch. 35 (2nd edn, 1990); Filip de Ly, *International Business Law and Lex Mercatoria* (1992); Feloc Dasser, "Internationale Schiedsgerichte und Lex Mercatoria", *Rechtsvergleichender Beitrag Zür Diskussion Über Ein Nichtstaatliches Handelsrecht* (Zurich, 1989); *UNIDROIT Principles of International Commercial Contracts* (International Institute for the Unification of Private Law, 1994).

come up with a more illustrative scenario than that found in *Clarendon* v. *State Bank of Saurashtra.*[83] A Swiss beneficiary of a $2.2 million letter of credit issued by a state bank in India had to pursue almost four years of judicial proceedings, with three different court decisions, merely to obtain an appellate order remanding the case to a lower court for disposition on the merits of the documentary credit claim.

9.50 To the beneficiary, the legal questions raised in the case could hardly have seemed other than arcane and irrelevant to interpretation of the letter of credit itself: federal court "subject matter jurisdiction," the Foreign Sovereign Immunities Act, and the applicant's status as an indispensable party to the litigation under the Federal Rules of Civil Procedure. The merits of the case hinged on whether the Uniform Customs and Practices for Documentary Credits requires (as it does) that an issuing bank give prompt notice of refusal to honour a credit by reason of discrepant documents, in the instant case a bill of lading dated a day earlier than called for in the credit.[84]

Arbitration clauses

9.51 To reduce the cost and delay of such extensive and time-consuming litigation, parties to letters of credit might agree to submit their controversy to arbitration under the rules of an institution that has developed experience in documentary credit disputes.[85] Special care must be taken in drafting an arbitration clause in a conflict between more than two parties. For example, if a dispute involves an applicant or beneficiary as well as the issuing and confirming banks, the arbitration clause should provide for consolidation of all related claims before a single arbitral tribunal.

DOCDEX

9.52 The International Chamber of Commerce offers parties to documentary credit transactions not only the possibility of arbitrating their disputes under its arbitration rules, but also the opportunity to settle controversies through a panel of experts. Developed through almost two years of intensive deliberation by an ICC working party, the "Documentary Credit Dispute Expertise Rules" (DOCDEX) were approved in final form by the ICC Banking Commission in November 1996, and will be administered by the ICC Centre for Expertise in collaboration with the Banking Commission.

9.53 Under the DOCDEX rules, a request for dispute resolution may be filed

83. 77 F.3d 631 (2d Cir. 1996).

84. Under the UCP the issuing bank must either hold the documents at the disposition of the presenter or return them.

85. Such institutions include the International Chamber of Commerce, the London Court of International Arbitration, the American Arbitration Association, and the recently created Institute of International Banking Law and Practice located in Maryland.

unilaterally by an aggrieved party, or jointly by all parties to the dispute. The ICC will appoint three independent experts from a list maintained by the ICC Banking Commission. After payment of the advance on costs, the ICC Centre for Expertise will transmit the file to the experts for a decision, made on the basis of documents alone.[86]

9.54 The DOCDEX Rules state that the experts' decision "is not intended to conform with any legal requirements of an arbitration award". Therefore it is doubtful that very many courts would subject the decision to arbitration statutes or treaties, even if one of the parties so requested. The parties are free to consider it legally binding or as having moral force only. If the parties fail to state how they will characterise the decision, the default rule presumes bindingness.

Distinguishing experts from arbitrators[87]

9.55 The DOCDEX insistence that its decisions are not intended as arbitration awards raises the question of how exactly they should be characterised. Notwithstanding Shakespeare's suggestion that what we call something does not matter,[88] it does make a significant difference whether a contractually designated decision-maker is characterised as an "arbitrator", or in the alternative as an "expert", "adjudicator", "evaluator" or "appraiser".[89]

9.56 An arbitrator's award generally will benefit from the network of enforcement provisions created by multinational treaties and national arbitration statutes. On the other hand, an expert's opinion can be enforced abroad only in a new action under the relevant foreign law, subject to whatever contract defences may exist.[90] Arbitrators will generally benefit from immunity from suit for errors or omissions, while appraisers and experts will not.[91] Under some legal systems an arbitral award might be subject to appeal under statutory provisions for judicial review on the merits of an award,[92] while decisions of experts would fall outside the scope of such appellate schemes.[93]

86. The Rules cover only issues arising under the Uniform Customs and Practices for Documentary Credits or the Uniform Rules for Bank-to-Bank Reimbursement under Documentary Credits ("URR"). Thus an allegation of fraud would fall outside the scope of the expert's mission.

87. See generally Charles Jarrosson, *La Notion D'Arbitrage*, ss.202–297, pp. 112–157 (1987); Michael Mustill & Stewart Boyd, *Commercial Arbitration*, 38–50 (2nd edn, 1989); Paul Michard, Introduction to *Martindale Hubbell International Arbitration Directory* (1996), pp. xiii–xiv.

88. "What's in a name? That which we call a rose by any other name would smell as sweet." *Romeo and Juliet*, Act 2, Sc. 2, l. 85.

89. Experts and analogous decision-makers tend to be used in matters related to consideration for shares in a privately held company, or post-closing adjustments following certification of profits.

90. See generally Jean-François Bourque, "L'expérience du Centre International d'Expertise de la CCI et le développement de l'expertise internationale", 1995 *Revue de l'arbitrage* 231.

91. See generally Julian D.M. Lew, "Immunity of arbitrators under English law", in *The Immunity of Arbitrators* 21 (J. Lew, ed., 1990).

92. See, e.g., English Arbitration Act 1996, s.69.

93. See, e.g., *Jones* v. *Sherwood Computer Services* [1992] 1 WLR 277 (review of expert's decision only for fraud or failure to perform correct function). Compare *Mercury Communications* v. *General Telecommunications* [1996] 1 WLR 48 (House of Lords accepted review of expert's error).

9.57 It is often easier to describe the consequences of characterising a decision-maker as an arbitrator than to describe how the characterisation should be made. The existence of a dispute and the adversarial nature of the proceedings are often cited as indicating the exercise of arbitral functions rather than expert valuation.[94] Even if a dispute has arisen, however, a decision-maker may be characterised as an expert rather than an arbitrator. Courts usually determine whether a decision-making process constitutes arbitration by looking to the factors that make the process appear like a judicial hearing. The assumption is that arbitrators are substitutes for judges. In the United States elements indicating arbitration include an ultimate determination of legal liability and a hearing at which evidence is taken from the parties.[95] Courts on the Continent have looked to similar features.[96]

9.58 Whether or not the parties intended to bring their dispute resolution under the arbitration statute will usually be relevant to characterisation. However, the label given to the adjudicatory process will not always be determinative. For example, courts have denied New York Convention coverage to determinations of the price of shares at the break-up of a joint venture, even though the process was labelled arbitration.[97]

9.59 Still another approach to distinguishing between an arbitrator and an expert might focus on the nature of the claim rather than the adjudicatory process. Along this line, arbitration would be indicated when the questions posed to the decision-maker approximate a request for judicial relief. For example, a building contractor and his customer, fighting over the non-payment of a bill, might ask the decision-maker, "Was the roof completed?". In the alternative, the question might be, "Does Customer owe $10,000 to Contractor?". An expert would be more likely to answer the first question, while the second would normally be for an arbitrator.

94. It is sometimes said that the role of experts is to avoid disputes, while the function of arbitrators and judges is to decide them. See Supreme Court of Canada decision in *Sport Maska* v. *Zittner* [1988] 1 SCR 564, at p. 588. Evaluators of inventory of bankrupt company held not to benefit from immunity as arbitrators. See also discussion of the award rendered in ICC Case No. 6535, involving a construction contract, 1993 *Journal du Droit International (Clunet)* 1024, comment by Dominique Hascher.

95. See, e.g., *Sanitary Farm Dairies* v. *Gammel*, 195 F.2d 106 (8th Cir. 1952); *Shepard & Morse Lumber* v. *Collins*, 256 P.2d 500 (Or. 1953); *Omaha* v. *Omaha Water Co.*, 218 US 180 (1910). See generally Samuel Williston, *16A Treatise on the Law of Contracts*, §1919.

96. See generally references cited in Charles Jarrosson, *La Notion d'Arbitrage*, ss.202–297, pp. 112–157 (1987). See also decision of the Swiss Tribunal fédéral in *X et Y* contre *Z*, 26 Nov. 1991, ATF 117 Ia 365. See discussion in Paolo Michele Patocchi & Elliott Geisinger, *Code de Droit International Privé Suisse Annoté*, 433 (1995), concerning Art. 176 of the Swiss Loi fédérale sur le droit international privé.

97. See, e.g, *Frydman* v. *Cosmair*, 1995 WL 404841 (SDNY 1995). The decision was rendered under Art. 1592 of the French Code civil (*arbitrage d'un tiers*). As a consequence the enforcement of the decision could not be removed to federal court under 9 USC §§203 and 205.

Debt rescheduling and public sector lending

9.60 The British economist John Maynard Keynes reportedly remarked, "If you owe a man £100, you have a problem. If you owe him £1 million, he has a problem".

9.61 Restructuring a country's external debt often implicates amounts so sizeable that, to paraphrase Keynes, it is the bank not the borrower which has the problem. Debtor nations may have enough economic muscle to reject jurisdiction clauses designating the lender country's own courts. For example, rescheduling agreements with Brazil accepted New York governing law, but provided arbitration as a dispute resolution mechanism.[98]

9.62 Multilateral lending to states and state enterprises has likewise tended to include arbitration clauses in loan and guarantee documentation.[99] For example, the Standard Terms and Conditions of the European Bank for Reconstruction and Development adopt the UNCITRAL Arbitration Rules, and designate the International Court of Justice as the appointing authority.[100] The World Bank's General Conditions Applicable to Loan and Guarantee Agreements provide for arbitration under an ad hoc procedure.[101]

9.63 Bilateral public sector lending has also relied on arbitration. For example, during the period of Franco-Iranian co-operation in nuclear energy, the French Atomic Energy Commission agreed to provide Iran with services, expertise and access to uranium, in return for which Iran made loans to the French, including $1 billion credit extended to the Atomic Energy Commission. The loan agreement signed by Iran was governed by Iranian law, but provided that "[a]ny disputes arising in connection with this Agreement . . . shall be settled finally in Geneva" under the Rules of Arbitration of the International Chamber of Commerce. When these arrangements went sour after the 1979 Iranian

98. See Deposit Facility Agreement between Banco Central do Brasil and Republica Federativa do Brasil (as guarantor) and Citibank, N.A. (as agent), §12.08(a)–(b), 22 September, 1988.

99. In contrast, private sector lending by the European Bank for Reconstruction and Development retains the option to elect, at the time of a dispute, either to arbitrate or to sue the borrower in its country of residence. If elected by the bank, arbitration will proceed according to the UNCITRAL Arbitration Rules, with a *situs* in London and the London Court of International Arbitration as the appointing authority. See generally John W. Head, "Evolution of the governing law for loan agreements of the World Bank and other multilateral development banks", 90 *American Journal of Int'l law* 214 (1996).

100. S.8.04, September 1994 version of the Standard Terms and Conditions, European Bank for Reconstruction and Development. Other elements of the arbitral procedure provided in the Standard Terms include a three-member arbitral tribunal, the Hague as the seat of arbitration and proceedings in English.

101. S.10.04, International Bank for Reconstruction and Development, 1985 Version of General Conditions Applicable to Loan and Guarantee Agreements.

revolution, arbitration and ancillary litigation ensued in both Geneva and Paris.[102]

DRAFTING THE ARBITRATION CLAUSE

General principles

9.64 The cardinal rule of drafting an international arbitration agreement is to avoid the type of ambiguity or equivocation that will delight a party wishing to drag its feet. In some cases a defective arbitration clause may be unenforceable.[103] In other cases, courts may repair a defective clause by presuming the parties' intent as to elements that are missing[104] or ambiguous.[105] Either way, the uncertainty adds an unnecessary layer of contention to business relationships.[106]

9.65 In addition to an unambiguous submission to arbitration of *all* disputes connected with the contract, five aspects of an arbitration clause are vital:

1. a workable mechanism for appointing arbitrators;
2. the place of arbitration;
3. the standard for fixing the arbitrators' fees;
4. the language of the arbitration; and
5. the number of arbitrators.

102. See ICC Arbitration No. 3683 and 5124; Swiss Tribunal fédéral *CEA* v. *Republique Islamique d'Iran*, ATF 116 II, May 17, 1990, reported in *Semaine Judiciaire*, 1990, No. 26, at 566; Judgment of 20 March 1989, French Cour de cassation, 1re Chambre civile, 1989 Rev. Arb. 653–667 comment P. Fouchard, and Judgment of June 28, 1989, Cour de cassation, 1re Chambre civile, 1989 Rev. Arb. 653–57 comment P. Fouchard. A separate French franc loan was made to a related entity called Eurodif, with an award rendered 22 December 1990. See "Eurodif est condammé à payer 940 millions de francs à l'Iran", *Le Monde*, 1 January 1991, at 16.

103. See *Bauhinia Corp.* v. *China Nat'l Mach. & Equip. Import & Export*, 819 F.2d 247 (9th Cir. 1987). See also *Nat'l Iranian Oil Co.* v. *Ashland Oil*, 817 F.2d 326 (1987), in which the court deemed itself without power to enforce an arbitration clause providing for arbitration in Iran.

104. See *Jain* v. *De Méré*, 51 F.3d 686 (7th Cir. 1995) (holding court could compel arbitration notwithstanding that contract failed to specify either location of arbitration or method for appointing arbitrators).

105. See *Paul Smith Ltd* v. *H & S International Holding Inc.* [1991] 2 Lloyd's Rep. 127. Contract provided for both arbitration and submission to the exclusive jurisdiction of the courts of England. Reference to English courts was interpreted as a specification of the curial law governing the arbitration, covering matters such as interim measures of protection, vacancies in the arbitral tribunal and the removal of arbitrators for misconduct.

106. See *Mediterranean Enterprises, Inc.* v. *Ssangyong Corp.*, 708 F.2d 1458 (9th Cir. 1983) (language calling for arbitration of "any disputes arising under" joint venture agreement held not to cover claim of inducing breach of contract under related agency contract). Compare *SA Mineracao da Trinidade-Samitri* v. *Utah Int'l, Inc.*, 745 F.2d 190 (2d Cir. 1984) (clause providing for arbitration "whenever any question or dispute shall arise or occur under" the agreement held broad enough to include claims of fraudulent inducement to contract); *J.J. Ryan & Sons, Inc.* v. *Rhone Poulenc Textile SA* 863 F.2d 315 (4th Cir. 1988) (standard ICC clause providing for arbitration of "all disputes arising in connection with" a distribution agreement held to cover controversies related to ancillary agreements between the parties, as well as claims related to defendant's interference with contracts between plaintiff and its customers).

Additional desirable items include a choice-of-law clause (both substantive and procedural[107]), provisions for pre-award attachment and interim judicial injunctive relief, and automatic consolidation of related arbitral proceedings. It is occasionally useful to include qualifications for arbitrators, time limits for constituting the tribunal and rendering the award, clarification of the arbitrator's power to grant punitive damages and allocate attorneys' fees, a "last best offer" procedure (so-called baseball arbitration) and a requirement of reasoned awards.

9.66 Many of these items can be covered by reference to the procedural rules of an arbitral institution, which will fill some of the gaps in the parties' arbitration clause. (See Appendix I to this chapter.) Among the more widely known institutional rules are those of the American Arbitration Association (AAA), the International Chamber of Commerce (ICC) and the London Court of International Arbitration (LCIA). Other arbitration rules that occasionally will be used include those of the Geneva Chamber of Commerce and Industry (GCCI), the International Centre for the Settlement of Investment Disputes (ICSID) and the United Nations Commission on International Trade Law (UNCITRAL).

The arbitral *situs*

9.67 By permitting refusal of recognition to awards set aside where rendered, the New York Convention entrusts the place of arbitration with power either to uproot an award or to vest an award with presumptive international currency. Thus the choice of an arbitral *situs* is perhaps the most important component of an international arbitration agreement other than designation of the rules for selecting the arbitrators.

9.68 Judicial review of awards at the place where rendered normally falls into several categories. The first model admits appeal on the legal merits, as well as procedural irregularities such as arbitrator bias and excess of authority. The second limits courts to review of procedural fairness only. Under a third but less

107. It is best to be explicit that issues related to the arbitration and the arbitration agreement will be decided by the law of the arbitral *situs*. When the law selected to interpret the principal contract is applied to the arbitration clause as well, a court asked to recognise an arbitration clause in one jurisdiction (e.g., in New York) may sometimes stay arbitration until the validity of the clause is determined by a tribunal in the country whose law was selected (e.g., Venezuela). See decision by Judge Rakoff in *Pepsico* v. *Officina Central de Asesoria*, SDNY, 96 Civ. No. 7817, 28 October 1996. The court ultimately granted Pepsico's motion to compel arbitration after a decision on the validity of the arbitration clause by a court in Caracas. See *Pepsico* v. *Ayuda Tecnia*, SDNY, 96 Civ. No. 7817, decision of 25 February 1997, reprinted in 12 *Mealey's International Arbitration Reports* (No. 3, March 1997), See also *Volt* v. *Stanford*, 489 US 468 (1989), where California state law was held to apply to both the merits of the dispute and the arbitration procedure, with the consequence that an arbitration was stayed under California law pending resolution of related court proceedings.

popular paradigm for international arbitration, the arbitral *situs* provides no grounds at all on which an award may be set aside.[108]

9.69 The best place for arbitration is normally in a country where the judiciary will safeguard the procedural integrity of the arbitral process, but not insist on correcting an arbitrator's honest mistake on the substantive merits of the dispute. A right of appeal on points of law tends to maximise judicial certainty, but only at the price of finality. In arbitration the parties assume some risk of a "bad award", in the sense of an arbitrator getting it wrong on the facts of the law. However, the parties do not usually (if ever) agree to arbitrator excess of authority, bias, or departure from fundamental procedural fairness.

9.70 Courts in France,[109] Switzerland[110] and the United States,[111] as well as countries that follow the UNCITRAL Model Arbitration Law, all provide for judicial monitoring of an arbitration's procedural regularity, but do not allow appeal on the award's substantive legal merits.[112] England's recently adopted Arbitration Act allows review of jurisdictional matters and procedural fairness,[113] but also permits appeal on points of law unless otherwise agreed by the parties.[114]

Unilateral clauses?[115]

9.71 From the perspective of litigation strategy, the best of all worlds for the lending institution would be to have an option either to elect arbitration or to go to court.[116] Such a unilateral right to arbitrate permits significant flexibility with respect to elements that are hard to forecast when a contract is signed. For example, a lender may want to assess, after a dispute arises, whether extensive documentary discovery is in its interest. In the negative, court proceedings could be waived in favour of arbitration, with the concomitant likelihood of less discovery.

9.72 Whether such unilaterally optional clauses will be enforceable is not

108. See Belgium's Code Judiciaire, Art. 1717. Compare Art. 192 of Switzerland's conflict-of-laws code (Loi fédérale sur le droit international privé), permitting but not mandating a similar exclusion of all judicial review in some cases.

109. See French Nouveau code de procédure civile, Art. 1502.

110. See Swiss Loi fédérale sur le droit international privé, Art. 190. In some cases parties may opt to exclude any judicial review. See Art. 192. Under cantonal law, however, arbitral awards may be set aside for "evident violation of law or equity". See Intercantonal Concordat, Art. 36(f).

111. 9 USC §10.

112. France and Switzerland, as well as the UNCITRAL Model, also list "public policy" (*ordre public*) as a ground for challenge to awards. The appropriateness of public policy as a basis for setting aside an award where rendered (as opposed to refusal to enforce the award at the asset *situs*) is open to question.

113. Arbitration Act 1996, ss.67 (substantive jurisdiction) and 68 (serious irregularity).

114. Arbitration Act 1996, s.69.

115. See generally Laurent Niddam, "Unilateral arbitration clauses in commercial arbitration", 1996 Arb. Dispute Res. L.J. 147 (1996).

116. For an example, see private sector lending practice of European Bank for Reconstruction and Development.

entirely certain. Rightly or wrongly, the principle of "mutuality" (of remedy and of obligation) has occasionally been invoked to invalidate a one-sided arbitration agreement. Some decisions have taken the view that if both parties are not bound then neither is bound.[117] Other cases have been willing to enforce optional clauses.[118] Regardless of the correct answer from a policy perspective, a unilateral clause may be an invitation to litigation.

9.73 The principle of mutuality can work both ways, however. In at least one case mutuality was pressed into service to justify enforcement of a forum selection clause for the benefit of a defendant who was not a party to the agreement.[119]

9.74 In contrast to arbitration, court selection clauses covered by the Brussels and Lugano Conventions seem to admit unilateral jurisdiction selection.[120] This principle accords with cases enforcing a contractual right to choose between several different courts.[121]

UNCERTAINTIES IN FINANCIAL ARBITRATION

The International Monetary Fund Agreement

9.75 The Articles of Agreement of the International Monetary Fund ("IMF") may in some cases circumscribe an arbitrator's power to hear the dispute. The IMF Articles prohibit Member States from imposing exchange controls on

117. See, e.g, *Hull* v. *Norcom, Inc.*, 750 F.2d 1547 (11th Cir. 1985). Arbitration clause in employment agreement subject to New York law not enforceable because employer retained right to go to court; result would probably be different today in light of *Sablosky* v. *Gordon*, below. See also *Lopez* v. *Plaza Finance*, 1996 WL 210073 (ND Ill. 1996) (arbitration clause not enforceable in instalment loan agreement where debtor could not arbitrate disputes related to events of default); *Stevens, Leinweber, Sullens Inc.* v. *Holm Development*, 795 P.2d 1308 (Ct. App. Ariz. 1990); *R.W. Roberts Construction* v. *St. John's River Water Mgt. Dist.*, 423 So.2d 630 (Fla. App. 5th Dist., 1982); *Stirlen* v. *Supercuts*, California 1st Appellate District, No. AO 70573 (9 January 1997), reported in 7 WA & MR 293 (December 1996) (employment contract).

118. See *Sablosky* v. *Gordon Co.*, 73 NY2d 133 (1989), 138–139; *Becker Autoradio* v. *Becker Autoradiowerk*, 585 F.2d 39, 42 (3d Cir. 1978); *Doctor's Associates* v. *Distrajo*, 66 F.3d 438, 451 (2d Cir. 1995); *Willis Flooring* v. *Howard S. Lease Construction*, 656 P.2d 1184 (Alaska 1983); *Kalman Floor Co.* v. *Jos. L. Muscarelle Inc.*, 481 A.2d 553 (NJ Superior AD 1984); *Cindy's Candle Co.* v. *WNS Inc.*, 714 F.Supp. 973 (ND Ill., ED, 1989); *W.L. Jorden & Co.* v. *Blythe Industries Inc.*, 702 F.Supp. 282 (ND Ga. 1988).

119. See *Frietsch* v. *Refco*, 56 F.3d 825, 827–828 (7th Cir. 1995). Defendant brokerage firm, not party to contracts between investors and promoters of commodities investment pool, permitted to reply on contractual choice of German forum to preclude action in the United States for allegedly operating a Ponzi scheme. Judge Posner rejected "asymmetry of procedural choices".

120. See Art. 17(4), Brussels Convention.

121. See, e.g., *Medoil* v. *Citicorp.*, 729 F.Supp. 1456 (SDNY 1990) (customer could sue Citibank only at location of branch managing account, while bank could bring action also at customer's residence).

current transactions, absent IMF approval.[122] The flip side of this restriction is that controls which do comply with the IMF Agreement must be respected.[123]

9.76 Certain countries have extended the scope of the IMF restrictions to any contract that affects a nation's international balance of payments, including loan agreements between residents and non-residents.[124] By contrast, the narrower interpretation of the IMF Articles limits its application to contracts that involve the swap of one currency for another.[125]

9.77 The broad application of the IMF Articles has two consequences for cross-border financial arbitration. First, exchange controls (if properly imposed) arguably apply regardless of the applicable law chosen by the parties. Like other mandatory norms of international public policy (often referred to as *lois de police*), legitimate exchange controls would seem to be non-waivable.[126] Second, national courts might refuse to enforce arbitration agreements implicating exchange controls, on the ground that the subject-matter is "not capable of settlement by arbitration" under the New York Convention.[127] Some authors, however, have taken the position that the IMF Articles ought *not* to constitute such a bar to the arbitrability of international loan disputes.[128]

9.78 Of course, if an arbitrator enforces an agreement that does in fact violate the IMF Agreement, then the award might later be refused recognition. But this does not mean that the arbitrator should be prohibited *ab initio* from interpreting the IMF Articles. The need for a level playing field on which transnational loans may be enforced argues for allowing arbitrators to hear cross-border credit controversies regardless of subsequent public policy implications.

122. IMF Art. VIII(2)(a). Current transactions include interest on loans and payments of moderate amounts for loan amortisation.

123. IMF Art. VIII(2)(b) provides that "exchange contracts" contrary to valid exchange controls shall be unenforceable. Debate has focused on whether to interpret "exchange contract" broadly to cover all agreements affecting balance of payments, including cross-border loans.

124. In Germany, see *Lessinger* v. *Mirau*, 22 ILR 725 (1955); in France, see *De Boer, Widow Moojen* v. *Von Reichert* (Paris, 20 June 1961), 1962 JDI 718; in Luxembourg, see *Société Filature et Tissage X Jourdain* v. *Epousé Heynen-Bintner*, 22 ILR 727 (1995). See note by Bernard Audit on two judgments by the French Cour de cassation, 1966, JDI 102. See also Joseph Gold, "Article VIII, Section 2(b) of the I.M.F. Articles in its international setting", in 6 *Law of International Trade Finance* 65, 86 (1989); P. Cresswell *et al.*, *Encyclopedia of Banking Law*, §F1604 (London, 1987).

125. In US see *Libra Bank* v. *Banco Nacional*, 570 F.Supp. 870 (SDNY 1983). In England see *United City Merchants* v. *Royal Bank of Canada* [1983] AC 168.

126. See Pierre Mayer, "Mandatory rules of law in international arbitration", 2 *Arbitration International* 274 (1986); Pierre Mayer, "Les lois de police etrangères", 1981 J. Dr. Int'l 277; Bernard Audit, *Droit International Privé* §§92–113 (1991).

127. See New York Convention, Arts II(1) and V(2)(a).

128. See Otto Sandrock, "Internationale Kredite une die internationale Schiedsgerichtsbarkeit", 48 *Zeitschrift für Wirtschafts und Bankrecht*, nos. 10 and 11 (12 and 19 March 1994); William W. Park, "L'arbitrage et le recouvrement des prêts consentis à des débiteurs étrangers", 37 *Revue de droit de l'Université McGill* 375 (1992). These authors note that courts have shown an increasing tendency to recognise arbitration of other public-law issues and to enforce arbitration agreements in international contracts even if the subject-matter would make the agreement unenforceable in a purely domestic context.

Consumer transactions

9.79 Like any freedom, the right to choose a dispute resolution mechanism is justified by the values it furthers. Arbitration can in some cases promote fairer and more efficient adjudication, while in other situations it might deprive an unsophisticated party of basic procedural safeguards.

9.80 In this connection, the validity of arbitration agreements in consumer transactions has been subject to limitation and challenge.[129] Some courts have refused to enforce arbitration clauses in consumer loan contracts.[130] Others have upheld consumer finance arbitration agreements.[131] The heart of the matter seems to be whether such arbitration agreements are genuinely consensual.[132] Arguments for enforcement would seem weakest when the arbitration clause has been mailed with a customer's monthly statement in printed form unlikely to attract particular attention.

9.81 Cases that struggle with arbitration in non-banking consumer transactions have reached similarly inconsistent results, sometimes holding arbitration clauses void for lack of informed consent,[133] while on other occasions

129. See, e.g., Arts 13–17, Brussels Convention on Jurisdiction and Enforcement of Judgments in Civil and Commercial Matters, 27 September 1968, as amended, 1990 OJ (C189) 1, and Lugano Convention on Jurisdiction and Enforcement of Judgments in Civil & Commercial Matters, 16 September 1988, 1988 OJ (L319) 9.

130. See *Geneva Bell* v. *Congress Mortgage*, Cal. App. 1st Dist., 17 May 1994, 24 Cal. App. 4th 1675 (1994), *ordered depublished*, 30 Cal. Rep. 2d 205 (1994). The court in *Geneva Bell* refused to compel arbitration absent a "clear and informed" waiver of the right to a jury trial (homeowner claims against mortgage lenders for fraudulent business practices). See also *ITT Consumer Financial Corp.* v. *Patterson*, 14 Cal. App. 4th 1659, 18 Cal. Rptr. 2d 563 (1993), *petition for cert. denied*, US Supreme Court No. 93–952, 7 March 1994, 114 S.Ct. 1217 (arbitration clause used in documentation for relatively small loans was an unconscionable limit on the borrower's opportunity to be heard); *Lopez* v. *Plaza Finance Co.*, 1996 WL 210073 (ND Ill. 1996) (no enforcement of arbitration agreement in instalment loan).

131. *Badie* v. *Bank of America*, (California Superior Court, San Francisco, No. 944916), *decided*, 18 August 1994; bench opinion discussed in 63 BNA Banking Report 293 (29 August 1994) and 5 World Arb. and Mediation Rep. 231 (October 1994); *Meyers* v. *Univest Home Loan*, 1993 WL 307747 (ND Cal. 1993) (consumer loan), *McCarthy* v. *Providential Corp.*, 1994 WL 387852 (ND Cal. 1994) (senior citizen "reverse mortgage").

132. One lawyer acting for a borrower summed up the matter as follows: "I like to say that ADR is like sex: it's great if both parties consent, but can't be allowed if one party is forced into taking part." See "Consumer Arbitration", 4 World Arb. and Mediation Rep. (BNA) 192, 193 (1993) quoting Patricia Sturdevant, attorney for the plaintiffs in *Badie* v. *Bank of America*. See also "Consumer Arbitration", 5 World Arb. and Mediation Rep. (BNA) 231 (1994).

133. See *Prudential Ins.* v. *Lai*, 42 F.3d 1299 (9th Cir. 1994), *cert. denied*, 116 S.Ct. 61 (1995) (arbitration clause not enforced in employment discrimination suit). The medical context has provided particularly fertile ground for arbitration. The arbitrability of malpractice claims against doctors, hospitals and insurers and health maintenance organisations has been considered in *Wheeler* v. *St Joseph Hospital*, 133 Cal. Rptr. 775 (Cal. App 4th Dist., 1976) (arbitration agreement not enforced); *Madden* v. *Kaiser Foundation Hospitals*, 17 Cal.3d 687, 131 Cal. Rptr. 882 (1976) (reversing order denying arbitration and remanding for further proceedings); *Colorado Permanente Medical Group* v. *Evans*, Col. Sup. Ct., 12 Nov. 1996, No. 95C270 (HMO arbitration clause unenforceable for failure to comply with statutory form requirement).

recognising the clause.[134] At least two cases have enforced arbitration clauses packaged in boxes of mail-order goods.[135] In all events, the voluntary nature of forum selection agreements tends to be a highly fact-specific matter.[136]

9.82 European Union consumer protection regulations[137] have been applied to both pre-dispute and post-dispute arbitration agreements.[138] These regulations invalidate unfair contract terms which, depending on the circumstances, can include provisions that were not individually negotiated and which cause a "significant imbalance in the parties' rights and obligations" to the consumer's detriment.[139] In some countries analogous legislation pre-dates the European Union Directive.[140] While such regulations may need refinement, they represent a first step toward safeguarding procedural rights for the weaker party in a transaction.

134. See *Wilson* v. *Kaiser Foundation Hospitals*, 190 Cal. Rptr. 649 (1983) (arbitration clause in medical agreement enforceable in claim for prenatal injuries by child who became member of health plan at birth); *Golenia* v. *Bob Baker Toyota*, 915 F.Supp. 201 (SD Cal. 1996) (claim under Americans with Disabilities Act held arbitrable); *Johnson* v. *Hubbard Broadcast*, 940 F.Supp. 1447 (D. Minn. 1996) (arbitration agreement enforceable against former employee who brought race discrimination claim); *Rojas* v. *TK Communications*, 87 F.3d 745 (5th Cir. 1996) (sexual harassment claim held arbitrable); *Stedor Enterprises* v. *Armtex*, 947 F.2d 727 (4th Cir. 1991) (enforcement of arbitration agreement in fabric sale confirmation even though document unread and unsigned).

135. See, e.g., *ProCD, Inc.* v. *Zeidenberg*, 86 F.3d 1447 (7th Cir. 1996) (terms of arbitration clause inside software box); *Hill* v. *Gateway 2000*, 105 F.3d 1147 (7th Cir., 1997) (arbitration clause in box containing computer ordered by mail and not returned within 30 days; court stated that "a contract need not be read to be effective". *Id.*, at 1148).

136. On consent in contract, see generally Randy Barnett, "A consent theory of contract", 86 *Columbia Law Review* 269 (1986); Randy Barnett, "Conflicting visions: A critique of Ian MacNeil's relational theory of contract", 78 *Virginia Law Review* 1172 (1992). On consent to arbitration agreements in a labour contract, see Stephen Ware, "Employment arbitration and voluntary consent", 25 *Hofstra Law Review* 83 (1996).

137. European Council Directive 93/13/EEC, OJ No. L95, 21 April 1993, p. 29.

138. For the extension of these regulations to arbitration in England, see Arbitration Act 1996, s.89.

139. UK Unfair Terms in Consumer Contracts Regulations 1994, regs 3 and 4. Consumers include individuals acting for purposes outside their business. *Id.*, reg. 2. One schedule to these Regulations contains an illustrative list of contract terms that may be regarded as unfair, and therefore non-binding. This list includes an oddly worded reference to terms that require consumers to "take disputes exclusively to arbitration not covered by legal provisions". Sch. 3, para. 1(g). It is not immediately clear what is meant by this curious phraseology, lifted verbatim from the European Directive whose mandates were implemented by the British rules.

140. See, e.g., French Code Civil, Art. 2061 ("*La clause compromissoire est nulle s'il n'est disposé autrement par la loi.*") Compare provisions allowing post-dispute agreements to arbitrate (*compromis*) (Code Civil, Art. 2060), as well as pre-dispute arbitration between merchants (*commerçants*) (Code de Commerce, Art. 631).

Multiparty and multicontract problems[141]

9.83 Although the rules of some arbitral institutions provide for voluntary consolidation of related arbitrations,[142] this does not obviate the need to obtain the consent of the party to be joined. For better or for worse, the Federal Arbitration Act does not authorise forced consolidation of different arbitration proceedings, even if they present similar questions of law and fact.[143] Therefore a company may be whipsawed by inconsistent results in connected financial disputes, unless arbitration takes place in a state that does provide for joinder of related claims.[144]

9.84 Occasionally an arbitration may have several parties on one side of the proceedings. For example, in a contractual relationship involving more than two companies, several entities could find themselves as defendants together. In such a procedural configuration, particular care must be taken in establishing the arbitral tribunal. Conflict or stalemate may occur if two defendants must agree on a single party-nominated arbitrator. Attempts to impose one arbitrator on two parties have sometimes been resisted as a denial of "equality of treatment".[145]

Federal–state conflicts

9.85 In the United States, federal arbitration law will usually pre-empt application of more restrictive state rules.[146] However, it is often less than self-evident exactly what state laws will be considered restrictive, particularly when they have no analogue in the Federal Arbitration Act. For example, some courts refuse pre-award attachment in non-maritime arbitration, reasoning that by agreeing to arbitration parties have implicitly excluded intervention by

141. See generally, Michael Mustill, "Multipartite arbitrations: An agenda for lawmakers", 7 *Arbitration International* 389 (1991); Philippe Leboulanger, "Multi-contract arbitration", 13 (No. 4) *Journal of International Arbitration* 43 (1996).

142. See, for example, Art. 13.1 of the Arbitration Rules of the London Court of International Arbitration.

143. See *United Kingdom* v. *Boeing*, 998 F.2d 68 (2nd Cir. 1993).

144. See, e.g., Massachusetts Gen. Laws, c. 251, §2A, calling for consolidation as provided in the Massachusetts Rules of Civil Procedure, which permits joinder of actions "involving a common question of law or fact." See *New England Energy* v. *Keystone Shipping*, 855 F.2d 1 (1st Cir. 1988), holding that federal courts sitting in Massachusetts may order consolidation of related arbitrations pursuant to state statute. Compare California Code of Civil Procedure, §1281.3; Hong Kong Arbitration Ordinance, Ch. 351, §6B (applicable to domestic arbitration); Dutch Code of Civil Arbitration Law Procedure, §1046.

145. See, e.g., *Siemens and BKMI* v. *Dutco*, French Cour de Cassation, 7 Jan. 1992, Ch. Civile No. 1, 1992 Rev. Arb. 470.

146. See *Doctor's Associates* v. *Casarotto*, 116 S.Ct. 1652 (1996); *Allied-Bruce Terminex* v. *Dobson*, 115 S.Ct. 834 (1995). Pre-emption will occur not only in federal courts, but also in state court actions involving interstate commerce; see *Southland* v. *Keating*, 465 US 1 (1984).

national courts until an award is rendered.[147] Other courts view pre-award attachment as a way to maximise the efficiency of the arbitral process.[148]

9.86 With respect to the initial formation of arbitration agreements, state law cannot erect obstacles to the validity of arbitration clauses that do not apply to other contractual commitments. The United States Supreme Court recently struck down a state "notice requirement" calling for arbitration clauses to be in capital letters on the first page of the contract.[149] The Court found such threshold limitations on arbitration agreements to undermine the goals and policies of the Federal Arbitration Act.

9.87 Aside from this limitation, however, state law generally governs whether, and what, two contracting parties agreed to arbitrate.[150] Federal law will normally pre-empt state rules on contract formation only when state law discriminates against arbitration.[151] Some authorities argue that international arbitration agreements are subject to the law agreed upon by the parties, or to a supranational standard that incorporates only "internationally recognized defenses" to contract enforcement, such as duress, fraud and waiver.[152]

9.88 More rather than less conflict between federal and state law can be expected, as some states attempt to implement consumer protection measures, and others enact their own international arbitration statutes in the form of the UNCITRAL Model Law. The Federal Arbitration Act, unlike the arbitration law of several European countries, contains no distinction between domestic and international arbitration, nor a provision for sheltering consumers from abusive arbitration agreements.

147. See *McCreary Tire & Rubber* v. *CEAT*, 501 F.2d 1032 (3rd Cir. 1974) (pre-award attachment denied); *Cooper* v. *Ateliers Motobecane SA*, 57 NY2d 408 (1982). See generally David Wagoner, "Interim relief in international arbitration", *Dispute Resolution Journal* 68 (October 1996).

148. See *Carolina Power & Light* v. *Uranex*, 451 F.Supp. 1044 (ND Cal 1977) (pre-award attachment allowed).

149. See *Doctor's Associates* v. *Casarotto*, 116 S.Ct. 1652 (1996). See Stephen Ware, "Arbitration and unconscionability after *Doctor's Associates* v. *Casarotto*, 31 *Wake Forest Law Review* 1001 (1996). A similar approach was taken by the First Circuit in *Securities Industry Association* v. *Connolly*, 883 F.2d 1114 (1st Cir. 1989).

150. See *Kaplan* v. *First Options*, 115 S.Ct. 1920 (1995) (the Supreme Court, however, added a qualification to the effect that "courts should not assume that the parties agreed to arbitrate arbitrability [i.e., existence and scope of arbitrators' jurisdiction] unless there is 'clear and unmistakable' evidence that they did so". *Id.* at 1924.) See also dicta in *Perry* v. *Thomas*, 482 US 483, at 492 n. 9 (1987). Analysis of the role of state law generally turns on the "savings clause" in s.2 of the Federal Arbitration Act, limiting enforcement of arbitration agreements by the qualification "save upon such grounds as exist at law or in equity for the revocation of any contract". It is unclear from the text of s.2 whether federal or state law should supply the grounds "at law or in equity" for invalidating the arbitration clause.

151. Some authorities, however, argue that *international* arbitration agreements are subject to the law agreed upon by the parties or to a supranational standard that incorporates only "internationally recognized defenses" to contract enforcement, such as duress, fraud and waiver. See generally Gary Born, *International Commercial Arbitration in the United States* (1994), at 269–277.

152. See *Rhone* v. *Achille Lauro*, 712 F.2d 50, at 53 (3d Cir. 1983), holding arbitration clause valid notwithstanding possible invalidity under Italian law.

Arbitral jurisdiction[152a]

Loan workouts: a case study

9.89 How, when and by whom an arbitrator's jurisdiction is determined can have a critical impact on almost any arbitration. The United States Supreme Court has recently addressed this matter in *First Options of Chicago* v. *Kaplan*,[153] a case that arose from an investment company's loan restructuring. A workout agreement providing for arbitration of any disputes arising from the debt rescheduling was signed by the company but not by its shareholders. Nevertheless, an arbitral tribunal, considering a claim with respect to unpaid debts, pierced the corporate veil to render an award against the owners as well as their company.

9.90 In considering the allocation of functions between judges and arbitrators, a unanimous Supreme Court affirmed a lower court ruling that the owners had not agreed to be bound to arbitration. In the case at bar the arbitrator's jurisdiction was a question for the courts.

9.91 The court in *First Options* also suggested in dicta that in some cases courts must defer to the arbitrators' decision on their own jurisdiction.[154] If the scope of arbitral jurisdiction was itself submitted to arbitration, the Court said, arbitrators' jurisdictional determination would be shielded from independent judicial scrutiny.[155]

9.92 While this dictum may make sense in some contexts, there are certain situations in which it says either too much or too little. If awards may still be reviewed for excess of authority under the Fedral Arbitration Act, judicial deference to arbitrators' decisions on jurisdiction may be an illusion. On the other hand, courts straining to give meaning to the dictum (and to reduce their workload) might interpret the pronouncement liberally to permit an inappropriate degree of arbitral autonomy.

9.93 It has always been problematic to draw the thin line between an arbitrator's simple (and non-reviewable) error of fact or law, and an arbitrator's excess of authority (normally subject to judicial review). After *First Options*, however, judges will ask not only whether arbitrators exceeded their jurisdiction, but also whether the excess of jurisdiction deserves judicial deference.

152a. See generally William W. Park, "Determining arbitral jurisdiction: allocation of tasks between courts and arbitrators", 8 *American Review of International Arbitration* 133 (1997).

153. 115 S.Ct. 1920 (1995). See generally William W. Park, "The arbitrability dicta in *First Options* v. *Kaplan*", 12 *Arbitration International* 137 (1996).

154. The potentially troublesome dictum (which in some situations may eclipse the holding of the case) reads as follows: "If [the parties agreed to submit arbitrability to arbitration] then the court's standard for reviewing the arbitrator's decision about the matter should not differ from the standard courts apply when they review any other matter that the parties have agreed to arbitrate . . . That is to say, the court should give considerable leeway to the arbitrator, setting aside his or her decision only in certain narrow circumstances."

155. In such cases, the court said, review must be conducted according to the "narrow" standard found in s.10 of the Federal Arbitration Act, which lists grounds for *vacatur* that include fraud, excess of authority, partiality or corruption, and arbitrator misbehavior prejudicing the rights of any party.

9.94 An agreement giving arbitrators sole competence to rule on their jurisdiction would make sense if contained in a subsequent contract that refers to arbitration disputes about jurisdiction arising under a pre-existing arbitration agreement. For example, a bank might assert that an arbitration clause bound a borrower's parent corporation as well as the subsidiary, on the theory that the subsidiary had contracted the loan as agent for the parent. After a dispute had arisen, nothing would prevent the parent from agreeing to ask an arbitrator to determine whether it was in fact bound by the arbitration clause. The arbitral tribunal to whose authority the parent has consented under the second agreement would be convened to determine whether the parent bound itself under the first agreement.[156]

Compétence–compétence

9.95 Questions of arbitrator jurisdiction are sometimes analysed according to a chameleon-like concept referred to as *compétence–compétence* (literally "jurisdiction concerning jurisdiction"), which links together a constellation of disparate notions about when arbitrators can rule on the limits of their own power.

9.96 In its simplest formulation, *compétence–compétence* means no more than that arbitrators can look into their own jurisdiction without waiting for a court to do so. In other words, there is no need to stop arbitral proceedings to refer a jurisdictional issue to judges.[157] However, the arbitrators' determination about their power would be subject to judicial reivew at any time, including when a motion is made to stay court litigation or to compel arbitration.

9.97 French law goes further, however, and delays court review of arbitral jurisdiction until *after* an award is rendered. If an arbitral tribunal has already begun to hear a matter, courts must decline to hear the case. When an arbitral tribunal has not yet been constituted, court litigation will go forward only if the alleged arbitration agreement is clearly void (*manifestement nulle*).[158]

9.98 In Germany before adoption of the UNCITRAL Model Arbitration Law *Kompetenz–Kompetenz* has been used to describe a situation not unlike that contemplated in the dicta of *First Options* v. *Kaplan*. German case law once suggested that by contract an arbitral tribunal may be given power to rule on its own jurisdiction in a binding way, without subsequent judicial review.[159] However, this type of "arbitrability agreement" often opened the door to more problems than it resolved.

156. This is exactly what happened in *Astro Valiente Compania Naviera* v. *Pakistan Ministry of Food & Agriculture (The Emmanuel Colocotronis) (No. 2)* [1982] 1 All E.R. 823.

157. See *Christopher Brown Ltd* v. *Genossenschaft Oesterreichischer Waldbesitzer* [1954] 1 QB 8.

158. See Art. 1458 of the Nouveau code de procédure civile.

159. See decisions of the Bundesgerichtshof discussed in Peter Schlosser, *Das Recht der Internationalen Privaten Schiedsgerichtbarkeit* (1989), at §556. The current reform of arbitration law in Germany, however, changed the operation of *Kompetenz–Kompetenz*.

9.99 To some extent, what is at issue here is the timing of judicial review. Going to court at the beginning of the proceedings can save expense for a defendant improperly joined to the arbitration on the basis of a clause that is either invalid or too limited in scope. On the other hand, judicial resources may be conserved by delaying review until the end of the process, when the parties may have settled. In this connection, Article 16 of the UNCITRAL Model Arbitration Law gives the arbitral tribunal an explicit right to determine its own jurisdiction in the form of an interim award subject to challenge within 30 days.

Separability

9.100 *Compétence–compétence* analysis is sometimes confused with notions of separability, which permits arbitrators to invalidate the main contract (e.g., for illegality or fraud in the inducement) without the risk that their decision will also invalidate the source of their power. The doctrine of separability does not, however, give the arbitrator the right to pass upon alleged infirmities in the arbitration clause itself.

9.101 To illustrate the difference between separability and *compétence–compétence*, assume that an arbitration clause has been included in a "Consulting Agreement" entered into by an American corporation seeking to obtain a public works contract in a foreign country. The American company might resist arbitration on two grounds: (i) the person who signed the agreement was not authorised to do so, and (ii) the agreement was void because payments thereunder were earmarked to bribe government officials.

9.102 Separability notions would permit the arbitrators to find the main contract void for ilelgality without destroying their power to do so under the arbitration clause, but would not permit the arbitrators to decide whether the individual who signed the agreement was authorised to do so. On the other hand, *compétence–compétence* principles would permit the arbitrators to examine the validity of the signature, but would not save an award declaring the contract void for illegality.

9.103 Unfortunately, not all legal academics, practitioners and judges have taken care to distinguish separability from notions about the arbitrators' power to determine their own jurisdiction.[160] Properly understood, however, separability should not prevent a party from resisting arbitration on the ground that consent was lacking, or that the arbitrators exceeded the scope of their mission.[161] For example, a court could still vacate an award based on a contract signed by someone without authority, since the lack of authority would render

160. For a case taking the right approach to matters of arbitral jurisdiction (at least from this author's perspective) see *Three Valleys* v. *E.F. Hutton*, 925 F.2d 1136 (9th Cir. 1991).

161. For a recent codification of the separability doctrine, see the English Arbitration Act 1996, s.7. The Act carefully avoids the type of confusion that has arisen in some minds about separability by also providing that English courts will not enforce an arbitration agreement that is "null and void, inoperative, or incapable of being performed". *Id.*, s.9(4).

inoperative the arbitration clause itself. Arbitrators get the final word on the principal agreement, not the arbitration clause.[162]

CONCLUSION

9.104 The identity of the person who will decide a financial controversy often matters as much as, or more than, the legal standards that purport to govern the merits of the dispute. Rules by themselves have little power to prevent an unjust decision by an antagonist jury or a xenophobic judge. Equally as important, the fairest and most favourable decision will mean little in practice unless it can be enforced against the loser's assets.

9.105 Against these twin concerns—biased adjudicators and unenforceable judgments—lawyers in the financial services industry increasingly are called to evaluate the relative reliability of arbitration agreements as contrasted to court selection clauses. The effectiveness of each of these dispute resolution mechanisms will depend largely on its context, both geographic and transactional.

9.106 In some countries, court judgments will benefit from not a single enforcement treaty, nor will jurisdiction clauses receive dispositive effect from any statute. Moreover, court selection agreements may prove ineffective when judges are unable or unwilling to allow the parties to thrust a case upon the court, due either to limits on subject-matter jurisdiction or to *forum non conveniens* notions.

9.107 On the other hand, the New York Convention mandates enforcement of arbitration agreements and awards throughout the world. And *forum non conveniens* and subject-matter jurisdiction limits are unlikely to prevent arbitrators from hearing a case, assuming their fees can be paid.

9.108 Arbitration, of course, suffers from its own sources of uncertainty. For example, in many jurisdictions there exists no easy way to consolidate related claims. And in some countries judicial decisions have unfortunately obscured the process for monitoring arbitrator excess of jurisdiction.

9.109 Before drafting a forum selection clause, therefore, counsel will need to focus on several questions. Can a judgment be rendered in a location where the debtor has assets? If not, will an international treaty mandate enforcement of the judgment of a court with jurisdiction to hear the dispute? Is the debtor's country likely to impose exchange controls? Will the courts entertain lender liability or punitive damage claims against the banker? How costly and time-consuming

162. In most cases, it will be possible to contest arbitral jurisdiction either at the beginning of the arbitration (for example, by bringing a competing action in court) or after the award is rendered. In either case, courts will usually have the opportunity to decide whether the arbitration clause was invalid or inoperative, whether *ab initio* or due to subsequent events. With respect to the timing of judicial review, France is the only major legal system that says courts must wait until the end of the arbitration to look at arbitral jurisdiction. See Nouveau code de procédure civile, Art. 1458.

will a court action prove to be? Will summary judgment procedure be available to the lender?

9.110 Depending on the answers to these questions, an arbitration clause can sometimes prove more reliable and efficient than a court selection agreement. First, when a borrower's assets are located in countries that have not concluded judgment treaties with the expected litigation forum, the New York Arbitration Convention may be a more effective enforcement mechanism than local rules about enforcement of foreign judgments. Second, when loans are subject to possible exchange controls, an arbitration clause reduces the likelihood of an Act of State defence to loan enforcement. Third, an arbitrator may be more reasonable than a jury in considering a punitive damages claim, or a lender liability action against a banker who has refused to advance additional funds or extend the term of a loan. Finally, arbitration occasionally commends itself in resolving documentary credit disputes more efficiently, and with more expertise, than does a judicial proceeding.

9.111 The interplay of these diverse elements in financial transactions makes it dangerous to rely on a "one size fits all" dispute resolution clause, based on habit rather than informed analysis. Financial lawyers will need to learn to relish a substantial amount of nuance in crafting dispute resolution clauses appropriate to the contours of each particular type of transaction. Solutions adopted now, when financial arbitration remains embryonic, will create a path dependency that will affect reliability in financial transactions for years to come.

WILLIAM W. PARK

APPENDIX I

MODEL ARBITRATION CLAUSES

COMMERCIAL LOAN AGREEMENT

9.112

1. All differences, controversies or claims arising in connection with, or questions related to the present Loan Agreement shall be finally settled under the Rules of Arbitration of the London Court of International Arbitration (LCIA)[1] by an arbitral tribunal composed of three arbitrators appointed in accordance with said Rules.

2. In all cases the Presiding Arbitrator shall be a lawyer fluent in English [and/or alternate language], experienced in international financial matters and not of the same nationality as either party.

3. The place of arbitration shall be [ ].

4. The language of the arbitration shall be [ ].

5. The parties hereby exclude any right of appeal to any court on the merits of the dispute.

6. Judgment on the award may be entered in any court having jurisdiction over the award or any of the parties or their assets.

7. This Agreement shall be governed and construed according to the laws of [ ] [and/or reference to UCP 500 for documentary credit disputes], provided that any dispute relating to this arbitration agreement or its implementation, including any challenge to the arbitral award, shall be governed by the laws of [ ].[2] The arbitral tribunal shall not decide in *amiable composition*, *ex aequo et bono* or according to any other principles that substitute equitable considerations and fairness for the substantive law and/or rules applicable to the merits of the dispute.

8. Nothing contained in this arbitration clause shall prevent either party from seeking interim measures of protection in the form of pre-award attachment of assets, or from seeking injunctive relief to enforce in courts of competent jurisdiction rights related to pledges, mortgages and other security interests.

9. In the event that disputes arise under both this present Agreement and any other document or instrument executed in connection with the transactions contemplated hereby, or in the event any dispute arises implicating more than two parties, such disputes shall be resolved in a consolidated arbitral proceeding by a single arbitrator appointed by the LCIA.

1. Alternative arbitral institutions include, by way of illustration, the International Chamber of Commerce, the American Arbitration Association and the Chambre de Commerce et d'Industrie de Genève.

2. For difficulties that can arise from failure to specify an appropriate law applicable to the arbitration agreement and procedure, particularly in a federal system, see *Volt* v. *Stanford*, 489 US 468 (1989) and *Pepsico* v. *Officina Central de Asesoria*, SDNY, 96 Civ. No. 7817, 28 October 1996.

WORLD BANK GENERAL CONDITIONS

International Bank for Reconstruction and Development

General Conditions Applicable to Loan and Guarantee Agreements

Article X, Section 10.04. Arbitration.

9.113

(a) Any controversy between the parties to the Loan Agreement or the parties to the Guarantee Agreement, and any claim by any such party against any other such party arising under the Loan Agreement or the Guarantee Agreement which has not been settled by agreement of the parties shall be submitted to arbitration by an Arbitral Tribunal as hereinafter provided.

(b) The parties to such arbitration shall be the Bank on the one side and the Borrower and the Guarantor on the other side.

(c) The Arbitral Tribunal shall consist of three arbitrators appointed as follows: one arbitrator shall be appointed by the Bank, a second arbitrator shall be appointed by the Borrower and the Guarantor or, if they shall not agree, by the Guarantor; and the third arbitrator (hereinafter sometimes called the Umpire) shall be appointed by agreement of the parties or, if they shall not agree, by the President of the International Court of Justice or, failing appointment by said President, by the Secretary-General of the United Nations. If either side shall fail to appoint an arbitrator, such arbitrator shall be appointed by the Umpire. In case any arbitrator appointed in accordance with this Section shall resign, die or become unable to act, a successor arbitrator shall be appointed in the same manner as herein prescribed for the appointment of the original arbitrator and such successor shall have all the powers and duties of such original arbitrator.

(d) An arbitration proceeding may be instituted under this Section upon notice by the party instituting such proceeding to the other party. Such notice shall contain a statement setting forth the nature of the controversy or claim to be submitted to arbitration and the nature of the relief sought and the name of the arbitrator appointed by the party instituting such proceeding. Within thirty days after such notice, the other party shall notify to the party instituting the proceeding the name of the arbitrator appointed by such other party.

(e) If within sixty days after the notice instituting the arbitration proceeding, the parties shall not have agreed upon an Umpire, any party may request the appointment of an Umpire as provided in paragraph (c) of this Section.

(f) The Arbitral Tribunal shall convene at such time and place as shall be fixed by the Umpire. Thereafter, the Arbitral Tribunal shall determine where and when it shall sit.

(g) The Arbitral Tribunal shall decide all questions relating to its competence and shall, subject to the provisions of this Section and except as the parties shall otherwise agree, determine its procedure. All decisions of the Tribunal shall be by majority vote.

(h) The Arbitral Tribunal shall afford to all parties a fair hearing and shall render its award in writing. Such award may be rendered by default. An award signed by a majority of the Arbitral Tribunal shall constitute the award of such Tribunal. A signed counterpart of the award shall be transmitted to each party. Any such award rendered in accordance with the provisions of this Section shall be final and binding upon the parties to the Loan Agreement and the Guarantee Agreement. Each party shall abide by and comply with any such award rendered by the Arbitral Tribunal in accordance with the provisions of this Section.

(i) The parties shall fix the amount of the remuneration of the arbitrators and such other persons as shall be required for the conduct of the arbitration proceedings. If the parties shall not agree on such amount before the Arbitral Tribunal shall convene, the Arbitral Tribunal shall fix such amount as shall be reasonable under the circumstances. The Bank, the Borrower and the Guarantor shall each defray its own expenses in the arbitration proceedings. The costs of the Arbitral Tribunal shall be divided between them, borne equally by the Bank on the one side and the Borrower and the Guarantor on the other. Any question concerning the division of the costs of the Arbitral Tribunal or the procedure for payment of such costs shall be determined by the Arbitral Tribunal.

(j) The provisions for arbitration set forth in this Section shall be in lieu of any other procedure for the settlement of controversies between the parties to the Loan Agreement and Guarantee Agreement or of any claim by any such party against any other such party arising thereunder.

(k) If, within thirty days after counterparts of the award shall have been delivered to the parties, the award shall not be complied with, any party may: (i) enter judgment upon, or institute a proceeding to enforce, the award in any court of competent jurisdiction against any other party; (ii) enforce such judgment by execution; or (iii) pursue any other appropriate remedy against such other party for the enforcement of the award and the provisions of the Loan Agreement or the Guarantee Agreement. Notwithstanding the foregoing, this Section shall not authorize any entry of judgment or enforcement of the award against any party that is a member of the Bank except as such procedure may be available otherwise than by reason of the provisions of this Section.

(l) Service of any notice or process in connection with any proceeding under this Section or in connection with any proceeding to enforce any award rendered pursuant to this Section may be made in the manner provided in Section 11.01. The parties to the Loan Agreement and the Guarantee Agreement waive any and all other requirements for the service of any such notice or process.

EUROPEAN BANK STANDARD TERMS

European Bank for Reconstruction and Development
Standard Terms and Conditions

Article VIII, Section 8.04. Dispute resolution.

9.114

(a) The parties to the Loan Agreement and the Guarantee Agreement shall endeavour to settle amicably any dispute or controversy between them arising out of such agreements or in connection therewith. To this end, at the initiative of any party to either such agreement, the other party or parties shall meet promptly with the initiating party to discuss the dispute or controversy and, if requested by the initiating party in writing, shall reply in writing to any written submission made by the initiating party concerning the dispute or controversy.

(b) If any such dispute or controversy, or any claim relating thereto, cannot be amicably settled as provided for in subsection (a), it shall be settled by arbitration in accordance with the UNCITRAL Arbitration Rules in force at the time the arbitral proceedings commence, subject to the following:

- (i) The number of arbitrators shall be three (3);
- (ii) The appointing authority for the purposes of the UNCITRAL Arbitration Rules shall be the President of the International Court of Justice;
- (iii) The place of arbitration shall be The Hague;
- (iv) The language to be used in the arbitral proceedings shall be English;
- (v) The law to be applied by the arbitral tribunal shall be public international law, the sources of which shall be taken for these purposes to include:
  - (A) any relevant treaty obligations that are binding reciprocally on the parties;
  - (B) the provisions of any international conventions and treaties (whether or not binding directly as such on the parties) generally recognized as having

codified or ripened into binding rules of customary law applicable to states and international financial institutions, as appropriate;

(C) other forms of international custom, including the practice of states and international financial institutions of such generality, consistency and duration as to create legal obligations; and

(D) applicable general principles of law;

(vi) Notwithstanding the provisions of the UNCITRAL Arbitration Rules, the arbitral tribunal shall not be authorized to take any interim measures of protection or provide any pre-award relief against the Bank and none of the parties to the Loan Agreement or Guarantee Agreement may address to any judicial authority a request for any interim measures of protection or pre-award relief against the Bank; and

(vii) The arbitral tribunal shall have authority to consider and include in any proceeding, decision or award, any dispute or controversy properly brought before it by the Bank, the Borrower, the Guarantor or the Project Entity, insofar as such dispute or controversy arises out of the Loan Agreement or the Guarantee Agreement; but subject to the foregoing no other parties or other disputes shall be included in, or consolidated with, the arbitral proceedings.

(c) Notwithstanding the provisions of this Section, nothing contained in these Standard Terms and Conditions shall operate or be regarded as a waiver, renunciation, or other modification of any right, privilege, or immunity of the Bank under Chapter VIII of the Agreement Establishing the Bank or under any applicable laws.

(d) In any arbitral proceeding arising out of the Loan Agreement or the Guarantee Agreement, the certificate of the Bank as to any amount due to the Bank under this Agreement shall be prima facie evidence of such amount.

MULTILATERAL INVESTMENT GUARANTEE AGENCY

General Conditions of Guarantee for Loans

Article 3. Dispute resolution and applicable law.

9.115

3.1 Any dispute between the Guarantee Holder and MIGA arising out of or in connection with the Contract (other than disputes regarding the determination of the Reference Rate of Exchange under Article 15) shall be settled by arbitration in accordance with the Arbitration Rules.[3] Arbitration proceedings shall be held in Washington, D.C.

3.2 No award may require MIGA to pay to the Guarantee Holder more than the Maximum Aggregate Liability plus interest under Article 22, and the cost of the arbitral proceeding.

3.3 The award of the Arbitral Tribunal shall be final and binding on the parties and enforceable in any court of competent jurisdiction. The parties shall carry out the award without delay.

3.4 Subject to Section 3.5, the Arbitral Tribunal shall apply the Contract and Convention, and to the extent that issues in dispute are not covered by the Contract or the Convention, general principles of law.

3.5 All provisions of the Contract shall be presumed to be consistent with the Convention and Operational Regulations. Such presumption may not be challenged by either MIGA or the Guarantee Holder.

3. The "Rules of Arbitration for Disputes under Contract of Guarantee of the Multilateral Investment Guarantee Agency" provide for appointment of one arbitrator by each party, and the appointment of the president of the tribunal either on concurrence of both parties or by the Secretary General if concurrence is not posible. See Arts 10 and 11 of the Rules of Arbitration.

APPENDIX II

SELECTED BIBLIOGRAPHY

9.116

American Arbitration Association, *Resolving Commercial and Financial Disputes* (1993).

Mark Augenblick & Delissa Ridgway, "Dispute resolution in world financial institutions", 10 (No. 1) *Journal of International Arbitration* 73 (1993).

Piero Bernardini, "The use of arbitration in banking and financial transactions", International Bar Association Section on Business Law, Committee D and Committee E, 12th Biennial Conference (Paris, September 1995).

E. Michael Bradley & William C. Rand, "The use of arbitration in banking and financial transactions", International Bar Association Section on Business Law, Committee D and Committee E, 12th Biennial Conference (Paris, September 1995).

James R. Butler, *Arbitration in Banking: State of the Art* (Robert Morris Associates) (1988).

Bernard Chambreuil, "Arbitrage international et garanties bancaires", 1991 *Revue de l'arbitrage* 33.

City Disputes Panel Handbook, London, 1994.

Carsten Ebenroth & Thomas Dillon, "Arbitration clauses in international financial agreements, 10 (No. 2) *Journal of International Arbitration* 5 (1993).

Michael Ferry, "Is it time for mandatory arbitration in contracts?", *Business Law Today*, May–June 1995, p. 22.

Dwight Golann, "Taking ADR to the bank: Arbitration and mediation in financial services disputes", 44 *Arbitration Journal* 3 (December 1989).

Bernard Hanotiau, "La pratique de l'arbitrage international en matière bancaire", in *Les Modes non-Judiciaires de Règlement des Conflits* 69 (1995).

Michael Hoellering, "Legal and practical aspects of arbitrating banking disputes", in *Commercial Arbitration* 21 (1988).

Hans van Houtte, "Arbitration involving securities transactions", International Bar Association Section on Business Law, Committee D and Committee E, 12th Biennial Conference (Paris, September 1995).

John Kerr, "Arbitrability of securities claims in common law nations", 12 *Arbitration International* 171 (1996).

Bruno Leurent, "Garanties bancaires et l'arbitrage", 2990 *Revue de Droit des Affaires Internationales* 401.

Deborah Masucci, "Securities arbitration—a success story: What does the future hold?", 31 *Wake Forest Law Review* 183 (1996).

William W. Park, *International Forum Selection* (1995).

William W. Park, "L'Arbitrage en matière financière", 40 *Revue de Jurisprudence Commerciale* 41 (1996).

William W. Park, "Particularités de l'arbitrage en matière bancaire et financière", 1994 *Semaine Judiciaire* 621 (Geneva) (1994).

William W. Park, "L'arbitrage et le recouvrement des prêts consentis à des débiteurs étrangères", 37 *McGill Law Journal* 375 (1992).
William W. Park, "When the borrower and the banker are at odds", 65 *Tulane Law Review* 1323 (1991).
William W. Park, "The arbitrability dicta in *First Options* v. *Kaplan*", 12 *Arbitration International* 137 (1996).
David E. Robbins, *Securities Arbitration Procedure Manual* (1990).
David E. Robbins, "Seven deadly sins that lead to arbitration disaster", (PLI, 1993).
Oscar A. Ruiz del Rio, "Arbitration clauses in international loans", 4 (No. 3) *Journal of International Arbitration* 45 (1987).
Otto Sandrock, "Internationale Kredite und die internationale Schiedsgerichtsbarkeit", *Zeitschrift für Wirtschafts und Bankrecht* (12 & 19 March 1994) (Vol. 48, Nos. 10 and 11) 405 and 445.
Otto Sandrock, "Is international arbitration inept to solve disputes arising out of international loan agreements?", 11 (No. 3) *Journal of International Arbitration* 33 (1994).
Lloyd N. Shields, "The role of mandatory arbitration for financial institutions", 46 *Arbitration Journal* 49 (December 1991).
"Symposium on arbitration in the securities industry", 63 *Fordham Law Review* (1995).

CHAPTER 10

RECEIVERSHIPS AND EXTRAJUDICIAL REMEDIES

INTRODUCTION

10.1 The exercise by creditors and other claimants for money payments of self-help remedies to recover what they claim without first obtaining judgment in a competent court has never stood high in judicial favour, and the history of the self-help remedies which were conceded by the early common law has been one of continual diminution by judicial attrition. The one outstanding exception to this has been the realisation of mortgages and charges over any kinds of property by the exercise of powers of sale and powers to appoint receivers conferred by, or under, the mortgage or charge.

10.2 The self-help remedies conferred by law which remain and which immediately spring to mind are distress or distraint on the goods of the debtor or alleged debtor, the recaption of retaking of goods of the claimant which have been wrongfully taken by another, the exercise of a common law lien or right of retention over goods of a debtor of the claimant and the set-off of a debt owed by a creditor of the claimant against a debt which the claimant owes to him, coupled with the tender of the balance of the amount which the claimant owes, if it is greater than the debt which is owed to him. All of these remedies and the few other self-help remedies which still exist have been subjected by successive judicial decisions to qualifications and conditions, the most important of which is that no forcible entry on the land of another person must occur in the exercise of a self-help remedy. The remedy of distress, for example, may only be exercised by a landlord against his tenant to recover arrears of rent, or by certain tax authorities authorised by statute to distrain for taxes payable to them, but if there is a likelihood that entry on the land where the goods to be distrained are located will be forcibly resisted, the person levying the distress may not proceed without a court order empowering him to do so, and if the distress is for unpaid rent in respect of most kinds of residential accommodation, a court order is essential in any event. Again, the remedy of recaption cannot be exercised without the claimant first obtaining judgment against the wrongful detainer of the goods if a forcible entry on the detainor's land is likely to occur, or if the retaking of the claimant's goods involves a trespass on the land of a person other than the detainor.

10.3 In fact, the only self-help remedies conferred by law which are not inhibited by the need to avoid forcible entries or trespasses on land are those where the subject-matter of the remedy is already in the possession or under the control of the claimant who exercises the remedy. A creditor who has a lien over goods of his debtor in those restricted situations where a lien attaches to the goods by law (for example, the lien of a repairer of goods or equipment for the cost of the repair, or of a warehousekeeper for the cost of storing goods, or the lien of a bank over negotiable instruments held by it for a customer who is indebted to the bank), can realise the subject-matter of the lien by selling or disposing of it and paying himself out of the proceeds, or if the subject-matter is money, by simply paying himself out of it. Similarly, but for different reasons, the exercise of a right of set-off cannot give rise to the possibility of a forcible entry or trespass, and so no court order is required before a right of set-off is asserted. In such cases the limiting factor on the availability of the self-help remedy is that imposed by the restrictions on the persons who, and the circumstances in which, the remedy can be exercised. Liens can only be claimed by certain categories of creditors to recover amounts payable to them for their services, and rights of set-off may be exercised only by claimants for liquidated amounts which are immediately payable, and the set-off can be effected only against debts for liquidated sums which are immediately payable by the creditors to the person against whom the set-off is asserted.

10.4 The restrictions which judicial decisions have imposed on the availability and the exercise of the few self-help remedies which the law still concedes make it tempting for claimants to seek to reserve self-help remedies to themselves by contractual provisions. Express contractual provision or, at least, mercantile usage was the foundation for the lien and power of resale now generally enjoyed by an unpaid seller of goods who is still in possession of them, and was likewise the foundation of the right of a pledgee who advances money on the security of a deposit of goods to sell them if the borrower does not repay the debt secured according to its terms. These rights are now implied in every contract of sale or pledge, unless the contract otherwise provides, and they may therefore now be treated as extensions of the self-help remedies conferred by law. Implied contractual rights of self-help are not numerous, however, even though they may be important to a particular category of creditors, for example the implied pledge or lien which a bank has over shipping documents delivered to it under a letter of credit, and over the goods to which the documents relate, when the customer of the bank who procured the issue of the letter of credit has not put it in funds to pay the amount which it is obliged to pay to the beneficiary of the letter of credit.

10.5 Because of the limited availability of contractually implied self-help remedies, a claimant can usefully extend the remedies available to him by law only by stipulating for them in the contract with his debtor. Examples of such extensions are: (a) the contractual liens and powers of sale which are often reserved to suppliers of goods to a customer on a regular basis where the powers are expressed to extend to all goods which the supplier agrees to deliver, but which have not actually been delivered, whether the amounts unpaid by the purchaser relate to those goods or to other goods which have already been delivered; and (b) the power, often contractually reserved to a seller of goods who retains the ownership of them until they are paid for, to retake the goods if the purchaser defaults in payment and to resell them in order to satisfy the unpaid price. This latter remedy again is one which can be exercised without a court order only if there is no likelihood of a breach of the peace resulting, and if no trespass on a third person's premises will occur in effecting the retaking.

10.6 The self-help remedies which are of particular concern to banks are the lien which a bank has at common law over securities or investments belonging to its customer, the documents relating to which have been deposited with the bank by him (whether the securities are negotiable or not) and the power of a bank to realise such securities which are negotiable; the right of a bank to set off debit and credit balances on separate accounts held with it by the same customer in the same right or, in other words, to consolidate the accounts held by such a customer; and the implied pledges of the kind already referred to where the bank finances the acquisition of goods, securities or investments by its customer and the shipping of other documents relating to them are received by the bank from its customer or from the seller to him. In this connection a bank is assisted by the fact that certain transferable documents of title to goods (particularly bills of lading and warehouse warrants issued by warehouses in certain ports governed by local Acts of Parliament) are treated as the equivalent of the goods to which they relate, with the consequence that the depositary bank which has financed the acquisition may reimburse itself, not only by selling the documents of title received by it, but also by selling the goods which they represent.

10.7 One particular form of self-help remedy which a bank or any other lender may exercise by virtue of a contractual provision is probably, from a bank's point of view, the most extensive and useful remedy which it may employ to recover a loan made by a bank to a company. It is the contractual remedy of appointing a receiver (or a receiver and manager) of a company's business undertaking, or of part of that undertaking or of assets comprised in it, in order to realise a charge or mortgage created by the company in favour of the bank, whether the loan or advance secured by the charge is made by the bank to the company or to any other company or individual (e.g. a loan to a parent company of a group secured by charges over the assets of its subsidiaries). If the appropriate contractual provisions are included in the loan agreement, debentures or a trust deed creating the mortgage or charge, a receiver may be appointed with the widest powers to realise the assets comprised in it, or to manage the whole or part of the company's undertaking with a view to recovering the amount owing out of receipts, or by eventually selling the undertaking or assets at an enhanced price. The remainder of this chapter will be concerned with such receiverships.

RECEIVERSHIPS: ORIGIN AND CHARACTER

10.8 Receiverships, for the purpose of recovering loans or advances made to companies, are closely associated in practitioners' minds with the enforcement of floating charges created by companies, but they are by no means confined to such charges. Receiverships may be initiated to enforce any kind of mortgage or charge, whether fixed or floating, and whatever kind of assets the charge encumbers.

10.9 The jurisdiction of the Chancery Court to appoint receivers with power to collect the income of the property on which a debt is secured, or to effect the sale of such property under an order of the court, goes back to the eighteenth century, and the only limit on the Chancery jurisdiction was the self-imposed one that the court would not intervene if the secured creditor had an adequate remedy at common law, for example if he held a legal mortage of land and was entitled after the contractual date for redemption to take possession of the land himself in order to collect the income from it.[1] Since the Judicature Act 1873 came into force in 1875, however, all divisions of the High Court have had jurisdiction to appoint receivers in appropriate circumstances. The court now appoints them at the request of both legal and equitable mortgagees and at the instance of persons who have only charges over property or assets, which must, except in the case of a charge by deed over land which is expressed to be created by way of a legal mortgage, inevitably be equitable in character.[2]

10.10 For a short period following the decision by the Court of Appeal in Chancery in 1870 that a floating charge created by a company over the whole or part of its assets and undertaking was valid in equity, and would be enforced as a fixed charge attaching to assets of the class charged which were owned by the company at the time when it went into liquidation, the holders of such floating charges who wished to enforce them on the company's default, or on their security becoming at risk of being lost or rendered inadequate although the company had not gone into liquidation, resorted to the Chancery Court to appoint a receiver with power to realise the assets charged. The court appointed such a receiver in a number of cases.[3] By the mid 1870s, however, lenders to companies sought to avoid the delay entailed in applying to the court to appoint a receiver of the assets and undertaking of a company which had been charged in their favour by inserting in the loan agreement or debentures powers for them to appoint a receiver out of court, who was authorised by the loan agreement or debentures to realise the company's assets and to carry on its business

1. *Berney* v. *Sewell* (1820) 1 Jac. W 648.
2. *Tillett* v. *Nixon* (1883) 25 Ch. D 238; *Re Crompton & Co. Ltd* [1914] 1 Ch. 954.
3. See, for example, *Perry* v. *Oriental Hotels Co.* (1870) 5 Ch. App. 420; *Peek* v. *Trimsaren Iron Co.* (1876) 2 Ch. D 115; *Boyle* v. *Bettws Llantwit Colliery Co.* (1876) 2 Ch. D 726.

undertaking with a view to an eventual realisation.[4] The circumstances in which a receiver might be appointed without an application being made to the court were listed exhaustively in the loan agreement or debentures under which the loan was made, or in the debenture trust deed which was now coming into use when a large-scale issue of debentures was made. During the last 20 years of the nineteenth century practitioners elaborated the list of circumstances in which a receiver might be appointed, so that they included not only the company's failure to pay the principal and interest on the loan on the due dates and any breach by the company of its covenants or obligations, but also a long list of adverse events the occurrence of any of which might make it difficult for the company to fulfil its financial or other obligations, or would indicate that the company was heading for a situation where it might become difficult for it to meet its obligations, or if the company went into liquidation under an order of the court or voluntarily.[5]

10.11 During the 1890s and the early years of the twentieth century the courts worked out in a succession of cases the adverse events affecting a company which had created a floating charge over its assets, that would induce the court to appoint a receiver of those assets on the application of a lender or debenture holder on the ground that there was a serious risk that the assets subject to the charge would be lost or would prove inadequate (in other words, that the security would be in jeopardy). The court was largely helped in cataloguing such events by the contemporary specification of them in loan agreements, debentures or debenture trust deeds as entitling the lender or debenture holders to appoint a receiver without the aid of the court. The fact that such a receiver could be appointed, however, was held to be no reason for the court to refuse to appoint a receiver itself.[6] Nevertheless, because a receivership initiated without an application to the court was usually cheaper and more expeditious than one resulting from an appointment by the court, it was in practice only when an appointment out of court could be made only with the consent of the holders of a certain minimum fraction of debentures issued in a series that applications were made to the court by minority debenture holders, who could not elicit the support of sufficient of their fellow debenture holders to effect an appointment out of court.

10.12 One significant feature of the appointment of a receiver by the court or out of court as a consequence of a jeopardising event occurring, however, is that it is not the occurrence of that event which causes the floating charge to crystallise and attach specifically to the assets of the company (even if the event is the cessation of the company's business activities): crystallisation occurs only on the appointment of the receiver because of the occurrence of that event.[7] This is

4. See *Re Henry Pound, Son and Hutchins Ltd* (1889) 42 Ch. D 402.
5. See *Hodson* v. *Tea Corpn Ltd* (1880) 14 Ch. D 859; *Wallace* v. *Universal Automatic Machines Co. Ltd* [1894] 2 Ch. 547.
6. *Re Henry Pound, Son and Hutchins Ltd*, above.
7. *Government Stocks and Other Securities Investment Co.* v. *Manila Rly Co.* [1897] AC 81.

not so, of course, if a floating charge crystallises by the company going into liquidation; crystallisation then occurs on the relevant winding-up order being made or a winding-up resolution being passed, and the fact that a receiver is only later appointed does not postpone the date of crystallisation.

10.13 The fact that a floating charge does not crystallise when an event occurs which justifies the appointment of a receiver by the court or out of court, but only when a receiver is actually appointed in consequence of that event, is one of the reasons why loan agreements, debentures and trust deeds which create floating charges nowadays often provide that the charge shall crystallise immediately on the occurrence of any of the designated events, or on notice being given to the company by the lender or lenders in consequence of one of those events (a provision for automatic crystallisation). Such a provision has been held by the courts to be valid, and its effect is to invalidate as against the lender or debenture holders purported dispositions of the company's assets by its directors after the occurrence of the relevant event or the giving of notice to the company of its occurrence, unless the lender, debenture holders or receiver consents.[8] As a matter of nomenclature, clauses in loan agreements, debentures or covering trust deeds creating floating charges which list the events which will entitle the lender, debenture holder or trustee of the trust deed to appoint a receiver, or which will cause the immediate crystallisation of the floating charge on their occurrence or on notice being given to the company thereafter, are often misleadingly called default clauses, even though not all the events specified in them involve breaches of obligations by the company. A better name for such clauses would be "enforceability" or "crystallisation" clauses, corresponding to the acceleration clause inserted in documents relating to unsecured loans or unsecured loan stock, in order to make the loan immediately repayable on the occurrence of specified adverse events.

10.14 Although there are many points of similarity between the appointment of receivers by the court and out of court with power to realise assets of a company (such as freehold and leasehold land and premises owned by the company at any time before its secured indebtedness is discharged, or book debts owing to it at any such time), there are also material differences between them. Power to appoint a receiver out of court must be conferred explicitly by the instrument creating a floating charge, or to enable a receiver appointed under a charge over specific assets to realise them by sale or otherwise. The statutory power of a mortgagee or chargee by deed of any property to appoint a receiver under the Law of Property Act 1925, ss.101(1) and 109 (re-enacting the Conveyancing Act 1882, ss.19(1) and 24) enables him to appoint a receiver only for the purpose of collecting the income of the property charged and applying it in paying the secured debt. Such a receiver cannot realise the property, and even

8. *Re Woodroffes (Musical Instruments) Ltd* [1986] Ch. 366; *Re Brightlife Ltd* [1987] Ch. 200; *Re Permanent Houses (Holdings) Ltd* [1988] BCLC 563.

the statutory power to appoint a receiver to collect income cannot be exercised by a lender secured only by a floating charge.[9]

10.15 The explicit power in a loan agreement, debenture or trust deed to appoint a receiver out of court to realise assets comprised in a charge must, of course, specify exhaustively the events in which the appointment may be made, and an appointment may not be made in any other circumstances, even though the security is at risk of loss or the company has failed to fulfil its contractual obligations. On the other hand, the court's jurisdiction to appoint a receiver with power to realise the assets charged by a specific or floating charge or, in the case of a floating charge over a company's assets and undertaking, to carry on the company's business with a view to eventual sale (in which case the receiver will also be appointed by the court to be a manager), is not limited to the occurrence of the events of default or enforceability listed in the instrument creating the charge. The court can make the appointment whenever the company has failed to pay any part of the principal of the loan or interest on it in accordance with its contractual undertaking to do so, or when the security for the loan is exposed to a serious risk of loss.

10.16 Furthermore, the characters and capacities of receivers appointed by the court or out of court under the instrument creating the charge are different. A receiver appointed by the court is an officer of it, and not an agent of the secured lender or of the debenture holder who applied for his appointment or the debenture holders generally, nor is he an agent of the company.[10] Consequently, such a receiver is personally liable upon contracts which he enters into in the course of his receivership (with a right to be indemnified out of the assets in respect of which he was appointed if the contracts were proper ones for carrying out his functions), and the receiver is also personally liable to the company and third persons if he or persons employed by him commit acts which are wrongful as regards them in the course of the receivership.[11] In contrast, a receiver appointed out of court under a power conferred by an instrument creating a mortgage or charge is deemed to be the agent of the person who appoints him, who is consequently responsible as his principal for the fulfilment of contracts entered into by him and for all wrongs committed by him or by persons employed by him in the course of the receivership (including his failure to realise the company's assets at the best price reasonably obtainable).[12] At common law the appointor of the receiver alone was liable as the receiver's principal upon contracts made by him for the purpose of the receivership, but by the Insolvency Act 1986, s.37(1) and s.44(1) (re-enacting Companies Act 1985, s.192(3)), a receiver or manager of the whole or any part of the property of a company under

9. *Blaker* v. *Herts and Essex Waterworks Co.* (1889) 41 Ch. D 339.

10. *Moss S.S. Co. Ltd* v. *Whinney* [1912] AC 254; *Parsons* v. *Sovereign Bank of Canada* [1913] AC 160.

11. *Burt, Bolton and Hayward* v. *Bull* [1895] 1 QB 276; *Boehm* v. *Goodall* [1911] 1 Ch. 155.

12. *White* v. *City of London Brewery Co.* (1889) Ch. D 237; *Robinson Printing Co.* v. *Chic Ltd* [1905] 2 Ch. 123; *Deyes* v. *Wood* [1911] 1 KB 806.

a floating charge who is appointed by an instrument and not by the court, is made personally liable upon all contracts entered into by him in carrying out his functions. A receiver appointed out of court remains personally liable for wrongs committed by him or persons employed by him against third persons, in addition to the vicarious liability of the person who appointed him to those third persons.[13]

10.17 Because of the liabilities which lenders or debenture holders, or trustees for them, would normally incur for breaches of contracts made by receivers appointed by them out of court and for wrongs committed by such receivers, it has been the practice since the last decade of the nineteenth century for loan agreements, debentures and trust deeds to provide that, for all purposes, a receiver appointed under a power conferred by the instrument shall be deemed to be an agent of the company, which shall alone be responsible for and bear the consequences of his acts and defaults. Such a provision exempts the lender or debenture holders from liability in respect of contracts entered into by the receiver, including those entered into by the receiver after his deemed agency has come to an end or the company going into liquidation, and it also exempts the lender or debenture holders from liability for wrongs committed by the receiver otherwise than on the express instructions of the lender or debenture holders.[14] By the Insolvency Act 1986, ss.37(1) and 44(1), however, the fact that a receiver or manager is deemed by the loan agreement, debentures or debenture trust deed under which he is appointed to be an agent of the company does not affect his personal liability upon contracts made by him for the purpose of the receivership. The fact that a receiver who is deemed to be and acts as an agent of the company ceases to be such an agent on the company going into liquidation does not terminate his powers of realisation and management, and he exercises them thereafter as a principal, and not as an agent of the person who appointed him or of the company.[15]

10.18 Before concluding a consideration of the nature of receivership, more detailed reference must be made to the creation of a new sub-species of receiver appointed out of court under a power conferred by a loan agreement, or by debentures or a debenture trust deed, namely the administrative receiver. This sub-species was established by the Insolvency Act 1986, and comprises, in practice, most of the receivers of companies' property and assets who are appointed out of court. Administrative receivers are defined by the Insolvency Act 1986, s.29(2), as receivers or managers

> of the whole (or substantially the whole) of a company's property appointed by or on behalf of the holders of any debentures of the company secured by a charge which as

13. *Re Goldburg* [1912] 1 KB 606.

14. *Re B. Johnson and Co. (Builders) Ltd* [1955] Ch. 634; *Standard Chartered Bank Ltd* v. *Walker* [1982] 3 All ER 938.

15. *Bowman* v. *David Samuel Trust Ltd* [1978] 1 All ER 616.

created, was a floating charge, or by such a charge and one or more other securities, or a person who would be such a receiver or manager but for the appointment of some other person as the receiver of part of the company's property.

An administrative receiver, therefore, is one appointed under a floating charge which extends to the whole or substantially the whole of a company's assets and undertaking (other than or in addition to those comprised in a fixed charge), and his appointment, too, must extend to the same wide range of assets, but the fact that the floating charge has already crystallised before his appointment, or that another person has already appointed a receiver of part (but not the whole or substantially the whole) of the company's property under a mortgage or charge which has priority to the floating charge, does not affect the status of the appointee as an administrative receiver.

10.19 An administrative receiver is deemed by law to be the agent of the company whose assets are the subject of the receivership, but his agency continues only until the commencement of its liquidation, and like any other receiver appointed out of court, he is personally liable upon all contracts made by him in carrying out his functions, both before and after the company goes into liquidation, with the consequence that the lender or debenture holders for whose benefit he is appointed are not so liable (Insolvency Act 1986, s.44(1)). The reason for the creation of the new category of administrative receivers is that they (unlike other receivers) are required to be qualified insolvency practitioners (Insolvency Act 1986, ss.388(1) and 390(2)), and that on their appointment the directors of the company and certain other persons are required to submit to them a statement of the company's affairs on which they are required to report to the company's creditors (ss.47 and 48). Additionally, an administrative receiver is given certain statutory powers for the purpose of his receivership (unless the loan agreement, debentures or debenture trust deed under which he is appointed otherwise provides) (s.42(1) and Sch. 1); and with leave of the court an administrative receiver may dispose of property of the company in respect of which he was appointed free from any security to which that property is subject (such as a prior-ranking specific mortgage or charge, or a prior-ranking floating charge whose holder has not appointed a receiver), if the court considers that this would promote a more advantageous realisation of the company's assets (s.43(1)).

10.20 It should be observed, however, that although an administrative receiver is defined, and his powers and functions are prescribed by the Insolvency Act 1986, the Act confers on a lender or debenture holders, who is or are entitled to a general floating charge over the whole or substantially the whole of a company's assets, no statutory power to appoint an administrative receiver. However, if by the loan agreement, debentures or debenture trust deed an express power is conferred on them to appoint a receiver of the whole or substantially the whole of the company's assets charged, a receiver whom they appoint to realise or manage the whole, or substantially the whole, of those assets will automatically be an administrative receiver, whether he is so described in his instrument of appointment or not.

THE CONDUCT OF A RECEIVERSHIP

Purpose of a receivership

10.21 The purpose of a receivership is that the receiver shall realise sufficient of the assets of the company comprised in the charge under which he is appointed to pay the total outstanding amount of the loan or debt secured on those assets, plus the cost of the receivership and, if the charge is or includes a floating charge, any preferential debts and liabilities of the company which the receiver is compelled by the Insolvency Act 1986, s.40 to discharge out of the company's assets in priority to the amount secured by the floating charge. If the receiver is empowered by the court or the instrument under which he is appointed to manage the company's business undertaking and does so, his receipts from the continued carrying on of the company's business, less his expenses properly incurred in doing so, will be added to the proceeds of eventually realising the company's assets, whether piecemeal or by the sale of the company's business as a going concern, and the proceeds of carrying on the business will be applied in the same way as the proceeds of sale of those assets. If the proceeds of realisation and the net receipts from the receiver carrying on the company's business suffice to meet all the amounts payable out of them by the receiver, any cash balance left in his hands and any unrealised assets of the company in his possession must be returned to the company, and must not be applied by the receiver's paying secured or unsecured liabilities of the company, which rank for payment only after the secured debt in respect of which the receiver was appointed.[16]

10.22 If a receiver sells or disposes of assets of the company which are subject to mortgages or charges, or to securities arising by operation of law (such as liens or the security obtained by judgment creditors who have attached assets of the company in execution), the receiver may either sell the assets subject to those charges or securities, so that they continue to affect the assets in the hands of the purchasers, or (and this is more likely) the receiver may discharge those charges or securities out of the proceeds of realisation of the assets and transfer an unencumbered title to the purchasers. This is so, of course, only if the amounts of those charges or securities rank for payment out of the assets in question in priority to payment of the debt secured by the loan agreement or debentures under which the receiver is appointed. In this connection, as has already been noted, an administrative receiver may be authorised by the court under the Insolvency Act 1986, s.43(1) to dispose of assets which are subject to a security ranking in priority to the floating charge under which the receiver was

16. *Re G.L. Saunders Ltd* [1986] 1 WLR 215.

appointed. In this case, the receiver must apply the proceeds of realisation primarily in discharging that prior-ranking security, and if the proceeds are less than the net amount which, in the court's opinion, would be realised on sale in the open market (presumably on a sale by a willing seller to a willing buyer), the receiver must make good the difference out of the company's other assets subject to the floating charge or, if necessary, personally, in order to discharge the amount of the security (s.43(3)).

Powers of receivers

10.23 The purpose of receiverships initiated by creditors to enforce mortgages or charges over a company's assets is always the same, namely, the realisation of their security. However, the law does not, with one exception, confer a list of powers on a receiver appointed out of court to achieve that purpose, in the way that the Insolvency Act 1986, ss.165 and 166 and Sch. 4 confers a catalogue of powers on liquidators in the winding-up of companies. The one exception is the administrative receiver, who is deemed to have the powers listed in the Insolvency Act 1986, Sch. 1, unless the loan agreement, debentures or trust deed under which he is appointed provide otherwise (Insolvency Act 1986, s.42(1)). The statutory powers of an administrative receiver are as wide as those of a liquidator, and in some respects are more extensive. For example, an administrative receiver has power to carry on the business of the company generally (and not merely for the purpose of winding up the company's affairs, as a liquidator may do); he also has power to establish subsidiaries of the company and to transfer to any of the company's subsidiaries (whether formed by him or by the company itself) the whole or part of the business and property of the company; and, in general, he has power to do all such things (including the carrying out of work) as may be necessary for the realisation of the property of the company. The powers of an administrative receiver can be added to or diminished by the provisions of the loan agreement, debentures or trust deed under which he is appointed, and unless that instrument requires the consent of the lender, debenture holders or the trustees of a debenture trust deed, or any other person, to the exercise of an administrative receiver's statutory or other powers, he may act on his own initiative without obtaining anyone's consent. The powers of a receiver appointed out of court, who is not an administrative receiver, must be defined exhaustively by the loan agreement, debentures or trust deed under which he is appointed, since no powers are conferred on him by statute, and no doubt, in practice, the powers of administrative receivers will continue to be set out exhaustively in the same way, despite the statutory provisions conferring powers on them.

10.24 A receiver of any description of a company's assets takes them in the condition they are in when the receiver is appointed, and he cannot claim legal or equitable rights in respect of them which the company itself could not enforce against third persons. For example, if a receiver is appointed under a charge which includes present and future book debts owing to the company in connection with its business, the company's customers who owe it such book debts may set off against the receiver's claims the amounts of debts or cross-claims which they could set off in actions brought by the company itself at the date when the charge crystallised, or if the charge is a specific or fixed charge over book debts, at the date when the charge was notified to them.[17] The amounts to be set off against the receiver's claims must either be liquidated amounts which are due and payable by the company at whichever of those two dates is appropriate, however, or they must be accrued liquidated or unliquidated claims against the company arising under the same contract or transaction with it as that under which the receiver claims, or a closely related contract or transaction.[18]

10.25 Another example of the principle that the receiver takes the company's assets and rights as they exist at the time of his appointment is provided by the practice in recent years of suppliers of goods to companies retaining the title to the goods by express provision in the supply contract, until the price of the goods or the total outstanding indebtedness of the company to the supplier has been fully paid. If, at the time of the receiver's appointment, the title to such goods has not vested in the company or in a person to whom the company has resold them and any period of credit allowed by the supplier to the company has expired, the supplier may reclaim the goods if they are still identifiable and the receiver does not pay the amount owed to the supplier, and if in those circumstances the receiver refuses to return them to the supplier or disposes of them to a third party the receiver will be liable to the supplier in damages for the tort of conversion.[19] If, on the other hand, the supplier of the goods to the company has by the supply contract also reserved to himself the right to the price or the hire rental at which the company has resold or hired out the goods or any products made with them to third persons, so as to entitle the supplier to payment of the amount owed to him by the company out of the resale price or the hire rental, the reservation will now, in almost all situations, amount to an equitable charge on the resale price or hire rental, and the suppliers' claim to it will be ineffective against the receiver, unless it has been registered against the company at the Companies Registry as a charge on its book debts owing from its own customers.[20]

10.26 An administrative receiver (like a liquidator or an administrator acting under an administration order) is protected against the absolute liability which would be imposed on him at common law for taking or disposing of any property which he believes belongs to the company (such as goods in its

17. *Parsons* v. *Sovereign Bank of Canada* [1913] AC 160; *Rother Iron Works Ltd* v. *Canterbury Precision Engineers Ltd* [1974] QB 1.

18. *Handley Page Ltd* v. *Customs and Excise Commissioners* [1970] 2 Lloyd's Rep. 459; *Business Computers Ltd* v. *Anglo African Leasing Ltd* [1977] 2 All ER 741).

19. *Clough Mill Ltd* v. *Martin* [1984] 3 All ER 982; *Hendy Lennox (Industrial Engines) Ltd* v. *Graham Puttick Ltd* [1984] 2 All ER 152.

20. *E. Pfeiffer Weinkellerei-Weinkauf GmbH & Co.* v. *Arbuthnot Factors Ltd* [1987] 1 WLR 150; *Tatung (UK) Ltd* v. *Galex Telesure Ltd* (1988) 5 BCC 395.

possession under a contract by which the seller retains the title until the price is paid) by provisions in the Insolvency Act 1986, s.234(3) and (4), under which the receiver escapes liability to the owner or other person entitled to the property if he acts in good faith and reasonably believes that he is entitled to take or dispose of the property. This provision extends to all kinds of property, such as land, investments, book debts and industrial property rights, as well as goods, but it does not, of course, confer a title to the property on the receiver or any person to whom he disposes of it. Nor will the provision protect a receiver who is aware of an adverse claim to the property (e.g. that of an unpaid seller who has retained the title to goods delivered to the company).

Executory contracts of the company

10.27 A receiver or manager is not bound personally by contracts entered into by the company before he is appointed, even though he carries out part of the company's obligations under such contracts, for example by delivering goods which the company has contracted to sell.[21] The only way in which a receiver or manager can become bound by such a contract is by a novation, under which he agrees with the other contracting party to perform the company's obligations under the original contract in consideration of that party releasing the company from those obligations. It is unusual for a receiver or manager to agree to such a novation in practice, but it would be possible to imply a novation from conduct by the receiver which clearly indicates to the other party that he may perform his obligations safely under the contract in reliance on the receiver performing the company's obligations (for example, delivering goods in reliance on the receiver stating that they will be paid for).[22]

10.28 Furthermore, a receiver appointed out of court (including an administrative receiver) becomes personally responsible for the performance of the company's future obligations under contracts of employment entered into by it with its employees if he adopts such contracts in carrying out his functions, but nothing done or omitted by the receiver within 14 days after his appointment is taken to amount to an adoption by him of such a contract (Insolvency Act 1986, s.37(1) and (2) and s.44(1) and (2)). This provision will apparently apply only if the receiver continues to accept the services of the company's employees for the purpose of the receivership, for example, where he continues to carry on the company's business after 14 days from his appointment. Contracts of employment are not defined for the purpose of the provision, but presumably they are confined to contracts of service, and do not include contracts for the supply of services by independent contractors.

10.29 It has been suggested by the court, in a case where the point was not essential for the decision, that a receiver who does not fulfil a contract made by

21. *Parsons* v. *Sovereign Bank of Canada* [1913] AC 160.
22. *Chatsworth Investments Ltd* v. *Cussins (Contractors) Ltd* [1969] 1 All ER 143.

the company before his appointment may be liable personally to the other contracting party for the wrong or tort of procuring a breach of contract by the company, if by his deliberate act he causes the company's obligations not to be fulfilled.[23] It is doubtful whether this is correct, at least when the receiver has good reason for not carrying out the company's obligations under the contract in order to protect the interests of the lender or debenture holders who appointed him. Furthermore, if the receiver is deemed to act as the agent of the company by the terms of the loan agreement, debentures or trust deed, it would seem that, like any other agent, he will not be personally liable for causing the breach of contracts which his principal, the company, has entered into, and that the other party will merely have an unsecured claim for damages against the company itself if its obligations are breached.[24] The other contracting party may not obtain an injunction against the receiver to prevent him from causing the company to break a contract into which it has entered, nor may he obtain an order requiring the receiver to perform the contract specifically; if an injunction or order of specific performance is obtained by the other party against the company in a situation where the contract can be enforced by injunction or can be specifically enforced, the court's order is not binding on the receiver or the lender or debenture holders for whose benefit he was appointed, and they are not guilty of contempt of court by not conforming to the order.[25] On the other hand, if contracts entered into by the company create or result in the creation of proprietary interests in favour of third persons, such as an option to purchase land or shares in a company which is exercised, the receiver will be personally liable to the persons entitled to such interests if he infringes them, and he may be restrained by injunction from doing so.[26] He may, however, rely on the statutory defence that he honestly and reasonably believed that the property belonged to the company in this situation.

Receiver's duties in realising company's assets

10.30 Although a receiver may not be personally liable to fulfil the company's obligations under a contract entered into by it, he should not cause damage to its goodwill by failing to fulfil those obligations if the goodwill has a saleable value; this is so even if the cost of performing the contract exceeds the benefits which the company will obtain under it, and that excess is less than the loss of goodwill which will be caused to the company if the contract is not carried out.[27] But a receiver is liable for causing harm to the company's goodwill by not fulfilling its outstanding contracts only if he can perform them by utilising the company's assets and resources already available; he is not required to incur personal

23. *Re Botibol* [1947] 1 All ER 26.
24. *Said* v. *Butt* [1920] 3 KB 497.
25. *Atlantic Airspace Ltd* v. *Handley Page Ltd* [1970] Ch. 193.
26. *Telemetrix plc* v. *Modern Engineers of Bristol (Holdings) plc* [1985] BCLC 213.
27. *Re Newdigate Colliery Co. Ltd* [1912] 1 Ch. 468; *Re Great Cobar Ltd* [1915] 1 Ch. 682.

liability by himself entering into further contracts so as to enable him to fulfil the company's existing contracts, for example by borrowing.[28]

10.31 The liability (if any) which a receiver incurs by failing to fulfil existing contractual obligations of the company is not incurred to the other contracting party, but only to the lender, debenture holders or trustees for them who appointed the receiver, and the liability is limited to making good the value of the company's goodwill which is lost in consequence of the contract not being fulfilled.[29] Liability is also incurred by the receiver to the company itself to the extent that the value of the lost goodwill, when added to the company's other assets, would more than suffice to discharge the loan secured by the charge under which the receiver was appointed and also the costs of the receivership; the surplus can be claimed by the company from the receiver.[30] Side by side with the receiver's equitable obligation to account for any diminution of the company's assets caused by his default, a receiver is liable in damages to the company if he causes it loss by the negligent conduct of the receivership, for example by realising its assets at a price less than that obtainable by the exercise of proper care.[31] Such a liability is also incurred by the receiver to guarantors of the indebtedness secured by the charge under which the receiver was appointed, and they can recover from him as damages the amount by which the contributions exacted from them under their guarantee has been increased by the receiver's negligence in failing to realise the company's assets or to collect debts payble to it with proper care.[32]

Liabilities of lenders and debenture holders in a receivership or liquidation

10.32 A lender, debenture holders or trustees for them who appoint a receiver do not generally incur any liability in consequence of the improper or negligent conduct of the receiver; this is because he is expressed in the relevant loan agreement, debentures or trust deed to be an agent of the company, and it bears the loss caused by his defaults. However, if the appointor of the receiver or the lender or debenture holders on whose behalf he is appointed instruct him to pursue a course of conduct, or to do or abstain from doing an act, which involves a breach of duty on his part, or which is likely to cause a loss to the company not justified by the need to protect the interests of the lender or debenture holders, the person or persons giving the instruction or advice will be liable to the company for the loss it suffers (for example, the too rapid realisation of its assets at depressed prices), and it will be irrelevant that by the loan agreement,

28. *Re Thames Ironworks, Shipbuilding and Engineering Co. Ltd* [1912] WN 66.
29. *Re Newdigate Colliery Co. Ltd*, above.
30. *Re Newdigate Colliery Co. Ltd*, above.
31. *Standard Chartered Bank Ltd* v. *Walker* [1982] All ER 938.
32. *Standard Chartered Bank Ltd* v. *Walker*, above.

debentures or trust deed the receiver is deemed to be the agent of the receiver.[33] Although a lender or debenture holders, or their trustees, may be under a duty to the company to exercise their powers or influence over a receiver appointed by them with proper regard to the company's interests, however, they are not under any duty towards the company to exercise their powers only if they reasonably envisage that the company will not suffer loss or detriment in consequence, and they are at liberty to act so as to protect their own interests, even if the company does inevitably suffer harm as a result of that action. Consequently, a lender or debenture holders may insist on prompt payment of what the company owes under the loan agreement or debentures, and may refuse to allow it a reasonable additional time to raise money from another source in order to dischrge that amount before appointing a receiver to enforce their security. The company then has no claim against the lender or debenture holders for doing this even if, given a reasonable opportunity, the company might have raised the money elsewhere.[34]

10.33 It is possible for a lender or debenture holders, or their trustees, to become shadow directors of a company to which they have made advances for the purposes of the Companies Acts 1985 to 1989, and the Insolvency Act 1986, if the board of directors of the company is accustomed to act in accordance with their directions and instructions (Companies Act 1985, s.741(2)). If lenders or debenture holders habitually give instructions or directions to the board of a company to which they have made advances or from which they have taken security for indebtedness and the board has habitually conformed to the instructions, the lender or debenture holders may be shadow directors of the company, even though the primary purpose of the lender or debenture holders in giving the instructions or directions is to protect their loan or security, or to ensure that the company continues to fulfil its contractual obligations to them or to maintain their security at a level which will suffice to satisfy the amount owed to them, if they eventually realise the security.[35] The instructions or directions accepted by the board must, of course, relate to the management of the company's affairs for the lenders or debenture holders to become shadow directors, and it would seem that they must be so comprehensive that all, or the most important, management decisions are taken out of the hands of the board.

10.34 The practical significance of lenders or debenture holders being shadow directors of the company is that if the company goes into an insolvent liquidation, they may be ordered by the court to make contributions to its assets which will be available to meet all its debts and liabilities (including its unsecured debts), but such contributions may be ordered only if at some time before the onset of the company's insolvency, the lenders or debenture holders should have realised that it could not avoid an insolvent liquidation, and they

33. *Standard Chartered Bank Ltd* v. *Walker*, above; *Re Potters Oils Ltd (No. 2)* [1986] 1 All ER 890.

34. *Shamji* v. *Johnson Matthey Bankers Ltd* [1986] BCLC 278; [1991] BCLC 36.

35. *Re a Company (No. 005009 of 1987), ex parte Copp* [1989] BCLC 13.

did not thereafter take "every step with a view to minimising the potential loss to the company's creditors as . . . [they] ought to have taken" (Insolvency Act 1986, s.214(1) to (3)). The danger in the lenders or debenture holders "policing" their loan or security too actively, therefore, is that they may find in the company's liquidation that the effectiveness and priority of their claims as secured creditors, and their powers to realise their security, are diminished by the contribution to the company's assets which they are ordered to make for the benefit of the general creditors of the company. Bearing in mind that the court may charge the contribution ordered from them on the amount which the company owes them and on any security which they hold for that amount (s.215(2)), the lender and debenture holders may find that instead of being creditors with priority for payment out of the security in the liquidation, they are made to rank only equally with the company's general creditors and that the total fund in which they share will have been partly constituted by themselves.

10.35 Lenders and debenture holders of a company will become shadow directors only if they habitually give instructions or directions to its board of directors as to the management of the company's affairs generally and the board habitually conforms to them. This may be avoided by the lenders or debenture holders giving their instructions to a receiver or manager appointed by them under an enforcement or default clause in the loan agreement or debentures which is sufficiently widely drawn to enable the appointment to be made when they consider that their loan or the security for it is at risk. The receiver or manager then takes over all the powers of the directors which are necessary for the receivership (including managing the company's business as a going concern), and the directors cannot interfere with the receiver's exercise of those powers, or exercise them themselves.[36] If it is the receiver who acts on the lenders' or debenture holders' instructions, they may be liable to the company at common law for negligence in the way indicated above, but they will not be shadow directors of the company, and so cannot be ordered by the court to contribute to its assets in a liquidation.

CONCLUSION

10.36 This chapter has been mostly concerned with receiverships of companies under loan agreements and debentures as a means of recovery available to lenders (especially banks) by way of self-help. Receiverships provide a remedy which is unique to the common law jurisdictions, that is the Commonwealth countries and the US. In the civil law countries it is not possible for a creditor to enforce a security for his debt without obtaining an order of the court, unless he is in possession of the security of the subject-matter under a pledge. Although the court may appoint a suitable person to manage those of the assets of a business

36. *Newhart Developments Ltd* v. *Co-operative Commercial Bank Ltd* [1978] QB 814.

undertaking which are comprised in a security, acting as an officer of the court with a view to an ultimate sale, this remedy is not much used in practice. The order of the court which is usually sought is for the sale of the assets comprised in the security under the court's directions.

10.37 The limited range of remedies for the recovery of secured loans under civil law systems results largely from the fact that a floating charge over the whole assets and undertaking of a company is not recognised as a valid security by them. Under German law it is possible for a company to make a global transfer of its present and future book debts, and it can make such a transfer by way of security (*Sicherungsvorausabtretung oder Globalzession*), but such a global security transfer of book debts can only be enforced by proceedings in court. Similar global transfers cannot be made in respect of present and future interests in land, or any other classes of assets of a company other than book debts. Moreover, an attempt to make such a global transfer of assets is highly dangerous, because by the German Civil Code, §419(1) and (2) if a person (including a creditor) takes a transfer of the whole of the assets of another person (including a company), whether the transfer is of the beneficial interests in those assets or by way of security, the transferee automatically becomes liable for all the debts of the transferor at the date of the transfer to the extent of the value of the assets transferred. French legislation of 1909 (Loi de 17 mars 1909 concernant la vente et la nantissement des fonds de commerce) permits companies to charge their business undertakings (*fonds de commerce*) as security for their indebtedness, but the assets comprised in the charge are confined to the company's goodwill, business name, fixed assets and equipment, trade marks and insignia (logos), patents and the lease of the company's business premises (if any), and the charge cannot, even by express mention, extend to the company's current assets (that is, its raw materials, consumables, manufactured and semi-manufactured goods, stock in trade or inventory and book debts). Moreover, a charge over a company's business undertaking can be enforced only under an order of the court for the sale of the charged assets comprised in it.

10.38 The limitation in civil law systems that any security (other than a pledge of goods or negotiable paper in the lender's possession) may be enforced only by a judicial sale or other judicial process is symptomatic of the reluctance of those systems to permit self-help remedies, because being based on Roman law, they regard the pursuit of legal remedies as necessarily involving litigation. Consequently, the number of occasions when self-help remedies are available under civil law systems to enforce rights of any kind are extremely limited. There is nothing in civil law equivalent to the common law remedy of a landlord to distrain for unpaid rent, although he is regarded as having a charge on the property comprised in a lease for unpaid rent and the charge can be enforced by judicial proceedings. The remedies of an unpaid seller of goods who has given no credit for the price are confined to retaining possession of the goods until they are paid for without himself being in breach of contract, although in French law the seller has the little-used right to retake the goods if the price is not paid for seven days after delivery. In practice, unpaid sellers who wish to have some security over the goods do so by contractual provisions reserving the title to the goods to themselves until they are paid for, but if the goods have been delivered to the seller, they can be recovered *in specie* only by judicial proceedings. English law and that of the other common law jurisdictions are more liberal in permitting self-help remedies, provided that no forcible entry on land is involved, but even so, the occasions when such remedies may be employed are relatively few. Whether the availability of self-help remedies by law is desirable or not is a matter on which opinions unavoidably differ, but there can be no doubt that the availability of receiverships under English law to enable the secured creditors of companies to recover the amounts owed to them without having to resort to a court to appoint the receiver or to order the realisation of the assets comprised in the security provides a valuable practical benefit for secured creditors, especially when the companies concerned are declining rapidly.

R. R. PENNINGTON

CHAPTER 11

BANKS IN DISTRESS—NON-PERFORMING LOANS RECOGNITION AND RESPONSE BY DEBTORS AND CREDITORS: LESSONS FROM THE AMERICAN EXPERIENCE

IMPACT ON DEBTORS

11.1 In a depressed economy, debtor companies tend to recognise and attack problem assets or financing on an individual basis. This tendency is exacerbated when one or more of the debtor's creditors, caught in the downward spiral of the systemic capital inadequacy crisis, behaves in a reactionary mode and focuses only on its own problems with the debtor and disregards the debtor's other credit relationships and problems. At some point, the debtor may come to the realisation that it is unable to maintain many separate negotiations for the resolution of its problems simultaneously on a coherent basis. The debtor will recognise that many of its problems are interrelated and that some of its lenders or investors are more aggressive in seeking collection and pursuing default remedies than others. The debtor will have been prone to resolve its problems with its most troublesome creditors on a preferential basis and to defer the resolution of problems or potential problems with its more patient creditors, to their mutual detriment.

11.2 Each creditor considers its loan transaction and prospects for collection from a narrowed perspective. As the debtor's financial condition deteriorates, each creditor seeks to spread its grip over the debtor's resources to maximise its prospects for collection. When the debtor seeks to respond to each creditor on an individual basis and where each creditor adopts its hegemony over the debtor's financial resources through cross-collaterlisation, requirements of completion deposits, establishment of performance hurdles or deadlines which limit flexibility and distort decision-making, additional collateralisation and the like, the debtor may find that, in the process, its financial resources are insufficient to meet the demands of all its creditors.

11.3 The formulation of an overall workout plan for a debtor in the environment of a systemic capital adequacy crisis and the responses generated by its financial institution creditors requires a change of focus or frame of reference by the debtor, as well as its creditors. Unless the debtor's efforts are co-ordinated properly and the work handled efficiently, the debtor's efforts will become paralysed and the expense undertaken in the preparation of a consensual workout plan will be wasted. No overall workout plan can be accomplished without successful individual workouts, through renegotiation of the affected loan or credit transactions. Conversely, the only way in which the debtor can achieve a successful workout is by placing these individual successful workout renegotiations in the context of an overall plan, which is designed to maximise return to all of the creditors on a fair and equitable basis and to motivate the debtor to follow through with the plan and ultimately avoid judicial reorganisation or liquidation. The plan must accommodate the financial and legal positions inherent in each individual workout negotiation situation, and each individual negotiation situation must be placed in the context of the overall workout plan.

11.4 Generally, the plan, in its initial stages, is a reflection of a coherent communication of the debtor's legal and financial condition. The effect of this broad-based communication to the creditors of the debtor will have the effect of repositioning many of the debtor–creditor relationships from their status prior to presentation of the plan. This process of repositioning will generally go through several stages in which the overall nature of the plan may shift based upon shifting individual workout negotiations and individual negotiations will vary in light of the economic implication of the plan upon the specific transaction and based upon the legal implications of the relationship and of the plan itself. The objective of a consensual reorganisation is to obtain the essential benefits of protection afforded under the federal bankruptcy laws without the attendant costs, stigma and potential loss of control. The basic equitable principles underlying a successful consensual reorganisation are the same basic equitable principles that underlie the completion of a successful reorganisation under Chapter 11 of the Bankruptcy Code.[1] A consensual reorganisation, however, is not the legal equivalent of a proceeding under the Bankruptcy Code. Any discussion of reorganisation under the Bankruptcy Code is beyond the scope of this chapter.

CONSENSUAL WORKOUTS

Advantages of consensual workouts for both debtors and creditors

11.5 Consensual workouts fix the rights of the parties and avoid the uncertainties of litigation and bankruptcy. Other advantages afforded by consensual workouts, as opposed to bankruptcy, include the following:

1. consensual workouts are more flexible; workouts permit all legitimate agreements to accomplish the consensual intent of the parties, limited primarily by depth and breadth of imagination;
2. consensual workouts preserve higher asset values; debtors are given incentives to maximise recoveries to limit deficiency liability;

1. See 11 USC, §§1101–1174 (1988).

3. consensual workouts are generally less expensive, both from an administrative perspective and from a legal perspective. Workouts limit costs and avoid burdens of litigation and bankruptcy;
4. consensual workouts often afford more benefits to creditors and debtors, both tangible and intangible:
   (a) management retains control of business;
   (b) debtor avoids "stigma" of bankruptcy;
   (c) debtor's principals may avoid or defer liability on personal guarantees;
   (d) creditor may obtain acknowledgment of outstanding indebtedness and of validity of liens and encumbrances;
   (e) creditor may obtain waiver of defences, setoffs and counterclaims;
   (f) creditor may obtain additional collateral and guarantees; and
   (g) creditor may correct deficiencies in loan or security documents.

Disadvantages of consensual workouts from the debtor's standpoint

11.6 Since a workout is a consensual arrangement, neither debtor nor co-operating creditors can bind non-assenting creditors nor halt litigation or foreclosure proceedings by unco-operative creditors. Substantial unanimity is required of all creditors. This unanimity is often difficult to obtain.

11.7 Claims by governmental entities (IRS, DOE, FDIC, FSLIC, FHA, SBA, RTC, OCC, OTS, etc.) are frequently more difficult to deal with in workouts because governmental or government-controlled creditors tend to be less flexible; their respective regulatory guidelines frequently do not permit flexibility.

11.8 Additional problems include:

1. the debtor is unable to reject burdensome leases or other executory contracts;
2. the debtor is unable to recover property in possession of foreclosing creditors or to defeat prior attachment, garnishment or levy;
3. the debtor is unable to recover preferential, fraudulent or voidable transfers that otherwise might be avoidable in bankruptcy; and
4. the debtor has no convenient forum (such as an experienced bankruptcy court) for expeditious resolution of disputes, enforcement of sales free and clear of liens and encumbrances, determination of priority of liens and the like.

Disadvantages of consensual workouts from the creditor's standpoint

11.9 Unlike bankruptcy, consensual workouts do not subject the actions of the debtor and its principals to judicial scrutiny and control. Participation in a consensual workout may perpetuate ineffectual or dishonest management. It may also permit continued erosion of collateral or other asset values if control of timing and price of liquidation remains with the debtor. Participation in a consensual workout does not prevent a subsequent bankruptcy filing if the workout fails.

Conditions for a successful consensual workout

11.10 Participation in a consensual workout makes no sense if the crucial components of a successful workout are not present. Those elements depend upon the attributes of the particular workout. For example, inability to survive in the long term is inconsequential if the workout contemplates an orderly liquidation of assets, as opposed to continuing business operations. Many consensual workouts initially envision long-term survival, but as negotiations progress, they evolve into more or less of an orderly liquidation. In evaluating a proposed consensual workout, some of the most important factors relating to its potential success include:

1. adequate liquidity (cash) available to fund the workout;
2. readjusted and realistic expectations by all parties;
3. adequate disclosure of information; a consensual workout is, in a sense, a private bankruptcy proceeding, where the scope of information provided by the debtor should be substantially equivalent to that disclosed in a formal bankruptcy filing;
4. flexibility of the legal rights and practical leverage of each of the participants;
5. appreciation of the legal rights and practical leverage of each of the participants;
6. absence of significant avoidable transfers which prefer one creditor over others in the same class, as well as equitable treatment of classes of creditors;
7. perceived fairness in the treatment of differing creditor and equity classes;
8. continuing co-operation of critical creditors, employees and management personnel;
9. confidence in management;
10. confidence in the debtor's business plan; and
11. ability to operate profitability within the applicable regulatory climate.

Pitfalls which creditors should seek to avoid in a consensual workout

11.11 Assuming that the key elements for a successful consensual workout are present, creditors should guard against:

1. inducing others to extend credit to the debtor;

2. paying debtor's employees without making adequate provisions for trust fund taxes or funding the payroll with knowledge that debtor's management will not surrender or withhold appropriate taxes;
3. failing to comply with bulk transfer provisions;
4. failing to take immediate possession of surrendered collateral;
5. becoming enmeshed in unintended admissions, waivers or releases during negotiations; and
6. exercising control over the debtor.

International application of the consensual workout process

11.12 A recent example of the application of the consensual workout principles articulated in this chapter may be found in Draft Circular No. S/98/, issued by the Hong Kong Association of Banks on 3 April 1998, entitled "Guidelines on Corporate Difficulties", the complete text of which follows.

GUIDELINES ON CORPORATE DIFFICULTIES

1. Introduction

(a) This circular contains formal but non-statutory guidelines covering how institutions should deal with customers in difficulties where the customer is dealing with multiple banks. There have been many instances where the constructive approach suggested below has made possible the survival of businesses which otherwise would have failed. These are supported by H.K.A.B., which would expect all members to use their best endeavours to follow these guidelines.

(b) The stakeholders in a business can comprise its shareholders, directors, employees, creditors (including bankers and suppliers) and customers. It is in all their interests that the business should survive if there is a reasonable possibility that it is viable. Only where there is not should it be liquidated. All concerned will prefer the company's bankers to opt first for a work-out (a process whereby, a debtor company having acknowledged that it is in financial difficulty, it is nursed back to health by the addition of capital or re-scheduling its debts). Other creditors will have to co-operate by not demanding repayment.

2. Underlying principles

(a) When it becomes public knowledge that a debtor company may be experiencing financial problems and the borrower has approached its banks, banks' initial attitude should be one of support. They should not withdraw facilities or hastily put the company into receivership, or issue Supreme Court writs demanding repayment.

(b) Further decisions should only be made based on information which is reliable and shared fully with all creditor banks (after obtaining the debtor's permission).

(c) The decision to offer the company financial assistance—or not—should be a collective one by creditor banks.

3. Implementation

(a) The underlying objective of any work-out should be to obtain for creditor banks the best deal that can be achieved.

(b) The work-out will need unanimity. Whilst banks are likely to be reluctant to permit an increase in their exposure on a customer so that other banks' facilities can be salvaged, they should be aware that, if they fail to co-operate in a work-out, the same might be done to them next time if the roles are reversed.

(c) The performance of the lead bank in a work-out is of prime importance. It should lead but not dominate excessively. It must ensure the provision of full information to all the banks involved. Preferably some mechanism for this should be laid down in the arrangements agreed between creditors. Care should be taken, for quoted debtors, to avoid breaching insider trading rules and keep the market orderly.

(d) Correspondingly, other creditor banks must be constructive and play their part by participating in meetings and providing comments promptly. Their representatives should be adequately senior to appreciate the underlying issues.

(e) For larger lending groups, it may be useful to consider establishing a steering committee. This can facilitate communications and provide quicker, representative feed-back than consultation with the entire group. Consideration may be given to having this body be the party to draft any agreement covering stand-still arrangements. It may also be the body to enlist expert assistance, e.g. of investigating accountants.

(f) Other creditors—see also 1(b) above; to this list might be added holders of bonds and commercial paper—may usefully participate in a work-out.

(g) A careful watch must be kept on costs. The expenses of a work-out, e.g. for lawyers and accountants, should properly be for the account of the debtor but creditor banks should take care that they are minimized and reasonable, given that otherwise the debtor's cash-flow will be unnecessarily worsened. Likewise the demands on the borrower for information must be reasonable.

(h) Care must be exercised regarding sales of debt, particularly to parties who have not been involved previously. Bringing them up to speed and ensuring their commitment can impede progress. Sellers should ensure that the buyers are aware of the guidelines in place and that they would be expected to adhere to them.

(i) any conflicts of interest should be declared openly and promptly.

(j) The arrangement between creditor banks must provide a mechanism for enforcing any breathing space for the debtor which is initially agreed. It should also cover the treatment of new money and ensure fair distribution.

(k) The terms of any re-structuring must be manageable for the debtor.

4. Role of Hong Kong Monetary Authority

(a) The H.K.M.A. has expressed its support for the above guidelines. It has indicated that in appropriate circumstances it stands ready to help to resolve differences of views which would threaten a work-out and to achieve an acceptable compromise. In this connection it would be prepared to listen to any involved party, irrespective of size or national affiliation.

EVOLUTION OF INSOLVENCY LAW AS A CONTEXT FOR CONSENSUAL WORKOUT

11.13 Awareness of the evolution of insolvency law brings context to current national, as well as international, problems of insolvency. Historically, the United States has addressed the problem of insolvency through its bankruptcy laws. The Bankruptcy Act of 1800 was the first bankruptcy law adopted by the

United States Congress.[2] The Bankruptcy Act of 1800 closely followed the English Statute of Bankrupts.[3] In turn, the origins of the English Statute of Bankrupts may be traced back to the laws of other European countries, the Italian city-states of the fourteenth century, and even further, to the Roman Empire.[4]

11.14 The various practices employed in dealing with the problem of a debtor who either refused, or was unable, to pay its debts date back as far as the extension of credit itself. In the primitive and ancient cultures, public opinion provided two sanctions by which a debtor could be compelled to perform his part of a contract. Each of these sanctions was extremely powerful. One sanction was religious, while the other was more primitive and severe: execution.[5]

11.15 In thirteenth-century England, the common law provided for imprisonment of the debtor until he "made agreement (with his creditors) or his friends for him".[6] Imprisonment was intended to compel payment of the debt and not to punish the debtor for his failure to pay.[7]

11.16 The most important early English bankruptcy law was the Statute of

2. R.L. Jordan & W.T. Warren, *Bankruptcy*, (1985) p. 20.

3. *Ibid.*

4. *Ibid.*, p. 17. On ancient Roman collection practices, "If the debtor be insolvent to serve creditors, let his body be cut in pieces on the third market day. It may be cut into more or fewer pieces with impunity, or, if his creditors consent to it, let him be sold to foreigners beyond the Tiber." Twelve Tables, Table III, 6 (*c.* 450 BC).

5. Levinthal, "The early history of bankruptcy law", 66 U. Pa. L. Rev. 223, 229 (1918). For instance, in India of old, and currently in Nepal, creditors engaged in the practice of "sitting d'harna" and, in ancient Ireland, creditors engaged in "fasting on" debtors. These practices involved the creditor placing himself before the debtor's doorway and remaining until the debt was paid. This practice was extremely effective, in light of the fact that debtor would have been instantly and severely punished by public opinion if he were to permit his creditor to suffer from exhaustion or die of starvation at his door. *Id.*, 229, citing Tarde, "Evolution of procedure", in A. Kocourek & J. Wigmore (eds) *Primitive and Ancient Legal Institutions* (1915), p. 700. The Hindus employed a system of self-help. In this system, the creditor could take his debtor and force him to perform labour for him or he could resort to violence and kill or maim the debtor, confine his wife, his sons or his cattle. Lang, "Origin of exogamy and totemism", in A. Kocourek & J. Widmore (eds) *Primitive and Ancient Legal Institutions* (1915), p. 230, citing Manu. XIII, pp. 48 *et seq.*

The Egyptians, however, only provided for the attachment of the debtor's property, not his person. The rationale for this was that the state might at any time require the debtor's service, in peace as an official or labourer, and in war as a soldier. *Ibid.*, pp. 230–231, on the authority of Diodorus, I, 79; Reveillout, *Cours de Droit Egyptien*, p. 42.

In time, legal process against insolvents evolved to the point where execution was had against the property of the debtor, rather than against the debtor himself. Undoubtedly, this was the result of a change in objective from retaliation to compensation. Tarde, p. 232. In ancient systems of law, whether the debtor was actually honest or dishonest, insolvency was seen as something that was irregular and fraudulent. However, in time the unfortunate insolvent was distinguished from the fraudulent bankrupt. See, e.g., Code of Hammurabi, §§116 and 117, where protection from creditors was provided to the debtor who was made insolvent by misfortune.

6. J. Cohen, "The history of imprisonment for debt and its relation to the development of discharge in bankruptcy", 29 U. Chi. L. Sch. Rec. 5, 6 (Fall 1983), citing 11 or 13 Edw.1 c.14 (1283 or 1285).

7. *Ibid.* While some may argue that imprisoning the debtor was punitive in nature, the debtor could always terminate his imprisonment by paying the debt.

Bankrupts.[8] The Statute of Bankrupts was directed toward punishment of fraudulent debtors[9] and only applied to debtors who were merchants, providing that a debtor who committed "an act of bankruptcy"[10] was to be reputed, deemed and taken for a bankrupt. Upon complaint, the Lord Chancellor could appoint a commission of "wise, honest and discrete" persons who were authorised to seize the property of the bankrupt and sell it for the payment, pro rata, of the debts of the bankrupt. The bankrupt, however, remained liable to the extent that his creditors were not paid in full. The commissioners had the power to imprison the bankrupt and, by virtue of a later statute, he could be subject to pillory and the loss of an ear as well.[11] The design of early English bankruptcy law was to protect creditors and to punish debtors who were trying to avoid payment of just debt.[12]

11.17 In the early eighteenth century the harshness with which bankrupts were treated was greatly reduced by statutes which provided for the granting of a discharge to the bankrupt of the debts owing at the time of bankruptcy.[13] This development was attributed to the notion that bankrupts were not always fraudulent, and sometimes failed because of circumstances beyond their control, and that such bankrupts were entitled to relief.[14] Society recognised that unlimited incarceration of the debtor did not usually lead to the reimbursement of his creditors.[15] In addition, creditors came to believe that a law which was "all penalty and no reward" was self-defeating: forcing bankrupts to relinquish all of their property to satisfy some creditors and then exposing them to unlimited imprisonment by others encouraged evasion, even by merchants who would otherwise have been willing to co-operate.[16] Finally, creditors acknowledged that mercantile credit was given in the interest of the creditor, as well as of the debtor, and that the giving of credit necessarily involved some risk and, therefore, it followed that the business of the merchant should insure against this risk by adding on a percentage for the credit which he advanced and that all a debtor ought to pledge to this credit was his estate, and not his future earnings or personal liberty.[17] Not until well into the nineteenth century did the notion of allowing a debtor to voluntarily declare bankruptcy become a part of English bankruptcy law as a means of finding relief from creditors.

11.18 Insolvent debtors have historically received different treatment,

8. 13 Eliz. c.7 (1571).
9. Jordan and Warren, *Bankruptcy*, p. 18.
10. "Acts of Bankruptcy" included the debtor's departure from his realm, his taking refuge in his home, his taking sanctuary and various other acts if his purpose was to avoid process with the intent of defrauding or hindering his creditors.
11. See Levinthal, "The early history of English bankruptcy", 67 U. Pa. L. Rev. 1, 16–18 (1919).
12. D.G. Boshkoiff, "Limited, conditional and suspended discharges in Anglo-American bankruptcy proceedings", 131 U. Pa. L. Rev. 69, 105–106 (1982).
13. 4 Anne c.17 (1705); 10 Anne c.15 (1711). These statutes applied only to merchants, however.
14. Jordan and Warren, *Bankruptcy*, p. 18.
15. Boshkoff, 131 U. Pa. L. Rev. 69 (1982).
16. Levinthal, "The early history of English bankruptcy", 67 U. Pa. L. Rev. 1, 18–19 (1919).
17. Cohen, 29 L. Sch. Rec. 5, 6 (Fall 1983).

dependent upon whether they were merchants. A merchant was entitled to bankruptcy in which, upon surrender of his available assets, he was discharged from liability to his creditors. Insolvency also applied to non-merchants, who however, after release, remained obligated to pay the remainder of their debt. Blackstone probably best expressed the rationale for restricting bankruptcy to the merchants when he stated:

> But [the laws] are cautious of encouraging prodigality and extravagance by this indulgence to debtors; and therefore they allow the benefit of laws of bankruptcy to none but actual traders; since that set of men are, generally speaking, the only persons liable for accidental losses, and to an inability of paying their debts without any fault of their own. If persons in other situations of life run in debt without the power of payment, they must take the consequences of their own indiscretion, even though they meet with sudden accidents that may reduce their fortunes: the law holds it to be an unjustifiable practice, for any person but a trader to encumber himself with debts of any considerable value. If a gentleman, or one in a liberal profession, at the time of contracting his debts, has a sufficient fund to pay them, delay of payment is a species of dishonesty, and a temporary injustice to his creditor; and if, at such time, he has an insufficient fund, the dishonesty and injustice is the greater. He cannot, therefore, murmur, if he suffers the punishment which he has drawn upon himself. But in mercantile transactions, the case is far otherwise. Trade cannot be carried on without mutual credit on both sides: the contracting of debts is therefore here not only justifiable, but necessary. And if by accidental calamities, as by loss of a ship in a tempest, the failure of brother traders, or by the non-payment of persons out of trade, a merchant or trader becomes incapable of discharging his own debts, it is his misfortune and not his fault.[18]

11.19 In the United States, the Constitution gives Congress the authority to enact laws concerning bankruptcy. Every bankruptcy law in the United States has been the product of some financial crisis or business depression,[19] and thus the bankruptcy legislation is a reflection of changes in economic conditions and viewpoints in the country. It has evolved through periods of pro-debtor tendencies, pro-creditor tendencies and compromises between each.[20] The United States generally has accepted the principle that bankruptcy as a process is required in the public interest of the nation, in addition to the effect of the law upon particular individuals upon whom the law was to operate. The interest of the nation lies in the continuation of business and the conservation of property for the benefit of creditors and the debtor, and not in the sale and distribution of the assets among the creditors, or even in the debtor's own immediate discharge from debt. The forced sale of property and the stoppage of business in times of financial crisis constitutes a loss to the nation at large, as well as to the individual debtors and creditors.[21] Thus, bankruptcy law has developed into a system which attempts to achieve three objectives:

1. to protect creditors from each other;

18. W. Blackstone, 2 *Commentaries on the Laws of England*, 417, 473–474 (1765–1769).
19. C. Warren, *Bankruptcy in United States History* (1935), p. 9.
20. *Ibid.*
21. *Ibid.*

2. to protect creditors from dishonest debtors; and
3. to protect the honest debtor from his creditors by means of discharge.[22]

11.20 Those laws that seek to protect creditors from one another attempt to prevent any one of the creditors from obtaining more than its proportionate share of the debtor's assets. Such a law provides for the collective execution of process directed against all of the property of the debtor for the benefit of, and at the common expense of, all the creditors. When the debtor is unable to pay all of its debts in full, the principle of contribution is invoked, and any loss due to insolvency is thereby spread among all of the creditors. The basis for this execution process is both social and economic. In order to achieve these objectives, a method of managing the debtor's estate during the pendency of the process is required. Some entity must be given control over all of the property of the debtor to collect, manage and distribute all the assets. When this process is handled through bankruptcy law, the expense of the process and depletion of the debtor's estate to the detriment of the creditors is significant.[23] The objective in a consensual workout is, through voluntary, transparent and forthright action by the debtor, to inspire in the creditors a high level of trust and confidence in the debtor's adherence to the fundamental principles of bankruptcy law and the likelihood of achievement of their mutual objectives by voluntary and consensual management, and thereby to avoid the polarisation and expense of a judicial achievement of those objectives and to thereby maximise repayment.

CONSENSUAL WORKOUT THEORY

11.21 Consensual workouts are based upon the fundamental assumption that the debtor has been honest and forthright in its operations and that current economic difficulties leading to workout or reorganisation are due to honest mistakes of business judgement or market conditions not susceptible of anticipation or accommodation by the debtor. The systemic problem of deteriorating capital adequacy is precisely such a circumstance. Resolution of the resulting financial problems between a debtor and creditor then need not necessarily be a violently adversarial process. A calm and dispassionate evaluation of the factors leading to the defined economic problem, however, should lead to a fairly clearly defined set of options under existing legal and financial structures for problem resolution. The mission of both the debtor and the creditor in a consensual reorganisation is to go past artificial adversarial

22. Levinthal, "The early history of bankruptcy law", 66 U. Pa. L. Rev. 225. It should be noted that not all systems of bankruptcy law seek to achieve this third goal.
23. Warren, *Bankruptcy in United States History*, p. 112, citing Am. L. Rev. VII (July 1873): "[F]rom the beginning to the end, there is one continuous, increasing plucking at the estate. Merchants have come to believe it best to settle with their debtors out of the bankrupt court. In its details, the law is perplexing, cumbersome, annoying, and expensive."

posturing and to seek to understand the underlying root of the economic problem and allocate the loss occasioned by that problem in accordance with the legal and economic facts. If both the debtor and the creditor see the facts clearly, their interests should be aligned in resolving the allocation of loss in accordance with those facts and the law in the most expeditious and efficient manner possible. These parties are in the position to suffer the most pain in the absence of such a consensual agreement and are in the position to gain the greatest economic benefits from its success. A successful consensual reorganisation requires, and is the product of, this alignment and agreement.

11.22 The organisation of the legal and economic facts into a workout plan, however, involves a complex interrelated set of decisions which, in each case, must be measured against the available alternatives. The test in each case for each of the constituent decision makers, both the debtor and the creditor, and the constituents within the debtor organisation, including partners, investors and employees, is to measure and prioritise the consequences of each decision under various alternatives. A consensual workout or reorganisation should produce an alignment of the constituents' best legal, economic and personal interests. A correct alignment among the constituents in the face of the legal and economic facts will produce a desire to complete the workout.

11.23 Performance incentives or inducements can be built in with respect to any or all of these constituents. Examples of such incentives or inducements include preferential treatment for risk-taking by creditors, incentive fees or participation in residuals and limitation or elimination of personal liability for debtors under certain circumstances. If the desire, action and performance by the debtor, combined with time and space afforded by a consensual workout plan, will not produce a greater repayment to creditors than a liquidation, the creditors will not permit any economic incentive or inducement, action and performance. The objective of the consensual workout and the definition of its success is the effectuation of the lowest cost and most efficient allocation of loss on the most equitable basis, considering the facts and the law, which produces the maximum repayment to creditors. Every decision and the consideration of every alternative must be considered against this test of success.[24]

11.24 Debtors should be cognisant that, in many cases, lenders do not act rationally. The motivation of loan officers and lender management is often inconsistent with their role in the workout process. Many decision-making motivations for these individuals are personal and relate to internal politics in or external pressures on their employer organisations or to regulatory pressures. Often, the responsible officers are not given any incentive to understand and do not understand their factual and legal position. The debtor must be mindful of

24. While this type of consensual workout has achieved widespread acceptance, and recent activity among the G-10 indicate some move to adopt the same principles for sovereign debt restructures, bank regulators have tended to treat bank indebtedness (deposits) which they have insured or guaranteed from a much more limited perspective. See articles; see also B. Eichengren *et al.*, *Crisis? What Crisis? Orderly Workouts to Sovereign Debtors* (1995).

the problems presented by these anomalous situations and of the effect of the state of mind of the various decision makers on their approach to the workout process.

11.25 Although it is the objective of a consensual workout to avoid adversarial positioning, it may be necessary for the debtor or for the creditors to utilise adversarial tools, such as bankruptcy proceedings, litigation and other aggressive actions, from time to time, to level the field of negotiations and protect consensual participants from creditors who seek to obtain an advantage without providing a corresponding benefit to the consensual workout process or to force reluctant or misguided participants to the bargaining table. This process is often required in one of two situations:

1. where responsibility for negotiations on behalf of a creditor must be moved out of the hands of a defensive loan officer, who may desire to avoid the issues and protect his personal position in the organisation; or
2. where responsibility for negotiations on behalf of a debtor rests with an individual whose ego and self-image dominate strategy.

In each of these situations responsibility and control must be delegated and moved into the hands of a professional problem solver.

11.26 Creditors will often take a very tough position from both a legal and a business point of view to discover the level of commitment and will of a debtor who proposes a consensual workout or reorganisation plan. The debtor must remain calm, stick with the workout plan and utilise appropriate adversarial proceedings sparingly, but with sufficient definition and purpose, to protect its position and move the workout process forward, stopping short of polarising positioning.

11.27 The plan formulation process must recognise creditor preferences for reaching separate individual workout agreements, rather than global agreements. Creditors consistently demonstrate a strong desire to avoid master creditor agreements which extend over a long period of time. Each plan, therefore, should seek to accommodate the individual creditor relationships to the maximum possible degree through consistent treatment and, if possible, to accomplish satisfaction of undersecured or unsecured claims through available assets which can be segregated on a fair and equitable basis. Only where unsecured and undersecured claims cannot be satisfied in this way should a collateral pooling mechanism be utilised. Creditors will often prefer to waive their unsecured claims or undersecured claims to avoid the complication of participation in a complex collateral pool, or they may be willing to advance new funds outside of the collateral pool context, but subject to a requirement for additional collateralisation or specific cross-collateralisation not related to the other unsecured or undersecured claims, in effect creating individual creditor-by-creditor collateral pools. An important component of the plan will be to clearly communicate to the creditors that undersecured or unsecured claims can be waived, or collateralised, if new consideration is given. In addition, if there is enough collateral to go around, and if it can be divided equitably and if there is an incentive to the debtor to go through with this process, a master, or global collateral pool may not be required.

11.28 The purpose of a collateral pool is to effect a mechanism to capture equity for repayment of unsecured or undersecured creditors, subject to any reasonable residual incentives reserved to the debtor. Collateral pools are an important plan component in consensual reorganisations, but collateral pools are not absolutely necessary if claims can otherwise be satisfied on a fair and equitable basis.

11.29 A consensual plan is no panacea. There is no magic to the process: just the hard work of uncovering, organising and recording the economic and legal facts, developing a detailed knowledge of the circumstances and communicating these clearly and persistently to the parties to the plan. The legal and economic facts will define the plan, and internal and external relationships will be changed, based upon the development of these factual and legal positions. Development of a consensual workout plan of reorganisation is difficult and requires the alignment agreement of a large number of disparate parties, each of whom will undoubtedly recognise some change in their legal and economic position from the position they thought they had before the process began. Those changes must be accepted and alternative decisions based on the commonly understood legal and economic facts must be measured, and in each case, against the legal and economic alternatives, the anticipated effectiveness of the plan and its costs measured against the cost of alternatives. Where there are reasonable prospects for the development and execution of a consensual workout plan, both the creditors and the debtor have the duty to pursue it and to honestly and vigorously seek its implementation.

IMPACT ON CREDITORS

11.30 Lessons learned by federal regulators in the Texas experience and in New England were applied with swiftness to banks in other regions of the country. Regulators relied heavily on the doctrine of bank safety and soundness in order to halt practices to which it objected. Prior to the Texas experience, the application of the standard of safety and soundness was unclear when applied to real estate loan portfolios and OREO and, by extension, to LBO portfolios. Although no clear consensus has yet developed in the courts, the application of the standard now has much more focus.

11.31 The statutory underpinning of safety and soundness is found in 12 USC, §1818, which authorises federal banking agencies to take enforcement action necessary to halt unsafe and unsound banking practices. Such enforcement actions range from informal administrative action, such as letters of commitment or broad resolutions, through memoranda of understanding, to cease and desist orders. These documents require the bank's board to direct specific positive action by management and proscribe continued unsafe and unsound practices and violations of law. The consequences of engaging in practices found to be unsafe and unsound or in violation of law can include restitution for losses by and/or civil monetary penalties against and/or temporary or permanent disbarment from the banking industry of members of management and the board of directors.[25] Enforcement actions often contain allegations of violations of law, fraud and breach of fiduciary obligations by directors and officers. The Financial Institutions Reform Recovery and Enforcement Act ("FIRREA")[26] and the Crime Control Act of 1990 ("CCA")[27] greatly expanded the enforcement authority of regulators and increased civil penalties for violations.

11.32 Regulators applied the standards of safety and soundness subjectively based on a retrospective factual analysis. Consequently, bank management and its board of directors were required to be pro-active and anticipatory in demonstrating to regulators their awareness of and serious concern for safe and sound practices. This awareness and concern must be carefully documented. This documentation constitutes the "*transparency*" at the asset level which is *indispensable* to calculations of bank capital adequacy. For example, documentation should show that the board and management are aware of the effect which explosive growth in non-performing assets can have on the financial condition of the bank. It should show that management has given consideration to and has evaluated alternative courses of action. It should demonstrate that a specific course of action has been adopted and put into effect. Most importantly, documentation should demonstrate that the board and management have exercised reasonable business judgement in dealing with the problem. Reasonable business judgement is generally regarded as the ultimate standard to which management may be held accountable. However, some recent public sentiment indicates a call for a higher and more rigorous standard of care by management in dealing with other people's money. Unless or until the requirement of a higher standard of care actually develops, the reasonable business judgement should be the test of managing the bank safely and soundly.

11.33 The early 1980s, late 1980s and early 1990s in the Southwest, New England and the Middle Atlantic states clearly demonstrated that the excesses in real estate, LBOs and ill-conceived mergers had created an absolute loss in value in many assets which were collateral for banks' loans. This loss was systemic and unavoidable. It could not have been escaped by "better underwriting". Indeed, underwriting to a large degree has *become irrelevant*.

25. See J. Crawford, "Scandal gives parties a chance to fire away at each other", 48 Cong. 2204, 2205 (1990). See also the Competitive Equality in Banking Act (CEBA) PL–100–86, 101 Stat. 552, (codified in various sections of 2, 12, 15 and 31 USC) (1987) and the Federal Deposit Insurance Corporation Improvement Act of 1991 (FDICIA) PL–102–242, 105 Stat. 2236 (codified in various sections of 12 and 15 USC) (1991).

26. PL–101–73, 103 Stat. 183 (codified in various sections of 12 and 15 USC) (1989).

27. PL–101–647, 104 Stat. 4789 (codified in various sections of 11, 12, 18 and 28 USC) (1990).

11.34 Thus, the task of bank asset management is to recognise and shift this unavoidable loss to others and away from the bank to the greatest extent possible. The shift of loss may be to the borrower or it may be to his other creditors who are not as aware nor as pro-active as banks.

BASIC PRINCIPLES OF LOAN RESTRUCTURES

Balancing collection efforts with effect on bank results

The dilemma: ultimate loss protection vs. non-performing asset minimisation

11.35

- Banks are guarded by rating agencies and bank stock analysts on current and projected levels of non-performing assets ("NPAs") compared to total assets, loss reserve and capital. High ratios cause higher cost of funds.
- Thus, management is deeply concerned about NPAs and reserves.
- The real loss is the ultimate loss on an asset. The rest is interim accounting.
- So which is more important? How do you balance these concerns?
- Establish a clear rule.

Regulator confidence

11.36

- Importance:
  - Benefit of doubt in close calls.
  - Higher cut-off.
- Examiners examine from centralised, organised files. Examiners give no credit for what's in your head or your desk file.
- Knowledge of credit and pursuit of a pro-active plan action must be demonstrated by road map memos.
- Examiners are the most experienced reviewers of appraisals today.

Rating agency expectations

11.37

- Rating agencies identify potential credit watch banks with regional statistics on vacancy, rent rates, absorption, general business conditions and job creation.
- They are particularly interested in a bank's tracking systems and early pro-active address of problems.

— They can have as much effect on bank earnings and capital as the examiners.

Important accounting issues and their effect on workout action

11.38 Although Mexico and many Latin American as well as other emerging countries do not follow American Generally Accepted Accounting Principles (GAAP), officials at the Mexican National Banking and Securities Commission announced on 11 March 1996 that by 1 January 1997 Mexican banks would be following accounting standards much closer to GAAP standards. When implemented,

> [a]ccording to Jose Garcia-Cantrera, Latin American bank analyst at Solomon Brothers, the new accounting rules could mean that past due loans increase by as much as 100 per cent, which would cut in half the amount of reserves a bank has against loans in default. (Reuters, 11 March 1996, Mexico City).

Suddenly, GAAP accounting issues are of immediate importance to Mexican bankers and borrowers. They will soon be of importance to other emerging countries.

Capitalisation of interest

11.39 Capitalised interest on loans is defined as uncollected interest which is added to the unpaid principal balance in accordance with a contractual loan agreement.[28]

11.40 It is common in construction lending for the loan agreement to contain a line item loan allocation for the costs of construction. One of the line items is often an "interest reserve" out of which advances are made periodically to pay interest charges on the outstanding balance of the construction loan. When construction is complete and all line item allocations including the interest reserve are fully advanced, the loan is repaid through permanent financing or sale of the project in the normal course of business. The result, of course, is that the loan including the interest allocation is paid.

11.41 Capitalised interest concerns arise when the project loan is not paid at maturity through permanent financing or sale as was expected. In these cases, the "interest reserve" has been fully advanced, the loan has matured, but the source of repayment is delayed. If the loan is renewed pending receipt of the source of repayment, the interest reserve by definition has been capitalised into the loan.

11.42 Another situation causing interest capitalisation concerns arises from opening a new loan or increasing the original loan to create a new interest reserve to carry the renewed loan pending its repayment. Depending on the

28. OCC Examining Circular 229.

source of repayment of the new loan, it too may be deemed capitalised interest on the original loan.

11.43 *Capitalisation of interest for reporting purposes is appropriate only when the borrower has the ability to repay the debt in the normal course of business.*[29] The preceding sentence does *not* mean that any construction loan which is not repaid at maturity must automatically be placed on non-accrual. It is not unusual in the real estate development business for permanent financings and sales to be temporarily delayed and for additional well-structured loans to be extended to pay interest on the original loan during the delay. The purpose of this section is to give workout officers guidance on the circumstances under which continued accrual is appropriate.

11.44 Capitalisation of interest on short-term real estate loans should be based upon the borrower's ability to discharge the indebtedness in the normal course of business considering the surrounding circumstances and based upon prudent credit judgement including source of repayment and value of collateral.

11.45 The appropriateness of interest capitalisation for accounting purposes is based primarily on the creditworthiness of the borrower and guarantors. In addition to the general criteria for creditworthiness, the following questions should be considered in determining whether capitalisation of interest is appropriable:

(a) Was interest capitalisation anticipated upon approval of the initial loan?
(b) Is the loan well secured: (i) by collateral that has a realisable value sufficient to discharge the debt (including capitalised interest) in full?; *or* (ii) by the guaranty of a financially responsible and capable party?
(c) Is repayment of the loan based on a reasonably ascertainable event in the future?
(d) Can the borrower obtain funds from sources other than the bank on similar terms and rates?
(e) Is there little or no doubt as to the ultimate collection of all principal and interest?

If the answer to these questions is predominantly affirmative, then capitalisation of interest may be acceptable. The primary test remains the overall credit quality of the loan. Credits of sound quality may merit interest capitalisation even if some of these questions are answered negatively. However, only in very unusual circumstances will a loan classified as substandard merit interest capitalisation.

29. *Ibid.*

Insubstance foreclosures

11.46 Loans should generally be considered insubstance foreclosures where they meet all of the following criteria:[30]

(a) the debtor has little or no equity in the collateral, considering the current fair value of the collateral; *and*
(b) proceeds for repayment of the loan can be expected to come only from the operation or sale of the collateral; *and*
(c) the debtor has either: (i) formally or effectively abandoned control of the collateral to the creditor; *or* (ii) retained control of the collateral but, because of the current financial condition of the debtor, or the economic prospects for the debtor and/or the collateral in the foreseeable future, it is doubtful that the debtor will be able to rebuild equity in the collateral or otherwise repay the loan in the foreseeable future.

11.47 The first two criteria are used to identify situations where most of the risks and rewards of ownership of the collateral have passed from the borrower to the bank. Even if the value of the collateral securing the loan has dropped so that there is little or no equity in that particular investment, the borrower or guarantor may currently have demonstrable sufficient strength or outside sources of cash to service and eventually retire the debt. In such case, the second criteria is not met and there is no insubstance foreclosure. Thus, value of collateral for a secured loan may drop to zero without a finding of ISF if the borrower or guarantor has the demonstrable current wherewithal to repay the loan from other sources. Likewise, if all loans to a borrower are cross-collateralised and total debt is reasonably exceeded by the value of all cross-pledged collateral, then the first criterion is not met and there is no finding of ISF.

11.48 The third criterion leaves room for subjective evaluation of the borrower's ability to rebuild equity in the collateral or otherwise repay the loan in the *foreseeable* future. This subjective evaluation should be prudently exercised by the workout officer and management. For example, when using forecasts to assess the borrower's ability to repay the loan or to assess the prospects for improvement in the value of the collateral, the workout officer making the determination should be mindful that the longer the time projected, the less reliable the projected results. Projections should be reasonably near term and be based on independently derived supportable assumptions.

11.49 Workout officers should be aware that determination of ISF affects only the bank's *accounting* for a loan as substantially repossessed. Legal title to the asset remains in the borrower until it is passed to the bank either consensually or through foreclosure. The loan is not in default solely by being

30. US Securities and Exchange Commission FRR §401.09(c) (FRR 28) (6AAP Release 17,9189); see also Statement of Financial Accounting Standards No. 15, paras 28 and 29.

found to be an ISF. It may be in the bank's best interest to obtain control over the price and timing of the sale of the collateral to eliminate an asset acquired for debt previously contracted as soon as possible, but action must be taken in a way to protect the bank from lender liability allegations. Therefore, it is extremely important for lending and supervised workout officers to maintain a course of dealing that minimises the bank's exposure to such allegations.

11.50 Even though an ISF real estate loan must be accounted for as OREO, compliance with 12 USC, §7.3025 is limited to the initial appraisal and annual reappraisal of the value of the underlying real estate. It is not necessary to obtain prior regulatory approval to fund a borrower's draw request,[31] although the bank may opt to refuse such funding under its loan agreement if the loan is in default.

Troubled debt restructures

11.51 A troubled debt restructure ("TDR") is one "in which the bank, for economic or legal reasons *related* to the *borrower's financial difficulties, grants a concession to the borrower that it would not otherwise consider*".[32]

11.52 Basic knowledge of TDR accounting is important to workout officers in: (a) preventing non-accrual status for certain loans and, (b) restoring existing non-accruals to performing status. *A finding that a restructure is a TDR requires the restructure to be carried on the bank's financial statement as a non-performing asset even if the loan is current as to interest.* TDRs are governed by FAS 15[33] which is extremely complex. This section undertakes only to outline the basic rules of TDRs and make certain suggestions rather than attempt a comprehensive review of FAS 15.

11.53 The point is to make workout officers aware that a restructure that makes perfect business sense may nonetheless be deemed a TDR by the bank's independent accountants, with the result that the goal of reducing non-accrual assets is not achieved. However, the workout officer should not negotiate a less favourable business deal in an attempt to achieve more favourable accounting treatment.

11.54 Because of the complexity of FAS 15, the advice and counsel of the bank's internal accounting staff should be sought as soon as a plan begins to take shape and before commitments are made to the borrower.

11.55 Note from the emphasis added in the definition of TDR that the touchstone is *granting concessions because of the borrower's difficulty.* For example, extending a loan at an interest rate equal to that generally charged for loans with similar risk would not be a TDR even if the rate were lower than the rate on the original loan.

31. Conference with legal staff OCC Southwestern District Office.
32. Banking Circular 195, 1 May 1985.
33. Statement of Financial Accounting Standards No. 15.

11.56 If the new terms of the troubled debt restructuring provide for a reduction of either interest *or* principal (referred to as a modification of terms), FAS 15 requires that the recorded amount of the loan on the bank's books (principal plus accrued interest) be compared to the total future contractual cash payments (including both principal and interest) expected to be collected. A loss is recognised *only* if the total of such future combined payments is less than the recorded amount of the loan. Otherwise, no loss is recognised and the only additional accounting requirement is to determine the new effective interest rate for income recognition purposes. However, the restructured loan will be carried as a non-performing asset.

11.57 Often the new effective interest rate is equal to the stated loan rate included in the restructured loan document. However, adjustments may be required if:

(a) the loan principal is reduced,
(b) the new contractual rates are on a graduated basis (e.g. 8 per cent first year, 10 per cent second year, etc.),
(c) due and unpaid interest is not added to principal or otherwise included in the contractual interest rate amount, or
(d) the repayment terms have other unusual provisions.

If an effective interest rate computation is required, it should be based upon future contractual payment terms excluding all payments which are contingently payable. This rate is calculated so as to yield a constant rate of interest over the remaining life of the loan. It is expected the rate will generally be less than the original loan rate and may be as low as zero without any requirement to recognise a loss.

11.58 Subject to the rules on capitalisation of interest discussed in paragraph 11.39ff, above, the bank may extend additional credit to a borrower at interest rates below the current market rate. Since this is a new loan to the same borrower, no special accounting rules apply. Accordingly, discounting or loss recognition is not necessary. However, if the new loan is granted in connection with the restructuring of an existing loan, it will be considered part of the restructuring and accounted for as previously described.

11.59 In all troubled debt restructuring the collectibility of future payments may be questionable. Therefore, a credit analysis should be performed to determine if any additional amounts should be charged to the allowance for loan losses. The analysis should include the borrower's ability to meet the new terms of the loan based upon projected cash flows, profitability and other credit factors.

How to force hidden problems to the surface

Strict enforcement of loan agreement

11.60

- — Require full compliance with all conditions to new advances (advising borrower, if necessary, that any prior waiver of certain conditions will no longer be granted).
- — Make sure that financial statements and borrowing base/construction progress reports are provided on time and accompanied by any required certificate of compliance.
- — Obtain detailed computation of any financial covenants required by loan agreements, such as current ratio, leverage ratio, tangible net worth, etc.
- — Obtain on a regular basis ageings of all payables and receivables and an analysis of concentrations.
- — Inspect borrower's book and records and properties as permitted by loan agreement.

No reallocation

11.61 In order to keep a loan on accrual, the lending officer is sometimes tempted to reallocate from, say, the tenant finish line items to the interest reserve after the initial interest reserve has been depleted. The debtor will offer convincing arguments that tenant finish requirements are lower or will be paid by the tenant. This type of action hides problems because the tenant finish is always *higher* than originally projected, not lower.

Borrower's deposits

11.62 Borrower deposit requirements are included in loan agreements to capture the borrower's cash into a project as soon as a line item cost overrun is known. Failure to exercise this right allows the borrower to divert his cash to other uses, thus exposing the bank to additional cost and probable loss to complete the end of the job.

Borrowing base overadvances

11.63 A clear sign of problems in an accounts receivable and inventory financing is when the borrowing base report, either directly or indirectly through an analysis of specific items contained therein, discloses that the principal balance of the loan exceeds the stipulated borrowing base. In nearly all situations, the borrower will argue that the overadvance is temporary in nature and will correct itself over time so that a waiver should be granted. In the overwhelming majority of cases, the overadvance will not cure itself over time, and the bank is well advised not to grant the waiver unless the borrower makes specific concessions designed to protect the bank's interests (e.g., lock box, additional collateral and/or personal guaranties).

Breaches of financial covenants

11.64 A primary purpose of financial covenants in a loan agreement is to provide an early warning signal of a borrower's potentially serious financial difficulties. Clearly, the financial covenants will fail to serve such purpose if their breach is treated by the bank as a mere "technical" default and readily waived. The breach of any financial covenant should be carefully analysed to determine if it represents an isolated occurrence based on special circumstances or is indeed a harbinger of future distress for the customer (and bank). If such breach raises concerns, consideration should be given to obtaining specific concessions from the borrower in exchange for granting a waiver. In any event, the waiver should always be given in writing and make clear that it applies only to the specific date or period involved.

Understanding economic and market forces

Market for the product

11.65 In troubled real estate markets, the debtor often depletes his resources in covering overheads or feeding projects with perceived positive potential. He has little left to support the bank's projects.

11.66 In these cases, the bank's primary source of interest carry and principal payment is the collateral itself. Thus, it is critical for the workout officer to know how to evaluate the project. This is discussed in detail in paragraph 11.133ff, below.

Current feasibility

11.67 Appraisals are important in evaluating collateral, but appraisals do not produce the cash to repay a loan. They only give an indication of what the collateral is worth on the day of the appraisal. Consider that appraisals are for accounting purposes. The workout officer needs to know current *feasibility* of the project. This is also expanded in paragraph 11.143ff, below.

Lease rules

11.68

- Importance of bank approval rights.
- Effect on value and saleability.
- Free rent rules.
- Lease profitability rules.

Sales of subsidiaries

11.69 In many highly leveraged transactions it is common for the lender to require the parent company borrower to grant liens on the stock or assets of subsidiary companies. While the cash flow of the consolidated group may be sufficient to pay interest on the loan, the sale of one or more subsidiaries may be needed to make principal payments. The sale of subsidiaries may not have been contemplated at the time the leveraged buyout originally occurred. In any case, the workout officer must carefully analyse the potential value of various subsidiaries and their prospects for sale, taking into account that the overhead charges allocated by the parent company to such subsidiaries may skew their apparent operating results. Such analysis will require a review of *consolidating* financial statements as well as the possible retention of an industry consultant.

Bank's rights to collateral

Negative pledge

11.70 The bank may have required a "negative pledge" which, although not acquiring a lien against the assets, limits the debtor's right to dispose of or encumber certain assets. The theory of a "negative pledge" is that the debtor agrees with the bank that it will not sell, lease, convey, or otherwise dispose of specified assets of the debtor or permit to exist any encumbrances with respect to such assets. The negative pledge may be coupled with the debtor's agreement to provide collateral to the bank (i.e., that the debtor will execute documents necessary to grant the bank a lien against certain property) upon the happening of certain events which typically may be tied to circumstances evidencing a deteriorating financial condition of the debtor. This type of arrangement may provide little comfort to the bank if the loan becomes troubled. To the extent that the debtor may be in default for failure to make any required payments to the bank or is otherwise in default to the bank, the debtor may have little motivation to deliver the requisite lien documents at that point, as its failure to do so will simply be another event of default. The bank may be in no better position than it would be if the loan were "unsecured", although the bank could perhaps argue that the debtor's agreement and obligation to provide collateral is specifically enforceable or that the collateral is held in a constructive trust for the benefit of the bank. Significant litigation expense would likely be incurred in such cases.

Assignment of partnership interests

11.71 In a restructure or in connection with the original loan, the bank may attempt to obtain or may have obtained a collateral assignment of a partnership interest held by the borrower. The assignment of the partnership interest should in most cases be a collateral assignment (security interest or lien on the partnership interest) and not an absolute assignment (bank owns partnership interest) in order to avoid obligating the bank for any partnership duties or liabilities. Prior to obtaining an assignment of a partnership interest, the partnership agreement should be reviewed with the bank's counsel in order to determine any issues relating to partner's consents to a transfer, securities law restriction and future capital contribution obligations of the partner. The collateral assignment of the partnership interest typically will provide the bank with a more valuable asset—the entire equity interest—than simply an assignment of proceeds from the partnership interest.

Assignment of proceeds

11.72 In connection with a restructure, a bank may attempt to obtain an assignment of proceeds from certain collateral, typically a partnership interest or some types of contracts (e.g. lot sale contracts, income-generating service contracts). The assignment of proceeds will typically only provide the bank with remedies or recourse in the event proceeds are received by the borrower from a partnership interest or from contracts and such proceeds are not delivered to the bank. The bank will not have obtained a security interest in or lien on the actual interest which produces the proceeds, so the true balance-sheet value of such an assignment may be nominal. In certain cases (e.g. service contracts) the bank may very well not want to obtain an assignment of a contract so as not to impose liability on the bank. One other consideration is that if bankruptcy is likely the proceeds received by the bank within the preference period prior to bankruptcy may be required to be disgorged.

Liens, senior and subordinate

11.73 Typically, the bank will obtain a first or senior lien on the primary collateral for its loan. In many instances, either in obtaining additional collateral for the original loan or in shoring up a troubled loan, the bank may have acquired a subordinate lien on an additional piece of collateral. The subordinate lien would be subject to one or more prior liens in favour of other creditors. An analysis of the actual value of the subordinate lien must include consideration of the total value of the collateral, the amount of debt secured by senior or prior liens against the collateral and the actual willingness of the bank to advance funds to protect its interest in the collateral in the event the borrower is in default in payments to a senior lienholder or in the event the senior lienholder exercises remedies against the collateral. Another consideration in the use of a subordinate lien is to "tie up" the collateral so that no consensual sale or conveyance of the collateral by the borrower can occur without the bank having the opportunity to require payment of the proceeds from the sale of the property to the bank prior to the release of its lien.

Related personal property

11.74 Often loans secured by real property will be additionally secured by personal property and fixtures used in connection with the real property. The bank should have valid security interests that have been perfected by financing statements currently filed and effective with the property filing offices. Liens on personal property are extremely important in relation to multifamily properties and hotel properties.

Remedies under UCC Article 9

11.75 Upon default in a loan secured by personal property which is subject to a valid and enforceable security interest under Article 9 of the Uniform Commercial Code, Article 9 affords the secured creditor the following non-judicial (i.e., self-help) remedies:

(a) the right to notify account debtors to make payment directly to the secured creditor;
(b) the right to repossess tangible collateral without causing a breach of the peace;
(c) the right to require the debtor to assemble the collateral and make it available at a reasonably convenient location designated by the secured creditor;
(d) the right to retain the collateral in satisfaction of the loan; and
(e) the right to sell, lease or otherwise dispose of the collateral by public or private proceedings.

11.76 The most significant remedy available under Article 9 is the secured creditor's right, after giving prior notice to the debtor and certain other interested parties, to conduct a private or public sale of all or a portion of the collateral without any judicial involvement.[34] While the power of sale under Article 9 represents an efficient method of liquidating collateral, there is imposed on the secured creditor the responsibility of assuring that every aspect of the sale is conducted in a "commercially reasonable" manner.[35] Article 9 does not expressly define what constitutes "commercially reasonable" conduct, and litigation has frequently resulted, seeking to determine whether a secured creditor's conduct was commercially reasonable in the specific circumstances presented. The importance of conducting the Article 9 sale in a commercially reasonable manner is that the secured creditor who fails to meet this standard may be denied the right to pursue any deficiency claim against the debtor or any guarantor and may be restrained from or ordered to conduct the sale in a specified manner or be liable for damages.[36]

34. UCC, §9–504.
35. UCC, §9–403(3); see also UCC, §9–507(2).
36. UCC, §9–507.

Bank's remedies—local law determination

11.77 The determination of the specific legal remedies available to the bank in the event of a loan default is made under the local law of the governing jurisdiction and is an inherent part of that state's economic and political structure. The workout officer must consult with the bank's legal department and local legal counsel to ascertain the legal advantages and disadvantages of specific workout structures and enforcement strategies.

Overview of borrower problems

Federal income tax liability

11.78 A properly counseled debtor will first be concerned with his liability for income tax arising from involuntary or voluntary conveyance of title to collateral or from forgiveness of debt. Income tax planning is a very significant element of virtually every real estate workout. In fact, in many workouts, the tax considerations become the single most important factor in developing a strategy and ultimate consummation of the workout. Although certain taxes incurred more than three years before the filing of a bankruptcy petition may be dischargeable in bankruptcy, more recent Federal income taxes, including taxes generated pursuant to the transactions involved in the workout, are not dischargeable. Consequently, it may be advisable for the debtor to pursue virtually any course that would minimise Federal tax liabilities, including incurring additional personal liability which may be subsequently discharged in bankruptcy.

(A) INFORMATION TO BE GATHERED

11.79 In order to apply the foregoing legal principles and to further develop the strategies described below, the following information must be examined:

(i) A detailed description of each asset owned by the debtor, including its fair market value, adjusted tax basis, and usage by the debtor (i.e., investment, personal, trade or business, inventory, etc.);
(ii) A detailed description of all fixed and contingent liabilities of the debtor, including whether they are recourse or non-recourse, guaranteed, seller-financing, etc.;
(iii) All agreements relating to the assets and liabilities of the debtor, including notes, loan agreements, guarantees and partnership agreements.

(B) ANALYSIS AND STRATEGIES

11.80 In a comprehensive real estate workout, the following steps of tax planning and analysis must be taken:

(i) evaluate the market value, indebtedness and adjusted basis of each property and determine the taxable gain or loss that would be recognised upon the voluntary or involuntary conveyance of each such property;
(ii) determine the taxable income of the debtor for the current taxable year to date and project the taxable income for the remainder of the year, other than income or loss that may be generated upon the disposition of the real properties;
(iii) determine the solvency or insolvency of the debtor;
(iv) determine the practical likelihood of bankruptcy and the willingness of the debtor to consider bankruptcy;
(v) consider and plan for the amount of gain or loss and timing of disposition of each and every property of the debtor.

Reputation, future earning power and family

11.81 A debtor will be concerned with his reputation in the community since it will greatly affect his ability to earn money in the future. These concerns are driven by his perceived need to preserve a reasonable life style for himself and his family. These are powerful psychological motivations and should not be treated lightly by the workout officer.

Alternatives

11.82 Absent fraud or other malfeasance, a borrower can accomplish his objectives by filing for bankruptcy, an action which is expensive and time-consuming for the bank, invariably leads to greatly reduced value of collateral if the stays are finally lifted or may expose the bank to a cram-down plan of reorganisation resulting in write-downs and permanently non-performing assets. Thus, heavy-handed action by a workout officer without consideration of the factors described above can adversely affect the bank. Conversely, if the bank is an undersecured or unsecured creditor, it may prefer the debtor to be in bankruptcy, in which case a different approach is appropriate. As noted in paragraph 11.133ff below, the facts generated in connection with the initial analysis of the existing status of the credit will dictate the workout plan.

Basic workout strategy

11.83 *Time is always critical.* First, it is important to the bank's well-being that non-performing and classified assets be reduced quickly. Second, if the workout plan requires foreclosure and resale, ultimate actual loss is minimised by doing so as quickly as possible especially in a deteriorating market. Finally, the bank benefits greatly by achieving its workout before other creditors are mobilised.

11.84 It is imperative to understand the bank's plan and focus on alternatives for achievement of the plan. The workout officer should prioritise actions to achieve the plan and move quickly and effectively with these actions. Remain calm and cool; avoid recriminations in meetings and exchanges where the borrower or guarantor faces the same facts you have uncovered. Do your best to avoid exchanges of legalism which polarise the objectives. Seek to align the borrower's and guarantor's plan with that of the bank. The officer should remember to stick to the loan documents and the bank's legal position within the context of the bank's plan. All parties should focus on a resolution and not waste money and time arguing about "who shot John".

Objective: Prevent non-performing asset classification

11.85 The first goal of every workout plan is to prevent the subject loans from being placed on non-accrual or to restore the subject loans to accrual status, if possible. If accrual is not possible, then the plan goal is to minimise interim charge-offs and ultimate actual loss.

Downside protection

11.86 It is axiomatic that the lender who: (i) addresses problems with the debtor first; (ii) acts consistently and in good faith; (iii) addresses debtor concerns; and (iv) is knowledgeable, reasonable and creative, will achieve a better solution to a troubled credit whether that solution is loan restructure or amicable acquisition of title to collateral. Debtors, however, are not always co-operative. Thus the workout officer must put the bank in the strongest position if restructure efforts fail and the relationship becomes acrimonious. Always first position the bank for maximum recovery if the events critical to the workout's success do not occur.

11.87 The following actions should be part of, or at least given consideration in formulating, every workout plan:

(a) Find the best available collateral and get it pledged to support future value declines, accrued unpaid interest or possible working capital loans. The best collateral is that which produces income in addition to value.
(b) Get all unsecured debt secured by anything of real value immediately.
(c) Control the cash flow of the bank's collateral by entering into a cash collateral agreement with the debtor under which he pays over monthly to the bank all net operating income without deduction for capital improvements, taxes or insurance. The expense component of monthly NOI should be tightly negotiated and the debtor should agree to strict accounting subject to audit by the bank. Refusal of the debtor to comply with the requirements is a clear indication of bad faith

necessarily requiring the workout officer to control cash flow through the bank's legal remedies.

(d) Get all loans to the debtor cross-collateralised and cross-defaulted as an early objective. If cross-collateralisation cannot be obtained at the asset level because of ownership by partnerships without common partners, at least obtain cross-collateralisation of all the common partnership interests. The workout officer can expect a sophisticated debtor to use granting of cross-collaterisation as a bargaining chip, for example for a working capital loan or release of liability. Any other deficiencies discovered in the analysis of the documentation should be corrected in any restructure modification agreement relating to a troubled credit.

(e) Get the bank's deal done before other creditors wake up. Start the preference period running.

Press remedies in the documents

11.88 Correctly drafted loan documents will provide for non-monetary covenants, undertakings and representations and warranties by the borrower. Non-compliance with these provisions usually constitutes a default after appropriate notices to the borrower and his failure to cure within the time limits provided. Often it is necessary to get the attention of an unco-operative borrower by methodical enforcement of the bank's rights and remedies under the loan documents. Such enforcement should stay strictly within the bounds of the documents (e.g., written notice, grace period, etc.) in order to avoid allegations of lender liability. By demonstrating its seriousness through methodical enforcement of rights and remedies, the bank encourages the borrower to be willing to negotiate restructure.

11.89 Even after restructure negotiations begin, the bank should continue to give all notices and other actions required of it by the documents. The bank can always suspend legal enforcement if negotiations are proceeding satisfactorily, but not lose time (and money) through a "start-stop-start" approach to enforcement if negotiations break down.

11.90 To avoid surprising the borrower (which often leads to emotional allegations of bad faith by him), the bank should inform the borrower at the outset of negotiations that it intends to follow this dual track course of action (legal enforcement while simultaneously negotiating).

Encourage borrower proposals

11.91 The borrower should be encouraged to propose solutions to the problem. By encouraging borrower's proposals the workout officer keeps the borrower involved and obtains insight into the borrower's management ability.

Be responsive, firm and sceptical

11.92 Be sceptical of the debtor's optimistic projections of lease up, rent rates, low tenant finish requirements, sales volume, sales prices and operating income. The market is *always* worse than the developer perceives. Feasibility analysis previously ordered will give the workout officer his own independent realistic view of the market. The restructure should be based on the realistic view.

11.93 Set performance benchmarks in the restructure which the debtor must meet to earn the right to continue the workout. Make them reasonably achievable, but not easy.

11.94 Often the debtor will propose a "cash flow" mortgage to the bank. In all but the rarest circumstances, the workout officer should reject such a proposal. Cash-flow mortgages leave the debtor in control of timing and pricing of sale, give him the opportunity to manipulate net operating income to the disadvantage of the bank (even if he has executed a cash collateral agreement) and leave the bank with all of the risk of value decline either from market deterioration or from debtor mismanagement. If a cash-flow mortgage is accepted, it must be made "defaultable" with a requirement of a minimum monthly payment regardless of cash flow and prompt payment by the debtor of taxes and insurance.

11.95 Some debtors with many lenders will propose a consensual reorganisation of their business in an attempt to reach a global resolution of all their debt (see paragraphs 11.21ff and 11.30ff, above). Even though these plans usually involve cash flow mortgages (called "pass-throughs"), they should not be rejected out of hand. It is a feature of such plans that they also include a "collateral pool" into which the debtor places all of his business assets for the benefit of all of his creditors and usually involve partial or complete release from liability. The plan requires equal treatment of all creditors and full disclosure. They are similar in many respects to bankruptcy but without judicial supervision. If the bank is undersecured even after cross-collateralisation, it may be beneficial to consider consensual reorganisation to gain access to the collateral pool. The plans are extremely complex and should be discussed thoroughly with the workout officer's manager.

One broken promise for another

11.96 Do not trade one broken promise to pay for a new promise to pay. Always obtain something tangible for *any* concession, however small.

Borrower affidavits

11.97 When problems begin to arise with respect to a lending relationship, a bank finds it increasingly difficult to get current financial information from the borrower. Its borrower may well be encountering difficulties with other creditors and will want to reveal as little information as possible about its current affairs while it considers possible courses of action to protect its interests as against all creditors. The bank's ability to evaluate the status of the loan and the prospects for repayment are made more difficult by its inability to determine the overall financial condition of the borrower. It is essential that the bank obtain a full and complete disclosure of the financial condition of the borrower as a part of and as a condition precedent to any workout arrangement. The borrower should provide a detailed sworn financial statement which describes and identifies all assets and liabilities and prior transfers of assets. The affidavit of financial condition, when examined against prior financial information received from the borrower, may assist the bank in identifying any fraudulent transfers which may have been made by the borrower and also should either provide the bank with support for the borrower's oral representations regarding its financial condition or reveal that the borrower has been untruthful or fraudulent during workout discussions. The borrower should be able to show that his financial affairs are such that a restructure of a problem loan can be successful in order for a bank to consider that alternative. Likewise, to the extent that a borrower who claims to have few assets from which the creditor may recover seeks to be released from liability in consideration of his co-operating with the bank in the bank's realisation on any collateral for the loan, the borrower should be able to evidence such financial condition to the bank.

Techniques to maintain loan performance

Unsecured loans, additional collateral, cross-collateralisation

11.98 A primary objective in any workout is to improve the bank's prospects for repayment by obtaining any new collateral which is available to be pledged to it. In the case of an unsecured loan, obtaining collateral, even if it provides considerably less than full coverage for the loan, will be the only means of acquiring a specific source of repayment and prevents the bank from being treated in the same manner as the borrower's trade creditors who, in a bankruptcy context, will receive only pennies on the dollar.

11.99 Even if the bank's loan is currently secured, there may be additional collateral which is available to be pledged to improve the bank's secured status. Obviously, assets which are currently unencumbered are the best form of collateral. However, it may be extremely advantageous for the bank to obtain a lien against assets which have previously been encumbered since the current or future value of such assets may exceed the amount of the first lien. In evaluating the borrower's assets which may be available to serve as collateral, do not hesitate to be creative. For example, a borrower's intangible assets, such as patents, copyrights, trademarks, servicemarks and franchise rights, could be very valuable but may not have been taken as collateral by other lenders who only loan against "hard" assets.

11.100 An extremely important objective in any workout is for the bank to obtain cross-collateralisation of all of its loans. Cross-collateralisation means that particular assets serve as collateral for more than one loan or indebtedness. For example, if a bank's relationship with its borrower consists of a revolving line of credit secured by accounts receivable and inventory, a term loan secured by equipment and real estate, and letters of credit secured by the proceeds of specific contracts, the workout officer's objective would be to revise the existing documents to make sure that all the assets which have been pledged by such borrower secure all three types of financing provided. The reason that cross-collateralisation is so important is that it will enable the bank to apply "excess" value attributable to collateral for one loan against the outstanding balance of another loan. Using the example discussed above, it is quite conceivable that if the borrower were to file for bankruptcy, its accounts receivable and inventory which secure the revolving line of credit would be insufficient to pay off such line of credit. On the other hand, liquidation of the borrower's equipment and real estate may result in proceeds in excess of the term loan. Unless the revolving line of credit and term loan were cross-collateralised, the bank would not be entitled to apply the excess proceeds of equipment and real estate to the outstanding balance of the revolving line of credit, thereby resulting in a loss on the revolving line of credit which would otherwise be avoided.

Cash collateral agreements

11.101 Often the bank will be faced, in a workout situation, with the opportunity to enter into an agreement with a borrower whereby the borrower will turn the revenues from the property over to the bank and the bank will be allowed to deal with the property by taking control of the property and managing it prior to the time that the bank actually acquires the property pursuant to a foreclosure action. Generally, the bank is presented with this opportunity in relation to income-producing real estate, and it may appear to be an ideal way to obtain possession of the revenue from the property and protect the collateral pending foreclosure. When the bank and a borrower agree to this type of arrangement, they usually enter into a cash collateral agreement to govern the collection and application of the rents from the property. The borrower generally attempts to obtain a full release and an indemnification from the bank in relation to the activities of the bank during the period that the bank is in possession of the property prior to the bank's acquisition of the property through foreclosure. Notwithstanding that a cash collateral agreement may seem to be the ideal arrangement in cases where the foreclosure process is lengthy, there are numerous pitfalls which the bank should consider.

11.102 Once the bank takes possession of the property it becomes a "mortgagee in possession". This term has slightly different meanings in various jurisdictions; however, the principles and warnings set forth below are generally applicable. A mortgagee in possession is one who takes possession of property pursuant to a contract (e.g., a cash collateral agreement) and is entitled to remain in possession until the bank's debt is paid in full.

11.103 Generally the standard of care of a mortgagee in possession is that of a constructive trustee and the mortgagee is under a duty to manage the property in a reasonably prudent and careful manner in order to keep the property in a good state of preservation and to make it productive. When a mortgagee comes into possession of the property in other than a lawful manner, then the mortgagee generally is responsible for the reasonable rental value of the property, if any, during the time the mortgagee is in possession. If the mortgagee's possession is lawful, then the mortgagee must account for the rents and profits received or which might have been received by the use of reasonable diligence and care. The mortgagee in possession may be liable as the landlord under the leases that cover the property and will be liable for negligent acts occurring on the property. Indemnities from borrowers are generally of little or no help in protecting the bank; however, insurance can cover some of the risk assumed by a mortgagee in possession.

11.104 Because of the bank's control over the borrower and the property resulting from its being a mortgagee in possession, there are a number of lender liability concerns which should be considered. If a borrower subsequently seeks the protection of the bankruptcy courts and the bank is found to be in control of the borrower's business, the bankruptcy court has the power to "equitably subordinate" the bank's lien to the liens of other creditors. If the bank is found to be in control of the borrower's business, it can be held liable under federal and state environmental statutes for the cost of cleanup of various hazardous wastes. Certain liability for federal withholding taxes also can be successfully asserted by the Internal Revenue Service if the bank controls the borrower's business. In addition, notwithstanding the fact that the bank may act properly, a borrower seeking to prevent foreclosure may raise allegations of improprieties related to the bank's possession of the property which the borrower may allege prevented the borrower from making payments on the debt.

11.105 There are circumstances when the bank will clearly desire to become a mortgagee in possession (e.g., where the borrower has abandoned the property). However, in most cases careful consideration should be given to the facts surrounding a proposed cash collateral agreement and the circumstances relating to the collateral, especially in light of the numerous liabilities which inure to a mortgagee in possession. If the risks are such that a cash collateral agreement is deemed to be appropriate and possession of the property is desirable, the provisions of the agreement with the borrower should be carefully drafted to protect the bank. The bank should attempt to structure a cash collateral agreement under which the borrower retains control of the property by leaving the borrower responsible for the management and operation of the property while obtaining the net revenues from the property.

Loan splitting

11.106 Given a $10,000,000 loan on an office building which is producing $600,000 in NOI from credit tenants, with no outside support available from the debtor/guarantor, and where no concessions on rate or terms other than extension of maturity are made: can the loan be internally restructured on the bank's books as a $5,000,000 performing loan ($600,000/$5,000,000 = market rate) and a $5,000,000 non-accrual loan? Generally no. If there is no outside debtor/guarantor support and the building produces $600,000 in NOI, it will be difficult to show a value in excess of the $10,000,000 loan amount. These factors would combine to produce an insubstance foreclosure (see paragraph 11.46ff above). If an independent, accurate appraisal of the building showed value in excess of $10,000,000, then the workout officer should discuss the possibility of this internal "restructure" with the bank's internal accountants.

11.107 One exception to the general rule is a change in circumstance after the loan has been placed on non-accural and been charged down. For example, a new creditworthy tenant could be obtained producing new cash flow which would carry and begin amortising the loan as charged down. In such case, the loan may be returned to accrual.

Trading borrowers

11.108 The original borrower arranges to sell the project for an amount equal to the current debt to unrelated buyers. The bank agrees to finance 100 per cent of the purchase price for the new buyers at below market rate but offers no other concessions such as limited liability to new buyers. The new loan is not technically a TDR under FAS 15 because it is not to the original borrower. However, the new loan may still be a non-performing asset if there was a finding that the original loan was an insubstance foreclosure because the downpayment requirement of 12 USC, §7.3025 and FAS 66 was not met. Even if there was no finding of insubstance foreclosure, the principal balance of the new loan may be required to be marked to market to reflect a below-market interest rate. These are only two of many complex considerations. Advice of the bank's internal accountants should be sought early on.

11.109 *Warning*: Workout officers are often tempted to negotiate with in-house and independent accountants to comply with the literal accounting rules and to twist the deal to meet accounting requirements. The new borrower immediately picks up on the bank's problems and extracts substantive concessions for his co-operation in helping the bank with its accounting issues. This often weakens the restructure and can lead to greater ultimate loss. Build hammers, not watches.

Additional compensation for added risk

11.110 Obviously, if the bank structures a workout with the borrower that reduces the bank's current return, causes it current loss or exposes it to future loss, the bank should be and is entitled to a higher reward. The bank contracted for interest risk and interest reward. If the bank's risk is converted to equity risk, it should participate to some degree in equity reward if such occurs because of a rising market.

11.111 However, the bank must beware of lender liability issues inherent in increasing its reward. The bank must maintain its position as a secured lender and not a partner of the debtor.

Marketing agreements with the borrower

11.112 As an alternative to forced liquidation of assets and litigation, a bank may consider affording the borrower a reasonable period of time in which to market the property prior to the bank's ultimate enforcement of its remedies pursuant to the loan documents. The bank may assist the borrower in its marketing efforts by obtaining from the borrower a non-exclusive right to market the property. The bank must exercise care in this area to avoid the exercise of control over the borrower which could subject the bank to potential claims.

Borrower conferences

Purpose

11.113 When arranging a conference with the debtor, the workout officer should specify the purpose of the meeting. The debtor should then be informed that the intitial meeting will commence with execution of the pre-workout agreement, which should be provided to the debtor in advance. He should be advised to come prepared to bring the bank up to date on his financial condition, cash flow, property status, other debt and other pertinent topics, and to present his own workout alternatives.

11.114 Debtors may approach this meeting with a "wait and see" attitude to get an understanding of what types of alternatives the bank will consider before they make a proposal. The meeting will be more productive if the workout officer encourages the debtor to make a proposal at the meeting.

How to prepare

11.115 In order to conduct a meaningful and fruitful working meeting, the workout officer must be prepared to enter into an open-minded discussion of the facts as presented by the debtor so he can fully understand the circumstances and review alterantives, some of which may be suggested by the debtor. By beginning the working conference in this manner, the workout officer can establish the "ground rules" for future discussions, the results of which will be more fruitful under these circumstances.

11.116 Because of the debtor's potential fears or anger, the conference may become antagonistic and unproductive. For this reason, the workout officer must have the discipline and professional attitude to maintain the purpose of the meeting and maintain the "ground rules" for meaningful resolution.

Use of attorneys

11.117 Many conferences relating to workout resolution can be handled directly between the workout officer and the debtor. Depending upon the nature of the workout, the size of the loan and the potential for non-accrual or loss, certain discussions should include an additional workout officer, preferably the group manager. If a debtor indicates he will arrive at a meeting with his attorney, the workout officer must review the situation with his manager to determine if it is appropriate for the bank to engage legal counsel at this juncture. By all means, when an attorney for the debtor is present, the workout officer should include in the conference his manager or legal counsel so two people are representing the bank.

11.118 Examples of instances when the meeting should include the bank's legal counsel follow:

- Debtor has made claims of lender liability.
- Litigation between the bank and the debtor is pending or being actively considered.
- Debtor has revealed plans to file bankruptcy.
- The workout officer considers there are issues for which a claim may arise in the future against the bank.
- Debtor's relationship is already antagonistic, in which case the bank may be best served by utilising legal counsel as the primary contact with the workout officer support.
- A discussion of legal issues is expected.

11.119 Prior to the meeting, either the workout officer, his manager, or another workout employee should be designated as the person to take notes and prepare a follow-up memorandum summarising the meeting.

Topics for discussion

11.120 Topics for discussion include:

- status of debtor's loans with other creditors;
- status of debtor's other real and personal property investments (leasing, cash flow);

— status of pending transactions or litigation which may positively or negatively affect the debtor's financial condition;
— possibility of raising additional equity, refinancing, sales;
— future plans;
— operating standards for the collateral property during the period of negotiations (What happens to the cash? Is the property secure?).

11.121 At the initial debtor conference, the workout officer should explain the bank's requirements regarding turnover of property NOI and present the debtor with the proposed cash collateral agreement discussed above. One objective is to make clear to the debtor that the bank intends to enforce its remedies thoroughly.

Memos of meetings and next steps

11.122 Immediately after the meeting, the person designated to summarise the meeting in report form generates a report memo. The original of the memo should be sent to the credit file with a copy sent to each participant. The memo should be factual, objective, and not draw any subjective conclusions as to the outcome of negotiations.

11.123 As a result of conferences with the debtor and his analysis of information provided, the workout officer will have obtained new information which must be investigated and verified in order to fully understand the debtor's financial condition and the potential for repayment from liquidation or refinancing of the collateral. As the workout officer assesses certain key factors, and defines more clearly the particular problems, resolutions can then be developed.

11.124 Essentially, there are four options which can apply in a workout:

— reinstatement of the loan;
— restructure;
— foreclosure;
— negotiation of a deed-in-lieu of foreclosure.

11.125 As stated above, the workout officer must remain mindful of the bank's objectives and the debtor's concerns discussed above in developing his proposed resolution.

Settlement agreements and releases

11.126 If a bank and a borrower determine that the loan will be restructured, it is important that the parties focus on the lending relationship going forward and that any disputes which have arisen during the term of the loan be laid to rest. As a part of a bank's agreement to restructure a loan, the bank should require the borrower to release the bank from, and indemnify the bank against, all claims and causes of action which the borrower may have against the bank in relation to the loan arising prior to the time of the restructure.

11.127 To the extent that resolution of a problem loan involves the bank's foreclosure of its lien against property or a conveyance to the bank by deed in lieu of foreclosure, the borrower and any guarantors may have negotiated a release from all or a portion of personal liability in connection with the loan. To ensure that the borrower and any guarantors do not interfere with the bank's exercise of its foreclosure rights, it may be appropriate to condition their releases on their not taking any such actions. Because the borrower's overall financial condition may be in jeopardy and there is the possibility of a bankruptcy filing by the borrower, it may also be appropriate to provide that the releases of the borrowers and any guarantors will not be effective in the event of a bankruptcy filing for a one-year or longer period following foreclosure to the extent that the foreclosure is set aside by a court of competent jurisdiction.

Multi-creditor loans and relationships

11.128 There are several distinct types of multiple creditor loans. In the lending community the word "participation" is often used generically to describe a multiple creditor loan. However, it is helpful to categorise the types of arrangements between creditors. Loan participations are those loans where the "lead lender" sells a participation to one or more other creditors in the loan made by the lead lender to a borrower. A participation is evidenced by a particiption agreement and a participation certificate executed by the participant and the lead lender. There is only one note and only one set of security documents. The participant's rights are contained in the participation agreement with the lead lender. A loan syndication, on the other hand, is an arrangement where each creditor has a direct-creditor relationship with the borrower. There are several types of syndications including agented credits, non-agented credits governed by an intercreditor agreement, and arrangements where each creditor has a separate agreement with the borrower. The problems encountered by the bank in the workout of a multiple creditor loan vary depending upon whether the bank is the lead lender, a participant or part of a bank group governed by an intercreditor agreement.

Considerations of lead lender or agent

11.129 Set forth below are some of the issues that should be considered by the lead lender or agent:

(a) *Documentation.* The bank should carefully review the documentation which relates to the participation or the syndication. The participation agreement, agent's agreement or intercreditor agreement will spell out the duties and obligations of the lead lender in relation to the other creditors that are participants in the loan. A thorough understanding of the position of the lead lender or agent and its duties and obligations is necessary for the bank to proceed through the workout process. Under no circumstances should the bank take an action which is not authorised by the loan documents or the documents governing the multi-creditor relationship. The bank's failure to honour the contractual obligations in the agreements can subject the lead lender or agent to liability to the other creditors and the borrower.

(b) *Is the participation interest a security?* If the participation interest is characterised as a security, the lead lender may have other responsibilities to the participants in relation to the loan. The note or the participation agreement may be a security under the Securities Act of 1933 or the Securities Exchange Act of 1934. If the participation interest is a security, the offer and sale of the security would be subject to the anti-fraud provisions of the applicable Securities Acts. Whether the participation interest in any given situation is a security depends upon many factors. Even if an exemption is relied upon, the bank must be sure to make full disclosure to the participants at all times during the administration and workout of the loan.

(c) *Conflicts of interest.* Generally, participations and syndications involve large lending relationships where the lead lender or agent has other loans to the borrower, guarantors or affiliates of the borrower. Full disclosure of the lead lender's relationships is essential when the loan is sold or syndicated. If during the workout process it is discovered that there is or were conflicts or potential conflicts, they should be dealt with openly and fully disclosed. It is important to remember that when the loan becomes troubled the participants will likely not share a common view as to what the proper course of action may be to resolve the problems with the borrower. The various participants will have different financial resources, different guidelines for loan workouts, different regulatory pressures and different concerns relating to earnings and liquidity.

(d) *Regulatory guidelines.* There are certain regulatory guidelines with which the workout specialist should be familiar in this area. The Comptroller of the Currency, Banking Circular No. 181 (Revised 2 August 1981 and 1984) sets forth certain informational guidelines in relation to which the lead lender should supply information to the participant including: (i) accrual status; (ii) status of principal and interest payments; (iii) financial statements, collateral values and lien status; and (iv) factual information in relation to the borrower's credit standing. If these guidelines have been followed by the lead lender, it will be a better position when the loan becomes troubled.

If a loan was classified during the last examination, is in a non-accrual status, is in default as to principal or interest or has been renegotiated or compromised due to the weakening financial condition of the borrower, the loan is a "low-quality" loan, and the purchase or sale of the loan may be considered to be unsafe and unsound. Care should be taken not to participate in or syndicate a loan that has any of these characteristics without full disclosure.

Loan repurchase arrangements will require the lead lender to include the amount for which the lead lender is obligated to repurchase as a part of the lead lender's portion of the loan for loan limit purposes. Any obligation to repurchase (whether written or oral) will be treated as an extension of credit to the lead lender by the participant, and must be documented in writing and so reflected on the books and records of both creditors. Arrangements which provide that the participant's interest will be funded and paid back on a last in–first out basis require the participant's interest to be added to the lead lender's portion of the loan for loan limit purposes.

The documentation between the creditors will not cover all of the issues that will face the lead lender or agent in the context of a workout of a troubled multi-creditor loan. Many of the issues which arise will require the creditors to resolve the practical business problems and make decisions that are beyond the scope or even the contemplation of the documents governing the rights and duties of the parties. The lead lender or agent must ensure that the decision-making process goes forward and that decisions are made by the requisite number of creditors (as provided in the documentation) in a timely manner. Often this will require great patience and negotiating ability.

Bank as a participant

11.130 There are a number of concerns that the bank must be aware of when it is a participant in a troubled loan. The first thing that the bank must determine is the legal relationship between the bank and the creditor that sold the bank its interest. Depending upon the documentation, the relationship between the lead lender and the participant may be: (a) tenants in common, (b) trustee–beneficiary, (c) partners, (d) creditor–borrower, or (e) principal–agent. Generally, if the bank (as a participant) has purchased a partial or fractional interest in the loan, the bank will own the right to the bank's proportionate share of future payments of principal and interest. The insolvency of the lead lender should not affect the bank in such a situation. However, if the relationship is characterised as a loan from the bank to the lead lender which is unsecured (most participations that are not sales are unsecured or, at least, the security interest is unperfected), the effect of the insolvency of the lead lender may be fatal to the bank's recovery.

11.131 With respect to a syndicated multi-creditor loan, if the bank holds its own note and is a party to each security agreement it should be well protected in the case of the lead lender's insolvency as the insolvent lead lender should have no legal interest in the bank's portion of the loan. The agent agreement or the intercreditor agreement should deal with the administration of the loan in the event of the agent's insolvency or the insolvency of one of the creditors.

11.132 If the bank is a party to a participant agreement, the provisions of which indicate that the arrangement is a sale, the position of the bank should be fairly safe. There are certain risks of which the bank should be aware, however, and which it should attempt to protect against: first it should avoid commingling the funds, second, the note should either indicate the interest of the bank on its face or a third party should hold the note to avoid the risk of the lead lender transferring the note to a holder in due course, and third, the participation agreement should bc amended, if necessary, to allow continued administration of the loan in the event of the insolvency of the lead lender. If the bank is a party to a participation agreement that characterises the arrangement as a loan by the bank to the lead lender, then the bank should seek to accomplish one of the following, if at all possible: (a) an amendment of the participation agreement to recharacterise the loan as a sale, or (b) assurance that the participation agreement contains an enforceable security agreement and perfection of the security interest, if possible, under applicable law. If these steps cannot be accomplished, careful negotiation with the lead lender that leads to a reworking of the intercreditor relationship will be necessary.

REMEDIAL ACTION BY BANKS

Initial analysis and evaluation

Overview

11.133 It is common for a troubled credit relationship to be transferred to the workout officer in a state of disarray. The workout officer is often faced with disorganised files, a fearful borrower/guarantor and no clear direction. The first step, then, in rehabilitating the relationship is to determine what the bank has in terms of collateral and outside sources of repayment and what the problems are. Clear understanding of the facts is an absolute necessity, for a clear and comprehensive understanding of the facts will dictate the plan of action. The workout officer should make no assumptions about the credit nor should he rely completely upon his predecessor's version of the facts. He must make his own complete investigation of the situation. Otherwise, he may develop a workout plan that blows up because it was predicated on unreliable information and incorrect assumptions.

11.134 The correct procedure for investigation revolves around creation of proper files which accurately reflect the credit relationship. In order to create proper files, the workout officer must necessarily:

— gather all information from all sources in the bank and outside the bank including all existing credit files, working files, desk files and so forth;

- — order or otherwise obtain unbiased information about the collateral and the feasibility of its providing all or part of debt service and ultimate repayment;
- — organise this disparate information chronologically within subject-matter (i.e., collateral, outside ability to pay);
- — eliminate duplicates and organise notes held on scraps of paper;
- — analyse the facts the file reflects as it is organised; and
- — synthesise the facts into a plan.

11.135 Information and analysis obtained or performed by the workout officer which is subject to attorney–client privilege should be segregated.[37] If the workout officer has any doubts or concerns with respect to the nature of the information in the file, its sensitivity in the event of litigation or the applicability of the attorney–client privilege, the bank's counsel should be consulted for advice.

11.136 File gathering, organisation, culling and written analysis has the important side benefit of demonstrating to internal and external reviewers that the workout officer has complete understanding of the credit relationship and a plan to rehabilitate or collect the loan or to realise on the collateral.

Credit file

11.137 Analysis of a troubled credit relationship is divided into two parts:

(a) the borrower's or guarantor's capacity to service and amortise his debt from sources outside the asset(s) financed including the availability of additional collateral or financial support; and

37. The attorney–client privilege generally refers to the client's privilege to refuse to disclose and to prevent other parties from disclosing confidential communications which are made to facilitate the rendition of professional legal services. Communications between the client or the client's representative and the lawyer or the lawyer's representative which are confidential are protected. See *United States* v. *Kovel*, 296 F.2d 918 (2d Cir. 1961) (it is necessary that the communication be confidential). Confidentiality requires an intention that the communication not be communicated to third parties. See *Dorothy K. Winston & Co.* v. *Town Heights Development, Inc.*, 376 F.Supp. 1214 (DC Dist. 1974) (the communication must be intended to be confidential). In some states the attorney–client privilege is given a strict construction because of its tendency to suppress the truth, see, e.g., *San Francisco* v. *Superior Court of San Francisco*, 37 Cal. 2d 227, 231 P.2d 26 (1951) (because of its tendency to suppress the truth, attorney–client privilege receives a strict construction), while in other states a more liberal construction is adopted, on the theory that a client should be free to discuss all circumstances of a matter with his attorney without fear that his statements will later be used against him. See, e.g., *People* v. *Shapiro*, 308 NY 453, 126 NE 2d 559 (1955) (court favoured a liberal construction on the theory that one consulting a lawyer should be encouraged to communicate all the facts without fear that his statements may possibly be used against him in the future). The privilege belongs to the client, see *Radiant Burners, Inc.* v. *American Gas Assoc.*, 320 F.2d 314 (7th Cir.), *cert. denied*, 375 US 929 (1963), and only the client may waive its right to the privilege, see *Baird* v. *Koerner*, 279 F.2d 623 (9th Cir. 1960) (attorney cannot divulge information that was communicated to him in confidence until the protection afforded by the privilege has been properly waived by the client). In order to insure protection of the confidentiality of the relationship between the attorney and client, policies should be adopted which limit the scope of the parties to whom information is disseminated and who are in attendance at meetings. The attorney work

(b) the assets' ability to provide repayment of debt through sale or refinancing.

11.138 A properly constructed credit file will contain the information and analysis necessary to determine borrower/guarantor capacity to pay.

11.139 The credit file must first be organised by subdividing it into appropriate sections, eliminating duplicate information, identifying and finding missing information and filing each section in chronological order.

11.140 As various components of the file are built, the workout officer should study and make reading notes from analytical memos, correspondence, borrower/guarantor financial statements and cash flow with focus on the borrower's or guarantor's:

- sources of cash;
- required and optional uses of cash;
- unpledged liquid assets such as tradable securities;
- debt to other lenders and their collateral;
- unpledged liquidable assets such as seasoned income-producing property; and
- unpledged cash-flowing assets such as seasoned notes receivable, available second liens on cash-flowing property or, much less desirable, interests in cash-flowing partnerships.

11.141 Outdated or extraneous information should be noted and properly filed, but no time should be spent on in-depth analysis.

11.142 Careful study and complete reading notes will facilitate analysis of the borrower/guarantor capacity to service the existing loan or any form of restructured loan.

Project files

11.143 The second part of the analysis of a troubled credit relationship comes from gaining thorough understanding and knowledge of the assets pledged. This is accomplished through collection, organisation and analysis of material necessary to build a project file for each collateral asset.

product privilege protects from the discovery process the work produced and developed by an attorney, for his client, in anticipation of litigation. The "work product" of an attorney in preparing for litigation includes the mental impressions, conclusions, opinions, and legal theories of the attorney or other representative of a party to the litigation, see Fed. R. Civ. P. 216(b)(3), and is reflected in such things as memoranda, statements, correspondence, interviews and briefs, see *Hickman* v. *Taylor*, 329 US 495 (1947). The work product doctrine encourages effective preparation for litigation consistent with the adversarial system, based on the theory that each side should prepare its case independently without unnecessary interference. *Ibid.* Particular litigation need not have actually been commenced in order for the doctrine to apply, but there must be some probability that particular litigation will occur. See *Diversified Industries, Inc.* v. *Meredith*, 572 F.2d 596 (8th Cir. 1977) *en banc* (1978). The degree to which specific litigation must be contemplated, and the question of whether the work product doctrine protects documents which were generated other than in the case in which discovery is sought, varies from state to state.

11.144 The workout officer should gather from every source in the bank all information relating to each collateral asset including:

- the original loan underwriting memo;
- draw requests and certifications;
- appraisals and feasibility studies, if any, made in connection with initial underwriting;
- all subsequent appraisals and feasibility studies;
- inspection reports;
- all contracts and closing statements in connection with prior partial releases of properties for sale such as buildings, lots or homes;
- rent rolls on income-producing collateral;
- all leases and lease summaries on income-producing collateral;
- year-to-date and current month operating statements on income-producing collateral;
- copies of service contracts such as janitoring, equipment, etc.;
- copies of all other third-party contracts, if any;
- all environmental studies and assessments, if any;
- all borrowing base reports and ageing reports of accounts receivable;
- letters of credit;
- all correspondence to and from the borrower/guarantor(s) relating to the property; and
- all internally generated memoranda describing the property.

11.145 The workout officer should request and receive the desk files of his bank predecessor, since these files often contain nuggets not found in official files. Any information listed above which is not in the bank's possession should be requested of the borrower in writing.

11.146 Concurrently, the workout officer should order:

(i) a title report to identify any mechanic's or materialman's liens or other claims filed of record on the property;
(ii) an *ad valorem* tax certificate from all applicable taxing authorities;
(iii) a certificate of insurance from the borrower if not already provided; and
(iv) a UCC search in all applicable jurisdictions with respect to any personal property collateral.

Environmental issues should be addressed at this point. The project file of each collateral asset should then be organised in the format outlined in Procedures. Extraneous and duplicate information should be discarded unless it contains an original signature.

11.147 Finally, the workout officer should order from a competent appraiser an updated appraisal of the collateral based on current market conditions and the current status of the collateral. The appraisal should be supplemented by a feasibility study which considers current market conditions. The appraisal gives guidance in determining correct accounting treatment of the loan. The feasibility study gives guidance in the development of a plan of restructure.

11.148 As the project file is being constructed, the workout officer should analyse appropriate documents to give him knowledge of:

- status of completion;
- current market for the product offered;
- waste or mismanagement by the borrower;
- recent sales volume (for sale properties);
- recent leasing activity and current operating costs (income properties);
- current and near-term identifiable cash flow produced by the property;
- claims of others on the property; and
- the value and saleability of the property.

Again, careful study and complete reading notes will facilitate analysis of the situation.

Legal files

11.149 The legal documentation of the loan should be in reasonbly good order if closed by the bank's own legal staff or outside counsel. Any missing documentation such as recorded deeds of trust, mortgages, UCC financial statements, paid tax receipts or insurance certificates should be obtained by collateral cage personnel under the workout officer's oversight.

11.150 The legal documentation of loans not closed by the bank's attorneys may be incomplete. In such case, collateral cage personnel with the assistance of a paralegal (if necessary) should gather all missing documents, cure filing defects and organise the file.

11.151 The workout officer should carefully review the notes, guaranties and loan agreement for *business* points to determine, for example, whether the guaranties are of payment and performance or only of collection, whether the guaranties are limited in any way, whether the construction loan agreement contains a provision requiring a borrower's deposit in certain circumstances and whether all loans are cross-collateralised or cross-defaulted. These and other points will become important leverage either to the bank or to the borrower in negotiations. The workout officer must know whether he is dealing from strength or weakness. Typical business deficiencies in loan documents include:

— no cross-default or cross-collateralisation;
— no right to approve leases;
— no borrower deposit requirement;
— no time limit on the right to cure defaults;
— no penalty interest provision;
— limitations on exercise of certain remedies;
— inadequate insurance provisions;

— inadequate restrictions on sale of personal property; and
— no lock-box provisions relating to receivables.

11.152 Legal sufficiency of the loan documents should be reviewed by the bank's counsel. After review, counsel should report any significant deficiencies to the workout officer along with required remedial action and a cost estimate therefor.

11.153 Loan participations purchased present additional complexity. Often, the lead lender has virtually unlimited decision-making powers in a workout, effectively foreclosing the bank's legal right to participate meaningfully in negotiations with the debtor. The participation agreement may contain a buy/sell provision under which the bank could take out the lead lender or force being taken out itself, invariably at a loss. However, being taken out at a loss may be less costly than being an unwilling participant in oafish negotiations by an unskilled, or worse, financially weak lead lender. Also, the lead lender may be constrained in debtor negotiations by its obligations to the other participant(s).

11.154 Legal leverage and significant documentation deficiencies should be identified and analysed with the assistance of the bank's counsel.

Physical inspection

11.155 Collateral assets should be personally inspected by the workout officer promptly upon his receipt of the case. The extent and nature of the physical inspection should be made only in accordance with the rights of the bank under the loan documents and applicable law. During inspection, particular attention should be paid to design, quality, maintenance, location, access, traffic, neighbourhood ambiance, evidence of competition such as "for lease" and "for sale" signs on surrounding properties and so forth. The workout officer should approach the collateral asset with the view of a tenant or buyer as the case may be. What features about the property would encourage or discourage its lease or sale?

11.156 During inspection, the workout officer should be alert for signs of obvious construction defects, deferred maintenance or environmental hazards. If he suspects any, professional engineers should be engaged to make a thorough investigation and written report immediately.

Environmental issues

11.157 Case law under the federal Comprehensive Environmental Response, Compensation and Liability Act ("CERCLA")[38] and comparable state statutes are developing toward the perceived deep pockets of lenders. For example, in *US v. Fleet Factors Corp.*,[39] the 11th Circuit Court found that a secured lender may

38. 42 USC, §§9601–75 (1988, Supp. IV 1992).
39. 901 F.2d 1550 (11th Cir. 1990), *cert. denied*, 498 US 1046 (1991).

incur liability under CERCLA merely by participating in the financial management of a facility to a degree which would indicate that it had the capacity to influence *the borrower's* treatment and disposal of hazardous waste.

11.158 Thus, it is incumbent on the workout officer to become thoroughly knowledgeable as to environmental procedures and pitfalls and to be aware of circumstances which could expose the bank to unlimited claims under environmental laws.

Special issues in construction loans

11.159 It is often in the bank's best interest to retain the debtor's interest and co-operation at least through completion of construction, since, if he is honest, he can usually complete the project faster and cheaper. If the bank has lost confidence or the debtor has given up, the following issues must be addressed if the bank intends to complete the project:

- contractor and subcontractor status;
- legal access to plans and specifications in absence of debtor;
- subcontractor liens and lien waivers;
- defences to mechanics' liens;
- new permits in name of bank;
- cost of construction delays;
- feasibility of restriction of project scope;
- preservation of payment and performance bonds.

The decision—workout or foreclosure?

ASSET DEVALUATION AND NON-PERFORMING ASSETS LEAD TO BANK FAILURE

11.160 A general pattern of events has unfolded in distressed banks as a result of systemic debt problems. These events and effects can be traced through various phases:

— Collateral values deteriorate.
— Assets become classified.
— Assets become non-earning, leading to non-renewability of a loan, then default and, if the collection process is initiated by the lender, the raising of defences by the borrower, borrower bankruptcy and borrower tax problems. These actions dilute the collateral values further.
— Collection costs increase.
— Revenue from the underlying loan collateral may be lost as the borrower keeps the revenues as a "forced working capital loan".

- Word of the situation reaches the securities markets and is exacerbated by media stories.
- The stock price of the financial institution drops.
- The rating agencies get worried and lower ratings on:
  - preferred stock,
  - senior debt,
  - commercial paper of the parent holding company, if any,
  - certificates of deposit and letters of credit of the financial institution.
- The financial institution's cost of funds increases.
- The financial institution's earnings (and hence those of the parent holding company, if any) decline because of:
  - increases in the allowance for lease and loan loss reserve,
  - increases in the costs to administer repossessed collateral,
  - loss of interest income from an increase in non-performing assets,
  - increases in the cost of funds,
  - restatement of prior period earnings resulting from the reversal of previously capitalised interest.
- The bank regulators arrive and accelerate the decline in the value of assets through the examination process, e.g., increases in substance foreclosures, non-performing assets, write-downs and increased reserves and repossessed collateral.
- Management of the financial institution becomes preoccupied with reacting to the examiners and the examiners' instructions and fails to focus on its other constituencies (e.g., bondholders, shareholders and personnel).
- Shareholders initiate litigation against the financial institution for understating the allowance for lease and loan loss reserves and overstating earnings.
- Customers' corporate treasurers begin to withdraw deposits in excess of insured or guaranteed amounts.
- All "hot" money is totally withdrawn by the customers' corporate treasurers.
- The financial institution begins secured borrowings from the central bank.
- Central bank borrowings reach critical levels (e.g., $300 million to $1 billion).
- The regulatory agencies impose restrictions and require corrective actions by the financial institution pursuant to a cease-and-desist order.
- Examiners determine that the market-to-market value of the assets of the financial institution are exceeded by the financial institution's liabilities (balance sheet insolvency).

— The examiners withdraw assurances to the central bank, and the loans from the central bank to the financial institution are then called.
— The financial institution cannot repay the loans when called, and it is closed and a receiver is appointed as a result.
— The financial institution's assets and liabilities are disposed of by the receiver pursuant to a purchase and assumptions or other resolution structures.
— In the United States, the sister institutions of the failed financial institution also fall because of the cross-guaranty provisions of FIRREA.

CONCLUDING OBSERVATIONS

11.161 This chapter explores the circumstances facing debtors and creditors in America in the grip of a national crisis of capital inadequacy. Although America had faced a relatively recent banking crisis in the mid 1970s, it paled in comparison to the most recent distress. Loan underwriting became irrelevant. The absolute loss in value of many assets which served as collateral for bank loans was systemic and unavoidable by the debtors and creditors. This systemic loss must be distinguished from the "systemic" banking crises alluded to by many commentators as the risk posed by one bank's failure to the solvency of other banks in the banking system. Although the systemic crisis of capital adequacy in America did, in fact, pose bank-to-bank system risks, the issues presented were far more fundamental to overall American financial stability and bank solvency.

11.162 The American systemic crisis of capital adequacy was manifest where capital reposes: in assets—assets which collateralise loans, and which comprise the asset side of a bank's balance sheet, and are the source of a bank's solvency and liquidity.

11.163 This chapter focuses on the "micro" manifestations of the problem. Debtors and creditors as well as regulators in other jurisdictions such as Scandinavia, Mexico, Latin America, Central and Eastern Europe, Japan, Thailand, Indonesia and South Korea must recognise that the fundamental problems of bank capital are not limited to America. The fundamental issues facing debtors and creditors in all of these jurisdictions are substantially similar.

11.164 The worldwide systemic problem of capital inadequacy and bank insolvency is not, fundamentally, an issue of bank mismanagement, fraud or crime, but represents a broad-based problem whose roots predate the recent American crisis and spread throughout both so-called "developed economies" and emerging and transitional economies. Lee Rawls, Assistant Attorney General of the United States, in his response on behalf of the US Department of Justice, in response to the Draft GAO Report on the Justice Department's Financial Institution Fraud Program, by letter dated 1 October 1992, stated:

By all accounts, the near-collapse of the thrift industry was the result of a series of complex factors. Yet no one has ever suggested that the work of federal prosecutors is in any way responsible for the thrift failures. Moreover, regardless of whose numbers one looks at, fraud has not yet been shown to be the "major" (the use of the word "major" to suggest that fraud brought down the thrifts is simply not accurate based on known data) factor in the industry's failures. Nonetheless, the Report conveys the notion that the collapse is primarily a criminal law enforcement issue. It is not. Blaming all of the S&L losses on "criminals" may be politically convenient but it is not responsible law enforcement and it is not accurate ... While fraud and real estate related fraud in particular... were certainly factors in some failures, it cannot fairly be said that they were the major factors in all or even a majority of the failures. Economic factors in the real estate and other markets seem to have played a far larger role than fraud ... Notwithstanding the unsupported assertions of the Report, the extent of fraud as a factor in S&L failures is simply not known at this time, and indeed may never be known. Moreover, it cannot be responsibly inferred without empirical and anecdotal study of the reasons for all the failures.[40]

11.165 As international pressure for "transparency" in financial information disclosures as well as consistency and clarity in accounting rules and laws relating to banking, credit and security creation and enforcement increase, borrowers, bankers, accountants and lawyers in emerging economies will find the principles and strategies presented in this chapter to be of increasing relevance and importance. Attention to the principles, practical issues and strategies presented here will be of benefit to debtors and creditors in other jurisdictions who now face the consequences of the global crisis of capital inadequacy.

GERALD N. OLSON

40. US GAO Report on Bank and Thrift Fraud, 8 January 1993, pp. 84 and 85. See also, however, the body of the report to which Mr Rawls responded. The author supports the views of the US Department of Justice.

APPENDIX I

FUNCTIONAL ORGANISATION CHARTS AND AREAS OF PRIMARY RISK, FOCUS AND ALTERNATIVE COURSES OF ACTION

CONSENSUAL REORGANISATION OF TROUBLED DEBTORS: FUNCTIONAL ORGANISATION CHART AND SERVICES AVAILABLE

11.166

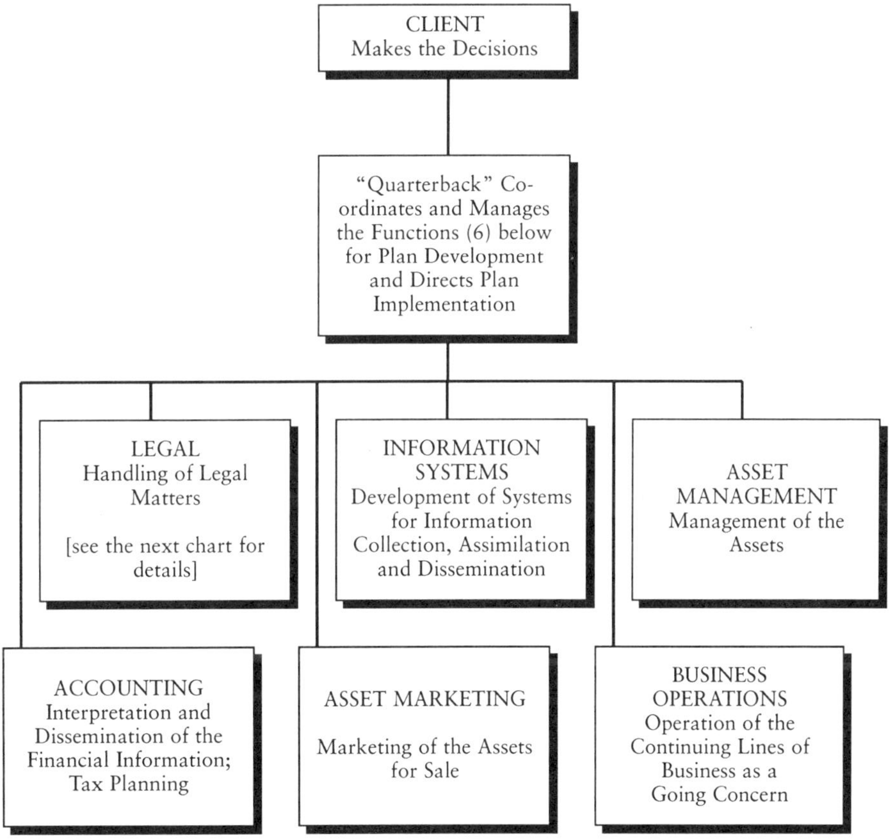

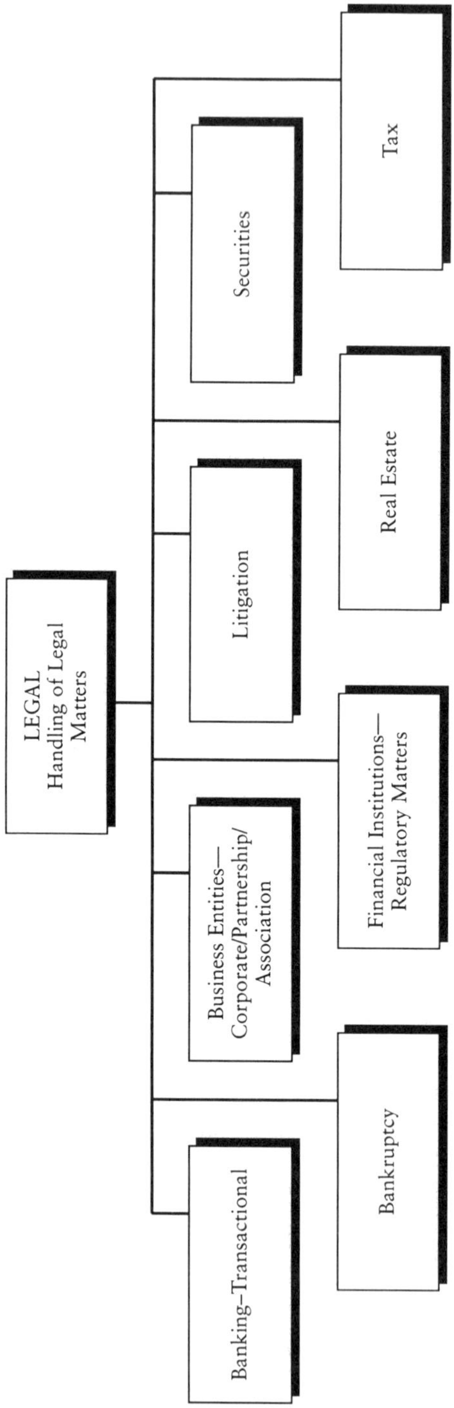
LEGAL
Handling of Legal Matters
Banking–Transactional
Business Entities—Corporate/Partnership/Association
Litigation
Securities
Bankruptcy
Financial Institutions—Regulatory Matters
Real Estate
Tax

CONSENSUAL REORGANISATION OF TROUBLED DEBTORS: AREAS OF PRIMARY RISK, FOCUS AND ALTERNATIVE COURSES OF ACTION

11.167

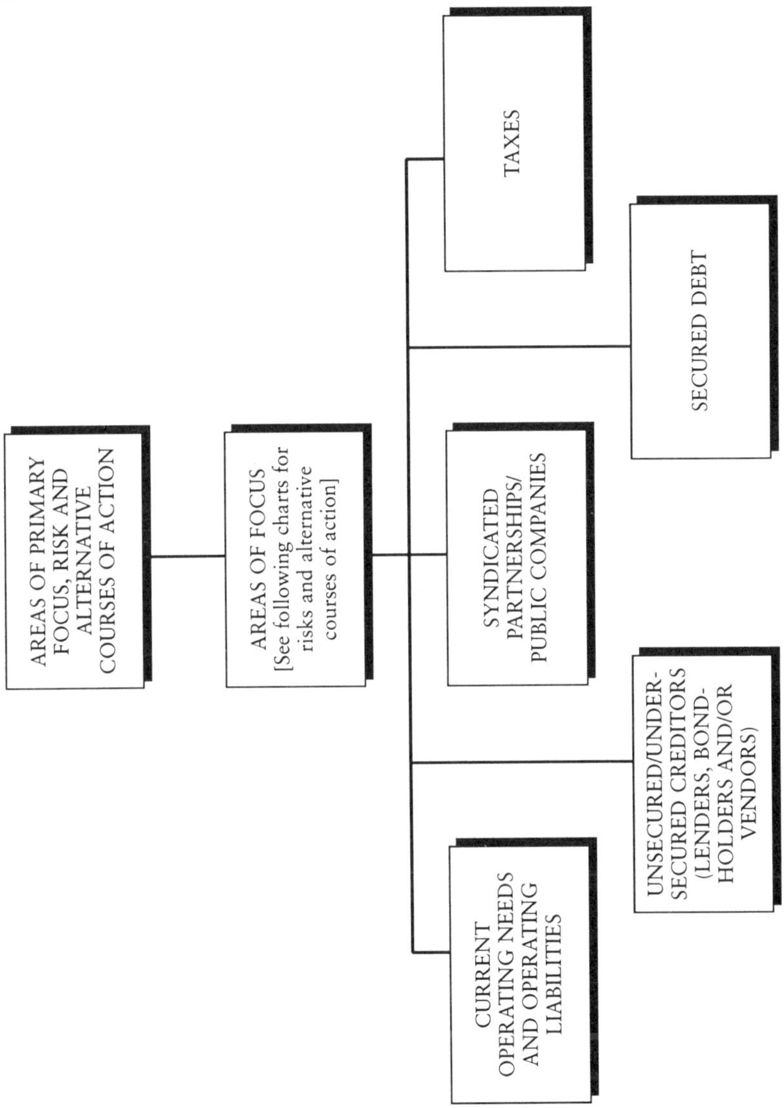

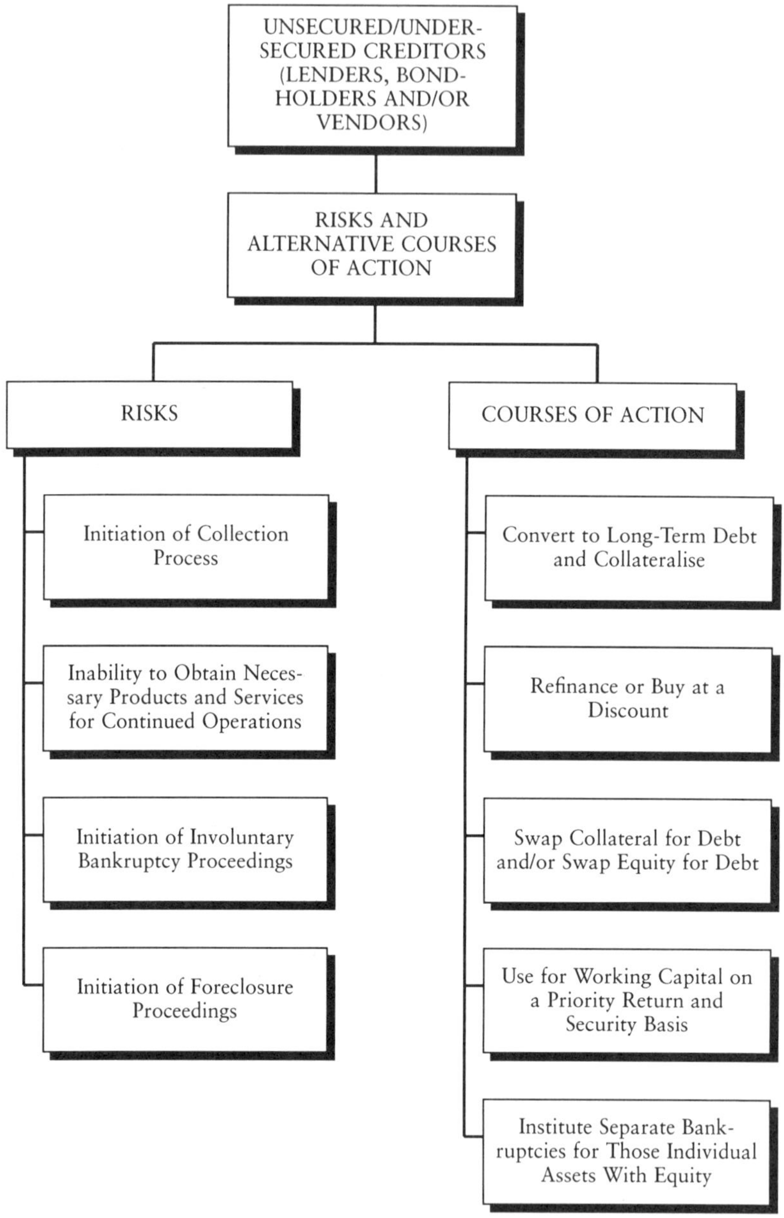
UNSECURED/UNDER-SECURED CREDITORS (LENDERS, BOND-HOLDERS AND/OR VENDORS)
RISKS AND ALTERNATIVE COURSES OF ACTION
RISKS
COURSES OF ACTION
Initiation of Collection Process
Inability to Obtain Necessary Products and Services for Continued Operations
Initiation of Involuntary Bankruptcy Proceedings
Initiation of Foreclosure Proceedings
Convert to Long-Term Debt and Collateralise
Refinance or Buy at a Discount
Swap Collateral for Debt and/or Swap Equity for Debt
Use for Working Capital on a Priority Return and Security Basis
Institute Separate Bankruptcies for Those Individual Assets With Equity

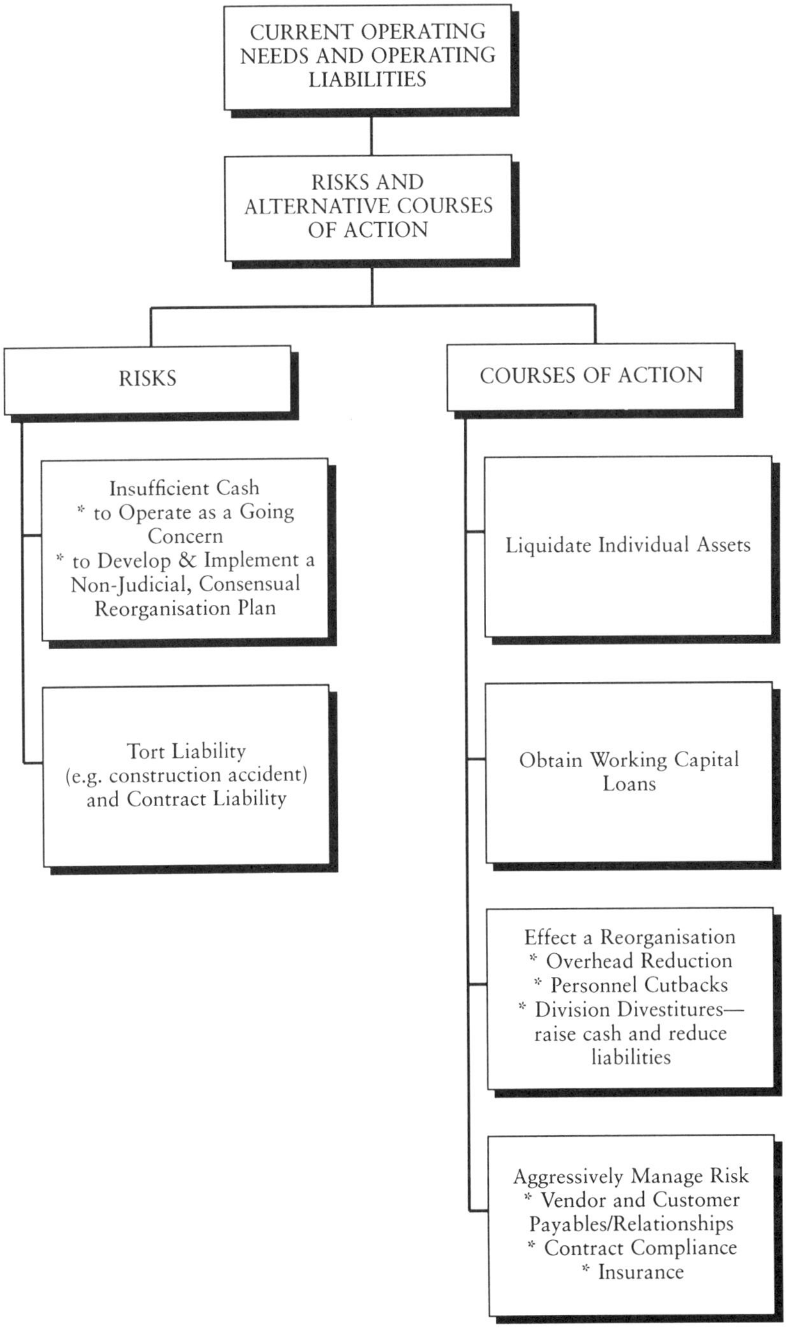
CURRENT OPERATING NEEDS AND OPERATING LIABILITIES
RISKS AND ALTERNATIVE COURSES OF ACTION
RISKS
COURSES OF ACTION
Insufficient Cash
* to Operate as a Going Concern
* to Develop & Implement a Non-Judicial, Consensual Reorganisation Plan
Tort Liability (e.g. construction accident) and Contract Liability
Liquidate Individual Assets
Obtain Working Capital Loans
Effect a Reorganisation
* Overhead Reduction
* Personnel Cutbacks
* Division Divestitures—raise cash and reduce liabilities
Aggressively Manage Risk
* Vendor and Customer Payables/Relationships
* Contract Compliance
* Insurance

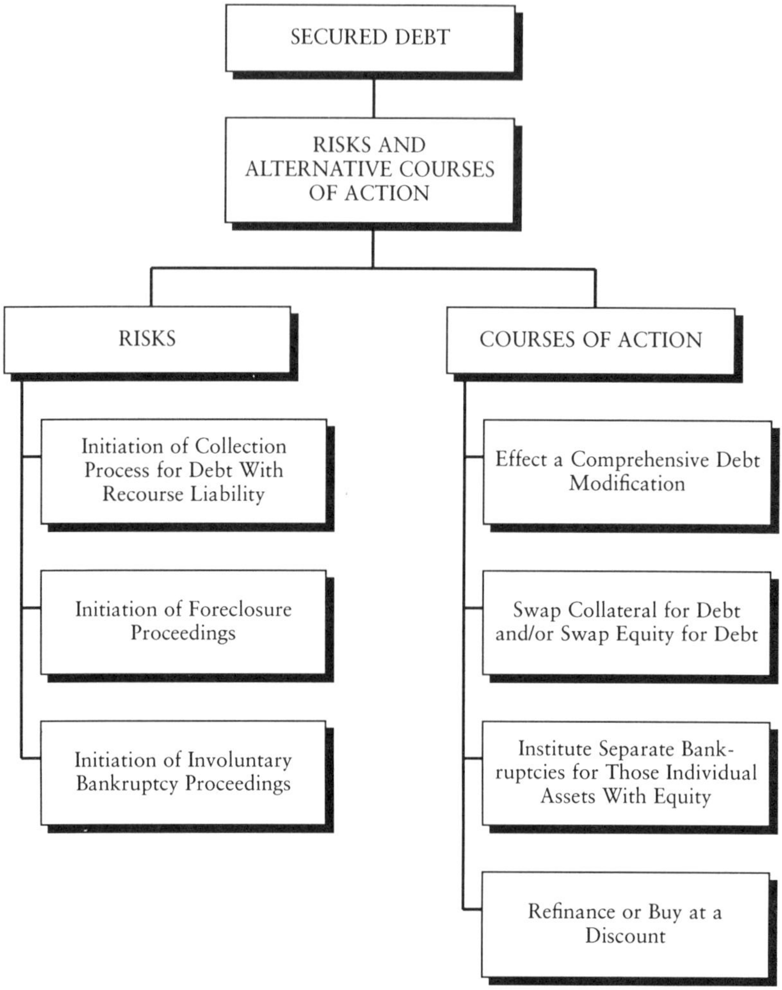
SECURED DEBT
RISKS AND ALTERNATIVE COURSES OF ACTION
RISKS
Initiation of Collection Process for Debt With Recourse Liability
Initiation of Foreclosure Proceedings
Initiation of Involuntary Bankruptcy Proceedings
COURSES OF ACTION
Effect a Comprehensive Debt Modification
Swap Collateral for Debt and/or Swap Equity for Debt
Institute Separate Bankruptcies for Those Individual Assets With Equity
Refinance or Buy at a Discount

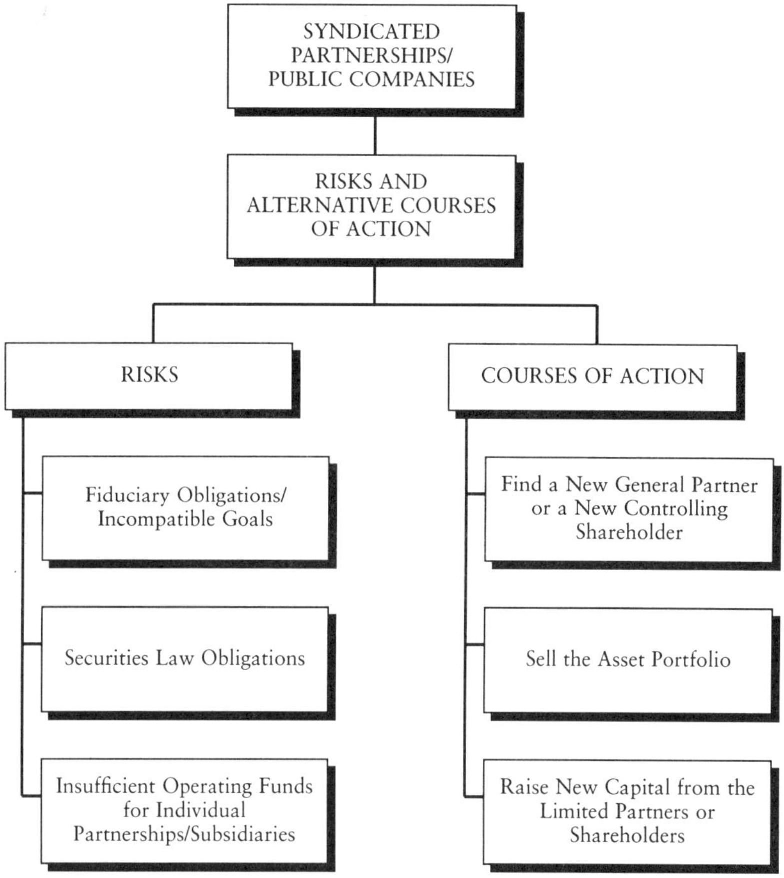
SYNDICATED PARTNERSHIPS/ PUBLIC COMPANIES
RISKS AND ALTERNATIVE COURSES OF ACTION
RISKS
COURSES OF ACTION
Fiduciary Obligations/ Incompatible Goals
Securities Law Obligations
Insufficient Operating Funds for Individual Partnerships/Subsidiaries
Find a New General Partner or a New Controlling Shareholder
Sell the Asset Portfolio
Raise New Capital from the Limited Partners or Shareholders

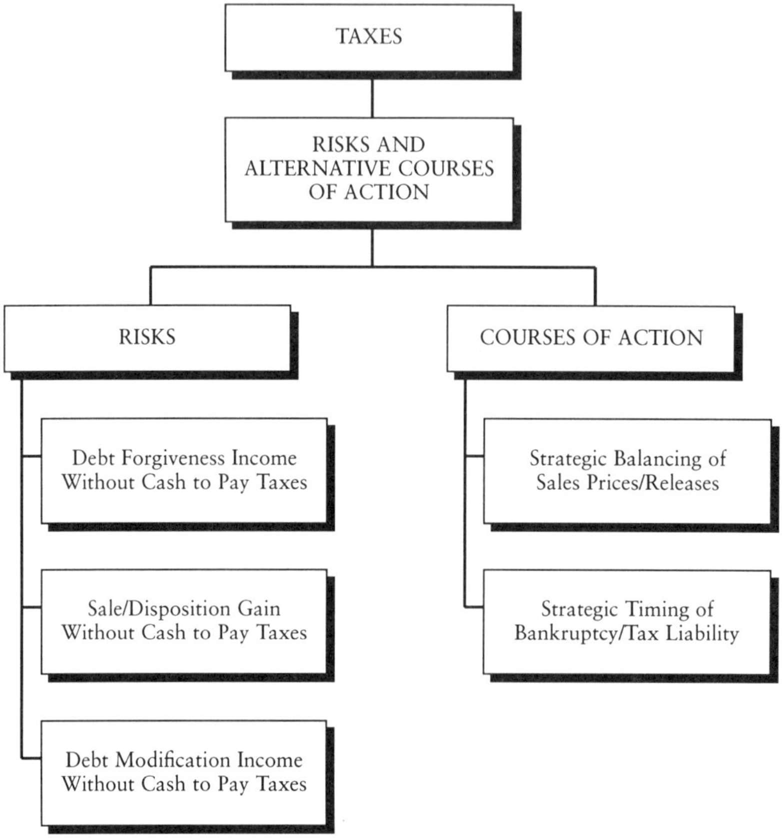
TAXES
RISKS AND ALTERNATIVE COURSES OF ACTION
RISKS
COURSES OF ACTION
Debt Forgiveness Income Without Cash to Pay Taxes
Sale/Disposition Gain Without Cash to Pay Taxes
Debt Modification Income Without Cash to Pay Taxes
Strategic Balancing of Sales Prices/Releases
Strategic Timing of Bankruptcy/Tax Liability

APPENDIX II

AFFIDAVIT OF FINANCIAL CONDITION

11.168

AFFIDAVIT OF FINANCIAL CONDITION
OF

____

STATE OF ________________ {

COUNTY OF ______________ {

____________________________________, being duly sworn, deposes and says: I am over the age of twenty-one (21) years and reside at

______________________________________,

I make this affidavit at the request of ____ ("Bank"), for the purpose of informing the Bank of my present financial condition. I know that the Bank's acceptance of this affidavit will be in reliance upon the accuracy and truth of the statements and representations made by me herein.

I have no property or assets and have no income except as hereinafter stated. [In connection with all listings and descriptions of assets owned, include the cost of acquisition of each asset.]

When this Affidavit describes assets that I "own" or "hold", or income that I "receive", the description includes without limitation (i) assets or properties which are owned or held by trustees, agents or nominees for my benefit, or on my own behalf, and income received by such persons for my benefit or on my behalf, and income received by such persons for my benefit or on my behalf; and (ii) assets or properties which are owned or held by my spouse, and income received by my spouse, except for assets, properties and income which constitute the separate property of my spouse under applicable laws.

The balance sheet attached hereto as Schedule 1 is true and correct in all respects, properly and fairly presents my financial condition and describes or includes all of my assets and liabilities (including, without limitation, contingent liabilities). Since the date of such financial statement, there have been no material adverse, or material positive, changes in my financial condition or position.

1. I receive no income from any source whatsoever, except [listed amount(s) and source(s)]:

2. I have no savings account, certificate of deposit or other time deposit in any bank, domestic or foreign, except [list name and address of institution and outstanding balance of account]:

3. I have no checking account or other form of demand deposit in any bank, domestic or foreign, except [list name and address of institution and outstanding balance of account]:

4. I receive no salary, except [list amount and source]:

5. I receive no fees for management assistance or other services rendered to any individual, partnership, firm or corporation, except [list amount and source]:

6. I receive no commissions from any source, except [list amount and source]:

7. I receive no stock dividends from any corporation, domestic or foreign, except [list amount and source]:

8. I am entitled to no bonus from any business, except [list amount and source]:

9. I have no safe deposit box or access to any safe deposit box, except [list name of and address of each institution, each safe deposit box number and the contents thereof]:

10. I own no real estate of any nature whatsoever, except [list address, legal description and date and cost of acquisition of all real estate owned]:

11. I have no ownership interest in any partnership, legal entity or corporation owning real estate, except [list name of partnership, firm, legal entity or corporation, interest owned and date and cost of acquisition]:

12. I do not own any mortgages or have any interest in any mortgages, except [list amount, interest, description of property mortgaged and identity of mortgagor]:

13. I own no building or loan certificates, or any shares in or assets in any savings and loan associations, except [list name of institution and ownership interest]:

14. I own no stocks, bonds, mutual funds or other securities, except [list, including date and cost of acquisition]:

15. I have no brokerage account with any broker, except [list name of broker, account number and outstanding balance in each account]:

16. I own no commodities, except [list, including date and cost of acquisition]:

17. I have no commodity account with any broker, except [list name of broker, account number and outstanding balance in each account]:

18. I have no account with any financial institution whatsoever, except [list name of institution, account number and outstanding balance in each account]:

19. I have no power of attorney or authority of any nature whatsoever, either over stocks, bonds, commodity accounts, or other form of securities, except [identify and describe any such property and beneficial owner thereof]:

20. I do not act as a trustee or fiduciary with respect to any property, either real or personal, except [identify and describe any such property and beneficial owner thereof]:

21. I do not own any bonds or evidence of debt of any governments, except [list all governmental debt issues owned and date and cost of acquisition]:

22. I own no insurance policy of any type, except [list name of company, face amount of policy, type of insurance, beneficiary and amounts borrowed thereon]:

23. I receive no dividends from any insurance company, except [list as in 22 above]:

24. I pay no premiums on any insurance policy, except [list as in 22 above]:

25. I am not the beneficiary of any insurance policy, except [list as in 22 above]:

26. I have no interest in any patents, inventions, tradenames, trademarks, copyrights, or royalty agreements, except [identify]:

27. I have no claim against any insurance company except [identify company, amount of claim and description of claim]:

28. I have no claim against or interest in any estate or any trust of any person, whether living or dead, except [identify estate or trust, amount of claim and description of claim]:

29. I have no claim against any person, whether living or dead, or any firm or corporation, except [identify individual or entity, amount of claim and description of claim]:

30. I am not a plaintiff or defendant in or otherwise prosecuting any action or proceeding in any court, except [list the style of each case, case number, and court in which each case is pending]:

31. I am not a party to any arbitration proceedings now pending before any Arbitrator or Board of Arbitration, except [identify each proceeding]:

32. I have no interest in any promissory notes, letters of credit, bankers' acceptances, drafts or other forms of commercial paper, except [identify maker or drawer and amount]:

33. I am not entitled to receive any money from any State, City or Federal government, or agency of department thereof except [list agency of department and amount]:

34. I am not entitled to any Federal, State or City income tax refund, except [identify and list amount]:

35. There are no judgments or decrees outstanding against me, except [list style of each case, case number and court which entered each judgment or decree]:

36. I have executed no guaranties of the indebtedness or obligation of any individual,

corporation, partnership or other entity, except [identify debtor, amount and holder of each guaranty]:

37. I have made no gifts within the preceding five (5) years, except [list property given, approximate value thereof in terms of cost of acquisition, date of gift and identity of recipient]:

38. I have made no conveyance of real or personal property for less than full value within the preceding five (5) years, except [list property transferred, approximate value thereof in terms of cost of acquisition, property or money received for such transfer (if any), date of transfer and identity of recipient]:

The foregoing statement includes not only outright conveyances of assets but also release and waivers of any valuable claims or contract rights which I owned or held against other parties.

39. During the past twelve (12) months, I have not made any payments to my trade creditors, outside of the ordinary [list amount and date of payment]:

40. During the past twelve (12) months, I have not made any payments to banks, financial institutions or other holders of my notes, bonds or funded indebtedness, except for: (i) payments to Bank; (ii) payments to creditors whose claims were, at the time of payment, fully secured by valid and perfected security interests in assets having a value at least as great as the amount of the indebtedness; and (iii) the following [list any other payments and dates]:

41. No real or personal property is held by others for my benefit, except [list property so held, approximate value thereof in terms of cost of acquisition, date of acquisition and identity of holder]:

42. I am not indebted to any bank, savings and loan associations, credit union, finance company, brokerage house or individual, except [list name of institution or individual, amount of indebtedness and date indebtedness was incurred]:

43. I own no airplane, automobile, boat, trailer or any motor vehicle of any nature whatsoever, except [list serial number and date and cost of acquisition]:

44. I have no personal property other than my clothing and personal effects, except [include description, serial number (if any) and date and cost of acquisition]:

45. I do not own or have any interest in any work of art, except [include description, date and cost of acquisition]:

46. I own no house, dwelling place, condominium apartment or cooperative apartment, except [list address, date and cost of acquisition]:

47. I have not had any financial statement prepared for or by me, nor have I issued any financial statement to any bank, financial institution, banking corporation, firm, or person within the last five (5) years, except (attach a copy of any such financial statement]:

48. I am not a custodian of property for any minor or other individual or entity, except [include description of such property and identity of beneficial owner]:

49. I own no property, real or personal, in Switzerland or any other foreign country or territory of the United States, except [include description of each item and its location, address and legal description of real property, serial numbers (if any) and date and cost of acquisition]:

50. I have no bank accounts, savings accounts or deposit accounts in banks in any foreign countries, except [list name and address of institution and outstanding balance of account]:

51. I have no jewelry or like property having a value (whether calculated separately or collectively) which exceeds the sum of $500, except [list description and date and cost of acquisition]:

52. I own no interest in any precious metals (i.e., gold, silver, platinum, etc.) or like property having a value (whether calculated separately or collectively) which exceeds the sum of $500, except [list description and date and cost of acquisition]:

53. Except for the property herein set forth above, I own no property of any nature whatsoever having a value in excess of $500, except [list description and date and cost of acquisition]:

54. My fixed monthly expenses are as follows [list amount and description of each fixed expense]:

55. My annual salary from all sources is [list amounts and sources]:

56. I have delivered to Bank true and correct copies of the tax returns (and all amendments thereto) which I have filed with the Internal Revenue Service for the following years:

57. I know of no other material facts relating to my financial condition except:

Sworn to before me this ______ day of ______________, 199_____.

(SEAL)

____

NOTARY PUBLIC

My Commission Expires:_________________

CHAPTER 12

ADMINISTRATION AND INSOLVENCY: THE UNITED KINGDOM APPROACH

BACKGROUND

12.1 Perhaps the most important practical distinction between the UK and US approaches to ailing companies is that under the UK system the court will only appoint a licensed insolvency practitioner to be administrator or to be supervisor under a voluntary arrangement. The concept of debtor in possession currently plays no part in English or Scottish law.[1]

12.2 This has the adverse effect that directors are reluctant to relinquish control by applying for an administration order until they are forced to do so by the twin sanctions of the Company Directors Disqualification Act 1986 and potential liability for wrongful trading.[2] Under section 6 of the former Act, the court will disqualify a director or shadow director[3] of a company which becomes insolvent from being a company director and from being engaged in the promotion, formation or management of a company for 2 to 15 years, if his conduct as a director makes him unfit to be concerned in the management of a company. The factors to be taken into account are set out in Schedule 1 to the Act and include any breach of duty to the company.

12.3 Wrongful trading arises if, at some time before insolvent liquidation, its directors knew or ought to have concluded that there was no reasonable prospect that the company would avoid insolvent liquidation.[4] Moreover, companies are obliged by the Companies Acts to prepare annual accounts and the directors will be assumed for these purposes to know the financial position of the company if they ought to have prepared accounts which would have

1. Contrast the Examiner procedure under Irish law. The desirability of some modification of UK procedures is under review.

2. Concepts not known in the US.

3. "Shadow director" is defined by the Insolvency Act 1986, s.251 to mean "a person in accordance with whose directions or instructions the directors of the company are accustomed to act" but it does not apply to a person if the directors act on advice given by that person in a professional capacity. Rescuing banks must be careful to limit their activities to monitoring—preferably through lawyers and accountants—and not issue directions or instructions to the board. See *Re PFTZM Ltd* [1995] BCC 280.

4. Insolvency Act 1986, s.214.

disclosed it.[5] It is a defence if the person concerned took every step with a view to minimising the potential loss to the company's creditors that he ought to have taken. A director whose advice and recommendations to cease trading go unheeded should consider resignation. If he does not resign, he is exposed to potential liability for wrongful trading, but failure to resign does not necessarily make him unfit to be concerned in management for the purposes of disqualification proceedings.[6]

12.4 The risk of being liable for wrongful trading (and potential disqualification) forces directors to seek insolvency advice earlier than they might otherwise. If directors are properly advised, rescue by syndicates of banks is often a viable possibility. Unfortunately, there are still instances where directors are advised by lawyers without appropriate insolvency experience and sometimes apply for administration orders on such advice when a corporate rescue would have been more beneficial to all concerned.

12.5 The adoption of some form of debtor in possession procedures would undoubtedly expand the options available to directors and would be consistent with the general view that the prospects of successful rescue diminish with delay. The balance between that desirable goal and the perceived risks of abuse is a policy issue.

ADMINISTRATION ORDERS

12.6 Because an administration order seriously interferes with the rights of creditors, it can only be made if the court is satisfied that the company is or is likely to become insolvent and that the making of the order is likely to achieve one or more of the following purposes:

1. the survival of the company and part of its undertaking as a going concern;
2. the approval of a voluntary arrangement (or a Companies Act scheme of arrangement); or
3. a more advantageous realisation of assets than would be effected on a winding-up.

12.7 The survival of the company is usually only achievable in those rare situations where the problem is limited to a cash-flow difficulty. However, more advantageous realisation than would be effected on a winding-up is a test relatively easily fulfilled because an administrator has wider powers than a liquidator. In particular, administration facilitates the realisation of a business as a going concern. It will, therefore, often be more advantageous to have an administration order, provided that the attendant costs are justifiable. A number of administration orders are also made with a view to a voluntary arrangement (see below).

5. *Re Produce Marketing Consortium Ltd (No. 2)* [1989] BCLC 520.
6. *Re C S Holidays Ltd* [1997] BCC 172.

12.8 There must be a "real prospect" that one or more of the above purposes will be achieved.[7] In practice, the court is strongly influenced by a report from an insolvency practitioner about the financial position and prospects of the company. Funding of the administration is also an important consideration.

12.9 Section 9(3) of the Insolvency Act requires the court to dismiss a petition for an administration order if an administrative receiver has been appointed prior to the hearing, unless the debenture holder consents or the security is liable to be discharged. This has led to banks taking, in addition to fixed charges, floating charges over the whole or substantially the whole of the assets of the company.[8] This is another practice which has assisted the preservation of businesses and jobs because such a receiver also has the power to sell the business as a whole.

12.10 The advantages of an administration order over a receivership are that it is more likely to be recognised in foreign jurisdictions, that creditors are precluded from repossessing goods except with the consent of the administrator or the leave of the court and that security ranking in priority to the debenture cannot be enforced without the consent of the administrator or the leave of the court. In some cases these considerations will be sufficient to persuade a debenture holder to refrain from appointing an administrative receiver and to allow an administration to proceed, even though all the preconditions for a receivership appointment are satisfied.

THE EFFECT OF AN ADMINISTRATION ORDER

12.11 On the making of an administration order, any petition for winding-up shall be dismissed and any administrative receiver shall vacate office.[9] While the order is in force, no resolution may be passed to wind up the company, though in practice resolutions are passed to wind up the company conditional on the court approving the resolution and discharging the administration order. This has the problem that preferential creditors at the commencement of the administration may lose their status, unless special arrangements are made to see them paid. This needs to be done if the ensuing liquidation is voluntary rather than compulsory.[10]

12.12 Other effects are that no steps may be taken to appoint an administrative receiver or otherwise enforce security (widely defined) or repossess goods, and no proceedings may be taken or execution or distress levied against the company or its assets, except with the consent of the administrator or the leave

7. *Re Harris Simons Construction Ltd* [1989] 1 WLR 368.
8. See *Re Croftbell Ltd* [1990] BCLC 844.
9. Insolvency Act 1986, s.11. A receiver of merely part of the company's property (not an "administrative receiver") must vacate office if called upon to do so by the administrator.
10. See *Re Mark One (Oxford Street) plc* [1998] BCC 984.

of the court.[11] It is not necessary to show misconduct by the administrator.[12] Leave is a matter for the court's discretion but that discretion is exercised in accordance with established guidelines which attach great importance to the creditor's proprietary rights. The administrator must not use the stay of creditors' remedies as a bargaining counter. Leave will usually be granted if refusal would cause significant loss; alternatively, conditions may be attached to provide redress.[13] An administrator who abuses his position risks personal liability.[14]

12.13 Members or creditors who are unfairly prejudiced by an administrator's actions can apply to the court for relief under section 27 of the Insolvency Act 1986. This is not simply a matter of challenging the administrator's decisions: administrators are officers of the court and the court will not readily interfere with their commercial decisions.[15] An obvious example of unfair prejudice would be discriminatory treatment within a class of creditors having like interests.

THE POWERS OF AN ADMINISTRATOR

12.14 By section 14 of the Insolvency Act 1986, the administrator may do all things necessary for the management of the affairs, business and property of the company, and he also has power to remove and replace directors and to call meetings of members and creditors. However, in exercising his powers he is deemed to act as agent of the company and it has been held that he can be injuncted from repudiating a contract binding on the company.[16]

12.15 By section 15, the administrator can exercise his powers in relation to assets subject to a floating charge as if they were not subject to the security. As regards fixed-charge assets, he may apply to the court to authorise him to dispose of the property as if it were not subject to the security, provided the net proceeds or, if greater, the open market value is applied towards discharging the sum secured. In *Re ARV Aviation Ltd*[17] the court held that it would look at all the circumstances of the case and balance the prejudice felt by the secured creditor against the prejudice felt by unsecured creditors who would potentially benefit from the purpose for which the administration order was made. The administrator can, therefore, not only prevent security being realised, but also, in some circumstances, force its sale subject to supervision by the court.

12.16 If administrators are authorised by the court under section 15 to

11. S.11.
12. *Royal Trust Bank* v. *Buchler* [1989] BCLC 130.
13. *Re Atlantic Computers plc* [1992] Ch. 505.
14. *Re Sibec Developments Ltd* [1992] 1 WLR 1253.
15. *MTI Trading Systems Ltd* v. *Winter* [1998] BCC 591.
16. *Astor Chemical Ltd* v. *Synthetic Technology Ltd* [1990] BCC 97.
17. [1989] BCLC 664.

override fixed charges, problems can arise about how to apportion the price obtained for the business as a whole. The purchaser will primarily be influenced by tax considerations which may be irrelevant to the administrator and the creditors. The fixed chargee will need to have his security valued and be prepared to apply to the court to protect his own interests.

THE DUTIES OF AN ADMINISTRATOR

12.17 It is the duty of the administrator to take control of all the assets of the company, and to manage its business and affairs until his proposals have been approved by the creditors in accordance with any directions given by the court.

12.18 Under section 23, the administrator is to make proposals for achieving the purposes of the order within three months of the administration order or such longer period as the court may allow. The administrator must summon a meeting of creditors to decide whether or not to approve the proposals. However, the meeting can modify those proposals only if the administrator consents to each modification. Any creditor or member of the company who considers that he has been unfairly prejudiced by the proposals may apply to the court under section 27, but no such application can prevent the implementation of proposals unless it is made within 28 days after the approval of the proposals.

12.19 After his proposals have been approved, the administrator's duty is to manage the company in accordance with those proposals.

12.20 As a general rule, administrators should not make asset disposals before their proposals have been approved at the creditors' meeting if the disposals would pre-empt the creditors' decision. However, the court will authorise disposal in exceptional circumstances.[18]

12.21 It is the duty of the administrator under section 18 to apply to the court for the administration order to be discharged or varied, if it appears to him that the purposes specified in the order have been achieved or are incapable of achievement. The court then has a wide discretion to make such order as it thinks fit.

VOLUNTARY ARRANGEMENTS

12.22 Although it is possible for directors to propose a voluntary arrangement under section 1 of the Insolvency Act 1986, such an arrangement has to be supervised by a licensed insolvency practitioner. In practice, a voluntary arrangement will only succeed if dissenting creditors can be kept at bay and this often entails applying for an administration order. "Stand alone" voluntary

18. *Re P D Fuels Ltd* [1999] BCC 450.

arrangements of companies are difficult to achieve without this protection, unless the number of creditors involved is small. However, voluntary arrangements coupled with administration orders are useful because an administrator in his capacity as such has no power to make a pro rata distribution binding on all creditors.[19]

12.23 As in administration, the proposals must be put to a creditors' meeting. The requisite majority in a voluntary arrangement is three-quarters in value. In addition, for the approval of a voluntary arrangement, there must also be a members' meeting. The proposals under a voluntary arrangement cannot affect the right of a secured creditor to enforce his security and shall not prejudice a preferential creditor without his agreement. As in the case of proposals by an administrator, any creditor or member who is unfairly prejudiced by the proposals may apply to the court for relief, provided the application is made within 28 days of the reports of the meetings being made to the court. In order to obtain relief the aggrieved creditor or member must show that the prejudice arises from the terms of the arrangement and not extraneous circumstances.[20]

CONCLUSION

12.24 Historically, insolvency procedures were designed to collect the assets of the debtor and distribute them to the creditors entitled. Now there is a realisation of the need to rehabilitate business and save jobs, a process assisted by calling in expert help at an early stage. Rehabilitation usually requires an injection of new capital and a strengthening of management, and may, therefore, entail selling the business. The next development (already evident in the US) may well be a perceived need to protect the environment.[21]

12.25 The UK concept of debentures charging all the assets of a company to the banks has done much to protect the UK banking system, but at the expense of trade and other creditors. It is arguable that the law should be amended so that floating charges only validly secure new moneys as opposed to old debt, just as retention of title could usefully be restricted to the price for the particular goods retained.

HAMISH ANDERSON[22]

19. *Re St Ives Windings Ltd* (1987) 3 BCC 634. The position may be different when the administration of a company results in sufficient to pay creditors in full and to return the company to management by its own directors: *Re John Slack Ltd* (unreported, 2 July 1990).

20. *Sea Voyager Maritime Inc.* v. *Bielecki* [1999] 1 BCLC 133.

21. See *Re Mineral Resources Ltd* [1999] 1 All ER 746; *Official Receiver* v. *Environment Agency*, *The Times*, 5 August 1999.

22. The original version of this chapter in the first edition of this book was written by James Lingard.

CHAPTER 13

REHABILITATION AND INSOLVENCY: THE GERMAN APPROACH

1999: BIG BANG FOR GERMAN INSOLVENCY LAW

History: "The bankruptcy of bankruptcy"

Bankruptcy procedure old style: the battle of the secured creditors

13.1 For over a century the German law of insolvency has been governed by a time-honoured statute, the Bankruptcy Code of 1877 (Konkursordnung, henceforth "KO"). Despite being still regarded as a piece of legislation of technical excellence, the KO was not only showing signs of age, but increasingly worked the opposite way to its very purpose of supplying a fair and effective liquidation procedure for debtors who have become insolvent. A study covering the years from 1985 to 1988 found[1] that over 75 per cent of all bankruptcy petitions filed had to be dismissed in the event because the realisable assets of the debtor—the "bankrupt's estate"[2]—did not cover the expenses of the liquidation procedure.[3] In 1950, the same figure had amounted to only 25 per cent.[4] In the few cases where courts did issue a bankruptcy or winding-up order,[5] insolvency proceedings were conspicuous for their failure to achieve anything short of a fair distribution of assets among the creditors. Secured and priority creditors would take the lion's share, whereas ordinary unsecured creditors came out with an average 3–5 per cent of their total claims.[6]

1. All statistics are taken from: Regierungsentwurf Insolvenzordnung (InsO) (government-proposed Insolvency Bill) of 21 November 1991, Official Comment (*Begründung*), p. 1. Bundesratsdrucksache 1/92, p. 72.

2. "*Konkursmasse*". It is one of the peculiarities of German insolvency law to conceive of the debtor's assets available for distribution as a separate estate, excluding on the one hand property in the debtor's possession but belonging to others, or the debtor's post-insolvency income, but including any third-party property that has been gained through preferential treatment and which may therefore be retrieved by the trustee in bankruptcy. See Baur/Stürner, *Insolvenzrecht* (3rd edn, 1991), p. 12.

3. See s.107(1) KO.

4. See *supra*, note 1.

5. Contrary to English law, German law, prior to the Insolvency Act (Insolvenzordnung) 1994, never made any systematic distinction between insolvencies of private individuals and company winding-ups.

6. See *supra*, note 1.

13.2 To make sense of these puzzling statistics some brief remarks on the German law of secured transactions are in order.[7] Due to their high debt–equity ratio, most companies in Germany hold the bulk of their assets not in real property but in moveables, i.e. inventory of all sorts and accounts receivable. It is this part of their property which is utilised foremost to secure the company's short-term and middle-term credit financing.[8] To be more specific, the dominant type of collateral today was, and still is,[9] non-possessory collateral over goods and debts.

13.3 Suppliers of goods—to begin with the first main group of secured creditors—selling on a hire-purchase basis will secure such transactions by way of reserving their ownership of the goods delivered. In the purchaser's bankruptcy, goods delivered under such conditional sales may be recouped by the supplier as personal property.[10] Not in any respect is the supplier a participant in the bankruptcy proceeding: at most he may have to refund the purchaser's instalments to the bankrupt estate.

13.4 The matter becomes more complex if the purchaser is a manufacturer compounding or assembling materials which have been supplied by various sellers. For those cases the security instrument usually provides for an "extended" conditional sale,[11] according each supplier, as a substitute for their lost property, a pro-rata co-ownership in the end-product—again resulting in a separate realisation of the collateral in the manufacturer's bankruptcy. With the manufacturer selling the product in the usual course of business the supplier's collateral again ceases to exist, yet, according to standard practice, is substituted by an anticipated (pro-rata) assignment of the sales proceeds.[12]

13.5 It is at this point that the suppliers' needs for adequate security clash with the competing interests of lenders. As the mortgaging of real property hardly ever covers a borrower's overall financing needs and most of the personal property will be encumbered in favour of supplier-creditors,[13] lenders most often seek collateral way of an assignment of all accounts receivable, present and future (*Globalzession*).[14] By necessity, such assignments conflict with prior or later assignments in favour of suppliers. Both groups of creditors prefer to carry out transfers "undisclosed", i.e. not communicating them to the debtor's

7. The reader will find further useful hints on that topic in Chapter 1 of this volume by Philip Wood.

8. For long-term financing real property mortgages remain the preferred security device.

9. For the changes effected by the new law see *infra*, para. 13.24 *et seq.*

10. See §§ 1, 43 *et seq.* KO; for the new law see *infra*, para. 13.25 *et seq.*

11. *Verlängerter Eigentumsvorbehalt.*

12. Creating a lien in money claims is possible but impractical under German law, because it has to be disclosed to the third-party creditor.

13. The taking of collateral in form of chattel mortgages by lenders (*Sicherungsübereignung*) is a viable option only to the extent that the claims of suppliers have been satisfied. For details, see Jährig/Schuck, *Handbuch des Kreditgeschäfts* (5th edn, 1989) pp. 667–688.

14. *Ibid.*, pp. 700–704. See also Scholz/Lwowski, *Das Recht der Kreditsicherung* (7th edn, 1994), pp. 488–565. Note that German law does not acknowledge an all-inclusive collateral equivalent to the English floating charge.

customers until the debtor's financial condition becomes perilous. Therefore, it does not come as a surprise that double or even multiple assignments of the same accounts receivable have come to be common practice. Normally, this perennial conflict situation would be governed by the principle of "first come first served", putting lenders at an advantage over suppliers. However, when asked to address the legal conflict, the Federal Court (Bundesgerichtshof) in a succession of cases took side with the suppliers, invalidating global assignments to lenders as *contra bonos mores*,[15] even if the secured loan transaction had been executed prior to a supplier's "extended" conditional sale.[16]

13.6 Assigning sales proceeds or accounts receivable for security is—for reasons not to be explained in this chapter—by and large equivalent to granting a lien. Unlike a reservation of ownership, this technique does not segregate assignees from a later insolvency proceeding against the borrower/purchaser, but ensures them preferential satisfaction in priority to all other debts.[17] The old law granted the holder of such collateral the privilege of being able to realise his interest on his own, and at the risk and the expense of the bankrupt's estate, whereas the trustee in bankruptcy[18] could take action only if the secured creditor was in default.[19] Only in so far as the proceeds from realisation of the security interest did not match the unpaid balance of the debt would the lender or supplier have to take the role of an ordinary creditor.[20]

13.7 All this placed secured creditors in a position pre-eminent not only by their substantive but also by their procedural rights. Small wonder then that insolvencies under the KO were mostly little more than a battle between lenders and suppliers to grasp a larger piece of the pie.[21] Taken by itself, however, the position of secured creditors was far from being satisfactory.[22] Leaving the debtor in possession of the collateral facilitated his trading freely with the encumbered assets. Granting concurrent or double collateral in the same asset caused, and still causes, sizeable costs for creditors in identifying and sorting out their relative security interests. Empirical surveys show that both lenders and suppliers suffer considerable losses in the realisation of their security.[23]

15. Civil Code (Bürgerliches Gesetzbuch of 1900), § 138(1).

16. See Bundesgerichtshof, BGHZ 55, 35; 98, 315; modified in *Neue Juristische Wochenschrift 1999*, 940. Lenders have reacted to this ruling by explicitly releasing in their instruments such claims that are likely to become subject to a supplier's conditional sale ("waiver clauses"); see Schimansky/Bunte/Lwowski (eds.), *Bankrechtshandbuch* (1997), vol. 2, p. 2403.

17. *Absonderungsrecht*; see §§ 4, 47 *et seq.* KO.

18. The term "trustee in bankruptcy" includes the function of an "official receiver" in company winding-ups under UK law.

19. § 127(2) KO.

20. § 64 KO.

21. See also *infra*, para. 13.30.

22. See J. Drukarczyk, "Insolvenzrecht als Versuch marktkonformer Gestaltung von Verwertungsentscheidungen und Verteilungsregeln", *Zeitschrift für Wirtschaftsrecht* (ZIP) 1989, 341, 345.

23. *Ibid.*

Arrangement procedure

13.8 Insufficiency of realisable assets and unequal distribution were but two serious shortcomings of the old law of bankruptcy. As early as just after the First World War an awareness arose that the inevitable and forced liquidation of an insolvent debtor's property, particularly by dismantling a debtor's business as a going concern, was indeed a lamentable waste of economic resources and should no longer be the law's sole response to the complex issues of insolvency. The automatic machinery of liquidation had to be supplemented by an alternative collective remedy allowing for the survival of ailing, yet still viable businesses. Thus, after some interim measures, in 1927 new legislation was enacted instituting a supplementary insolvency proceeding ostensibly designed to avoid bankruptcy under appropriate circumstances and to protect the "honest but unfortunate" debtor. To implement this policy goal an insolvent debtor was permitted to seek a collective arrangement with his creditors under close supervision by a court.

13.9 Although the basic approach of this Arrangement Act (Vergleichsordnung, as amended 26 February 1935, henceforth "VglO")[24] was remarkable at the time and may be considered an early precursor of modern rehabilitation schemes, the Act proved to be anything but a spectacular success. Its practical relevance came to be almost negligible, with less than 1 per cent court-approved arrangements in the years subsequent to 1983, compared with 30 per cent in 1950 and 8 per cent in 1970.[25] Whatever could be said in favour of the rehabilitative philosophy of the Act was outweighed by numerous and serious inherent defects, which never let the arrangement procedure perform its intended function as a viable alternative to bankruptcy.[26] Thus, the debtor had to make his choice whether to file bankruptcy or to go for an arrangement at a moment when the prospects for rehabilitation could not be sized up with reasonable certainty. Once a bankruptcy order had been made, any petition for arrangement was precluded. Secondly, it was the debtor who had to make the opening move, submitting a proposal as to a revision and/or rescheduling of his indebtedness, whereas the creditors were constrained to a largely inactive role. Thirdly, secured creditors did not by operation of law participate in the collective bargaining which is the basis of any arrangement proceeding because

24. For details of the legislative history see Baur/Stürner (*supra*, note 2) p. 1; see also Bundesministerium der Justiz (ed.), *Erster Bericht der Kommission für Insolvenzrecht* (1985), p. 4.

25. See Official Comment (*supra*, note 1), p. 1. In recent times, to the knowledge of this writer, there has been just one single large-volume arrangement considered a success: the insolvency of the electronics and engineering group Allgemeine Elektrizitätsgesellschaft (AEG) in the early 1980s. The success was based upon a set of favourable preconditions: (a) the principal creditor banks waived substantial parts of the unpaid balance of their loans; (b) subsequent to the commencement of the arrangement procedure, the company's equity capital was, by resolution of the general assembly, first reduced and then re-increased, with most of the issued stock acquired by the creditor banks; (c) a comprehensive asset disposal programme was effected; (d) after the remainder of AEG's business units had regained profitability, the banks sold out to Daimler-Benz for a handsome profit.

26. For a brief summary of the shortcomings of the arrangement procedure *cf.* M. Balz, *Sanierung von Unternehmen oder von Unternehmensträgern?* (1986), p. 14 *et seq.*

they were supposed to lack an adequate incentive to compromise. As they are not only dominant in value but also have security interests in most of the assets the debtor needs to carry on his business, this provision frustrated any meaningful effort at rehabilitation. Finally, in corporate insolvencies there was no way of having the company's members/shareholders participate in the formal arrangement procedure. That frequently defeated attempts to make the rehabilitation of the debtor's business contingent upon a corporate restructuring—which may be the royal road to success.

13.10 It was a fair view of the current state of the German law of insolvency when, in 1975, one of Germany's most prominent insolvency practitioners proclaimed the "bankruptcy of bankruptcy".[27] Even if, however, a body of law fails to generate efficient results, the market will find ways and means of "contracting around". Creditors, debtors and insolvency practitioners alike indeed worked their escape routes out of the pitfalls of the black-letter law. Sometimes these were voluntary and consensual (i.e. out-of-court) collective arrangements which functioned as a "silent" liquidation or reorganisation scheme of a corporate debtor who was actually insolvent.[28] Occasionally, particularly in insolvencies of larger firms, there were bulk sales by a trustee in bankruptcy of a corporate debtor's entire business, or of single operating units, to another company, which sometimes had been formed by a group of dominant creditors or long-term customers for the very purpose of serving as a buyer in the rescue action[29] ("rehabilitation by way of liquidation"[30]).

A concise chronology of law reform[31]

13.11 The "bankruptcy of bankruptcy", heralded in 1975,[32] soon spread as a watchword for the first serious movement for law reform in about 100 years. The Federal Minister of Justice set the agenda for reform when, in 1978, he appointed a Committee for Insolvency Law made up of experienced insolvency practitioners, academic lawyers and representatives from business organisations, trade unions and the banking industry.

27. Joachim Kilger, "Konkurs des Konkurses", *Konkurs-, Treuhands-und Schiedsgerichtswesen* (KTS) 1975, 142.

28. Estimates are that such "silent liquidations" amounted to more than 40 per cent of corporate insolvency cases where a bankruptcy petition was filed. *Cf.* Gessner/Rhode/Strate/Ziegert, *Die Praxis der Konkursabwicklung in der Bundesrepublik Deutschland—eine rechtssoziologische Untersuchung* (1978), p. 539.

29. For more details see P.J. Groß, *Sanierung durch Fortführungsgesellschaften* (2nd edn, 1988).

30. To quote from the leading insolvency text book; *cf.* Baur/Stürner, *supra*, note 2, at p. 17.

31. For a more comprehensive historical account see Baur/Stürner, *supra*, note 2, 4; Prütting, in B. Kübler/H. Prütting (eds), *InsO—Kommentar zur Insolvenzordnung* (1998), Einleitung no. 17–44.

32. See *supra*, note 27.

The reports of the Committee for Insolvency Law

13.12 In 1985/86 the Committee submitted two voluminous reports, making a powerful case for fundamental reform and spelling out comprehensive recommendations for a new and integrated law of insolvency.[33] Since a great deal of this has been incorporated into the Insolvency Act 1999, I need not go into details here.[34] Some proposals for a more radical change, e.g. the absolute priority of rehabilitation in corporate insolvencies and the discharge by court order to be granted in personal bankruptcies, were in fact imports from the US Bankruptcy Code of 1976. Remarkable was the new approach of the Committee with respect to non-possessory security interests over moveables. To replenish the "impoverished" insolvent's estate, such collateral was to be made part of the estate. Holders of non-possessory collateral would not be permitted to recoup or realise the encumbered assets given that a rehabilitation procedure was pending. Moreover, under a rehabilitation scheme, their collateral was at risk of being "devalued" by up to 50 per cent, putting them, for the remaining balance, in the position of ordinary creditors. In a liquidation procedure, only the administrator was entitled to realise the security, discounting a 25 per cent "contribution" from the proceeds. Even mortgagees were to be charged a 10 per cent contribution. Finally, the report did away with any kind of preferential debt (namely remuneration of employees, social security contributions, debts due to Inland Revenue).

The Insolvency Bill of 21 November 1991

13.13 The conversion of the political climate in the wake of a change of government in 1982 could not leave the Committee's propositions unaffected. When the incoming administration in 1988 submitted a first Draft Bill authored by the Ministry of Justice,[35] the Bill bore the hallmarks of a more liberal, market-oriented philosophy, its theoretical approach drawing heavily on the American-based economic analysis of law with its emphasis on economic efficiency, its substantive goals aiming at greater procedural autonomy for the creditors and less committed to job preservation and employee (or union, for that matter) participation.

13.14 The movement for law reform seemed to have suffered a perilous blow when German unification came in late 1990. The Unification Treaty of 31 August 1990, while as a general rule effecting legal unification plainly by way of adoption of the former West German law, provided that the states in the territory of the former German Democratic Republic (GDR) retain, subject only

33. *Erster Bericht der Kommission für Insolvenzrecht* (Federal Ministry of Justice, ed., 1985); *Zweiter Bericht* (1986).

34. See *infra*, para. 13.16 *et seq.*

35. A semi-official "Diskussionsentwurf" (draft for discussion) of August 1988 was soon followed by a "Referentenentwurf Gesetz zur Reform des Insolvenzrechts" of 1 November 1989 (Federal Ministry of Justice, ed., 1989).

to a comprehensive reform of insolvency law in all of Germany, their existing insolvency law, the Gesamtvollstreckungsordnung (GesO) of 6 June 1990.[36] Therefore, it took most experts by surprise when in November 1991 the government came forward with an official Insolvency Bill (Regierungsentwurf Insolvenzordnung of 21 November 1991[37]).

13.15 Of monumental dimensions, the Insolvency Bill was accompanied by comprehensive and detailed official comments which will continue to provide a point of reference for some time to come. After two years of discussion in the legislative bodies, which for the most part brought about only minor technical amendments,[38] the Bill passed in July 1994 (Insolvenzordnung of 5 October 1994,[39] henceforth "InsO"). To facilitate a smooth transition to the new law its taking effect was postponed to 1 January 1999. Patently there has, at the time of writing, been no case law interpreting the InsO.

THE LEGAL POSITION OF BANK CREDITORS UNDER THE INSOLVENCY ACT 1999 (INSO)

Principles and policy considerations of the InsO

13.16 In its Official Comment, the Insolvency Bill was remarkably explicit about the principles and policy goals it seeks to implement.[40] It almost emphatically embraces a philosophy of "let the market take care of itself".[41] Whatever may survive of this philosophy in post-enactment day-to-day court practice, it has been pivotal for quite a number of both substantive and procedural principles forming the framework of the new law.[42] In this section, I will focus on aspects of particular relevance to banks.[43]

36. The GesO (reprinted in *Zeitschrift für Wirtschaftsrecht* (ZIP) 1990, 1231) had been passed by the first (and last) freely elected GDR Parliament when German unification had already become a political necessity. Its substance compounded elements of the old Konkursordnung of 1877 with bits taken from the West German law reform project. It should be emphasised that the GesO was not inter-temporal law such as being applicable solely to companies residing on GDR territory before unification took effect.

37. See *supra*, note 1.

38. Among those worth mentioning are the introduction of a special consumer insolvency proceeding and the omission of detailed provisions on international insolvencies, the latter anticipating an early coming into force of the European Insolvency Law Convention; notoriously, this expectation has proved too optimistic.

39. Promulgated in *Bundesgesetzblatt* I, 2866.

40. See Official Comment, Part A. See also the authentic interpretation of the reformers' policy goals by the former legal counsel to the Minister of Justice, Manfred Balz; M. Balz, "Die Ziele des Reformentwurfs", in B. Kübler (ed.), *Neuordnung des Insolvenzrechts* (1989), pp. 1–19.

41. Unmindful of the golden rule that legislators should make good law rather than embark on theoretical adventures.

42. For an economic analysis of the Draft Bill see J. Drukarczyk, "Insolvenzrecht als Versuch marktkonformer Gestaltung von Verwertungsentscheidungen und Verteilungsregeln", *Zeitschrift für Wirtschaftsrecht* (ZIP) 1989, 341.

43. Skipping such interesting details as the provisions relating to discharge or to the position of employees in their employer's insolvency.

Allocation of control rights: the paramountcy of creditor governance

13.17 The InsO shifts emphasis from the goal of fair distribution of the debtor's assets to the goal of providing an economically efficient realisation procedure with a minimum of transaction costs. Efficiency is best served if decision-making is committed to an unhampered collective bargaining among creditors, owners (company members, shareholders), and employees who, acting as mobile financiers, pursue and balance their respective interests. The principle of creditor governance is paramount: both the administrator (*Insolvenzverwalter*, §§ 56–66 InsO)—who has replaced the trustee in bankruptcy of the old law—and the insolvency court[44] are kept to a subordinate position.

13.18 At the core of autonomous decision-making by creditors and owners lies the choice between an insolvent liquidation and rehabilitation, be it of the debtor company or of the company's business. It is for the creditors' meeting to take the decision early on as to whether to liquidate the debtor's business or to keep it going at least temporarily.[45] By the same token, it is the creditor's meeting which instructs the administrator in working out an insolvency plan. While the Committee Report had considered rehabilitation of the corporate debtor the remedy of first order, whereas liquidation should avail as a remedy of last resort,[46] the InsO does not attempt to impose either remedy, but favours an autonomous choice by granting groups of priority creditors, or major company members, the privilege of proposing an insolvency plan of its own making.[47] Furthermore, as to the substance of insolvency plans, the InsO allows considerable leeway to depart from the legal order of distribution.[48] Only in default of any meaningful creditor initiative will a classical liquidation procedure by statutory rules and under the governance of the court ensue.[49]

13.19 The insolvency court is not, in the first instance, a defender of the public interest and an advocate of social policy, but a guardian over procedural propriety and fairness and an intermediary dealing with conflicting demands. Its decision to grant an insolvency order is rather formal in character. Its prime responsibility in the early stage of the procedure is to issue interim orders as it thinks fit for the transition period prior to the formal opening of the procedure.[50] Under exceptional circumstances, i.e. if there is an imminent danger of the insolvent's estate melting away, it may even, in a joint decision with the interim

44. A specialised division of the court of first instance, the Amtsgericht; see § 2 InsO.
45. § 157 InsO.
46. See *Erster Bericht* (*supra*, note 24), *Leitsatz* 1.3.4.4 (at p. 149 *et seq.*).
47. §§ 157, 218(2) InsO.
48. §§ 217, 254 InsO.
49. § 159 InsO.
50. Under § 21 InsO the court has the power, e.g., to appoint an interim administrator, to stay any measures of individual execution against the debtor, or to issue an injunction against the debtor avoiding any disposition of the debtor's property. After issuing an insolvency order but prior to the first convention of the creditors' meeting the insolvency court may appoint and convene a creditor committee such as to support and supervise the court's decisions (§§ 67, 69 InsO).

administrator, shut down the debtor's business right away.[51] Again, the court's power to confirm the insolvency plan (§ 248 InsO) aims at procedural control in the first place.[52] Only if they are invoked for the protection of a minority of creditors is the court permitted to exercise its overriding powers by setting aside a resolution of the creditor meeting which discriminates against individual or groups of creditors.[53]

13.20 Similarly, the administrator should not conceive of his role as a controller, but rather as a trustee for the creditors. Therefore, in all matters of importance, he has to seek approval of his decisions by the creditors' meeting or, prior to the first convention of the meeting, by the creditor committee.[54]

13.21 All put together, the InsO may be seen as a scheme to "privatise" the insolvency process, while it, however, remains under the auspices of state courts and "in the shadow" of a statutory framework.[55]

Facilitating rehabilitation in an integrated procedure

13.22 It is not only the option to submit an insolvency plan which is designed to facilitate rehabilitation. As one of the major shortcomings of the old code had been the fact that insolvency petitions frequently came too late, the InsO also had to redefine and to supplement the grounds for filing a petition. Among the "classical" grounds[56]—i.e. the debtor's inability to pay his debts as they fall due (illiquidity); for corporate debtors in addition, the deficiency of the assets as compared with liabilities (balance sheet insolvency)—illiquidity is no longer contingent on the debtor being unable to meet an "essential" part of his liabilities, nor is the opening of proceedings precluded by a debtor's merely transient illiquidity as far as it exceeds a few weeks.[57] Furthermore, the classical grounds have been supplemented by a novel ground of "imminent insolvency",[58] enabling debtors and creditors—especially employees—to enjoy the advantages of the formal procedure before the debtor's financial condition becomes hopeless. However, as only the debtor himself is entitled to file a

51. § 22(1) no. 2 InsO.
52. See § 250 InsO.
53. See § 78 InsO (general provision), § 251 InsO (resolutions approving insolvency plan). The protection of minorities in resolutions over insolvency plans had widely been criticised as too far-reaching and liable to give rise to blackmail actions by minority creditors; see B.M. Kübler, "Die Stellung der Verfahrensorgane im Lichte der Gläubigerautonomie", in B.M. Kübler (ed.), *supra*, note 40, at p. 74 *et seq.*
54. The creditor committee has, e.g., to give its approval to an early discontinuation of the debtor's business; see § 158(1) InsO.
55. *Cf.* H. Eidenmüller, "Der Insolvenzplan als Vertrag" in *Jahrbuch für Neue Politische Ökonomie* 1996, p. 164.
56. See §§ 102, 207, 209 KO.
57. For details see G. Pape, in B. Kübler/H. Prütting (eds), *supra*, note 31, § 17 margin nos. 8–13.
58. § 18 InsO. Insolvency is defined as being "imminent" if the debtor will presumably be unable to pay his existing debts by the time they fall due; *ibid.*, § 18(2).

petition on the ground of imminent insolvency,[59] there will remain some potential for purely private, i.e. contractual, rescue operations. A non-incorporated debtor may opt for an early petition if he has little to expect from a creditor-driven bailout and is at the same time going for the prospect of discharge concluding a formal proceeding.

13.23 The need for more flexibility and adaptability to changing circumstances made a compelling case for an integrated insolvency procedure. Not only does the InsO put an end to the compartmentalisation of insolvent liquidation (bankruptcy) and rehabilitation (arrangement), providing a unified procedural frame for either purpose: it lets the participants throughout make their choices short of forced liquidation as they think fit. One such option has, by tradition, been to effect a bulk sale. Again, the InsO has removed an obstacle to the separation of assets and liabilities which is the effect of a bulk sale. § 419 Civil Code (BGB) provided that any wholesale takeover of a property (or a substantial part thereof) would make the acquiring party jointly liable for the whole of the transferring party's obligations.[60] It had long been recognised, to be sure, that this rule was not to be applied to bulk sales in the course of a bankruptcy proceeding, because its purpose of preventing debtors from putting their assets beyond their creditors' reach will not be affected by such transactions.[61] As the provision still involved substantial risks for potential buyers, thus remaining a stumbling block on the way to successful voluntary rescue operations, it has been repealed by the InsO.[62]

Secured creditors

13.24 As has been observed at the outset of this chapter, the fatal flaw of the former bankruptcy law was that it did not ensure that the insolvent estate retained adequate assets such as to allow the commencement of a formal procedure in the first place; and it was the holders of non-possessory collateral who, by repossessing their assets early on, took the blame for "plundering" what was left of the insolvent firm's property. A further crucial point was to make secured creditors go along with reorganisation measures. They usually own, or hold charges, liens, or other collateral on, substantial parts of the firm's productive assets such as, e.g., real property, technical equipment or supplies.

59. By the recommendations of the Insolvency Law Commission, *supra*, note 33, the ground of imminent insolvency was designed to be universal. The drafters of the InsO did not follow this proposal because they were apprehensive of petitions by creditors aiming at "blackmailing" the debtor; see G. Pape, in B. Kübler/H. Prütting (eds), *supra*, note 31, § 18 margin no. 2.

60. The same is true for taking over a business unit (not necessarily being the vendor's entire property), with the purchaser carrying on the unit's firm name. Here, however, the acquiring party is permitted to disclaim its liability in the sales contract; the disclaimer will be binding on creditors if made public through the medium of the official firm register. See Commercial Code (Handelsgesetzbuch), § 25.

61. *Cf.* Möschel, in *Münchner Kommentar BGB* (3rd edn, 1994), § 419 margin no. 36. The same is true for the related provision in Commercial Code, § 25.

62. See Art. 33, Nr. 16 Introductory Act to InsO.

Among all creditors they have the least to gain from any kind of rescue operation. This disincentive to co-operate was aggravated by the fact that the old Konkursordnung granted secured creditors—as has been said before—a largely unassailable procedural position by permitting them to pursue their interests individually and more or less apart from the formal bankruptcy proceeding. It was then for the trustee in bankruptcy (or the administrator in arrangement procedures, respectively) to persuade the secured creditors that their interests too would be best served by effecting a standstill agreement rather than breaking away with individual repossessions or foreclosures.

13.25 To remedy this shortcoming the InsO did not adopt the proposal, advocated by radical critics of the former law, to substantially curtail, if not do away with, privileges growing out of non-possessory collateral.[63] Following through with its market-oriented philosophy, the InsO takes for granted the privilege of creditors-financiers to safeguard themselves against the hazards of their borrowers' default by means of a pre-insolvency contractual arrangement. At the same time it rejects any attempts to make insolvency law an instrument of redistribution among different classes of creditors.[64] To a certain extent, however, this "pure theory" fell victim to the political trade-offs to be made in the course of every legislative procedure.[65] As even employees and public authorities were divested of their status as priority creditors,[66] the outcome was a provision charging holders of non-possessory collateral with a lump sum contribution to "liquidation expenses" in the amount of 9 per cent of the moneys availing from the realisation of their assets.[67] Again, it must not be overlooked that the market will "contract around" this provision, with creditors trying to strain the margin of permissible over-collateralisation and/or demanding a higher interest rate such as to compensate them for any liquidation costs. Since holders of reserved title under a conditional sale of goods are not in this comfortable position, they have been exempted from paying any contributions.

13.26 While the InsO imposes hardly any restrictions on the substantive claims of secured creditors, it is all the more eager to involve them in the collective bargaining and decision-making which are the essence of the new insolvency procedure. The KO let them pursue their interests outside the bankruptcy proceeding with its specific pressure to compromise. Indeed, the KO vested them, by virtue of their holding claims on all assets essential to carry on

63. To a certain extent, this had been the approach of the Committee Report; see *supra*, para. 13.12.

64. More on the order of distribution in the following paragraph.

65. See Landfermann, "Regierungsentwurf einer neuen Insolvenzordnung", *Zeitschrift für Wirtschaftsrecht* 1991, 1661.

66. See *infra*, para. 13.27.

67. See § 170 InsO. Four per cent thereof for "identification expenses", 5 per cent for "realisation expenses"; see § 171 InsO. It is subject to proof that the real expenses exceed, or fall short of, the lump sum. For the realisation of chattel mortgages an additional discount for VAT has to be made, *ibid.*, § 171(2).

the debtor's business, with some kind of veto power over any efforts at rehabilitation. The InsO provides for an automatic stay of individual remedies in the hand of secured creditors such as repossession of mortgaged chattels or collection of accounts receivable assigned for security.[68] Utilisation, administration and realisation of all non-possessory[69] collateral other than reserved ownership[70] are assigned to the administrator who is authorised to postpone realisation of moveables while they are needed to carry on the debtor's business. To be sure, imposing a co-responsibility for optimal realisation of the insolvent estate may amount to a partial expropriation of secured creditors. Accordingly, they are entitled to some compensation for their forced contribution. After a waiting period of up to three months they are permitted to claim post-insolvency interest on their debt.[71] If the administrator utilises an encumbered asset for the estate, he has to compensate holders of such security through periodic payments for the wear and tear.[72]

Order of distribution

13.27 For purposes of what it thought to be a fair distribution, the KO had established—beyond according absolute priority to secured creditors—13 different classes of preferential debt,[73] most prominent among them being the claims of employees, pension funds, social security and Inland Revenue. "Class societies" are almost inherently unjust; moreover, they are ill-suited to engage in co-operative problem-solving. Accordingly, the InsO abolished all preferential debts other than the costs and expenses of the proceeding and the liabilities incurred by the administrator while carrying on the debtor's business.[74] To hold or not to hold security is what makes all the difference. As an innovation in German insolvency law, however, the InsO creates a class of "subordinated debt", i.e. claims which were not even admitted to proof in a bankruptcy procedure under the KO, such as post-insolvency interest on debts or claims based on gratuitous promises.[75] More importantly, shareholders' claims for

68. §§ 50, 165–173 InsO.

69. Assets charged with possessive security are not part of the debtor's "operative" assets; hence, realisation of such collateral by creditors will not impede the administrator from carrying on the debtor's business. This is of practical importance for banks, which, by virtue of No. 19 of their standard form contract, hold charges in all of their customers' moveables being in their possession (e.g. negotiable instruments, stock certificates, bonds, etc.).

70. By a last-minute amendment, reservation of title by conditional sale of goods remains the only type of non-possessory security to be realised outside the insolvency procedure; § 47 InsO. Only by electing to perform the sales contract fully (i.e. paying the agreed price instead of a mere insolvency dividend) can the administrator impede retrieval of the delivered goods by the seller; see §§ 103, 107(2) InsO. By contrast, vendors' security rights arising from an extended conditional sale (*supra*, note 11) are treated like other non-possessory collateral. It remains to be seen if, and to what extent, this exemption will hamper efforts at rehabilitation.

71. § 169(1) InsO.

72. § 172 InsO.

73. §§ 60, 61 KO.

74. E.g. debts from working capital loans or purchases of goods. See § 55 InsO.

75. § 39(1) nos. 1–4 InsO.

repayment of a loan or a guarantee substituting equity have been made subject to subordination.[76] As this may impede lenders from assuming a more responsible role in a workout by taking an interim equity stake in a distressed company, a 1998 amendment to the Private Limited Companies Act (GmbH-Gesetz) has granted banks which are committing themselves to such actions a "rehabilitation privilege". Accordingly, § 32a(3) GmbH-Gesetz[77] provides that the rules relating to "loans in substitution of equity" shall not apply to lenders which acquire a stake in a company in distress for the sole purpose of overcoming such crisis.

Some selected problems

Leasing, factoring

13.28 § 55(2) of the Draft Bill 1989[78] had stipulated that any transaction intended to achieve effects similar to those of non-possessory collateral—notably capital goods leases or sale-and-lease-back transactions, both of them frequently financed by banks[79]—be treated equally with such collateral. The provision was designed to prevent transactions *in fraudem legis*, i.e. transactions designed to keep secured creditors from becoming involved in the insolvency proceedings. Without achieving substantive change, the InsO skipped this general clause. Generally, it is open to question—and contingent on the specific design of the lease agreement—whether capital goods leasing is a secured credit transaction in the first place.[80] Yet even if a bank financing the lease takes out a chattel mortgage in the leased good the administrator of the lessor's estate would not be entitled to repossession as the leased good is not part of the productive assets to be safeguarded for carrying on the debtor's (lessor's) business.

13.29 Factoring is a financial service carried out in two different ways. In a "factoring proper" relationship the purchase of accounts receivable is immune against cancellation by the factor, burdening the latter with the full risk arising from a customer's default or insolvency. Thus, factoring proper is a pure cash transaction. If, however, the factor has the power to cancel the purchase and to assign the receivables back to the customer once the payment becomes delinquent, the essence of the transaction is financing with the factor advancing cash subject to the collectibility of the purchased claim. Hence, the factor receives the same treatment as a lender who has been assigned accounts receivable for security. With the advent of the customer's insolvency the

76. § 39(1) no. 5 InsO. By contrast, the old law had not only subordinated such loans but treated them like real shareholdings.

77. As of April 1998.

78. *Supra*, note 35.

79. Even if the lease is not financed, leasing is considered a financial service, as the larger leasing companies often are subsidiaries or joint ventures of banks.

80. It may be one in so far as the bank financing the lease takes a chattel mortgage (*Sicherungseigentum*) in the leased goods.

factoring agreement will be cancelled for the pending period by operation of law (§ 116 InsO). With regard to receivables already assigned to but not yet collected by the factor, the factor can collect directly from the third-party debtor. However, since the contract is executory as long as the factor has not collected, the administrator may opt for non-performance and demand that the receivable be retroceded.[81]

Collateral pool agreements

13.30 Security pool agreements have originated from the practical difficulties arising when, mostly in large-scale insolvencies, a multitude of secured creditors concurs in seeking to realise their respective security interests in the same kind of assets or any portions thereof. As has been said before,[82] it is common practice of both lenders and suppliers to take collateral which is both (nearly) all-inclusive and revolving, thus generating discrete and highly fragmented rights and interests mainly in inventory and accounts receivable. Since most creditors, when realising their collateral, would not assume the burden of proving whether, e.g., the semi-finished products in warehouse X or Y are subject to lender A's or supplier B's charge, groups of secured lenders and suppliers selling on the basis of hire-purchase transactions joined in making security pool agreements,[83] at the outset primarily for the purpose of relieving the burden of proof and none the less ensuring an orderly and fair realisation of the encumbered assets. A common technique has bank creditors and suppliers and/or their credit insurance carriers agreeing on fixed quotas of distribution of the moneys available from realisation of the whole of encumbered assets. There is an ongoing debate as to what proportion of the pie might constitute a fair share for each of the two creditor groups.[84]

13.31 When pool agreements became popular in the 1970s, they were challenged because of their interference with third-party rights, namely the rights of creditors choosing not to participate. Today, the Federal Court (Bundesgerichtshof) and majority opinion reject this argument since the partners of a pool agreement do not intend to transfer more rights than each partner actually has,[85] and their co-operation for a joint enforcement of their individual rights is a legally valid option.[86] However, for a joint enforcement to work effectively, the organisers of a "mixed" pool[87] need to make every effort in

81. § 103 InsO; for details see A. Tintelnot, in B. Kübler/H. Prütting (eds.), *supra*, note 31, §§ 115, 116, margin no. 29.

82. See *supra*, note 14.

83. The interests of suppliers are frequently represented by credit insurance carriers.

84. *Cf.* Jährig/Schuck, *supra*, note 13 at 712–713.

85. It may, however, constitute a voidable preferential treatment if, in a pre-insolvency agreement, the debtor himself grants new security.

86. See Bundesgerichtshof in *Zeitschrift für Wirtschaftsrecht* (ZIP) 1982, 543, 545; *Neue Juristische Wochenschrift* (NJW) 1999, 2592, 2597. For the recent commentary literature, see M. Martinek, in *Bankrechtshandbuch*, *supra*, note 16, § 97 V.

87. Meaning pools with both lenders and suppliers participating.

order to have as many suppliers (i.e. co-owners of raw materials, semi-finished products, etc.) participate as possible.

13.32 As pool agreements came to be more or less unchallenged they have evolved as a powerful and multi-purpose instrument, particularly in the hand of lenders. When dealing with large-scale borrowers involving a larger number of lenders but a limited supply of potential security, banks will effect a pool agreement as soon as they make their respective loan commitments with the debtor.[88] While in the case of post-insolvency security pools the agreement is based on an inter-creditor accord, the debtor now has to be a party to the agreement, for the latter is an integral component of the secured transaction. For practical convenience, to secure payment of the claims of all participating lenders an all-inclusive security interest will be created in favour of one agent bank—mostly the principal lender—acting as a trustee for the other partners for all purposes of administration and realisation. The distribution measure will be pro rata and tied to a fixed trigger date. If, and to the extent that, the individual lines of credit have not been disbursed in full, netting-out operations will straighten out the undisbursed balances. Advances in excess of an agreed line of credit may, if not made with the others' consent, be compensated if there is a remaining balance after the claims initially agreed upon have been satisfied.[89]

13.33 Collateral pools will remain a major player in the new insolvency procedure.[90] By virtue of their large number, and because they hold security interests in most of the inventory, pool creditors have a powerful voice in the collective bargaining preceding any reorganisation. At the least, the participants in a pool agreement will be inclined to allow payments falling due to be deferred, enabling the administrator to maintain business operations for a limited period of time, such as to realise the fair market value of the encumbered assets instead of a lower break-up value availing in a forced liquidation. Where the assets combined in the pool are vital for a business unit to operate, the pool creditors are likely to gain, and wield, substantial influence on the management of the debtor company.On the other hand, the pool creditors may actively further a rescue operation, e.g. advancing working capital for paying the work force and maintaining production. Those working capital loans will then enjoy first priority in the order of distribution of the pool cash. Where several security pools are concurring, the administrator will seek to organise a "pool of pools" with pro-rata quotas for the distribution of the proceeds expected from a contemplated bulk sale.[91]

13.34 It seems that collateral pools under the new law will operate as post-insolvency pools in the first instance. Since holders of non-possessory

88. For details the reader is referred to Scholz/Lwowski, *supra*, note 14, at pp. 190–198.

89. Scholz/Lwowski, *ibid.* at pp. 193–194.

90. See Insolvency Bill, Official Comment, *supra*, note 1, Part A 3b comments on §§ 30, 266.

91. See B.M. Kübler, "Unternehmenskauf und Konkurs", *Zeitschrift für Unternehmens-und Gesellschaftsrecht* (ZGR) 1982, 498, at pp. 504–505.

collateral have been largely deprived of their privileged segregated status, pools designed to function as a device for a separate and self-determined realisation of security have had their day. Pre-insolvency pools will retain some importance so as to allow for a fair *ex ante* distribution of a limited supply of collateral among competing creditors. By contrast, post-insolvency pools will come to be a prime tool to aggregate split votes and concentrate bargaining power, especially when it comes to making insolvency plans aiming at rehabilitation.

Voting rights

13.35 Voting rights were one of the most controversial topics in the course of the law reform. Some argued that, in order to curb the dominance of principal creditors, the majority vote should be counted by heads at least for corrective purposes.[92] In the event § 76(2) InsO, while sticking to the "one claim, one vote" principle, required majorities on a creditor meeting to be calculated according to the amount of the consenting creditors' claims. For the purpose of voting on insolvency plans, the InsO establishes classes of creditors—basically secured, ordinary, and subordinated creditors[93]—each casting a separate vote by majority.[94] For a proposed plan to pass, § 244 InsO requires a dual majority of each creditor group, both by heads and by values of claims. Even when a proposal does not meet approval by a majority of one group, a consent is implied by law, if the obstructing group would not be made worse off by the proposed plan than without and if the majority of groups has approved.[95]

Working capital loans made to the insolvent estate

13.36 Interim administrators frequently call on the principal creditor bank to provide a short-term loan, taking for collateral the employees' undisbursed social security claims.[96] Financing of other working capital requirements may be made available by creditor groups organised as a security pool; new security may be granted from the proportion of future sale proceeds not yet assigned to other creditors. It is a matter of course that working capital loans made in the course of an insolvency procedure enjoy first priority in the order of distribution.[97] §§ 264–266 InsO extend this privilege both to middle-term loans (or

92. For details see B. Kübler, in Kübler/Prütting, *supra*, note 31, § 76 margin no. 1.
93. §§ 237, 238, 246 InsO.
94. § 243 InsO. As a matter of course, creditors are not entitled to vote if the insolvency plan does not affect their rights; see §§ 237(2), 238(2) InsO.
95. § 245 InsO, adopting the "cram-down" principle from US bankruptcy law.
96. Arrears of pay which have summed up in the last three months prior to the insolvency order are compensated by social security payments (*Insolvenzausfallgeld*); see §§ 183 *et seq. Sozialgesetzbuch* III (1999).
97. See §§ 53, 55(1) no. 1 InsO.

other credit) extended beyond the date when the insolvency procedure is closed and to those made during a "review period", subsequent to the approval of a rehabilitation plan.[98]

Financial derivatives, especially set-off and netting

13.37 Obviously financial derivatives were not a major concern of the KO of 1877.[99] Accordingly the subject had to be dealt with in § 104(2) InsO from scratch.

13.38 It was the professed intent of the drafters of § 104(2) InsO to bring the German insolvency law relating to financial derivatives into line with the rules, contractual practices and usages prevailing in other major financial centres, especially the UK.[100] By tradition, insolvency set-off under English law has been a more powerful tool to overcome the *pari passu* principle than in Germany.[101] Moreover, English law would generally leave intact contractual close-out netting clauses in the event of insolvency, whereas Germany prior to 1994 strictly adhered to the principle of mutuality. As such clauses are a staple in the international master agreements on trading with financial derivatives, the German legislator, set to protect the Frankfurt financial market against the risk of losing business, could no longer avoid the issue.

13.39 The new provision applies, in rather uninformative language, to "financial services which have a market or exchange price", and with a fixed maturity. The first qualification is designed to ensure that the parties are able to conclude a reverse transaction at any time, be it through an organised market (exchange) or "over the counter". § 104(2) InsO covers three—non-exclusive—types of such transactions:

— *forward transactions (financial futures)* in securities, money market instruments, foreign exchange, precious metals, including repo transactions and security lending;
— *swap transactions*, especially of foreign exchange and interest rates
— *options* to buy or to sell securities, security baskets, foreign exchange, indices, or precious metals.

While it is agreed that compound instruments such as "swaptions" are within the ambit of § 104(2) InsO, *credit derivatives* have been subject to controversy. In the form of "total return swaps"—i.e. where a bondholder swaps the future returns of his investment against a fixed return—they may be considered as plain swaps (of counter-party risks). By contrast, swaps of individual loans are not

98. The review period has to be mandated through the insolvency plan and may cover three years at most; § 268(1) InsO.

99. With the exception of a provision relating to forward sales of commodities (§ 18 KO).

100. For a brief account of the legislation process see J. Köndgen, in Kübler/Prütting (eds.), *supra*, note 31, § 104 margin nos. 1–6.

101. See only R. Goode, *Principles of Corporate Insolvency Law* (2nd edn, 1997), pp. 184 *et seq.*

covered by § 104(2) InsO, because they lack a "market or exchange price". A mere credit rating is no substitute for such a price.[102]

13.40 When an insolvency order is issued over either party to one of the above transactions prior to the agreed maturity, the obligation to deliver (a security, basket, foreign exchange, etc.) is cancelled automatically and converted into a monetary obligation to compensate the counter-party's expectation damages. At the same time, the mutual obligations are netted out, i.e. only the balance resulting from the set-off of the damages claim against the agreed price will effectively be paid. § 104(3) InsO mandates that the buyer's expectation damages be calculated by an "abstract" measure based on a hypothetical covering transaction effected as of the second workday subsequent to the opening of the insolvency proceeding.

13.41 Doubts have been raised as to whether the termination clauses in the two most important master agreements[103] can stand under the new law,[104] for they diverge from the InsO provisions in two respects: (a) they have the duty to deliver cancelled out at an earlier date preceding the opening of proceedings, e.g. of an out-of-court arrangement; (b) they allow calculation of the buyer's expectation interest by a different measure, e.g. the damage effectively suffered by the buyer. As a general rule, all statutory provisions relating to the impact of insolvency on executory contracts are mandatory (§ 119 InsO). Yet it appears that they are not retroactive so as to hinder terminations on a date earlier than the advent of insolvency. On the other hand, divergent contractual damage measures are obviously incompatible with the mandatory principle. Furthermore, if the contractual measure exceeds the statutory measure collecting contractual damages may indeed amount to an illicit preference.

13.42 The new provision on *close-out netting* (§ 104(2) 3d sentence InsO) is by and large a transformation of prevailing contractual practice into a statutory remedy. The set-off takes effect automatically. However, in order to avoid "cherry picking" by single-transaction set-off, the parties must have conducted their single mutual dealings under one master agreement. Note that the InsO presupposes a broad notion of mutuality but does not relinquish the principle of mutuality of parties. Therefore, multilateral netting remains a remedy not admissible under German insolvency law.

102. For details see J. Köndgen, *supra*, note 101, § 104 margin nos. 34–35.

103. For domestic transactions: Rahmenvertrag für Finanztermingeschäfte 1993, reprinted in: *Bankrechtshandbuch*, *supra*, note 16, vol 2 § 114 Anhang 1. For cross-border transactions: ISDA Master Agreement 1992.

104. For details see J. Köndgen, *supra*, note 101, § 104 margin nos. 37–40.

LEGAL ISSUES TO BE ADDRESSED IN A VOLUNTARY SUPPORT OPERATION

13.43 It remains to be seen if and to what extent the rehabilitative philosophy of the InsO will work out in practice.[105] Voluntary support operations, from the very outset, have been a topic deliberately left out of insolvency law reform. As has been said in Germany, pre-emptive rehabilitation to be successful has to be "timely, expeditious, and quiet".[106] None the less, there remains a host of legal issues to be addressed by banks participating in a voluntary support operation, lest the failure of such operation should result in a heavy burden of liability. The relevant body of law has been left largely unaffected by insolvency law reform; only the rules relating to fraudulent conveyances and preferences have been revised to a small degree.

Preferential treatment of bank creditors

13.44 The adjustment of pre-insolvency transactions of a debtor ("claw-back" provisions)—the *actio Pauliana* of Roman law—seems to be part of the common core of different national insolvency laws. Among the various types of transactions which a debtor heading for insolvency may be tempted to perform in order to give single creditors preferential treatment to the prejudice of the general body of creditors,[107] only a few are likely to involve banks. Thus, a secured loan transaction may constitute an unfair preference[108] in favour of the lender in a workout situation, if neither borrower nor lender acted in good faith as to the auspicious prospects of the rescue operation and the loan was designed solely to refinance and reduce the lender's commitment.[109] While such a situation appears to be rather exceptional, a lender's taking of new or additional collateral for pre-existing debt may be a more frequent practice. The latter is regarded as an unfair preference, even if pursuant to a previous general agreement to grant collateral,[110] because such agreement did not entitle the lender to take collateral in a specific kind of asset.[111] Even if pursuant to an agreement to grant collateral in a specified asset the transaction may be set aside

105. Preliminary empirical evidence suggests that the option to work out an insolvency plan is chosen in less than 10 per cent of the proceedings; see B. Kübler, "Die Insolvenzordnung aus der sicht eines Insolvenzverwalters", reported in *Zeitschrift für Bankrecht und Bankwirtschaft* 1999, 251.

106. Karsten Schmidt, *Möglichkeiten der Sanierung von Unternehmen durch Maßnahmen im Unternehmens-, Arbeits-, Sozial-und Insolvenzrecht* (1982), p. D 97.

107. *Cf.* §§ 130–35 InsO.

108. *Absichtsanfechtung*; see § 133 InsO. Under the new law, the relevant time for adjustment of such transactions may extend up to 10 years prior to the filing of an insolvency petition.

109. See Bundesgerichtshof (Federal Court) in *Neue Juristische Wochenschrift* 1984, 1893, 1898–1899.

110. Usually based upon No. 19 of the Standard Form Contract.

111. § 131(1) InsO. The relevant time is the month preceding the filing of an insolvency petition; the period covers up to three months if the debtor was already insolvent at the time the security was granted, regardless of the lender's knowledge—actual or constructive—of this fact.

in the event that it was executed during the last three months prior to the filing of an insolvency petition, and the lender had actual or constructive knowledge that the debtor was insolvent.[112] Because even constructive knowledge of the signals presaging the commencement of an insolvency procedure triggers the adjustment of a secured transaction, the new law may be seen to present a disincentive for lenders generously to make loans in a workout situation.[113]

Lender liability

13.45 The concept of lender liability is largely unknown to German lawyers.[114] I shall discuss under this label some miscellaneous causes of action supporting the liability of banks for improperly exercising certain rights and remedies in the course of a rescue operation.

Conflict of interest situations

13.46 When asked by a debtor company which has run into financial difficulties to make further advances, a bank faces the uncomfortable choice either to accelerate its loan if the debtor's condition seems hopeless[115]—at the risk of misjudging the debtor's potential for recovery, thus breaching its duty to act in good faith arising from the loan contract,[116]—or to make further advances at the risk of recklessly ignoring the alarm bells, thereby becoming liable to the general body of creditors in tort for impeding the timely commencement of an insolvency procedure.[117] Banks cannot expect the requisite guidance on how to resolve what is basically a conflict of interest situation from recent case law, nor can they rely on a majority opinion in the legal literature.[118] In a rare, clear-cut case, the Federal Court has held a major German bank liable in tort for recklessly pursuing its own interest at the prejudice of the general body of

112. § 130 InsO. Insolvency has to be cash-flow insolvency, as opposed to balance-sheet insolvency. Alternatively, the granting of collateral may be invalidated if it was effected subsequent to the filing of an insolvency petition, and the creditor had actual or constructive knowledge thereof. However, this case is unlikely to occur in a voluntary rescue operation.

113. See D. Rümker, in B. Kübler (ed.), *supra*, note 40, at p. 151.

114. See, however, J. Köndgen, "Risiken der Kreditinstitute bei der Sanierung von Unternehmen: Rechtsvergleichende Erfahrungen aus den USA, England und Frankreich", in: Hadding/Hopt/Schimansky (eds), *Sicherheitenfreigabe und Unternehmenssanierung—Aktuelle Rechtsfragen* (1995), p. 141.

115. If the debtor is indeed headed for an insolvent liquidation, the bank may accelerate its loan even if adequate security is still available; see Oberlandesgericht Celle in *Zeitschrift für Wirtschaftsrecht* (ZIP) 1982, 942.

116. The legal literature under appropriate circumstances advocates a contractual duty to refrain from "untimely" acceleration; cf. C.W. Canaris, *Bankvertragsrecht* (2nd edn, 1981), margin nos. 1341, 1262.

117. So-called "*Konkursverschleppung*"; the cause of action would be Civil Code (BGB) § 826—tort of "wilful or reckless infliction of harm". Recent case law increasingly construes "recklessness" as an equivalent to gross negligence; see Larenz/Canaris, *Schuldrecht* vol. II/2 (13th edn, 1994), p. 454.

118. The reader will find a comprehensive analysis of both the relevant case law and the literature in T. Möllers, *Die Haftung der Bank bei der Kreditkündigung* (1991).

creditors and the investing public. The defendant bank, which was also a shareholder to the debtor company, had, by a tricky manoeuvre, covertly reduced both its line of credit and its equity, at the same time taking an active part in raising new equity financing by underwriting an issue of stock to the general public.[119]

Interfering with corporate governance

13.47 When banks take the lead in a rescue operation they should be aware of the risks of overreaching. If they enter into a secured transaction granting them security in most of the debtor's assets and, at the same time, control over the debtor's business and financial affairs to the point that the debtor is a mere instrument in the hand of the lender, such a transaction may be invalidated by a court as being unconscionable.[120] Whether lenders who interfere with the debtor company's legitimate corporate governance may be held responsible for breach of their fiduciary duties as shadow directors is open to question. The doctrine of shadow directors has not gained strong footholds in the jurisprudence,[121] and there has been no case law applying it to lenders.

Lenders as shareholders

13.48 Finally, I will refer briefly to the special responsibility of banks acting in a dual role as both lender and company member. Even if the lender is not in the position of a controlling shareholder,[122] its claim for repayment of a loan granted to the company which is lacking adequate capital may be subordinated in the event of the company becoming insolvent.[123] The rationale behind these provisions is that a shareholder, once it elects to remedy its company's need for capital, must not do so other than through equity financing. Since much of the law relating to loans substituting equity is covered in Chapter 1 of this volume, I shall focus here on some recent developments.

13.49 In a landmark case of 1988,[124] the principal lender to the debtor

119. See Bundesgerichtshof in *Zeitschrift für Wirtschaftsrecht* (ZIP) 1986, 14 = *Wertpapiermitteilungen* 1986, 2. To the subscribers of new stock, liability was also grounded on the bank's underwriting a misleading prospectus; see Bundesgerichtshof in *Zeitschrift für Wirtschaftsrecht*, 1982, 923.

120. Bundesgerichtshof in *Wertpapiermitteilungen* 1955, 1667; Oberlandesgericht Celle, *supra*, note 115, at 950 came close to such a ruling, but in the event found that the lender had indeed closely monitored the debtor's conduct of his business but had not assumed operative control. See also J. Köndgen, "Financial Covenants", in: Prütting (ed.), *RWS-Forum Insolvenzrecht* (1997), p. 145 *et seq.*

121. See, however, Bundesgerichtshof, BGHZ 104, 44 (1988), holding a shadow director of a GmbH liable for failure to present a bankruptcy petition (a statutory duty imposed on corporate directors).

122. This may trigger the special duties imposed by the law relating to groups of companies which I cannot deal with in this place; for details, *cf.* H.P. Westermann, "Banken als Kreditgeber und Gesellschafter", *Zeitschrift für Wirtschaftsrecht* 1982, 379, 382 *et seq.*

123. See already *supra*, text following note 76.

124. Bundesgerichtshof in BGHZ 105, 168 (1988)—*Hamburger Stahlwerke*.

company had become a trustee over company shares by virtue of taking a major shareholder's shares as security for a syndicated loan extended to the company, with the assigning shareholder reserving his right to vote on company meetings. In addition, the bank had been appointed managing agent and trustee for the loan syndicate for all purposes of doing business with the borrower. The formidable question the Federal Court had to address was whether (a) the bank holding its share in the company only for transient financing purposes was subject to the same responsibility as an ordinary shareholder, and, in the affirmative, whether (b) the bank was excluded with its repayment claim to the full amount of the syndicated loan or only with its own, relatively small contribution.

13.50 With regard to the first part of the question, the majority opinion in Germany had long argued against a bank raising the defence that it became a shareholder only for the purpose of financing a support operation (so-called bank privilege).[125] Should this also be true if the lender holds the shares as a quasi-lien, even allowing the transferring shareholder to exercise the voting right? The Federal Court ruled in the affirmative arguing for a formal analysis, irrespective of the bank's motives for becoming a shareholder.[126] With regard to the latter argument, this ruling has become obsolete since a 1998 amendment to the GmbH-Gesetz[127] has suspended the application of the rules relating to "loans substituting equity" for lenders participating in a bailout.

13.51 The Federal Court avoided addressing the second question. The bank's defence was indeed not without its merits. The law does not, as a rule, require a shareholder to furnish additional equity whenever the company's capital base becomes insufficient. Only if he does choose to provide financing will this be treated as the equivalent of equity. Under this rationale, the bank had elected to finance the debtor company only to the extent of its relative quota of the loan,[128] allowing it to retrieve the remainder from the bankrupt's estate.

JOHANNES KÖNDGEN

125. See recently M. Lutter, "Neues zum Gesellschafterdarlehen?", *Zeitschrift für Wirtschaftsrecht* (ZIP) 1989, 477, 479.

126. The holding was widely acclaimed in the literature; see M. Lutter, *ibid.*, at 482–483; H.J. Priester, "Eigenkapitalersetzende Landesbankdarlehen", *Zeitschrift für Bankrecht und Bankwirtschaft* 1989, 30, 33.

127. *Supra*, note 77—so-called "rehabilitation privilege".

128. M. Lutter, *ibid.*, at p. 483.

INDEX